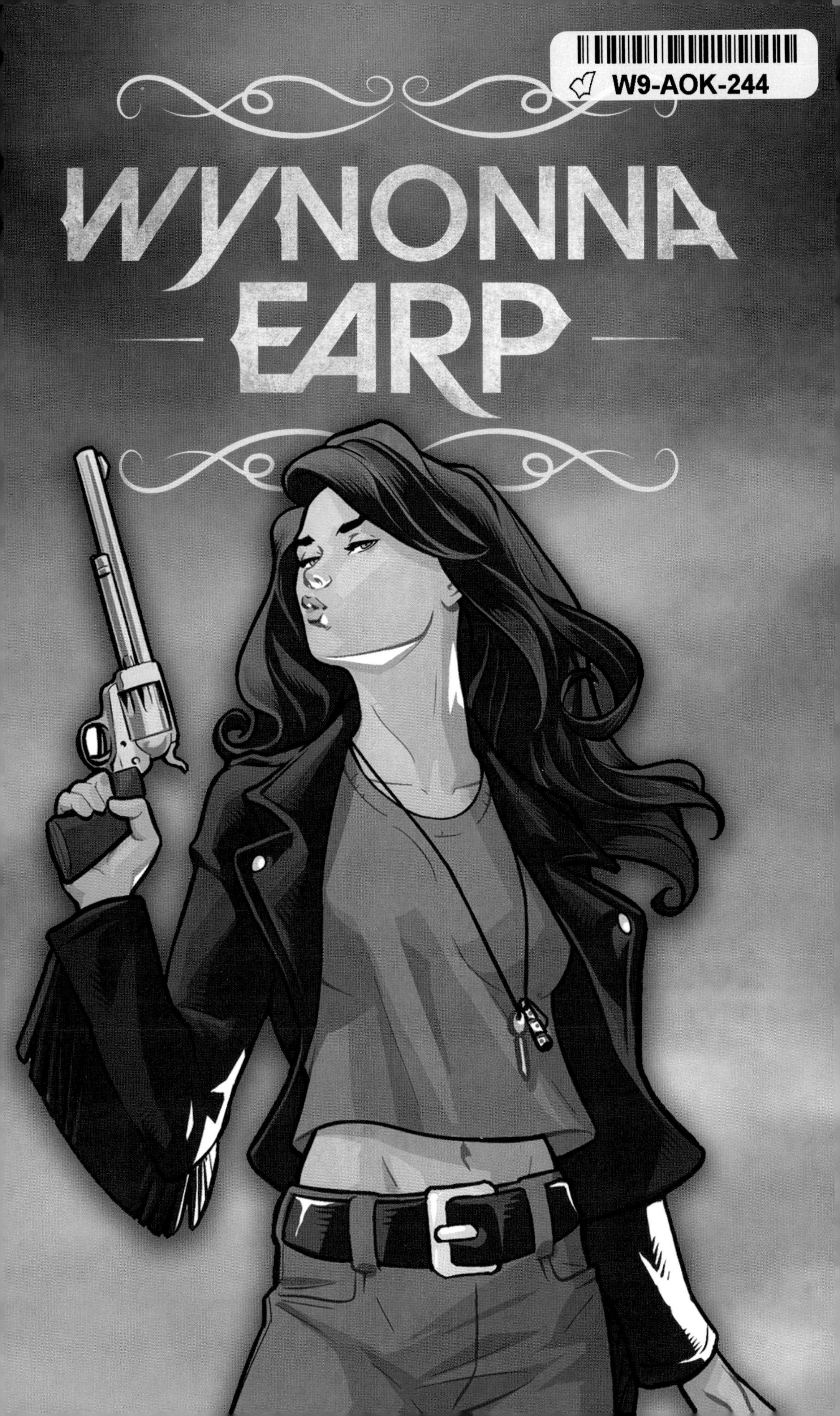
WYNONNA
EARP

Become our fan on Facebook **facebook.com/idwpublishing**
Follow us on Twitter **@idwpublishing**
Subscribe to us on YouTube **youtube.com/idwpublishing**
See what's new on Tumblr **tumblr.idwpublishing.com**
Check us out on Instagram **instagram.com/idwpublishing**

DESIGN BY
ROBBIE ROBBINS

SERIES EDITS BY
CARLOS GUZMAN

COLLECTION EDITS BY
JUSTIN EISINGER
AND
ALONZO SIMON

PUBLISHER
TED ADAMS

ISBN: 978-1-63140-749-9

19 18 17 16   1 2 3 4

Ted Adams, CEO & Publisher
Greg Goldstein, President & COO
Robbie Robbins, EVP/Sr. Graphic Artist
Chris Ryall, Chief Creative Officer/Editor-in-Chief
Laurie Windrow, Senior Vice President of Sales & Marketing
Matthew Ruzicka, CPA, Chief Financial Officer
Dirk Wood, VP of Marketing
Lorelei Bunjes, VP of Digital Services
Jeff Webber, VP of Digital Publishing & Business Development
Jerry Bennington, VP of New Product Development

For international rights, please contact
licensing@idwpublishing.com

WYNONNA EARP

Written by
Beau Smith

Art by
Lora Innes and **Chris Evenhuis**

Colors by
Jay Fotos

Letters by
Robbie Robbins

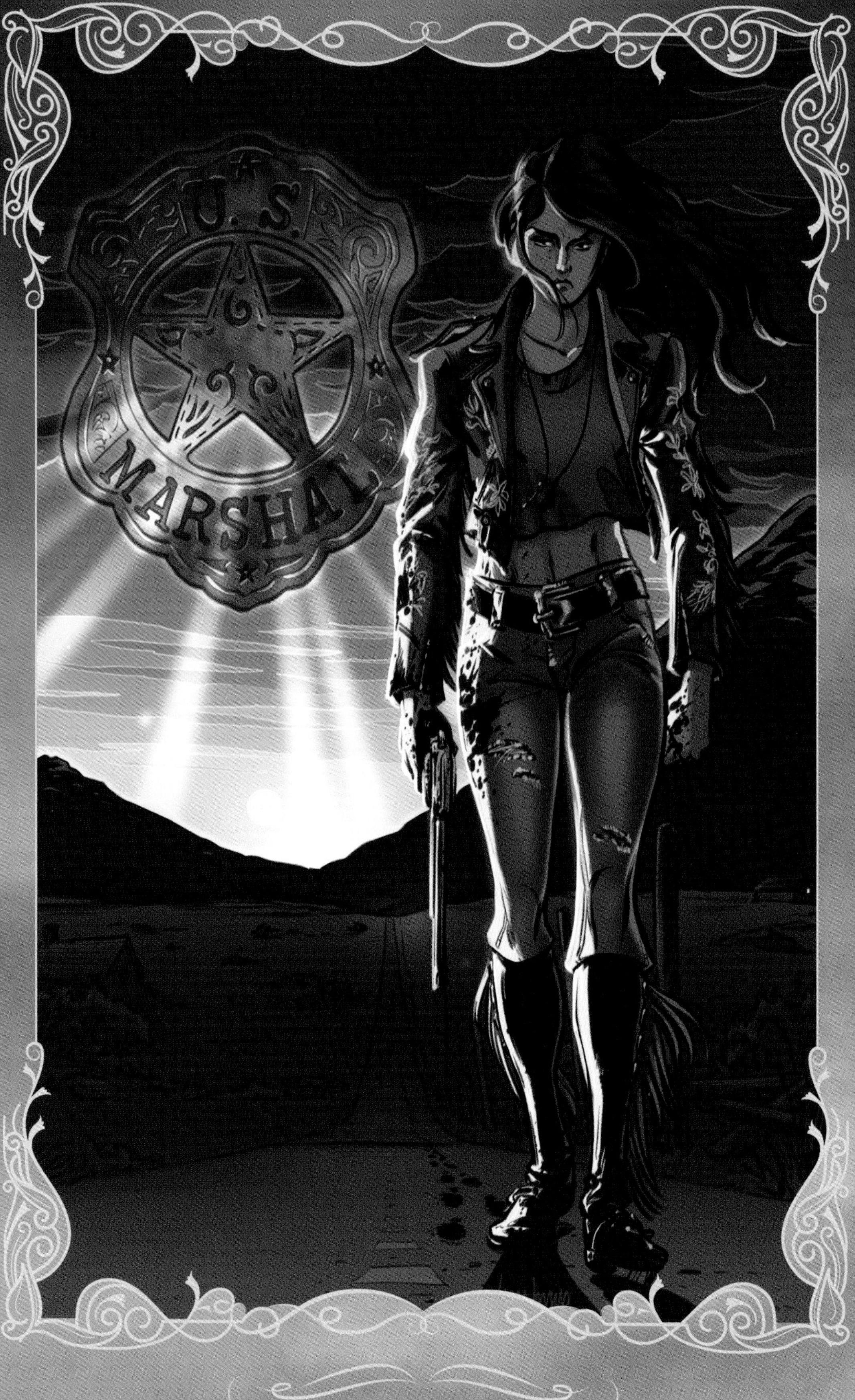
U.S.
MARSHAL

Art by **Lora Innes**

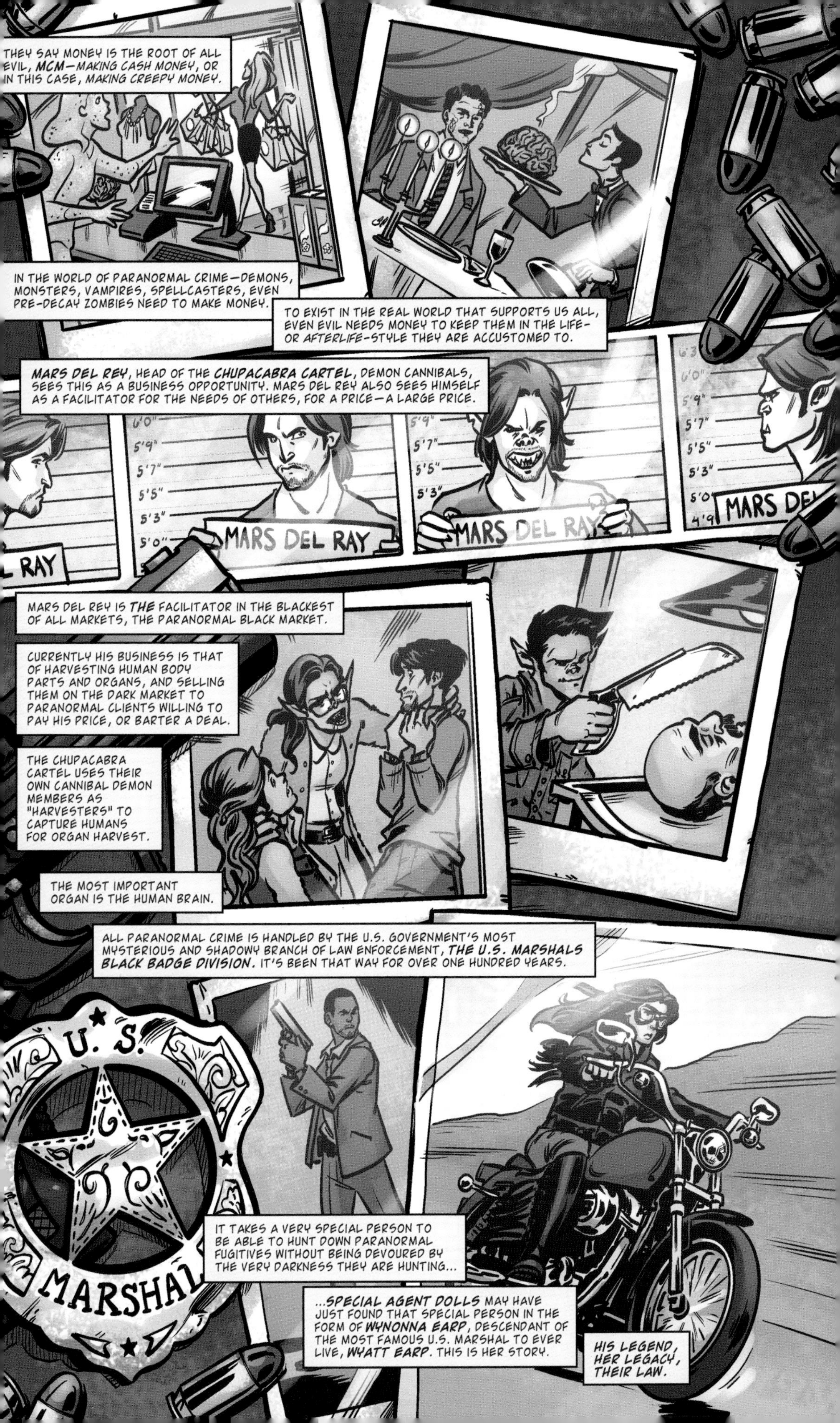
THEY SAY MONEY IS THE ROOT OF ALL EVIL, MCM—MAKING CASH MONEY, OR IN THIS CASE, MAKING CREEPY MONEY.
IN THE WORLD OF PARANORMAL CRIME—DEMONS, MONSTERS, VAMPIRES, SPELLCASTERS, EVEN PRE-DECAY ZOMBIES NEED TO MAKE MONEY.
TO EXIST IN THE REAL WORLD THAT SUPPORTS US ALL, EVEN EVIL NEEDS MONEY TO KEEP THEM IN THE LIFE- OR AFTERLIFE-STYLE THEY ARE ACCUSTOMED TO.
MARS DEL REY, HEAD OF THE CHUPACABRA CARTEL, DEMON CANNIBALS, SEES THIS AS A BUSINESS OPPORTUNITY. MARS DEL REY ALSO SEES HIMSELF AS A FACILITATOR FOR THE NEEDS OF OTHERS, FOR A PRICE—A LARGE PRICE.
L RAY
MARS DEL RAY
MARS DEL RAY
MARS DEL
MARS DEL REY IS THE FACILITATOR IN THE BLACKEST OF ALL MARKETS, THE PARANORMAL BLACK MARKET.
CURRENTLY HIS BUSINESS IS THAT OF HARVESTING HUMAN BODY PARTS AND ORGANS, AND SELLING THEM ON THE DARK MARKET TO PARANORMAL CLIENTS WILLING TO PAY HIS PRICE, OR BARTER A DEAL.
THE CHUPACABRA CARTEL USES THEIR OWN CANNIBAL DEMON MEMBERS AS "HARVESTERS" TO CAPTURE HUMANS FOR ORGAN HARVEST.
THE MOST IMPORTANT ORGAN IS THE HUMAN BRAIN.
ALL PARANORMAL CRIME IS HANDLED BY THE U.S. GOVERNMENT'S MOST MYSTERIOUS AND SHADOWY BRANCH OF LAW ENFORCEMENT, THE U.S. MARSHALS BLACK BADGE DIVISION. IT'S BEEN THAT WAY FOR OVER ONE HUNDRED YEARS.
U.S.
MARSHAL
IT TAKES A VERY SPECIAL PERSON TO BE ABLE TO HUNT DOWN PARANORMAL FUGITIVES WITHOUT BEING DEVOURED BY THE VERY DARKNESS THEY ARE HUNTING...
...SPECIAL AGENT DOLLS MAY HAVE JUST FOUND THAT SPECIAL PERSON IN THE FORM OF WYNONNA EARP, DESCENDANT OF THE MOST FAMOUS U.S. MARSHAL TO EVER LIVE, WYATT EARP. THIS IS HER STORY.
HIS LEGEND, HER LEGACY, THEIR LAW.

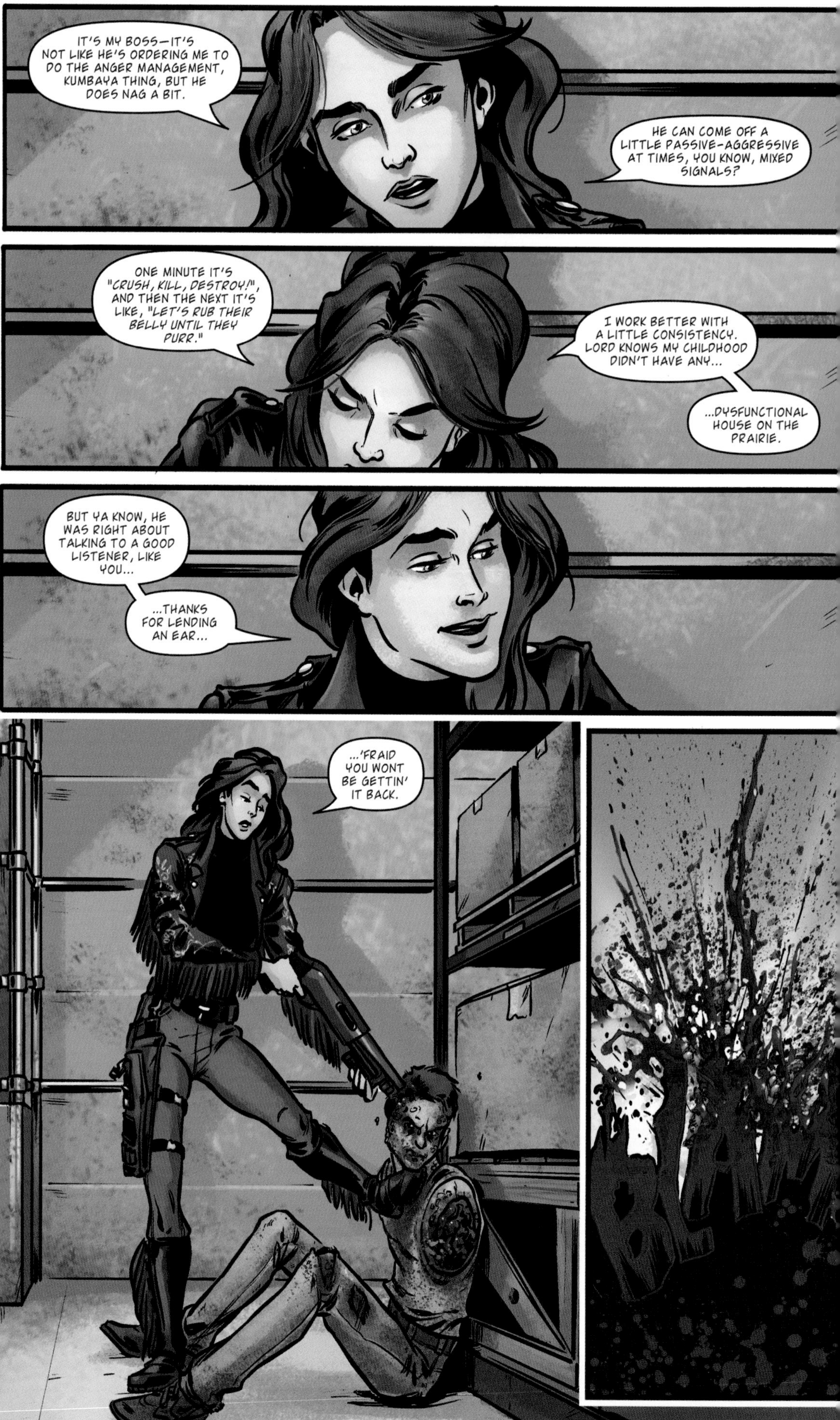
IT'S MY BOSS—IT'S NOT LIKE HE'S ORDERING ME TO DO THE ANGER MANAGEMENT, KUMBAYA THING, BUT HE DOES NAG A BIT.
HE CAN COME OFF A LITTLE PASSIVE-AGGRESSIVE AT TIMES, YOU KNOW, MIXED SIGNALS?
ONE MINUTE IT'S "CRUSH, KILL, DESTROY!", AND THEN THE NEXT IT'S LIKE, "LET'S RUB THEIR BELLY UNTIL THEY PURR."
I WORK BETTER WITH A LITTLE CONSISTENCY. LORD KNOWS MY CHILDHOOD DIDN'T HAVE ANY...
...DYSFUNCTIONAL HOUSE ON THE PRAIRIE.
BUT YA KNOW, HE WAS RIGHT ABOUT TALKING TO A GOOD LISTENER, LIKE YOU...
...THANKS FOR LENDING AN EAR...
...'FRAID YOU WONT BE GETTIN' IT BACK.

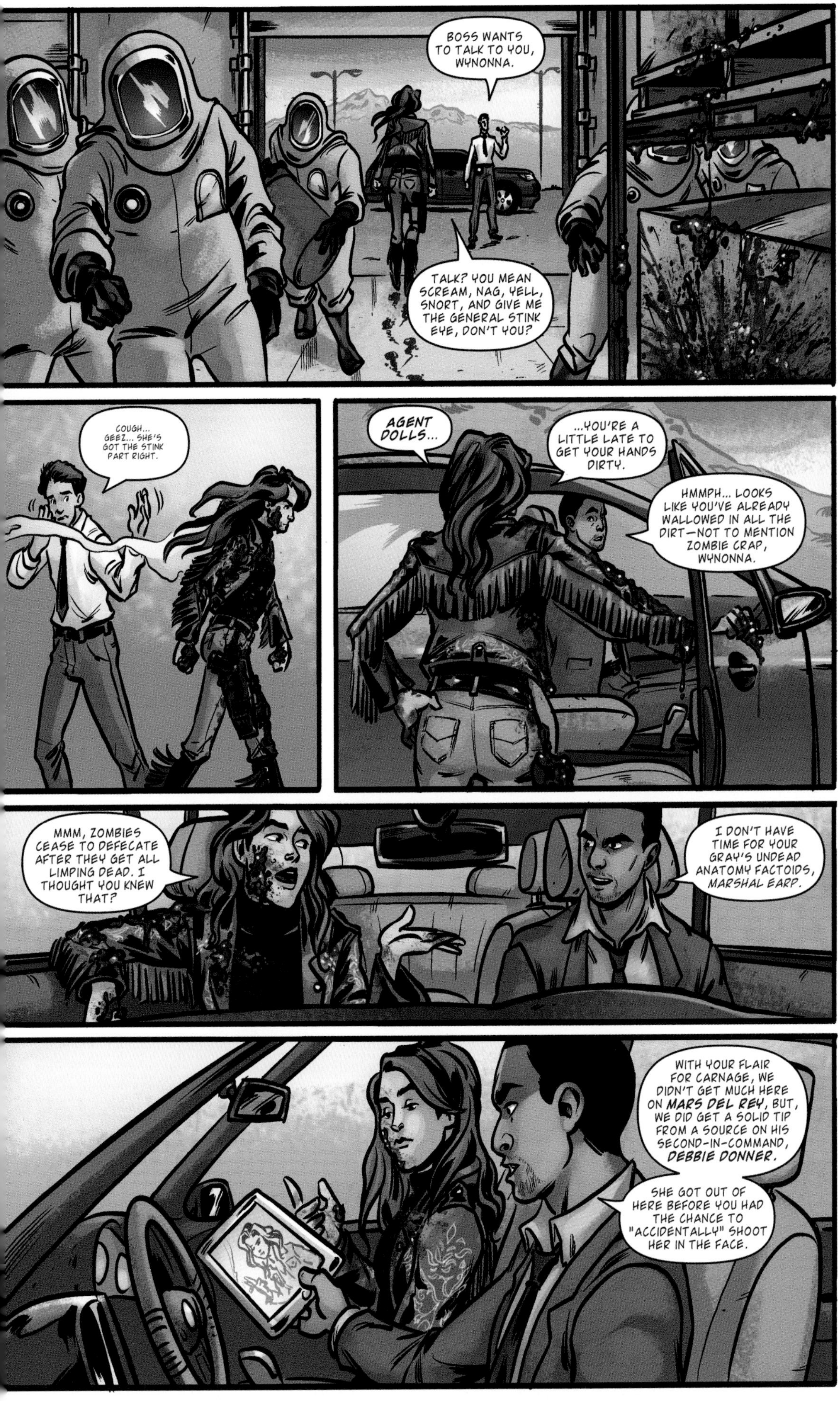
BOSS WANTS TO TALK TO YOU, WYNONNA.
TALK? YOU MEAN SCREAM, NAG, YELL, SNORT, AND GIVE ME THE GENERAL STINK EYE, DON'T YOU?
COUGH... GEEZ... SHE'S GOT THE STINK PART RIGHT.
AGENT DOLLS...
...YOU'RE A LITTLE LATE TO GET YOUR HANDS DIRTY.
HMMPH... LOOKS LIKE YOU'VE ALREADY WALLOWED IN ALL THE DIRT—NOT TO MENTION ZOMBIE CRAP, WYNONNA.
MMM, ZOMBIES CEASE TO DEFECATE AFTER THEY GET ALL LIMPING DEAD. I THOUGHT YOU KNEW THAT?
I DON'T HAVE TIME FOR YOUR GRAY'S UNDEAD ANATOMY FACTOIDS, MARSHAL EARP.
WITH YOUR FLAIR FOR CARNAGE, WE DIDN'T GET MUCH HERE ON MARS DEL REY, BUT, WE DID GET A SOLID TIP FROM A SOURCE ON HIS SECOND-IN-COMMAND, DEBBIE DONNER.
SHE GOT OUT OF HERE BEFORE YOU HAD THE CHANCE TO "ACCIDENTALLY" SHOOT HER IN THE FACE.

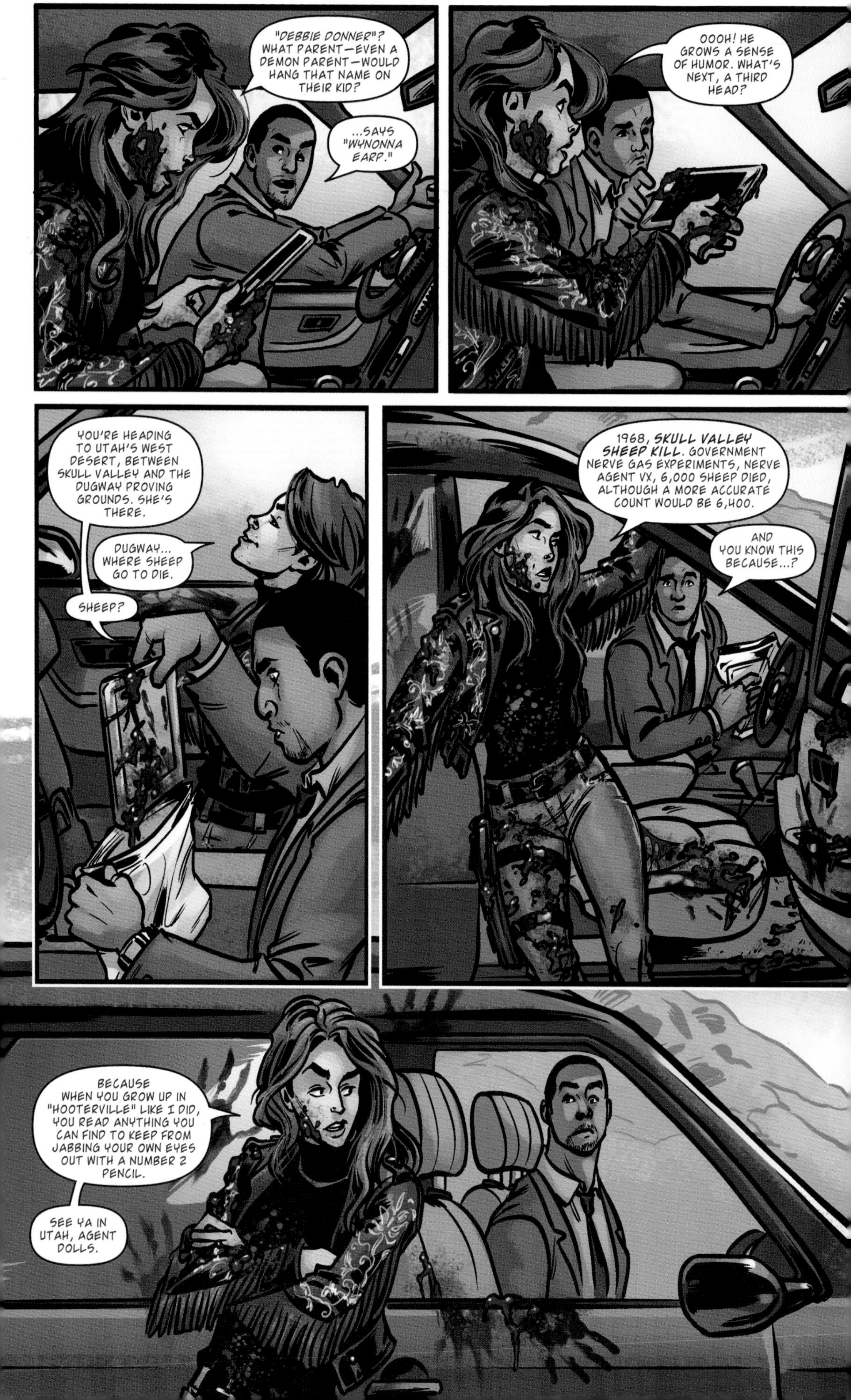
"DEBBIE DONNER"? WHAT PARENT—EVEN A DEMON PARENT—WOULD HANG THAT NAME ON THEIR KID?
...SAYS "WYNONNA EARP."
OOOH! HE GROWS A SENSE OF HUMOR. WHAT'S NEXT, A THIRD HEAD?
YOU'RE HEADING TO UTAH'S WEST DESERT, BETWEEN SKULL VALLEY AND THE DUGWAY PROVING GROUNDS. SHE'S THERE.
DUGWAY... WHERE SHEEP GO TO DIE.
SHEEP?
1968, SKULL VALLEY SHEEP KILL. GOVERNMENT NERVE GAS EXPERIMENTS, NERVE AGENT VX, 6,000 SHEEP DIED, ALTHOUGH A MORE ACCURATE COUNT WOULD BE 6,400.
AND YOU KNOW THIS BECAUSE...?
BECAUSE WHEN YOU GROW UP IN "HOOTERVILLE" LIKE I DID, YOU READ ANYTHING YOU CAN FIND TO KEEP FROM JABBING YOUR OWN EYES OUT WITH A NUMBER 2 PENCIL.
SEE YA IN UTAH, AGENT DOLLS.

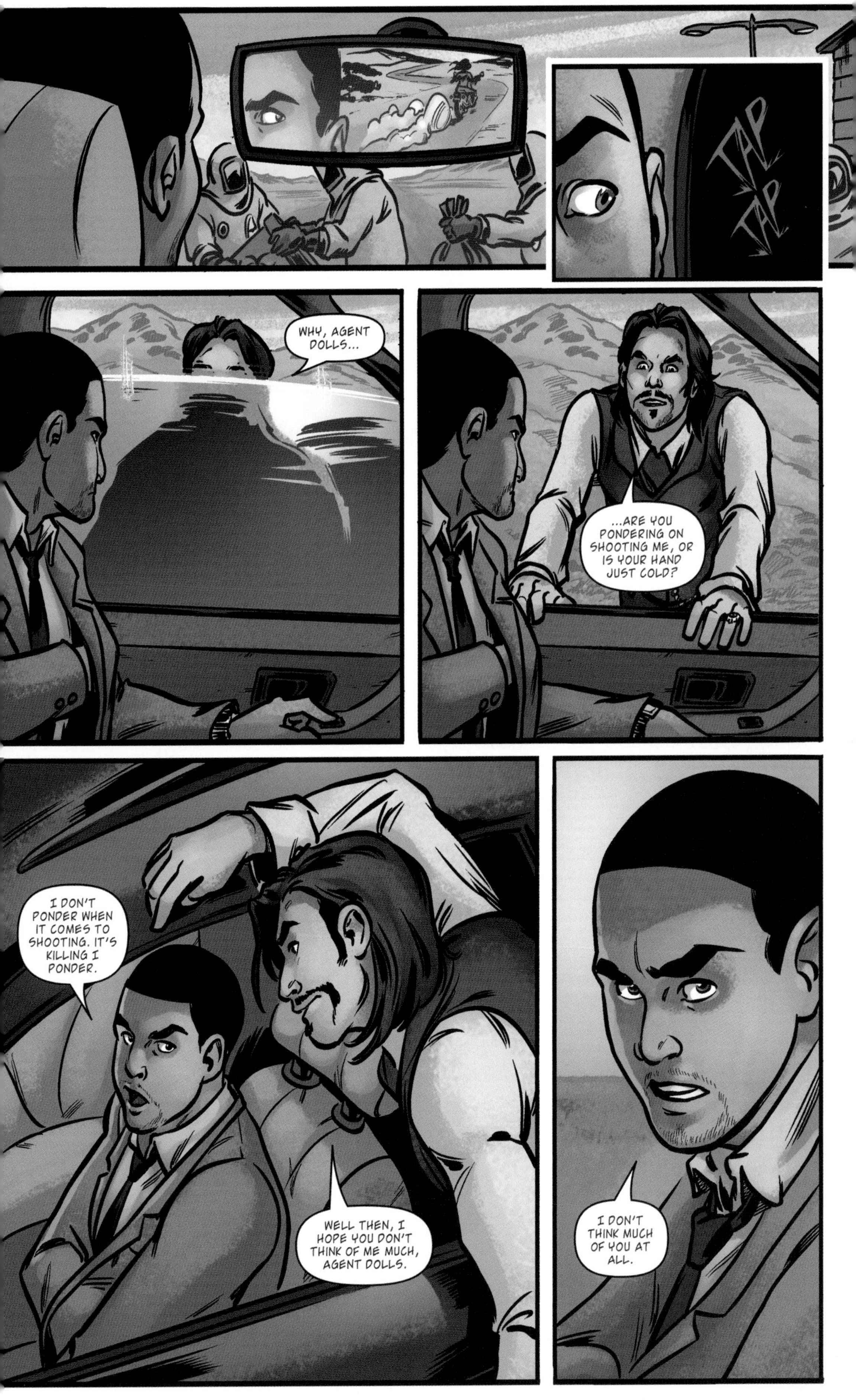
TAP
TAP
WHY, AGENT DOLLS...
...ARE YOU PONDERING ON SHOOTING ME, OR IS YOUR HAND JUST COLD?
I DON'T PONDER WHEN IT COMES TO SHOOTING. IT'S KILLING I PONDER.
WELL THEN, I HOPE YOU DON'T THINK OF ME MUCH, AGENT DOLLS.
I DON'T THINK MUCH OF YOU AT ALL.

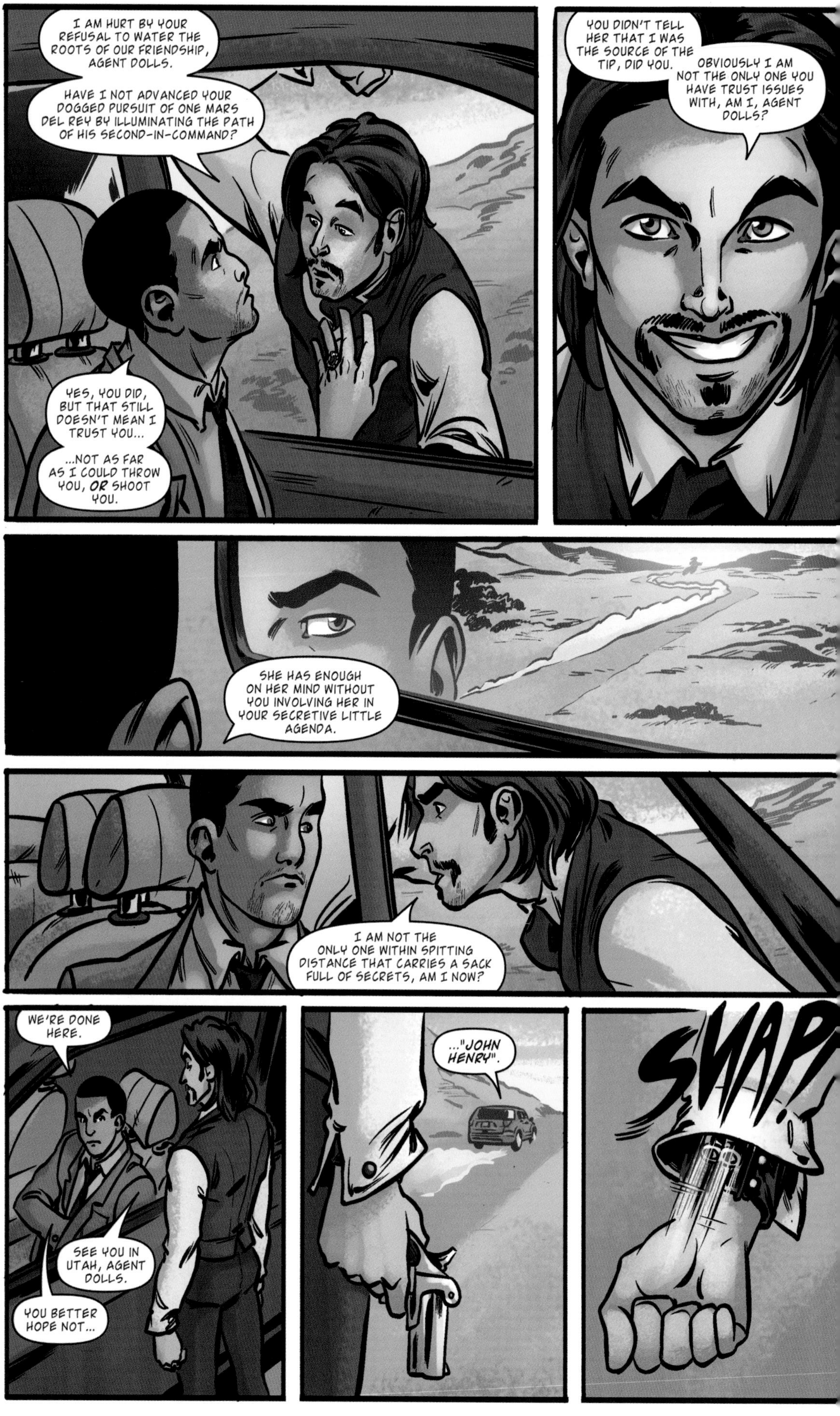
I AM HURT BY YOUR REFUSAL TO WATER THE ROOTS OF OUR FRIENDSHIP, AGENT DOLLS.
HAVE I NOT ADVANCED YOUR DOGGED PURSUIT OF ONE MARS DEL REY BY ILLUMINATING THE PATH OF HIS SECOND-IN-COMMAND?
YES, YOU DID, BUT THAT STILL DOESN'T MEAN I TRUST YOU...
...NOT AS FAR AS I COULD THROW YOU, OR SHOOT YOU.
YOU DIDN'T TELL HER THAT I WAS THE SOURCE OF THE TIP, DID YOU.
OBVIOUSLY I AM NOT THE ONLY ONE YOU HAVE TRUST ISSUES WITH, AM I, AGENT DOLLS?
SHE HAS ENOUGH ON HER MIND WITHOUT YOU INVOLVING HER IN YOUR SECRETIVE LITTLE AGENDA.
I AM NOT THE ONLY ONE WITHIN SPITTING DISTANCE THAT CARRIES A SACK FULL OF SECRETS, AM I NOW?
WE'RE DONE HERE.
SEE YOU IN UTAH, AGENT DOLLS.
YOU BETTER HOPE NOT...
..."JOHN HENRY".
SNAP!

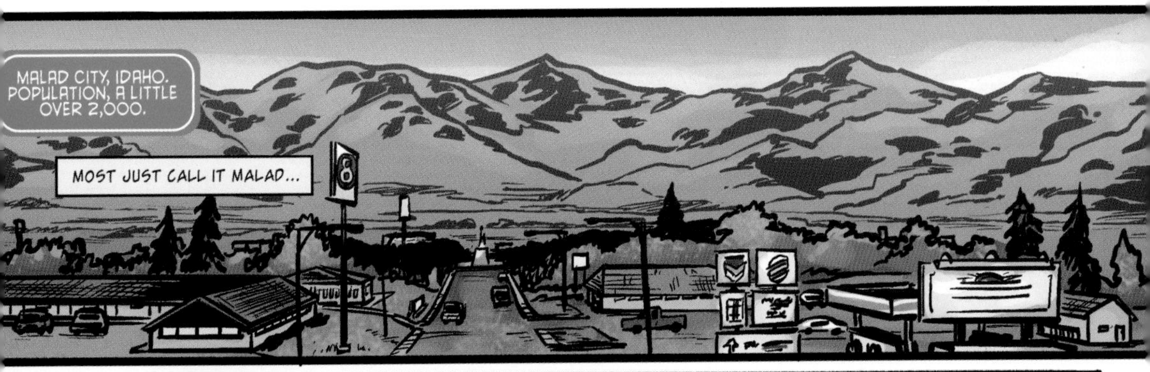
MALAD CITY, IDAHO. POPULATION, A LITTLE OVER 2,000.
MOST JUST CALL IT MALAD...

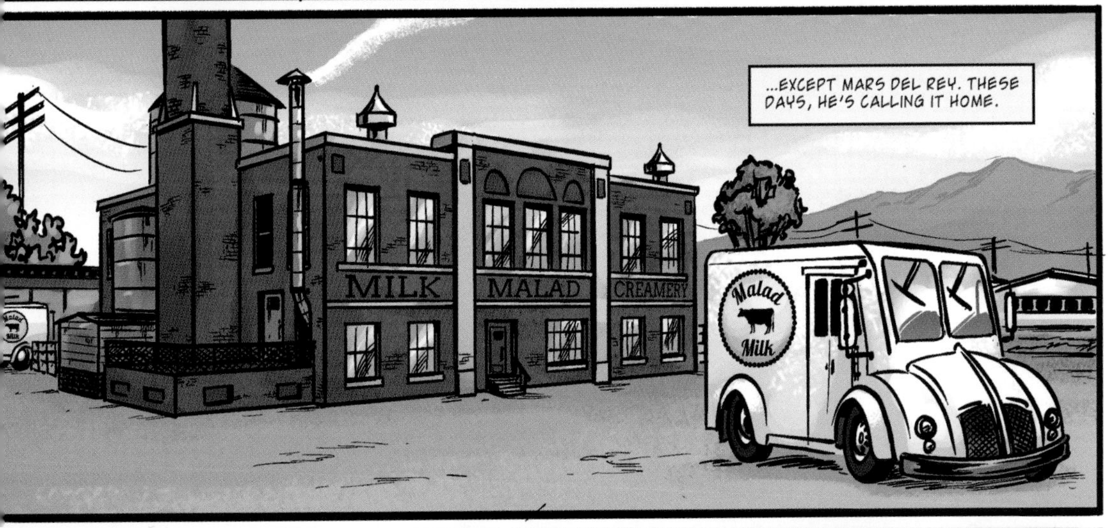
...EXCEPT MARS DEL REY. THESE DAYS, HE'S CALLING IT HOME.
MILK
MALAD
CREAMERY
Malad Milk

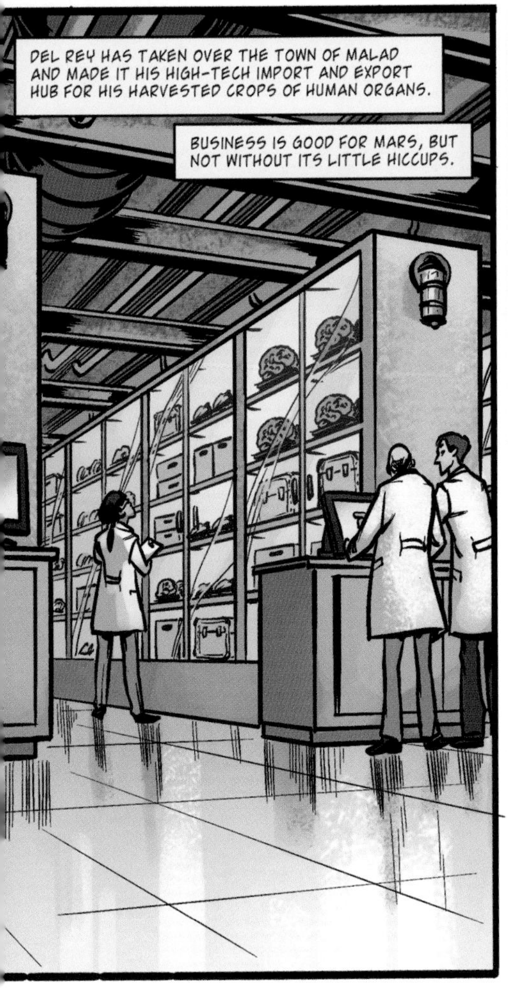
DEL REY HAS TAKEN OVER THE TOWN OF MALAD AND MADE IT HIS HIGH-TECH IMPORT AND EXPORT HUB FOR HIS HARVESTED CROPS OF HUMAN ORGANS.
BUSINESS IS GOOD FOR MARS, BUT NOT WITHOUT ITS LITTLE HICCUPS.

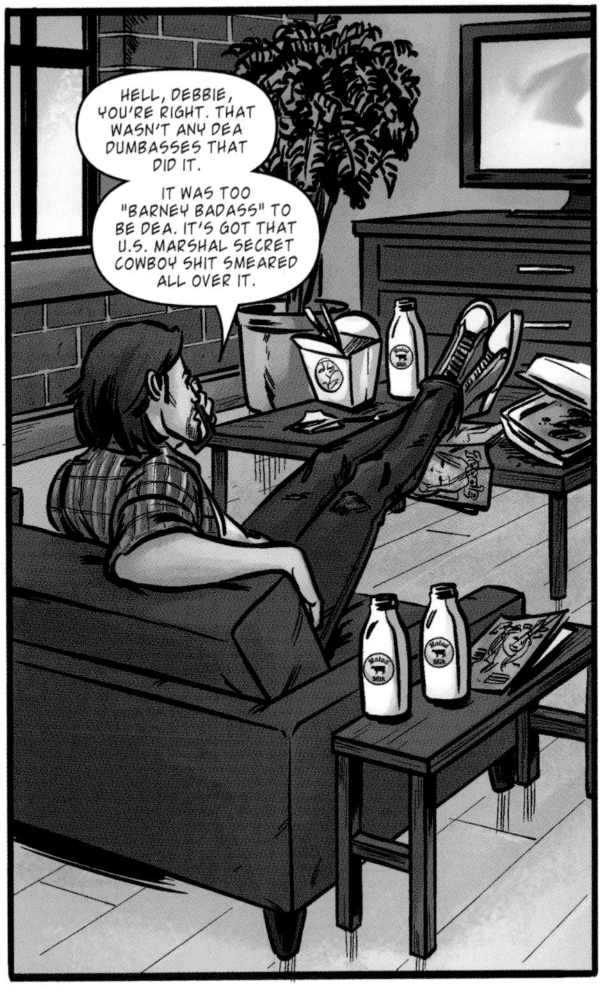
HELL, DEBBIE, YOU'RE RIGHT. THAT WASN'T ANY DEA DUMBASSES THAT DID IT.
IT WAS TOO "BARNEY BADASS" TO BE DEA. IT'S GOT THAT U.S. MARSHAL SECRET COWBOY SHIT SMEARED ALL OVER IT.

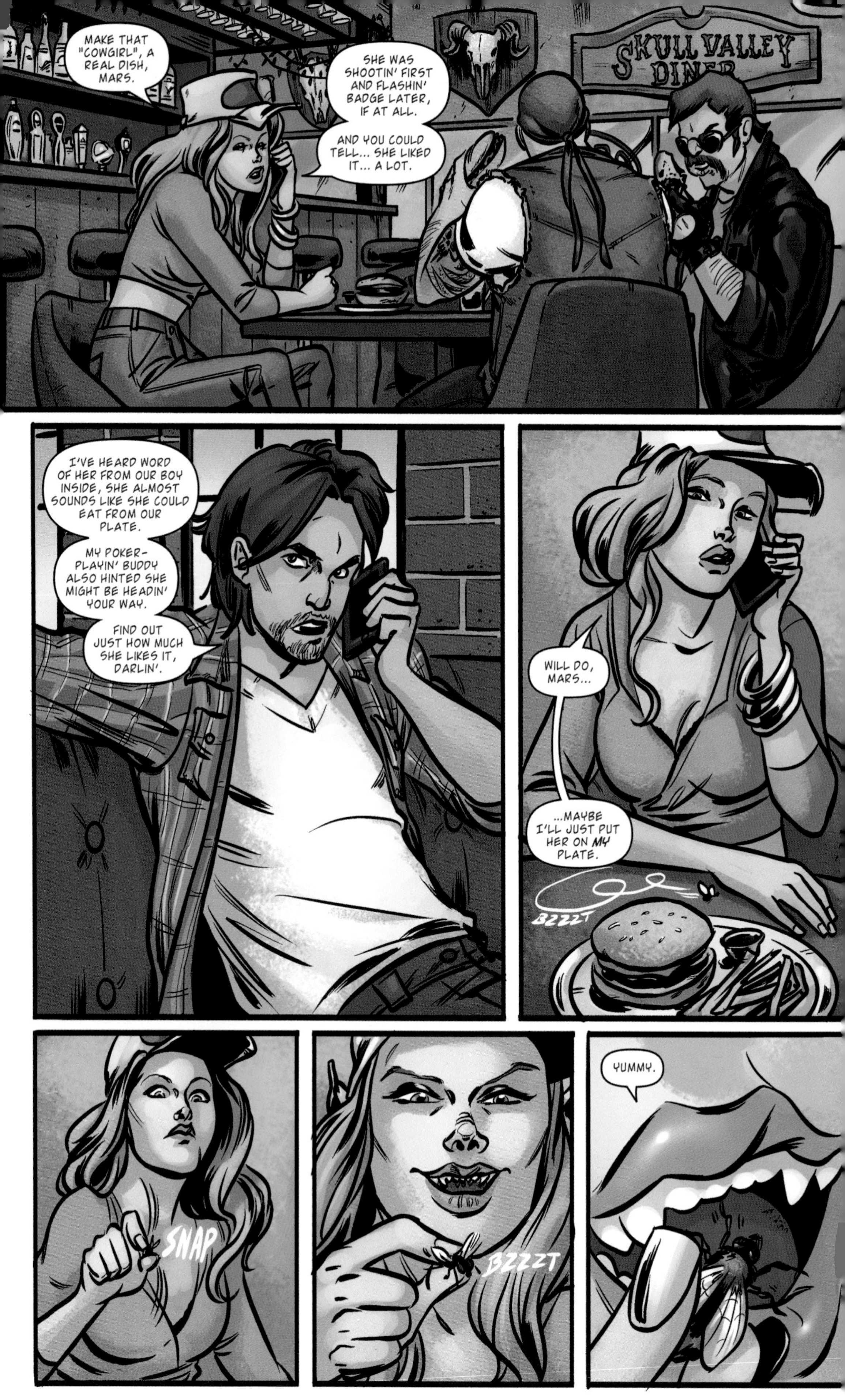
SKULL VALLEY DINER
MAKE THAT "COWGIRL", A REAL DISH, MARS.
SHE WAS SHOOTIN' FIRST AND FLASHIN' BADGE LATER, IF AT ALL.
AND YOU COULD TELL... SHE LIKED IT... A LOT.
I'VE HEARD WORD OF HER FROM OUR BOY INSIDE, SHE ALMOST SOUNDS LIKE SHE COULD EAT FROM OUR PLATE.
MY POKER-PLAYIN' BUDDY ALSO HINTED SHE MIGHT BE HEADIN' YOUR WAY.
FIND OUT JUST HOW MUCH SHE LIKES IT, DARLIN'.
WILL DO, MARS...
...MAYBE I'LL JUST PUT HER ON *MY* PLATE.
BZZZT
SNAP
BZZZT
YUMMY.

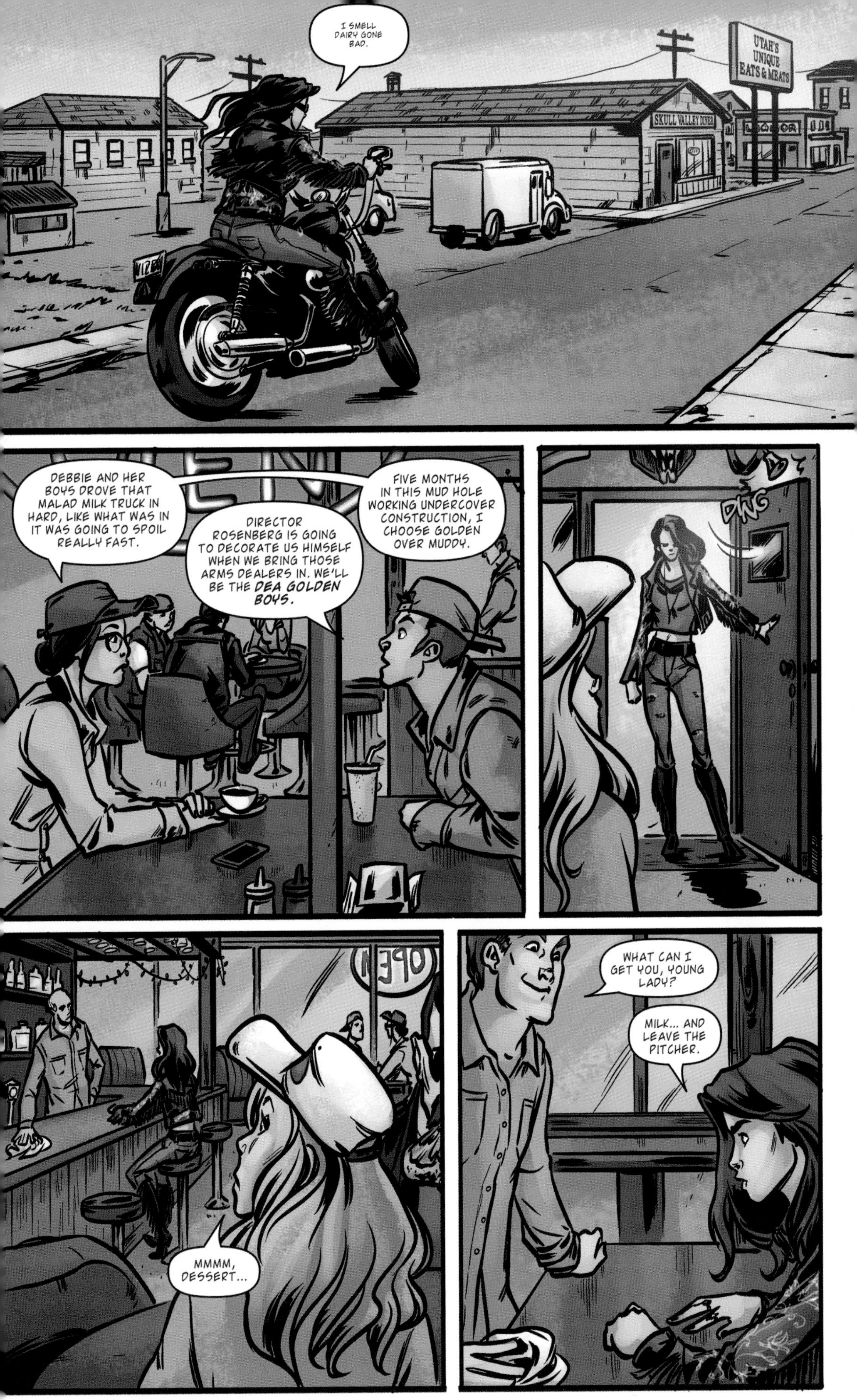
I SMELL DAIRY GONE BAD.
UTAH'S UNIQUE EATS & MEATS
SKULL VALLEY DINER
DEBBIE AND HER BOYS DROVE THAT MALAD MILK TRUCK IN HARD, LIKE WHAT WAS IN IT WAS GOING TO SPOIL REALLY FAST.
DIRECTOR ROSENBERG IS GOING TO DECORATE US HIMSELF WHEN WE BRING THOSE ARMS DEALERS IN. WE'LL BE THE DEA GOLDEN BOYS.
FIVE MONTHS IN THIS MUD HOLE WORKING UNDERCOVER CONSTRUCTION, I CHOOSE GOLDEN OVER MUDDY.
DING
MMMM, DESSERT...
WHAT CAN I GET YOU, YOUNG LADY?
MILK... AND LEAVE THE PITCHER.

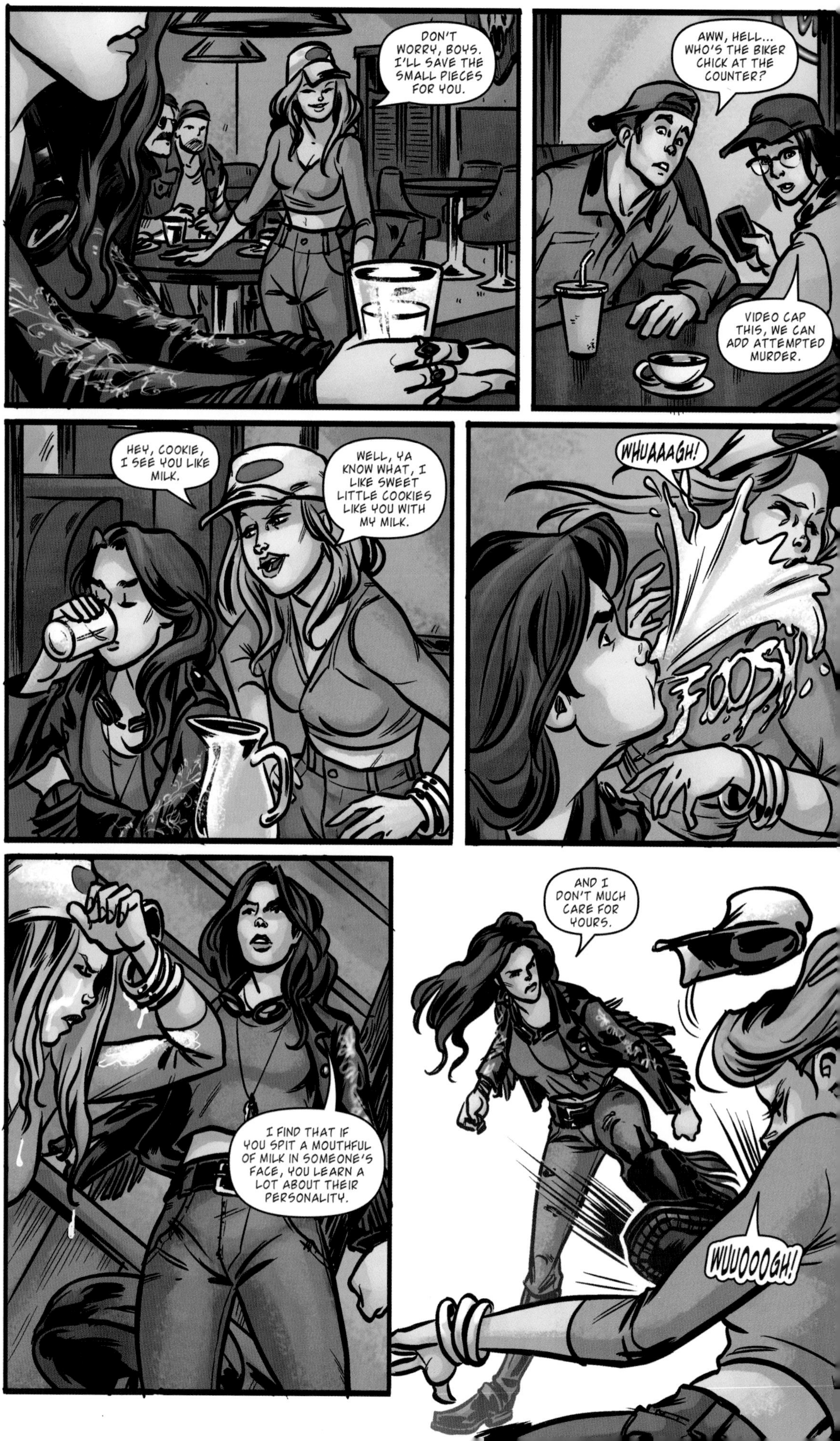
DON'T WORRY, BOYS. I'LL SAVE THE SMALL PIECES FOR YOU.
AWW, HELL... WHO'S THE BIKER CHICK AT THE COUNTER?
VIDEO CAP THIS, WE CAN ADD ATTEMPTED MURDER.
HEY, COOKIE, I SEE YOU LIKE MILK.
WELL, YA KNOW WHAT, I LIKE SWEET LITTLE COOKIES LIKE YOU WITH MY MILK.
WHUAAAGH!
FOOSH
I FIND THAT IF YOU SPIT A MOUTHFUL OF MILK IN SOMEONE'S FACE, YOU LEARN A LOT ABOUT THEIR PERSONALITY.
AND I DON'T MUCH CARE FOR YOURS.
WUUOOOGH!

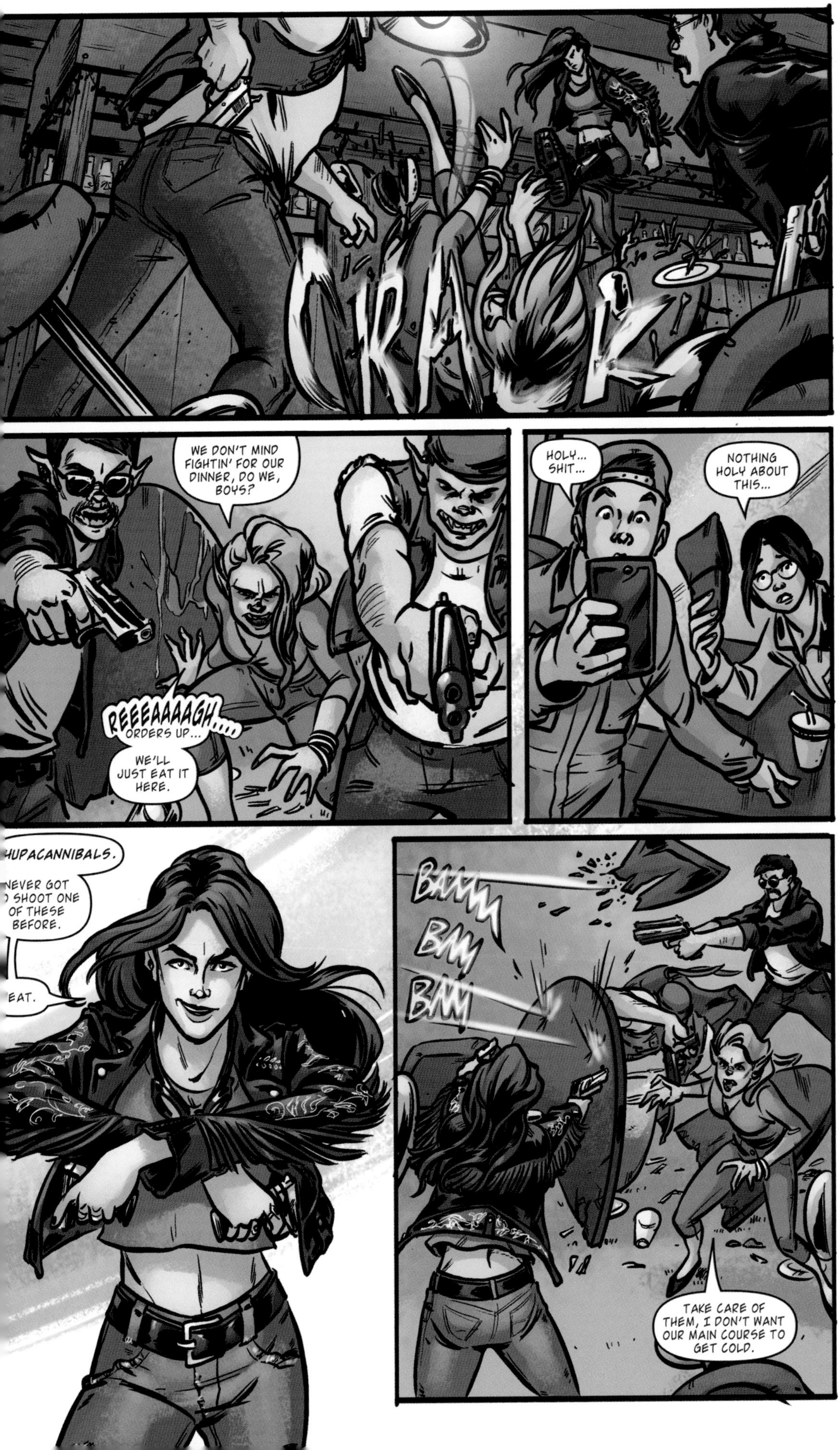
CRACK
WE DON'T MIND FIGHTIN' FOR OUR DINNER, DO WE, BOYS?
REEEAAAAGH.....
ORDERS UP...
WE'LL JUST EAT IT HERE.
HOLY... SHIT...
NOTHING HOLY ABOUT THIS...
HUPACANNIBALS.
NEVER GOT
SHOOT ONE OF THESE BEFORE.
EAT.
BAM
BAM
BAM
TAKE CARE OF THEM, I DON'T WANT OUR MAIN COURSE TO GET COLD.

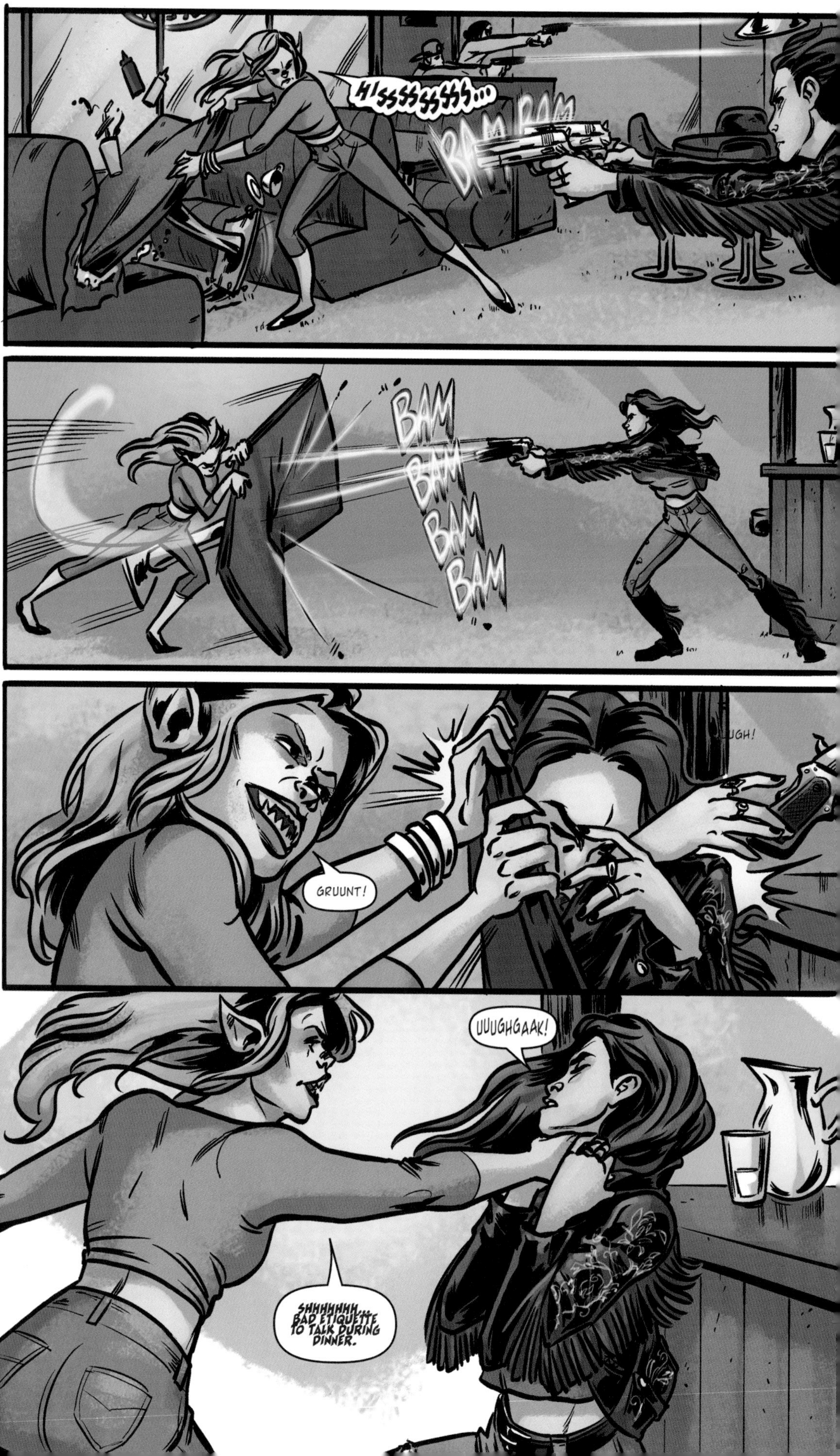
HISSSSSSSS...
BAM BAM
BAM
BAM
BAM
BAM
BAM
UGH!
GRUUNT!
UUUGHGAAK!
SHHHHHHH... BAD ETIQUETTE TO TALK DURING DINNER.

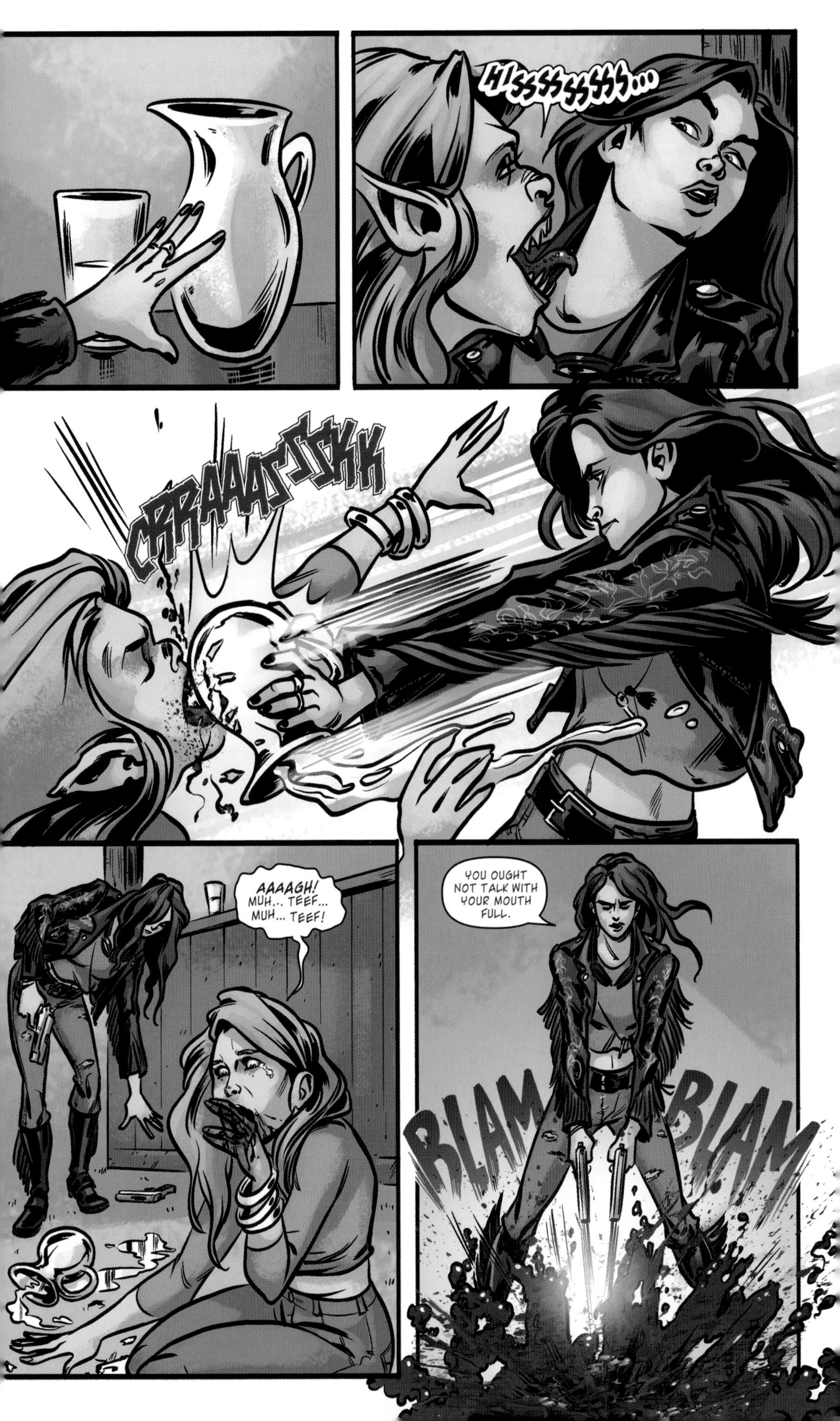
HISSSSSSSSS...
CRRAAASSSKK
AAAAGH!
MUH... TEEF...
MUH... TEEF!
YOU OUGHT
NOT TALK WITH
YOUR MOUTH
FULL.
BLAM
BLAM

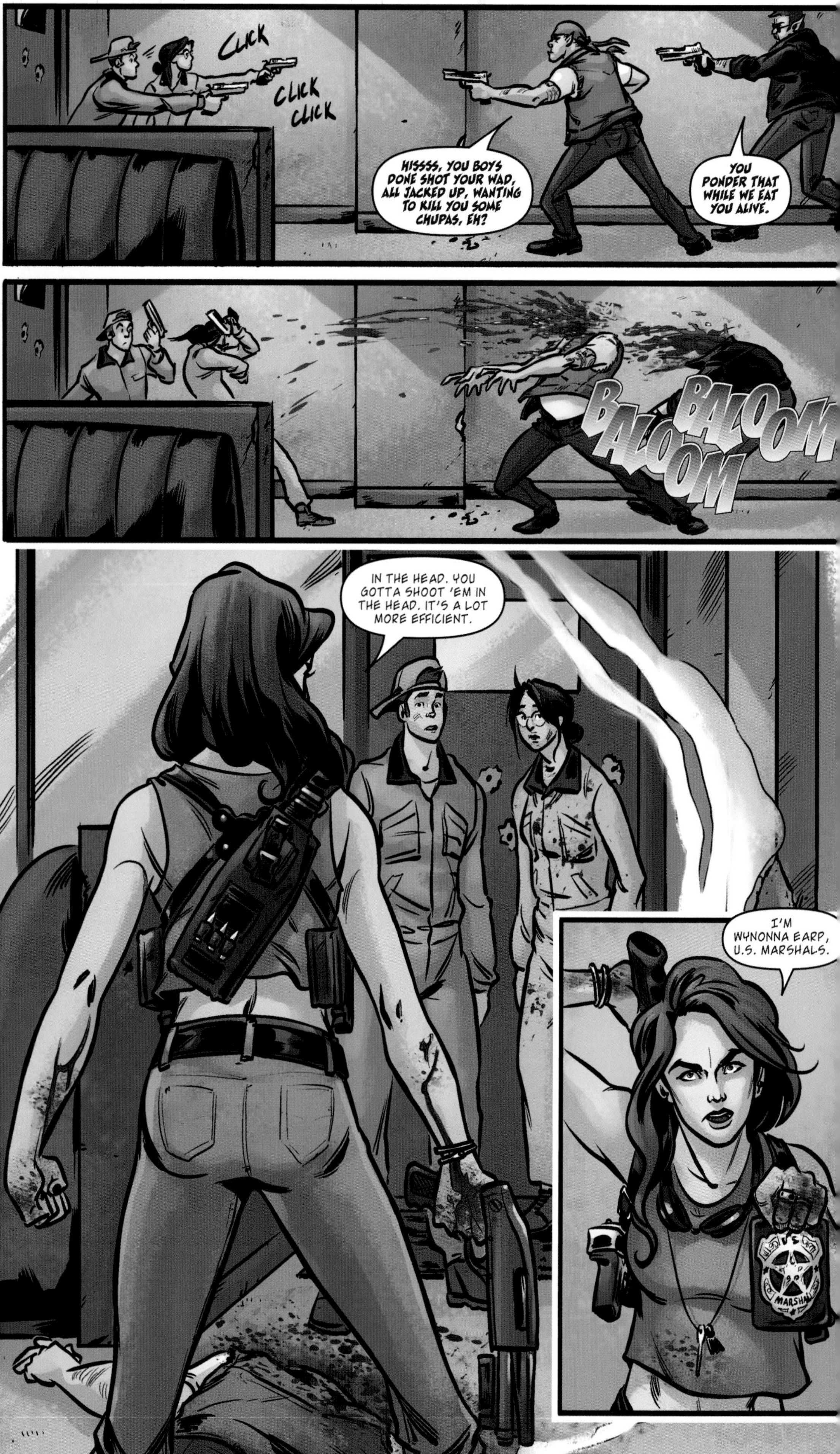
CLICK
CLICK
CLICK
HISSSS, YOU BOYS DONE SHOT YOUR WAD, ALL JACKED UP, WANTING TO KILL YOU SOME CHUPAS, EH?
YOU PONDER THAT WHILE WE EAT YOU ALIVE.
BALOOM
BALOOM
IN THE HEAD. YOU GOTTA SHOOT 'EM IN THE HEAD. IT'S A LOT MORE EFFICIENT.
I'M WYNONNA EARP, U.S. MARSHALS.

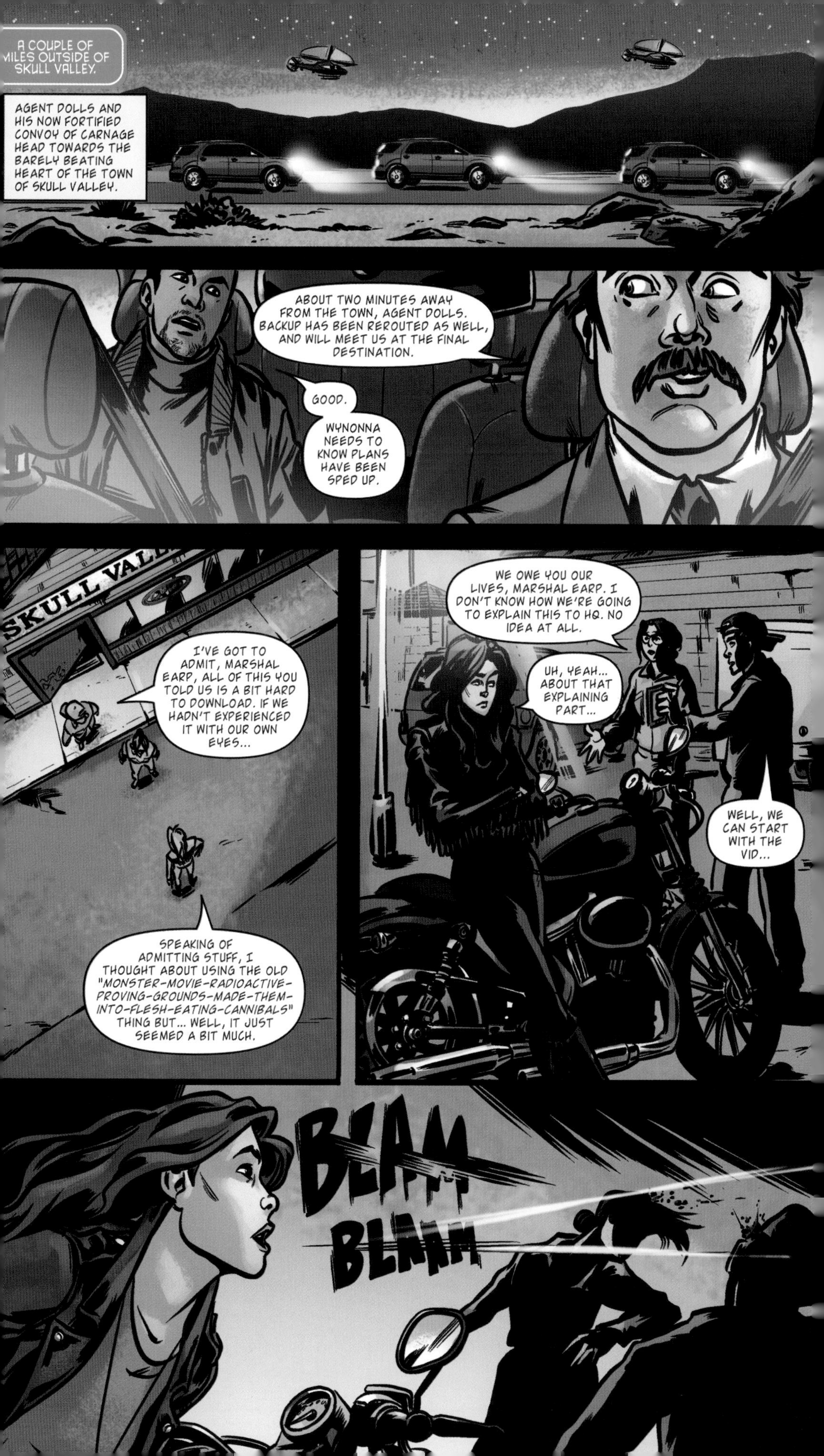
A COUPLE OF MILES OUTSIDE OF SKULL VALLEY.
AGENT DOLLS AND HIS NOW FORTIFIED CONVOY OF CARNAGE HEAD TOWARDS THE BARELY BEATING HEART OF THE TOWN OF SKULL VALLEY.
ABOUT TWO MINUTES AWAY FROM THE TOWN, AGENT DOLLS. BACKUP HAS BEEN REROUTED AS WELL, AND WILL MEET US AT THE FINAL DESTINATION.
GOOD.
WYNONNA NEEDS TO KNOW PLANS HAVE BEEN SPED UP.
SKULL VALL
I'VE GOT TO ADMIT, MARSHAL EARP, ALL OF THIS YOU TOLD US IS A BIT HARD TO DOWNLOAD. IF WE HADN'T EXPERIENCED IT WITH OUR OWN EYES...
SPEAKING OF ADMITTING STUFF, I THOUGHT ABOUT USING THE OLD "*MONSTER-MOVIE-RADIOACTIVE-PROVING-GROUNDS-MADE-THEM-INTO-FLESH-EATING-CANNIBALS*" THING BUT... WELL, IT JUST SEEMED A BIT MUCH.
WE OWE YOU OUR LIVES, MARSHAL EARP. I DON'T KNOW HOW WE'RE GOING TO EXPLAIN THIS TO HQ. NO IDEA AT ALL.
UH, YEAH... ABOUT THAT EXPLAINING PART...
WELL, WE CAN START WITH THE VID...
BLAM
BLAM

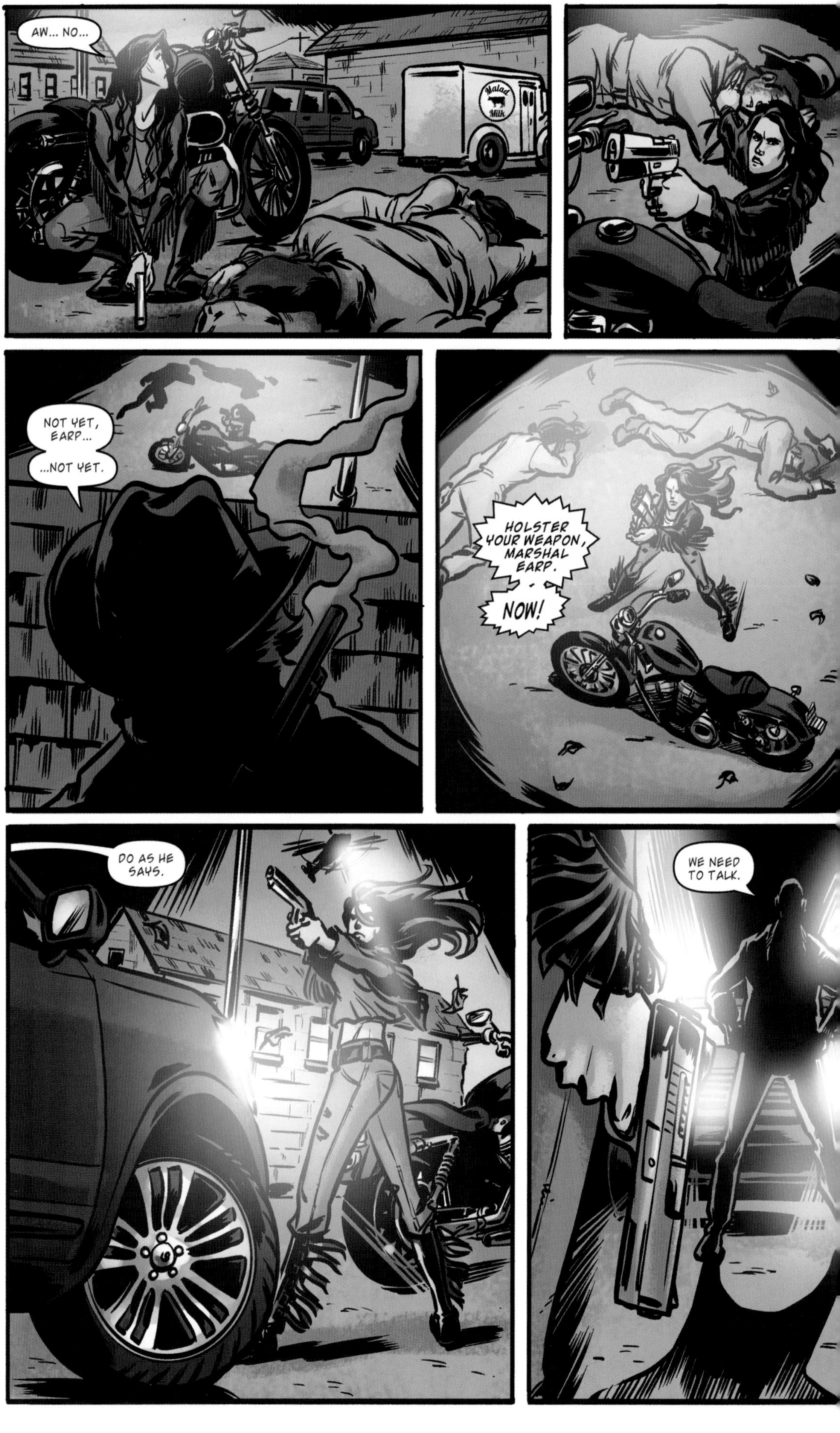
AW... NO...
Malad Milk
NOT YET, EARP...
...NOT YET.
HOLSTER YOUR WEAPON, MARSHAL EARP.
NOW!
DO AS HE SAYS.
WE NEED TO TALK.

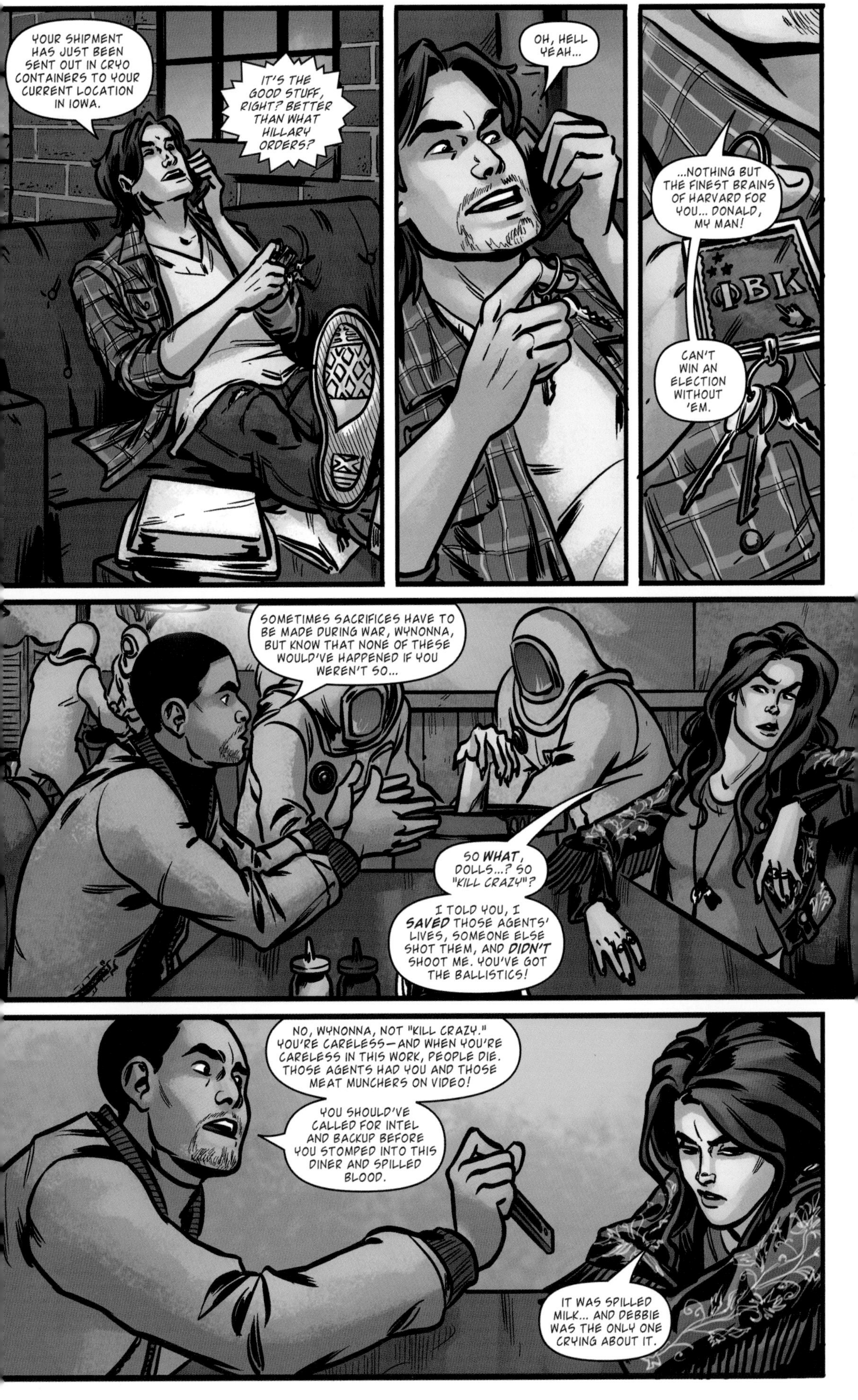
YOUR SHIPMENT HAS JUST BEEN SENT OUT IN CRYO CONTAINERS TO YOUR CURRENT LOCATION IN IOWA.
IT'S THE GOOD STUFF, RIGHT? BETTER THAN WHAT HILLARY ORDERS?
OH, HELL YEAH...
...NOTHING BUT THE FINEST BRAINS OF HARVARD FOR YOU... DONALD, MY MAN!
ΦBK
CAN'T WIN AN ELECTION WITHOUT 'EM.
SOMETIMES SACRIFICES HAVE TO BE MADE DURING WAR, WYNONNA, BUT KNOW THAT NONE OF THESE WOULD'VE HAPPENED IF YOU WEREN'T SO...
SO *WHAT*, DOLLS...? SO "*KILL CRAZY*"?
I TOLD YOU, I *SAVED* THOSE AGENTS' LIVES, SOMEONE ELSE SHOT THEM, AND *DIDN'T* SHOOT ME. YOU'VE GOT THE BALLISTICS!
NO, WYNONNA, NOT "KILL CRAZY." YOU'RE CARELESS—AND WHEN YOU'RE CARELESS IN THIS WORK, PEOPLE DIE. THOSE AGENTS HAD YOU AND THOSE MEAT MUNCHERS ON VIDEO!
YOU SHOULD'VE CALLED FOR INTEL AND BACKUP BEFORE YOU STOMPED INTO THIS DINER AND SPILLED BLOOD.
IT WAS SPILLED MILK... AND DEBBIE WAS THE ONLY ONE CRYING ABOUT IT.

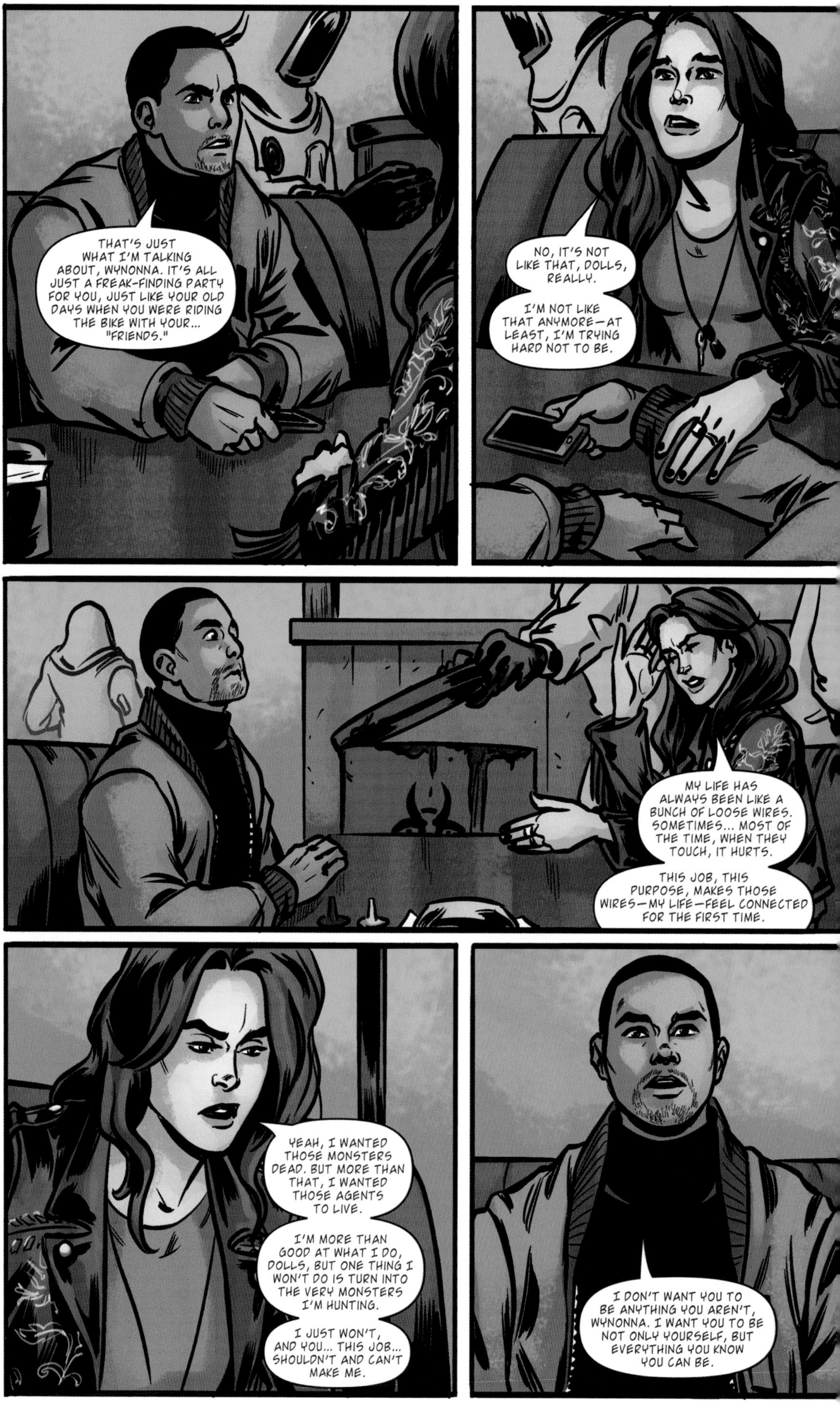
THAT'S JUST WHAT I'M TALKING ABOUT, WYNONNA. IT'S ALL JUST A FREAK-FINDING PARTY FOR YOU, JUST LIKE YOUR OLD DAYS WHEN YOU WERE RIDING THE BIKE WITH YOUR... "FRIENDS."
NO, IT'S NOT LIKE THAT, DOLLS, REALLY.
I'M NOT LIKE THAT ANYMORE—AT LEAST, I'M TRYING HARD NOT TO BE.
MY LIFE HAS ALWAYS BEEN LIKE A BUNCH OF LOOSE WIRES. SOMETIMES... MOST OF THE TIME, WHEN THEY TOUCH, IT HURTS.
THIS JOB, THIS PURPOSE, MAKES THOSE WIRES—MY LIFE—FEEL CONNECTED FOR THE FIRST TIME.
YEAH, I WANTED THOSE MONSTERS DEAD. BUT MORE THAN THAT, I WANTED THOSE AGENTS TO LIVE.
I'M MORE THAN GOOD AT WHAT I DO, DOLLS, BUT ONE THING I WON'T DO IS TURN INTO THE VERY MONSTERS I'M HUNTING.
I JUST WON'T, AND YOU... THIS JOB... SHOULDN'T AND CAN'T MAKE ME.
I DON'T WANT YOU TO BE ANYTHING YOU AREN'T, WYNONNA. I WANT YOU TO BE NOT ONLY YOURSELF, BUT EVERYTHING YOU KNOW YOU CAN BE.

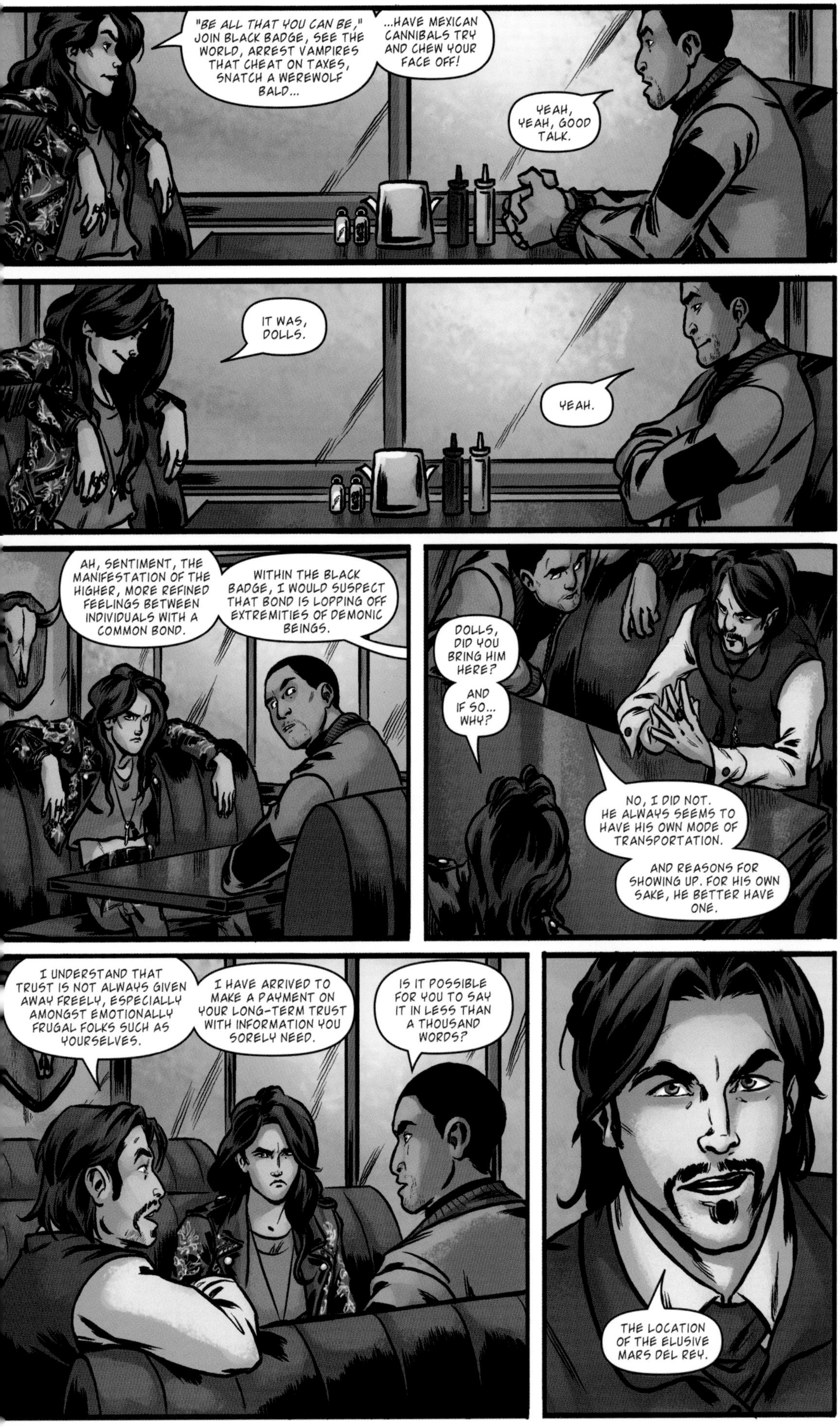
"BE ALL THAT YOU CAN BE," JOIN BLACK BADGE, SEE THE WORLD, ARREST VAMPIRES THAT CHEAT ON TAXES, SNATCH A WEREWOLF BALD...
...HAVE MEXICAN CANNIBALS TRY AND CHEW YOUR FACE OFF!
YEAH, YEAH, GOOD TALK.
IT WAS, DOLLS.
YEAH.
AH, SENTIMENT, THE MANIFESTATION OF THE HIGHER, MORE REFINED FEELINGS BETWEEN INDIVIDUALS WITH A COMMON BOND.
WITHIN THE BLACK BADGE, I WOULD SUSPECT THAT BOND IS LOPPING OFF EXTREMITIES OF DEMONIC BEINGS.
DOLLS, DID YOU BRING HIM HERE?
AND IF SO... WHY?
NO, I DID NOT. HE ALWAYS SEEMS TO HAVE HIS OWN MODE OF TRANSPORTATION.
AND REASONS FOR SHOWING UP. FOR HIS OWN SAKE, HE BETTER HAVE ONE.
I UNDERSTAND THAT TRUST IS NOT ALWAYS GIVEN AWAY FREELY, ESPECIALLY AMONGST EMOTIONALLY FRUGAL FOLKS SUCH AS YOURSELVES.
I HAVE ARRIVED TO MAKE A PAYMENT ON YOUR LONG-TERM TRUST WITH INFORMATION YOU SORELY NEED.
IS IT POSSIBLE FOR YOU TO SAY IT IN LESS THAN A THOUSAND WORDS?
THE LOCATION OF THE ELUSIVE MARS DEL REY.

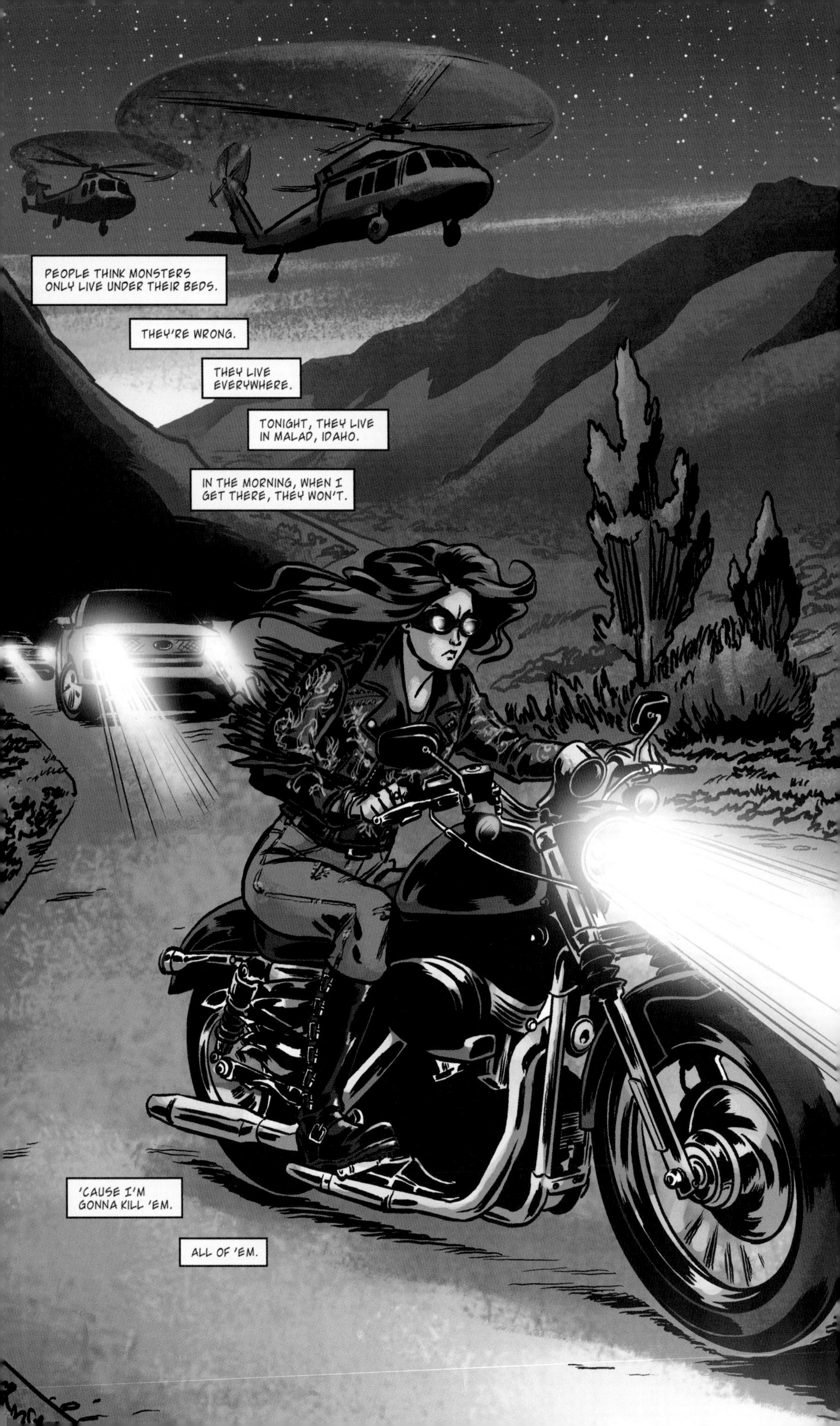
PEOPLE THINK MONSTERS ONLY LIVE UNDER THEIR BEDS.
THEY'RE WRONG.
THEY LIVE EVERYWHERE.
TONIGHT, THEY LIVE IN MALAD, IDAHO.
IN THE MORNING, WHEN I GET THERE, THEY WON'T.
'CAUSE I'M GONNA KILL 'EM.
ALL OF 'EM.

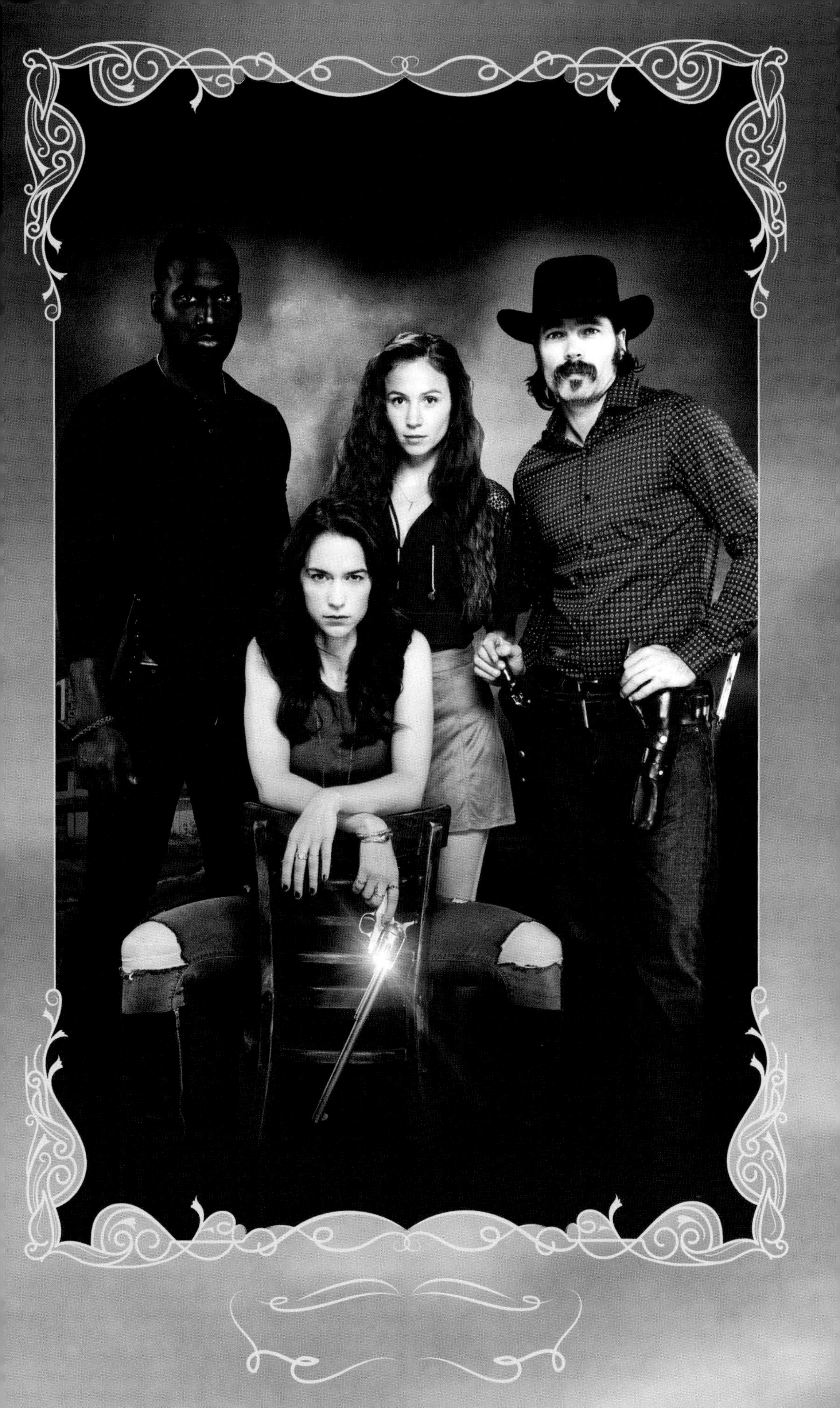

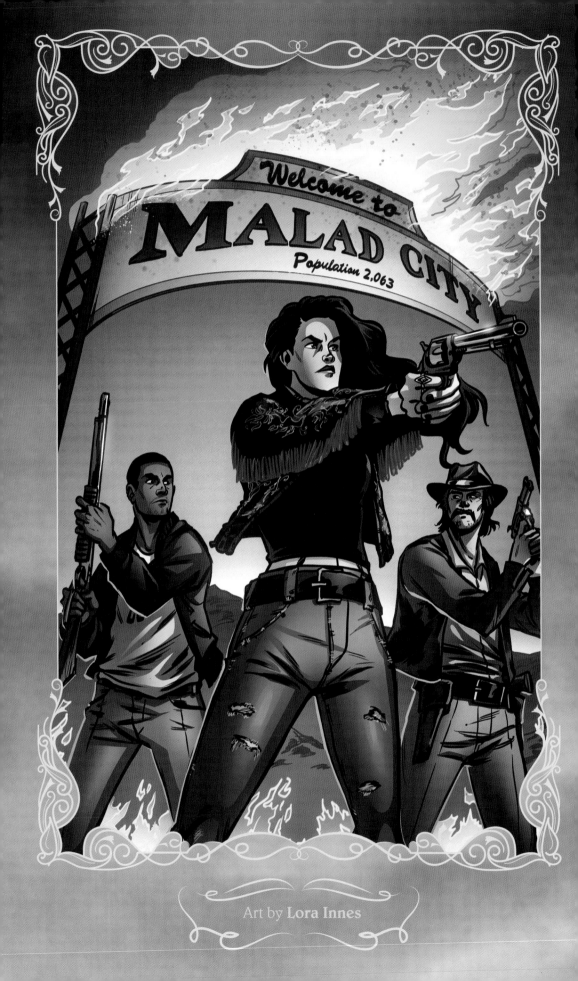

Welcome to MALAD CITY
Population 2,063

Art by **Lora Innes**

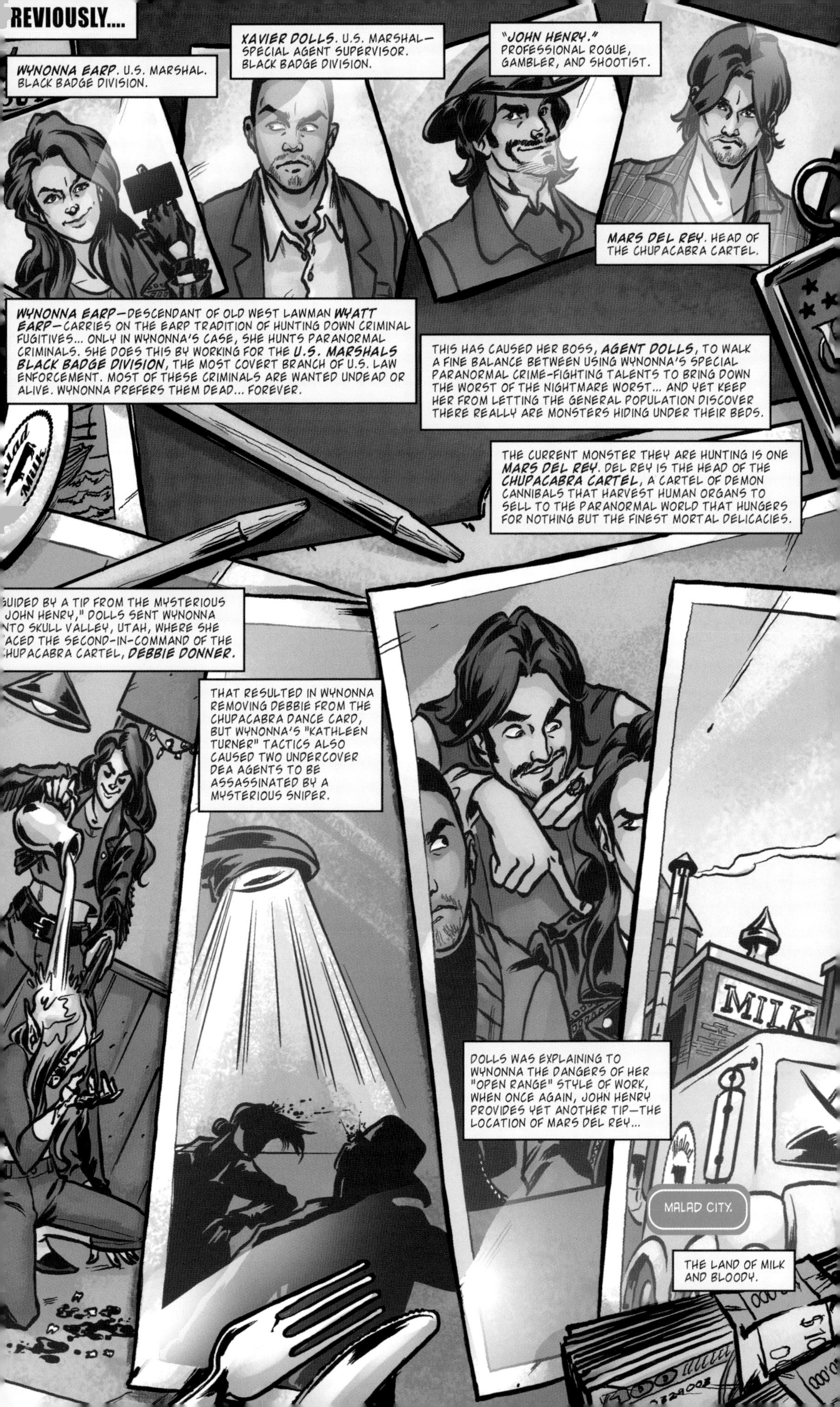
REVIOUSLY....
WYNONNA EARP. U.S. MARSHAL. BLACK BADGE DIVISION.
XAVIER DOLLS. U.S. MARSHAL—SPECIAL AGENT SUPERVISOR. BLACK BADGE DIVISION.
"JOHN HENRY." PROFESSIONAL ROGUE, GAMBLER, AND SHOOTIST.
MARS DEL REY. HEAD OF THE CHUPACABRA CARTEL.
WYNONNA EARP—DESCENDANT OF OLD WEST LAWMAN WYATT EARP—CARRIES ON THE EARP TRADITION OF HUNTING DOWN CRIMINAL FUGITIVES... ONLY IN WYNONNA'S CASE, SHE HUNTS PARANORMAL CRIMINALS. SHE DOES THIS BY WORKING FOR THE U.S. MARSHALS BLACK BADGE DIVISION, THE MOST COVERT BRANCH OF U.S. LAW ENFORCEMENT. MOST OF THESE CRIMINALS ARE WANTED UNDEAD OR ALIVE. WYNONNA PREFERS THEM DEAD... FOREVER.
THIS HAS CAUSED HER BOSS, AGENT DOLLS, TO WALK A FINE BALANCE BETWEEN USING WYNONNA'S SPECIAL PARANORMAL CRIME-FIGHTING TALENTS TO BRING DOWN THE WORST OF THE NIGHTMARE WORST... AND YET KEEP HER FROM LETTING THE GENERAL POPULATION DISCOVER THERE REALLY ARE MONSTERS HIDING UNDER THEIR BEDS.
THE CURRENT MONSTER THEY ARE HUNTING IS ONE MARS DEL REY. DEL REY IS THE HEAD OF THE CHUPACABRA CARTEL, A CARTEL OF DEMON CANNIBALS THAT HARVEST HUMAN ORGANS TO SELL TO THE PARANORMAL WORLD THAT HUNGERS FOR NOTHING BUT THE FINEST MORTAL DELICACIES.
UIDED BY A TIP FROM THE MYSTERIOUS JOHN HENRY," DOLLS SENT WYNONNA NTO SKULL VALLEY, UTAH, WHERE SHE ACED THE SECOND-IN-COMMAND OF THE HUPACABRA CARTEL, DEBBIE DONNER.
THAT RESULTED IN WYNONNA REMOVING DEBBIE FROM THE CHUPACABRA DANCE CARD, BUT WYNONNA'S "KATHLEEN TURNER" TACTICS ALSO CAUSED TWO UNDERCOVER DEA AGENTS TO BE ASSASSINATED BY A MYSTERIOUS SNIPER.
DOLLS WAS EXPLAINING TO WYNONNA THE DANGERS OF HER "OPEN RANGE" STYLE OF WORK, WHEN ONCE AGAIN, JOHN HENRY PROVIDES YET ANOTHER TIP—THE LOCATION OF MARS DEL REY...
MILK
MALAD CITY.
THE LAND OF MILK AND BLOODY.

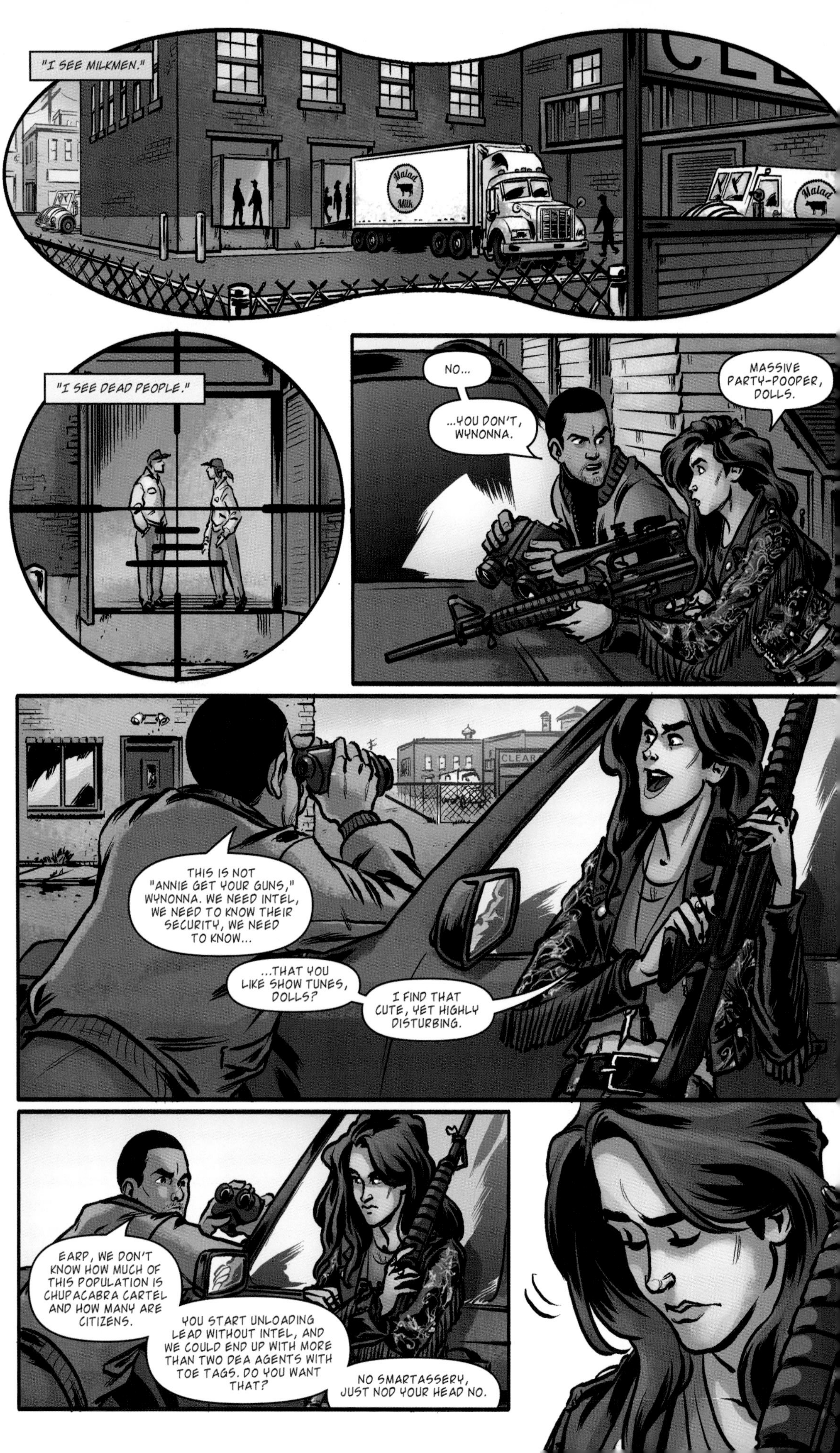
"I SEE MILKMEN."
Malad Milk
"I SEE DEAD PEOPLE."
NO...
...YOU DON'T, WYNONNA.
MASSIVE PARTY-POOPER, DOLLS.
CLEAR
THIS IS NOT "ANNIE GET YOUR GUNS," WYNONNA. WE NEED INTEL, WE NEED TO KNOW THEIR SECURITY, WE NEED TO KNOW...
...THAT YOU LIKE SHOW TUNES, DOLLS?
I FIND THAT CUTE, YET HIGHLY DISTURBING.
EARP, WE DON'T KNOW HOW MUCH OF THIS POPULATION IS CHUPACABRA CARTEL AND HOW MANY ARE CITIZENS.
YOU START UNLOADING LEAD WITHOUT INTEL, AND WE COULD END UP WITH MORE THAN TWO DEA AGENTS WITH TOE TAGS. DO YOU WANT THAT?
NO SMARTASSERY, JUST NOD YOUR HEAD NO.

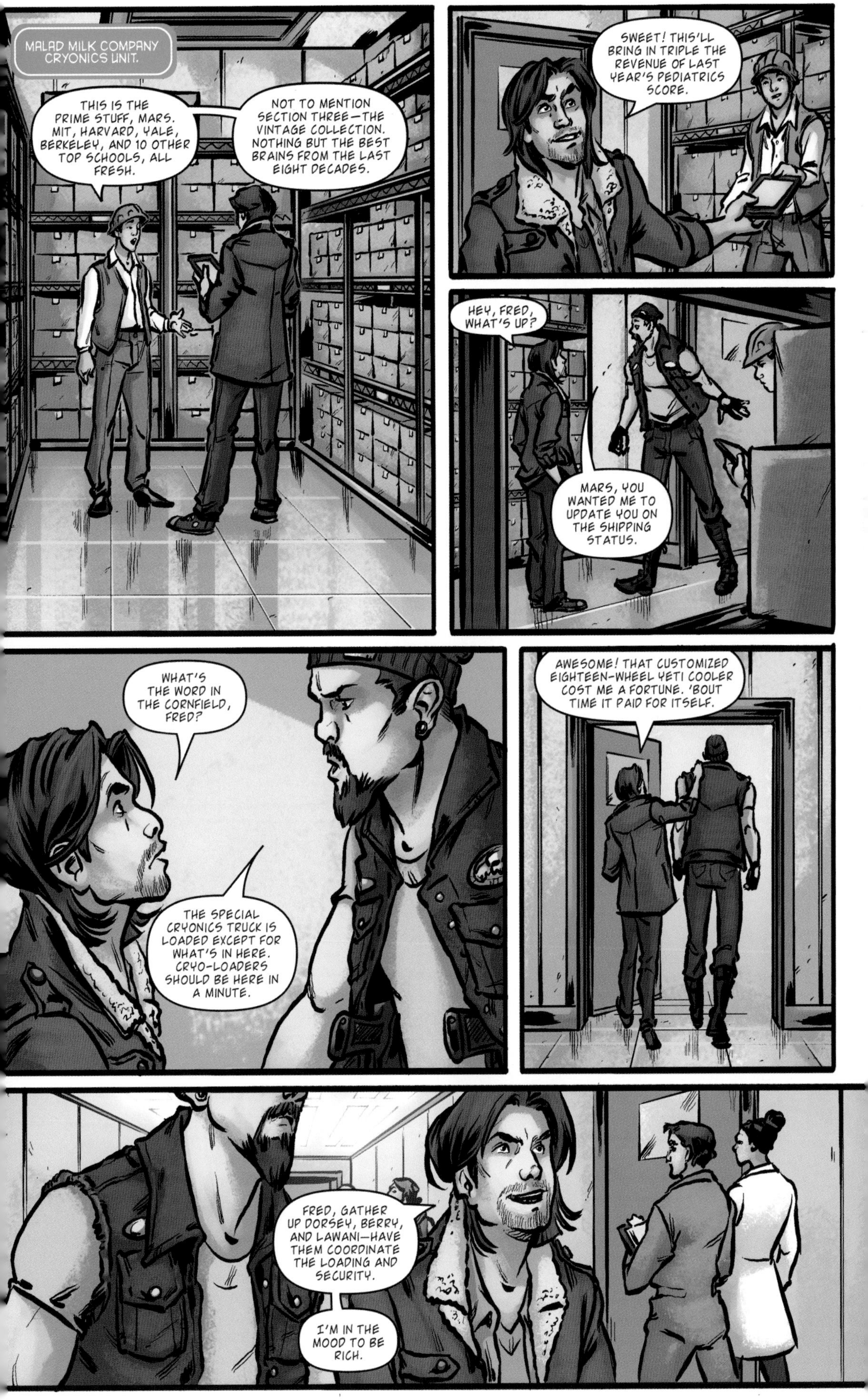
MALAD MILK COMPANY CRYONICS UNIT.
THIS IS THE PRIME STUFF, MARS. MIT, HARVARD, YALE, BERKELEY, AND 10 OTHER TOP SCHOOLS, ALL FRESH.
NOT TO MENTION SECTION THREE—THE VINTAGE COLLECTION. NOTHING BUT THE BEST BRAINS FROM THE LAST EIGHT DECADES.
SWEET! THIS'LL BRING IN TRIPLE THE REVENUE OF LAST YEAR'S PEDIATRICS SCORE.
HEY, FRED, WHAT'S UP?
MARS, YOU WANTED ME TO UPDATE YOU ON THE SHIPPING STATUS.
WHAT'S THE WORD IN THE CORNFIELD, FRED?
THE SPECIAL CRYONICS TRUCK IS LOADED EXCEPT FOR WHAT'S IN HERE. CRYO-LOADERS SHOULD BE HERE IN A MINUTE.
AWESOME! THAT CUSTOMIZED EIGHTEEN-WHEEL YETI COOLER COST ME A FORTUNE. 'BOUT TIME IT PAID FOR ITSELF.
FRED, GATHER UP DORSEY, BERRY, AND LAWANI—HAVE THEM COORDINATE THE LOADING AND SECURITY.
I'M IN THE MOOD TO BE RICH.

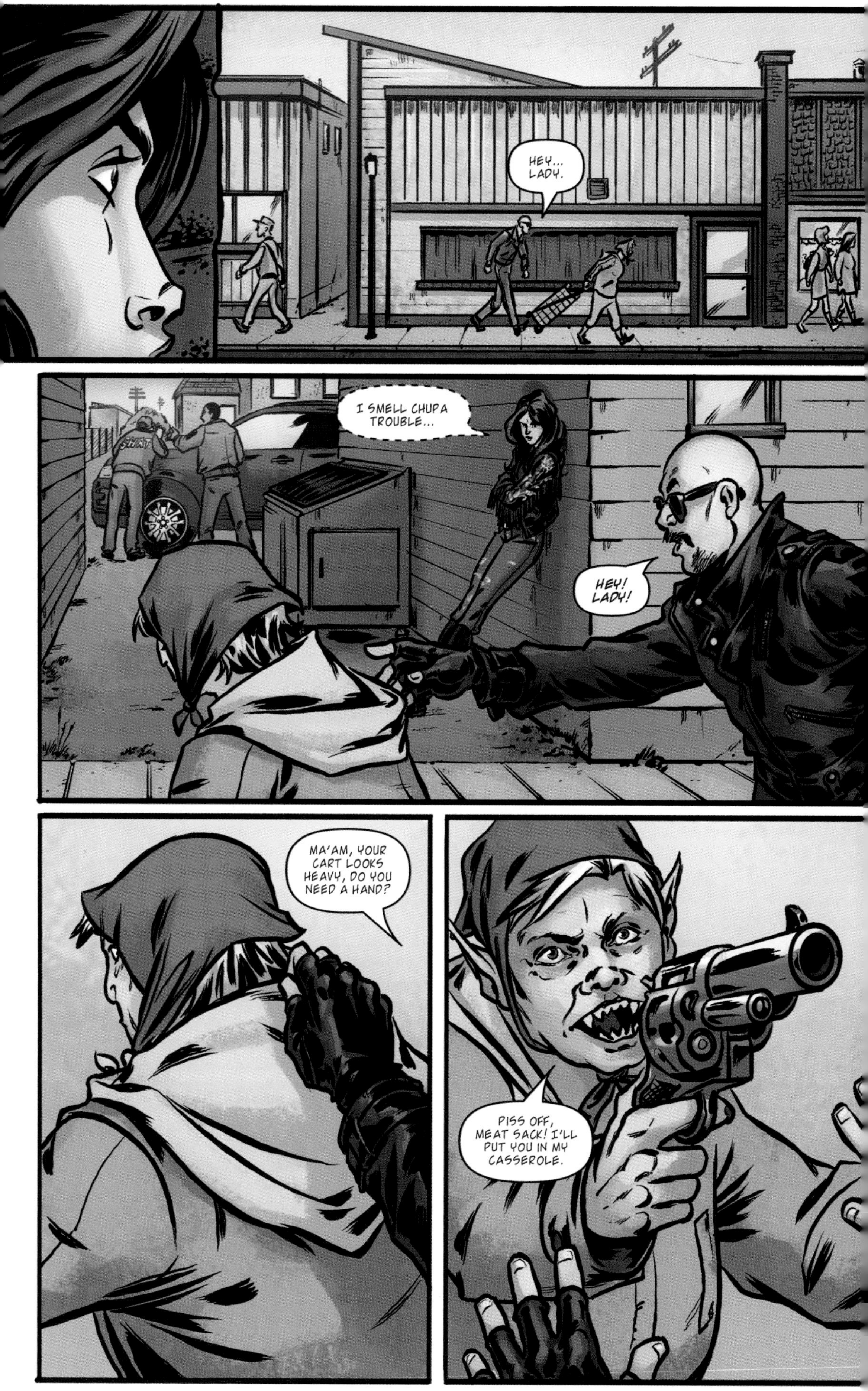

HEY... LADY.
I SMELL CHUPA TROUBLE...
HEY! LADY!
MA'AM, YOUR CART LOOKS HEAVY, DO YOU NEED A HAND?
PISS OFF, MEAT SACK! I'LL PUT YOU IN MY CASSEROLE.

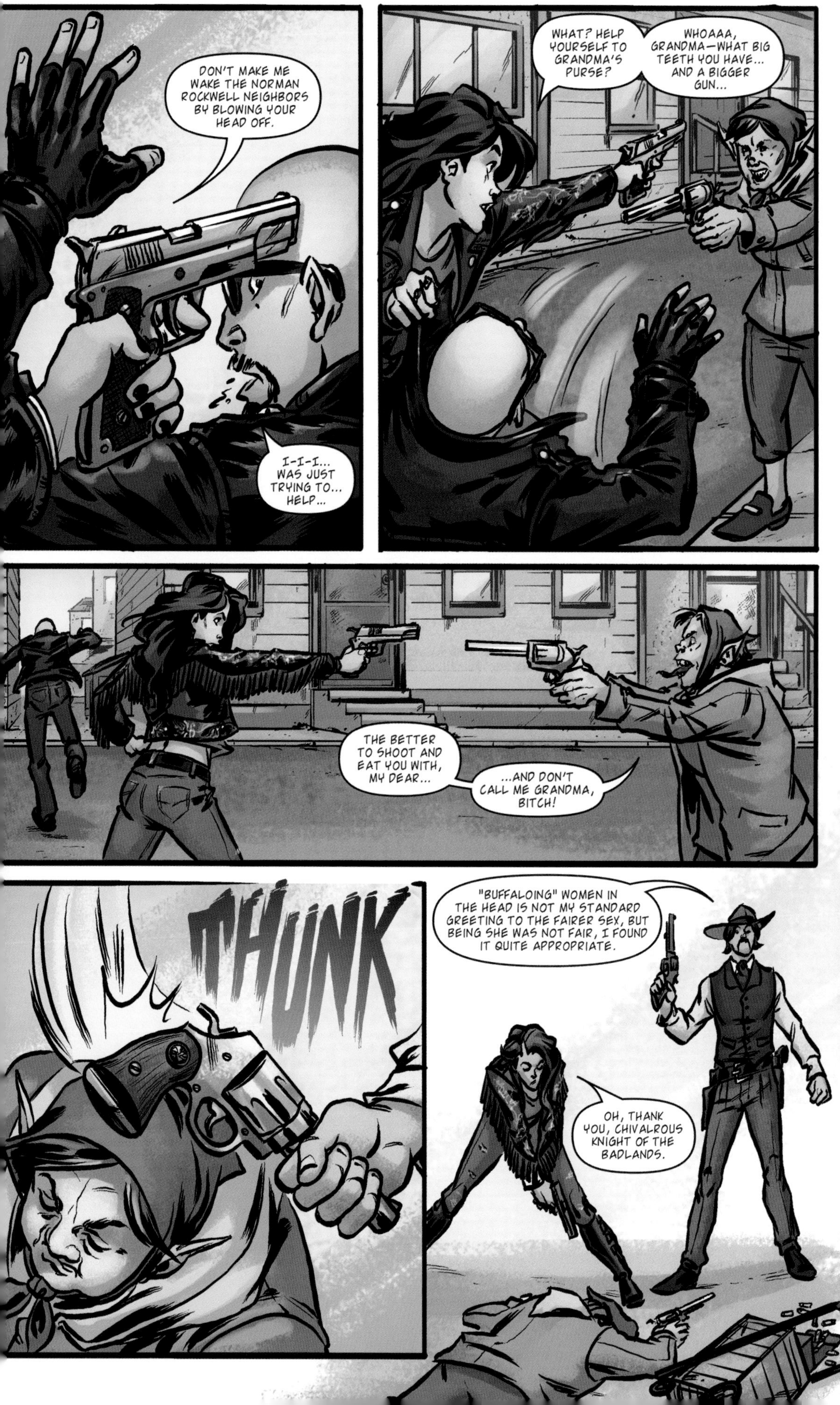
DON'T MAKE ME WAKE THE NORMAN ROCKWELL NEIGHBORS BY BLOWING YOUR HEAD OFF.
I-I-I... WAS JUST TRYING TO... HELP...
WHAT? HELP YOURSELF TO GRANDMA'S PURSE?
WHOAAA, GRANDMA—WHAT BIG TEETH YOU HAVE... AND A BIGGER GUN...
THE BETTER TO SHOOT AND EAT YOU WITH, MY DEAR...
...AND DON'T CALL ME GRANDMA, BITCH!
THUNK
"BUFFALOING" WOMEN IN THE HEAD IS NOT MY STANDARD GREETING TO THE FAIRER SEX, BUT BEING SHE WAS NOT FAIR, I FOUND IT QUITE APPROPRIATE.
OH, THANK YOU, CHIVALROUS KNIGHT OF THE BADLANDS.

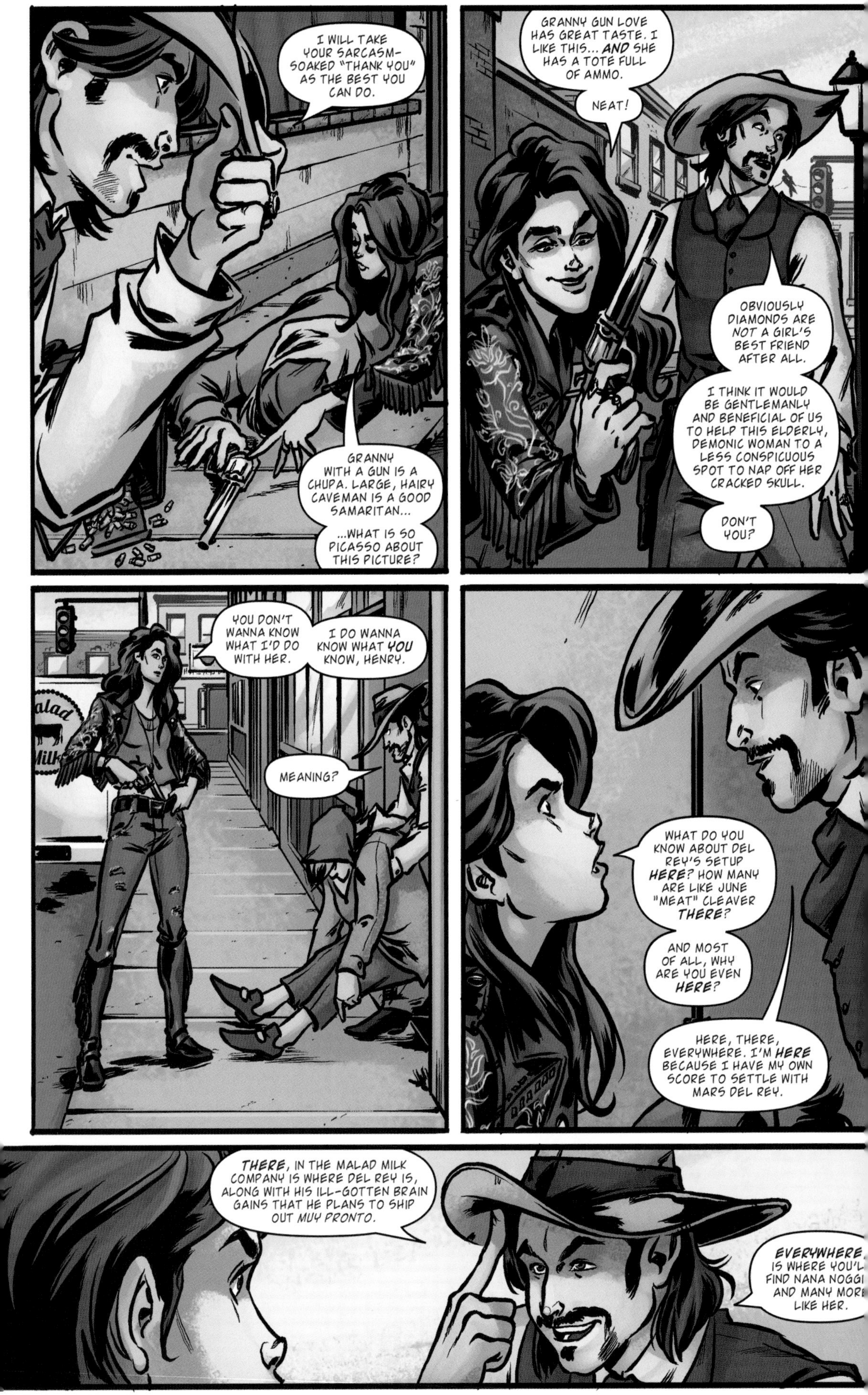
I WILL TAKE YOUR SARCASM-SOAKED "THANK YOU" AS THE BEST YOU CAN DO.
GRANNY WITH A GUN IS A CHUPA. LARGE, HAIRY CAVEMAN IS A GOOD SAMARITAN...
...WHAT IS SO PICASSO ABOUT THIS PICTURE?
GRANNY GUN LOVE HAS GREAT TASTE. I LIKE THIS... AND SHE HAS A TOTE FULL OF AMMO.
NEAT!
OBVIOUSLY DIAMONDS ARE NOT A GIRL'S BEST FRIEND AFTER ALL.
I THINK IT WOULD BE GENTLEMANLY AND BENEFICIAL OF US TO HELP THIS ELDERLY, DEMONIC WOMAN TO A LESS CONSPICUOUS SPOT TO NAP OFF HER CRACKED SKULL.
DON'T YOU?
YOU DON'T WANNA KNOW WHAT I'D DO WITH HER.
I DO WANNA KNOW WHAT YOU KNOW, HENRY.
MEANING?
WHAT DO YOU KNOW ABOUT DEL REY'S SETUP HERE? HOW MANY ARE LIKE JUNE "MEAT" CLEAVER THERE?
AND MOST OF ALL, WHY ARE YOU EVEN HERE?
HERE, THERE, EVERYWHERE. I'M HERE BECAUSE I HAVE MY OWN SCORE TO SETTLE WITH MARS DEL REY.
THERE, IN THE MALAD MILK COMPANY IS WHERE DEL REY IS, ALONG WITH HIS ILL-GOTTEN BRAIN GAINS THAT HE PLANS TO SHIP OUT MUY PRONTO.
EVERYWHERE IS WHERE YOU'L FIND NANA NOGGI AND MANY MORE LIKE HER.

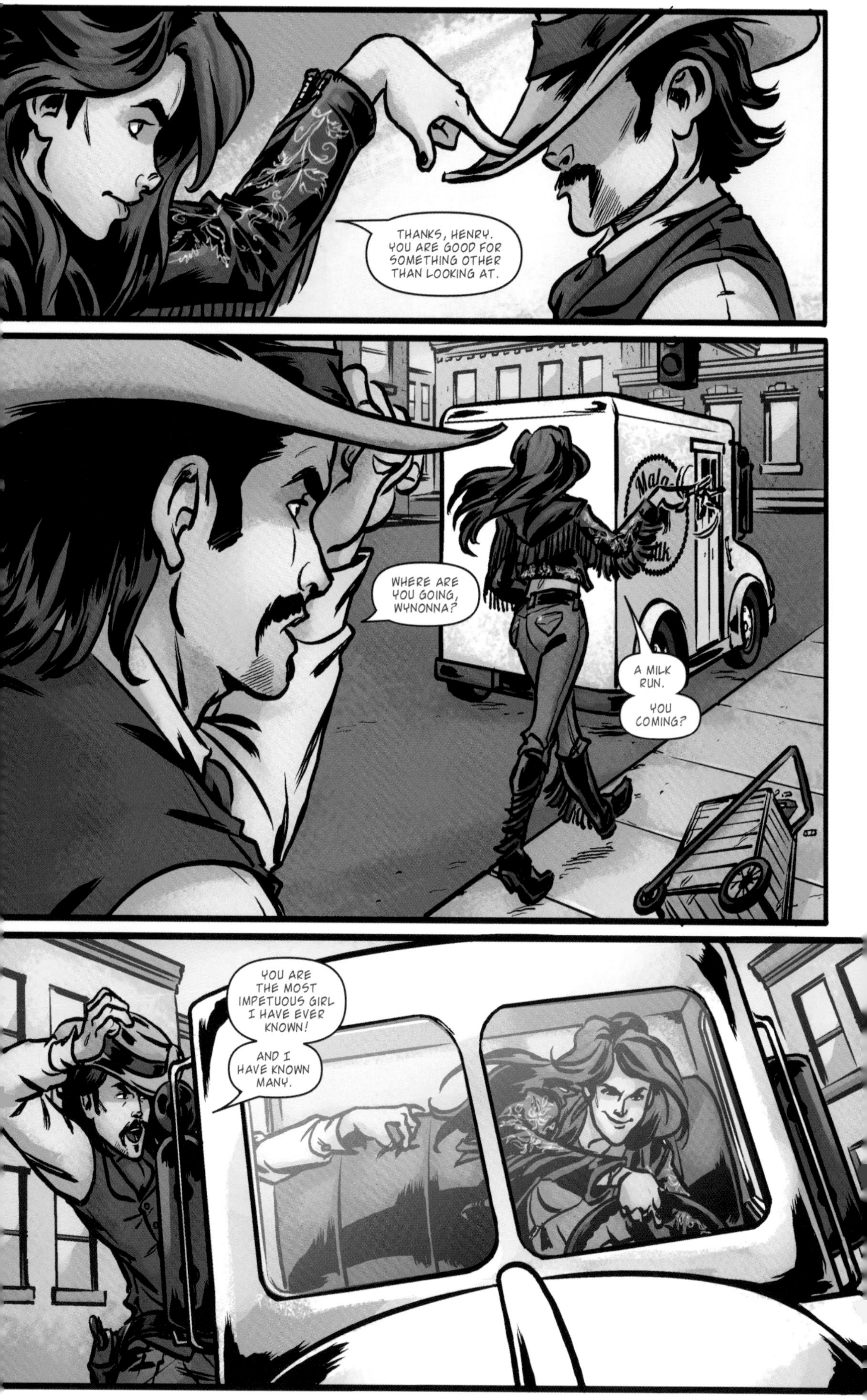
THANKS, HENRY. YOU ARE GOOD FOR SOMETHING OTHER THAN LOOKING AT.
WHERE ARE YOU GOING, WYNONNA?
A MILK RUN.
YOU COMING?
YOU ARE THE MOST IMPETUOUS GIRL I HAVE EVER KNOWN!
AND I HAVE KNOWN MANY.

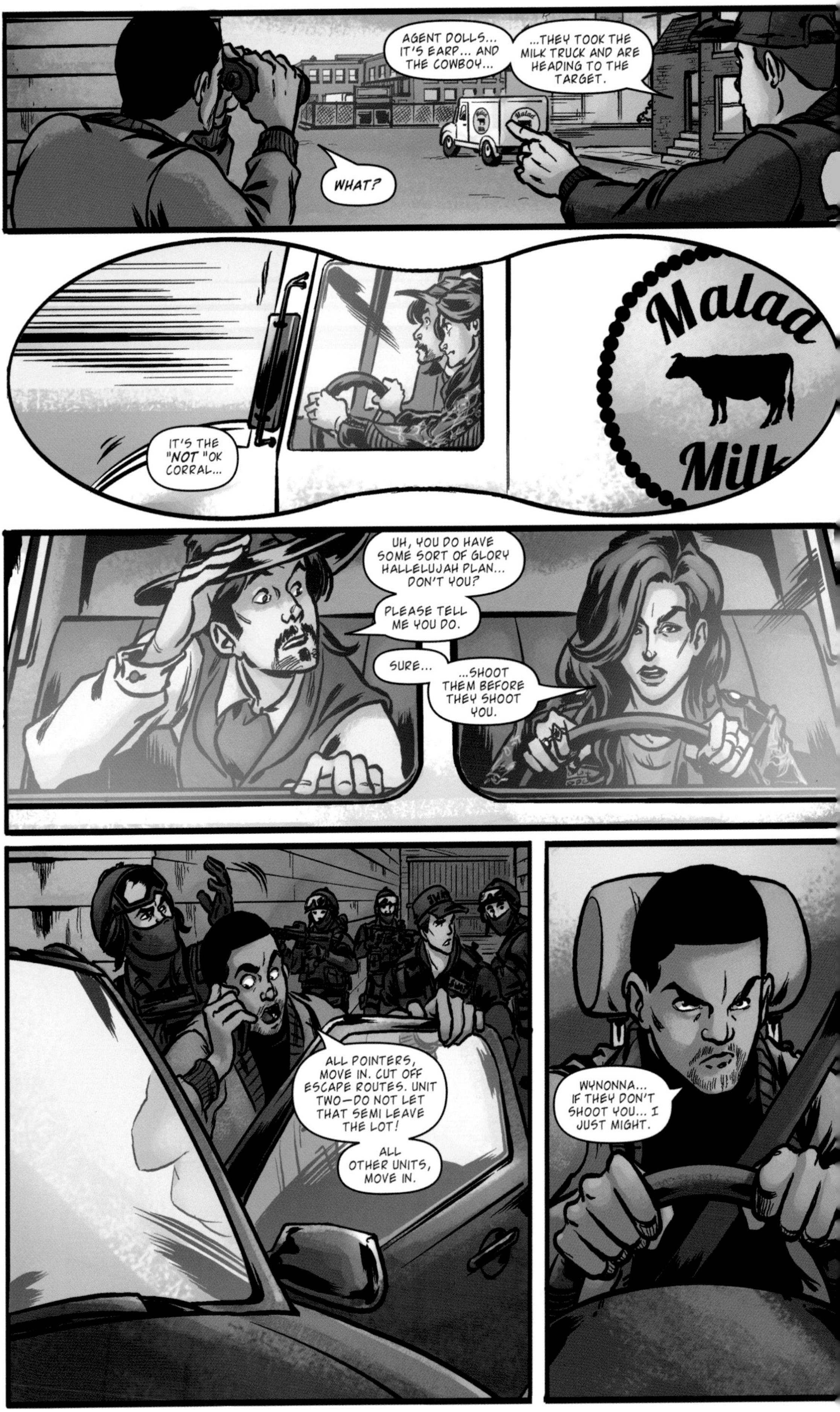

AGENT DOLLS... IT'S EARP... AND THE COWBOY...
...THEY TOOK THE MILK TRUCK AND ARE HEADING TO THE TARGET.
WHAT?
IT'S THE "NOT" OK CORRAL...
Malad Milk
UH, YOU DO HAVE SOME SORT OF GLORY HALLELUJAH PLAN... DON'T YOU?
PLEASE TELL ME YOU DO.
SURE...
...SHOOT THEM BEFORE THEY SHOOT YOU.
ALL POINTERS, MOVE IN. CUT OFF ESCAPE ROUTES. UNIT TWO—DO NOT LET THAT SEMI LEAVE THE LOT!
ALL OTHER UNITS, MOVE IN.
WYNONNA... IF THEY DON'T SHOOT YOU... I JUST MIGHT.

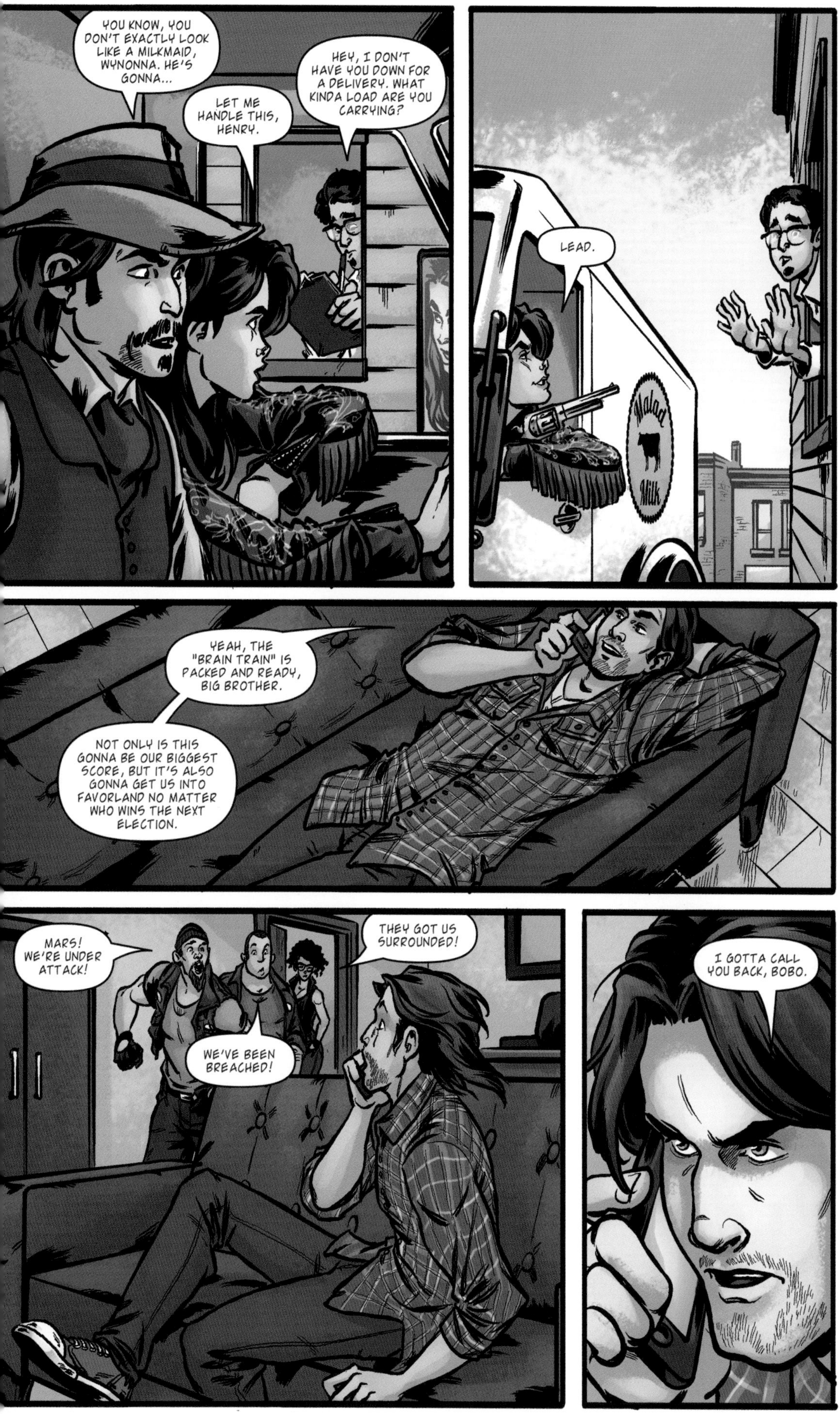
YOU KNOW, YOU DON'T EXACTLY LOOK LIKE A MILKMAID, WYNONNA. HE'S GONNA...
LET ME HANDLE THIS, HENRY.
HEY, I DON'T HAVE YOU DOWN FOR A DELIVERY. WHAT KINDA LOAD ARE YOU CARRYING?
LEAD.
Malad
Milk
YEAH, THE "BRAIN TRAIN" IS PACKED AND READY, BIG BROTHER.
NOT ONLY IS THIS GONNA BE OUR BIGGEST SCORE, BUT IT'S ALSO GONNA GET US INTO FAVORLAND NO MATTER WHO WINS THE NEXT ELECTION.
MARS! WE'RE UNDER ATTACK!
THEY GOT US SURROUNDED!
WE'VE BEEN BREACHED!
I GOTTA CALL YOU BACK, BOBO.

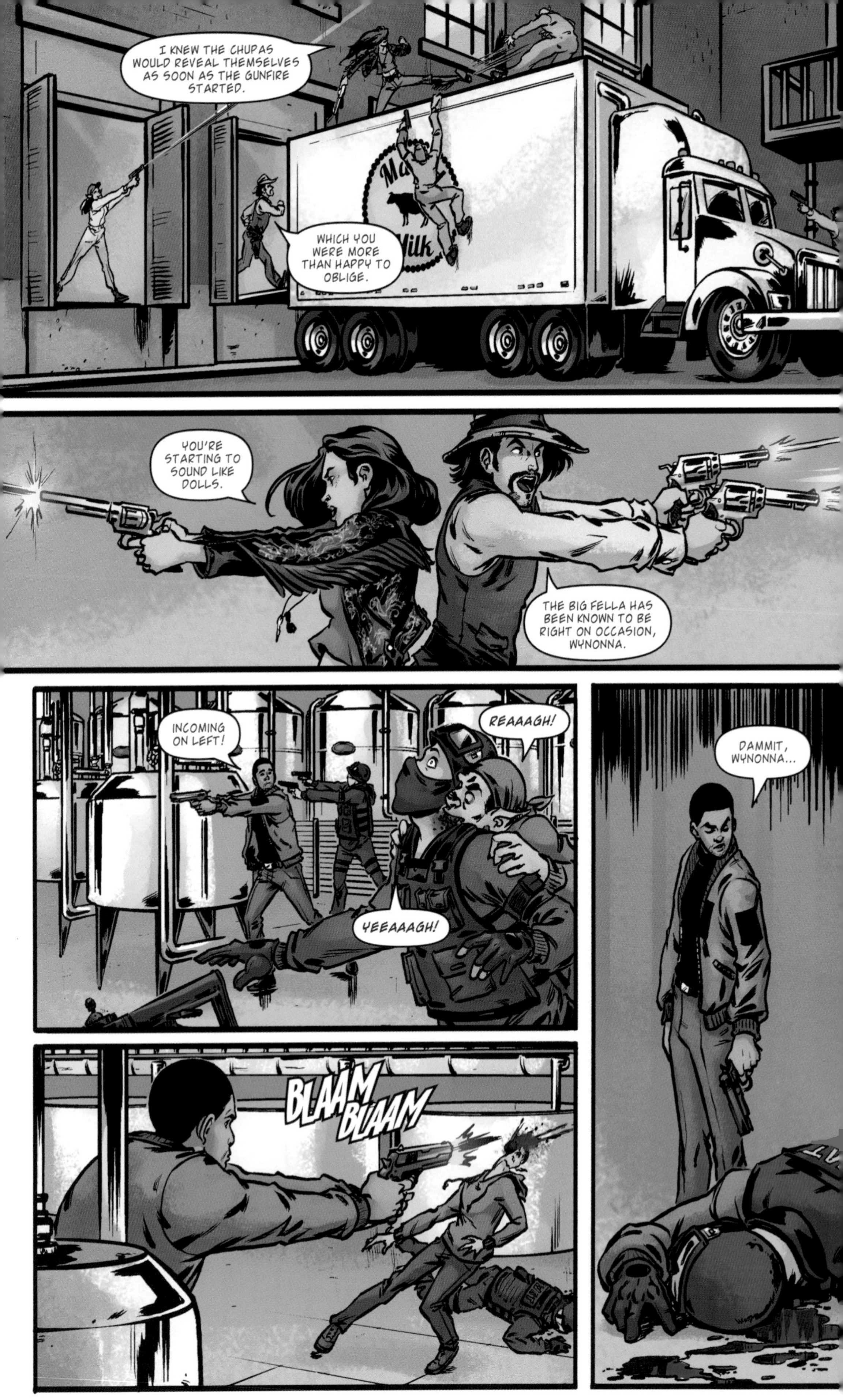
I KNEW THE CHUPAS WOULD REVEAL THEMSELVES AS SOON AS THE GUNFIRE STARTED.
WHICH YOU WERE MORE THAN HAPPY TO OBLIGE.
YOU'RE STARTING TO SOUND LIKE DOLLS.
THE BIG FELLA HAS BEEN KNOWN TO BE RIGHT ON OCCASION, WYNONNA.
INCOMING ON LEFT!
REAAAGH!
YEEAAAGH!
BLAAM BLAAM
DAMMIT, WYNONNA...

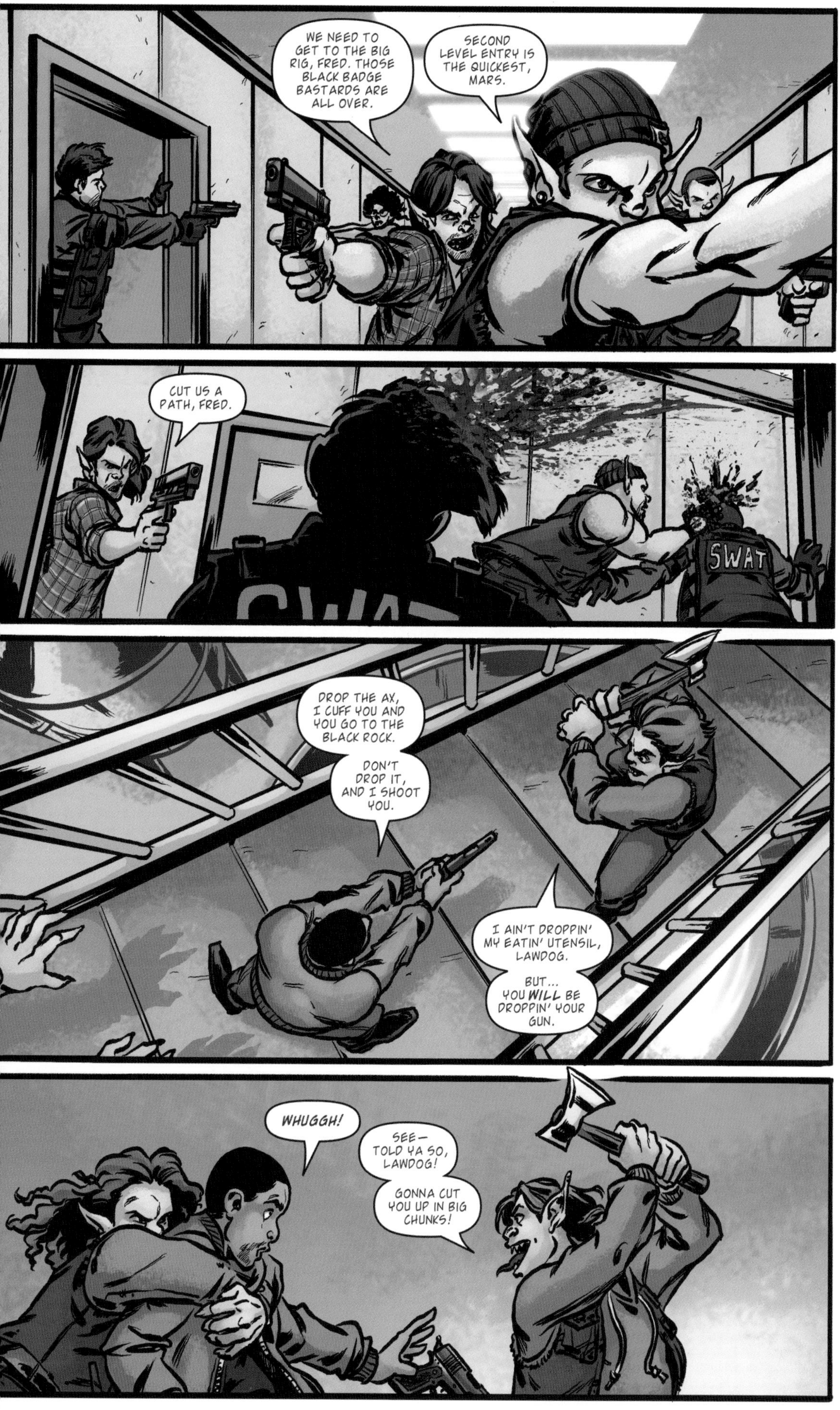
WE NEED TO GET TO THE BIG RIG, FRED. THOSE BLACK BADGE BASTARDS ARE ALL OVER.
SECOND LEVEL ENTRY IS THE QUICKEST, MARS.
CUT US A PATH, FRED.
SWAT
SWAT
DROP THE AX, I CUFF YOU AND YOU GO TO THE BLACK ROCK.
DON'T DROP IT, AND I SHOOT YOU.
I AIN'T DROPPIN' MY EATIN' UTENSIL, LAWDOG.
BUT... YOU **WILL** BE DROPPIN' YOUR GUN.
WHUGGH!
SEE— TOLD YA SO, LAWDOG!
GONNA CUT YOU UP IN BIG CHUNKS!

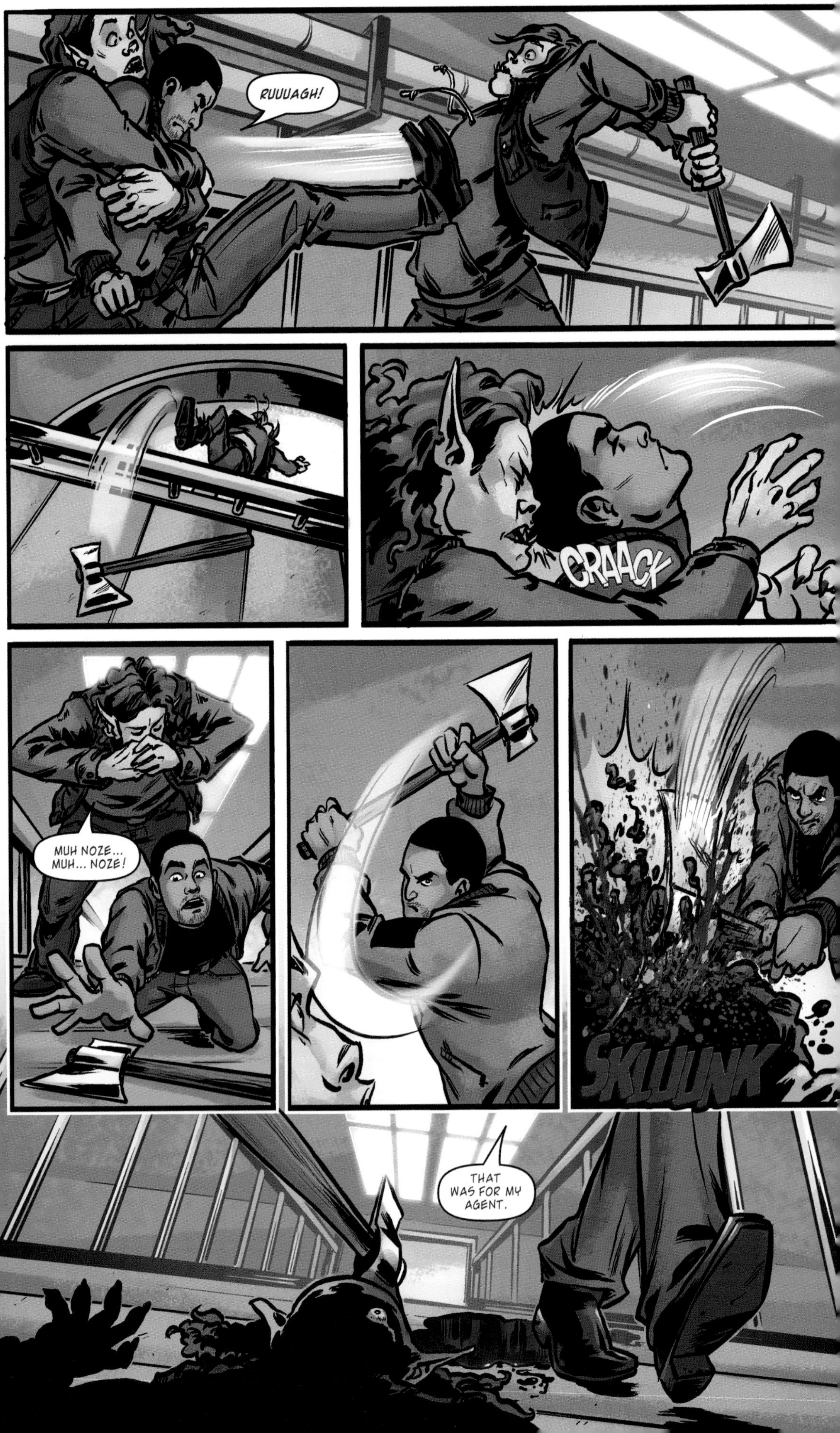
RUUUAGH!
CRAACK
MUH NOZE... MUH... NOZE!
SKLUUNK
THAT WAS FOR MY AGENT.

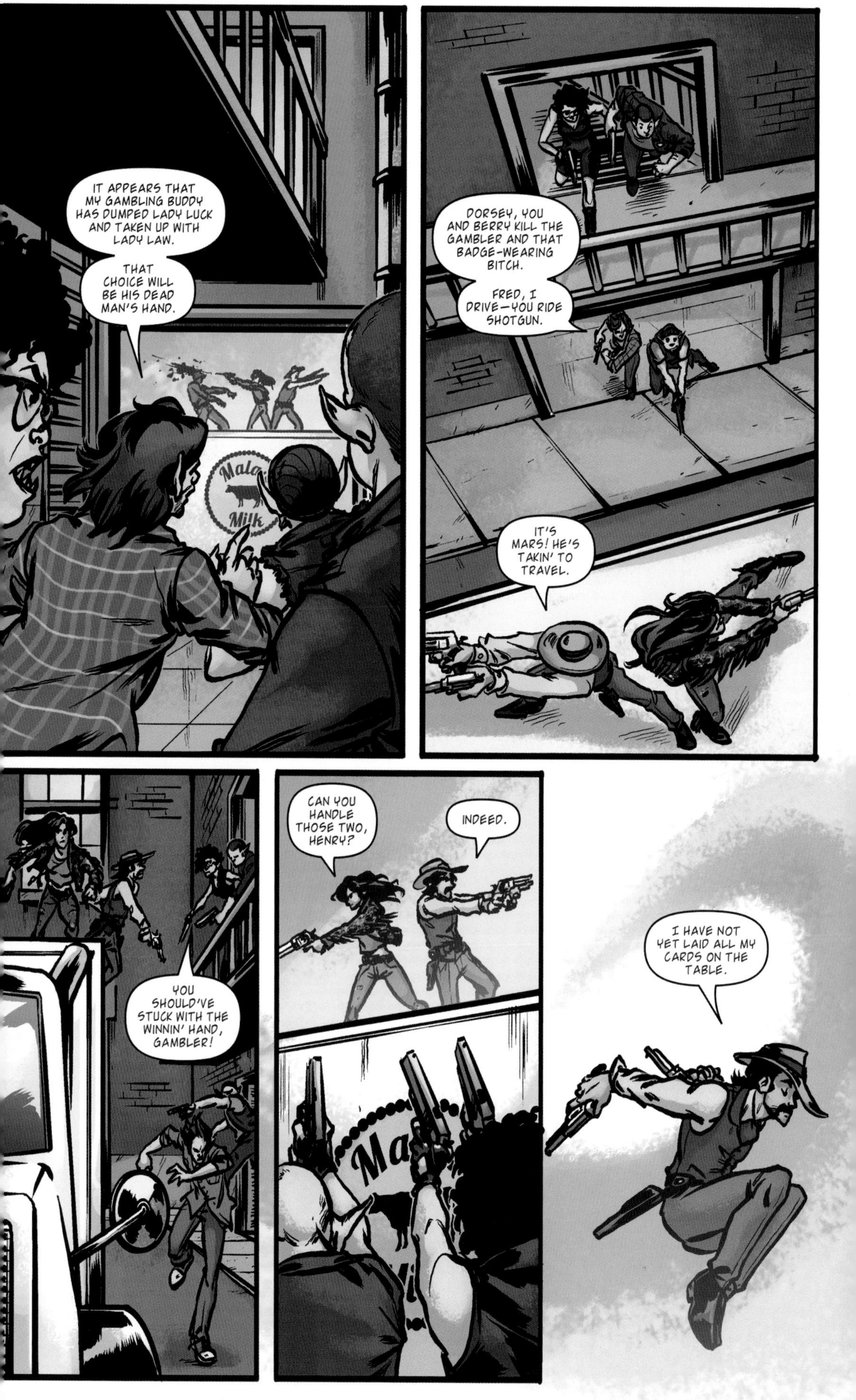
IT APPEARS THAT MY GAMBLING BUDDY HAS DUMPED LADY LUCK AND TAKEN UP WITH LADY LAW.
THAT CHOICE WILL BE HIS DEAD MAN'S HAND.
DORSEY, YOU AND BERRY KILL THE GAMBLER AND THAT BADGE-WEARING BITCH.
FRED, I DRIVE—YOU RIDE SHOTGUN.
IT'S MARS! HE'S TAKIN' TO TRAVEL.
YOU SHOULD'VE STUCK WITH THE WINNIN' HAND, GAMBLER!
CAN YOU HANDLE THOSE TWO, HENRY?
INDEED.
I HAVE NOT YET LAID ALL MY CARDS ON THE TABLE.

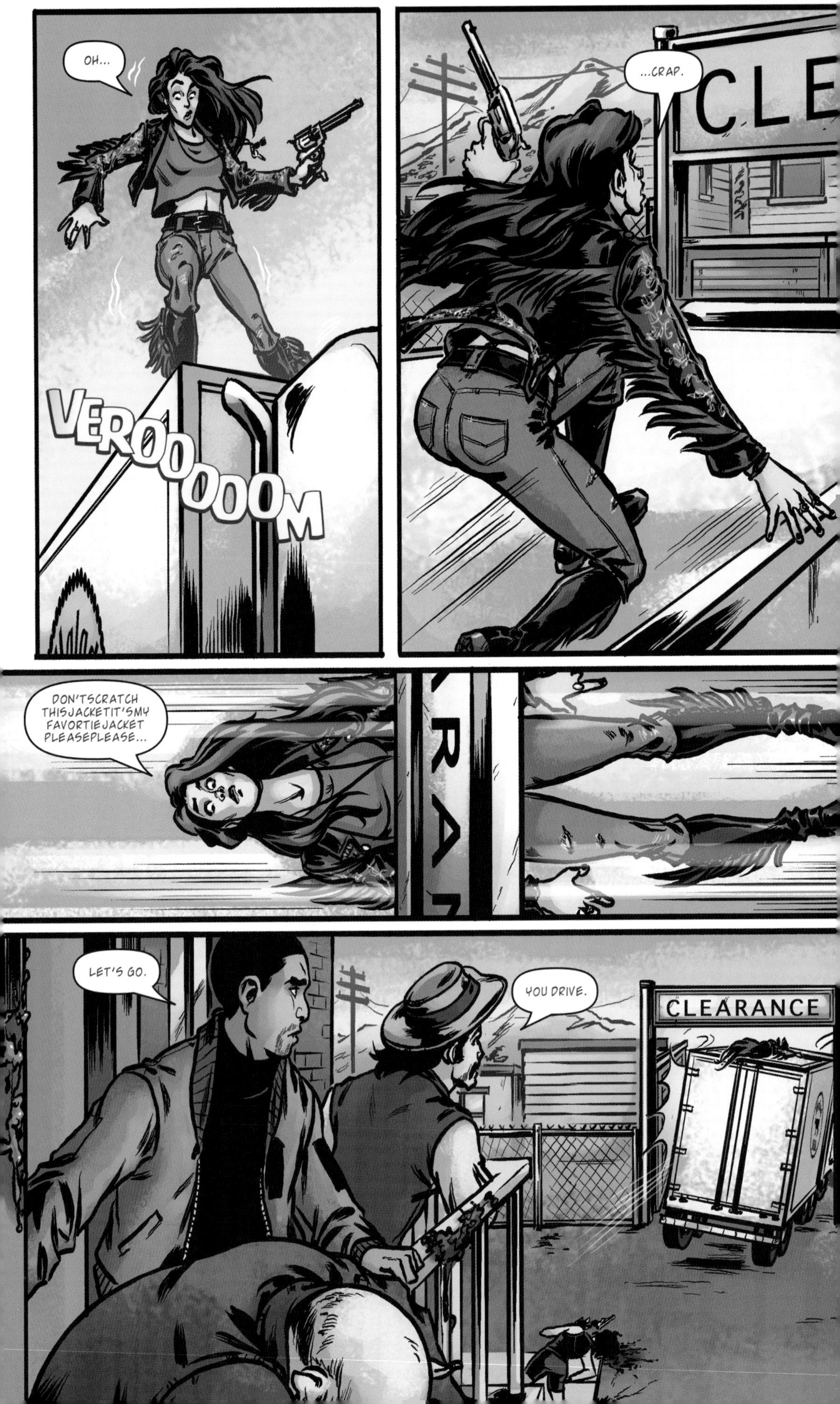
OH...
VEROOOOOOM
...CRAP.
CLE
DON'TSCRATCH THISJACKETIT'SMY FAVORTIEJACKET PLEASEPLEASE...
RA
LET'S GO.
YOU DRIVE.
CLEARANCE

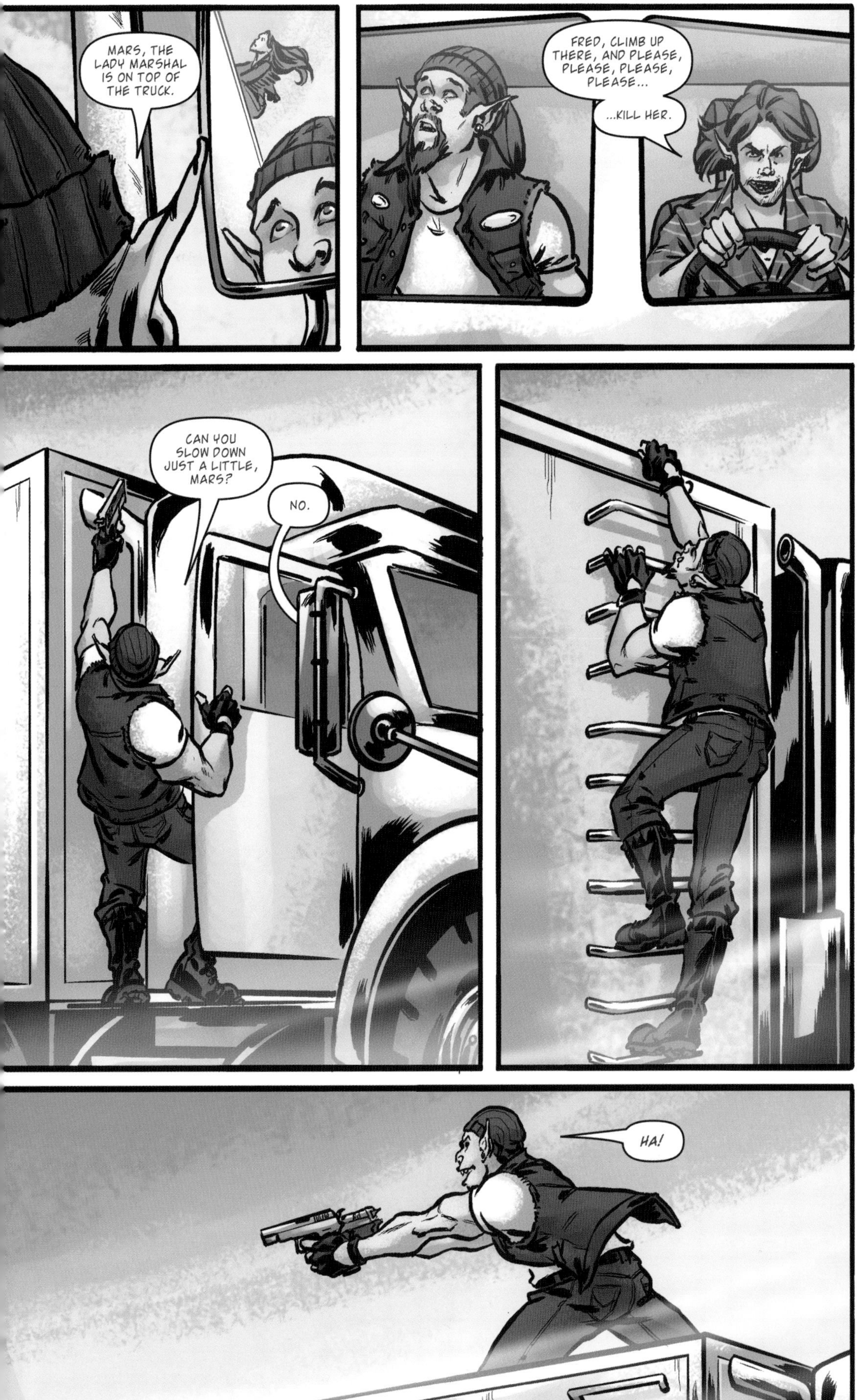
MARS, THE LADY MARSHAL IS ON TOP OF THE TRUCK.
FRED, CLIMB UP THERE, AND PLEASE, PLEASE, PLEASE, PLEASE...
...KILL HER.
CAN YOU SLOW DOWN JUST A LITTLE, MARS?
NO.
HA!

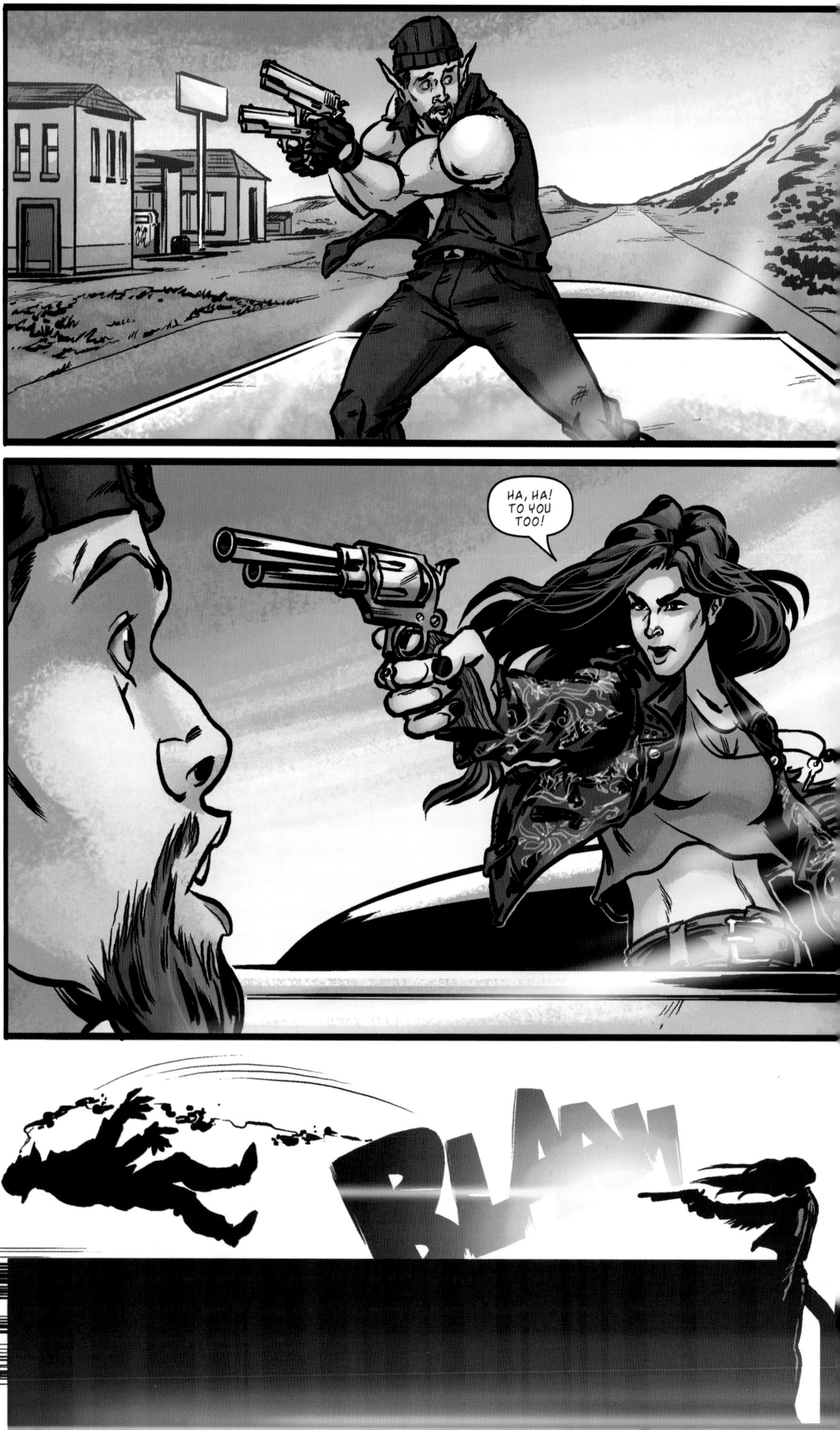
HA, HA! TO YOU TOO!
BLAAM

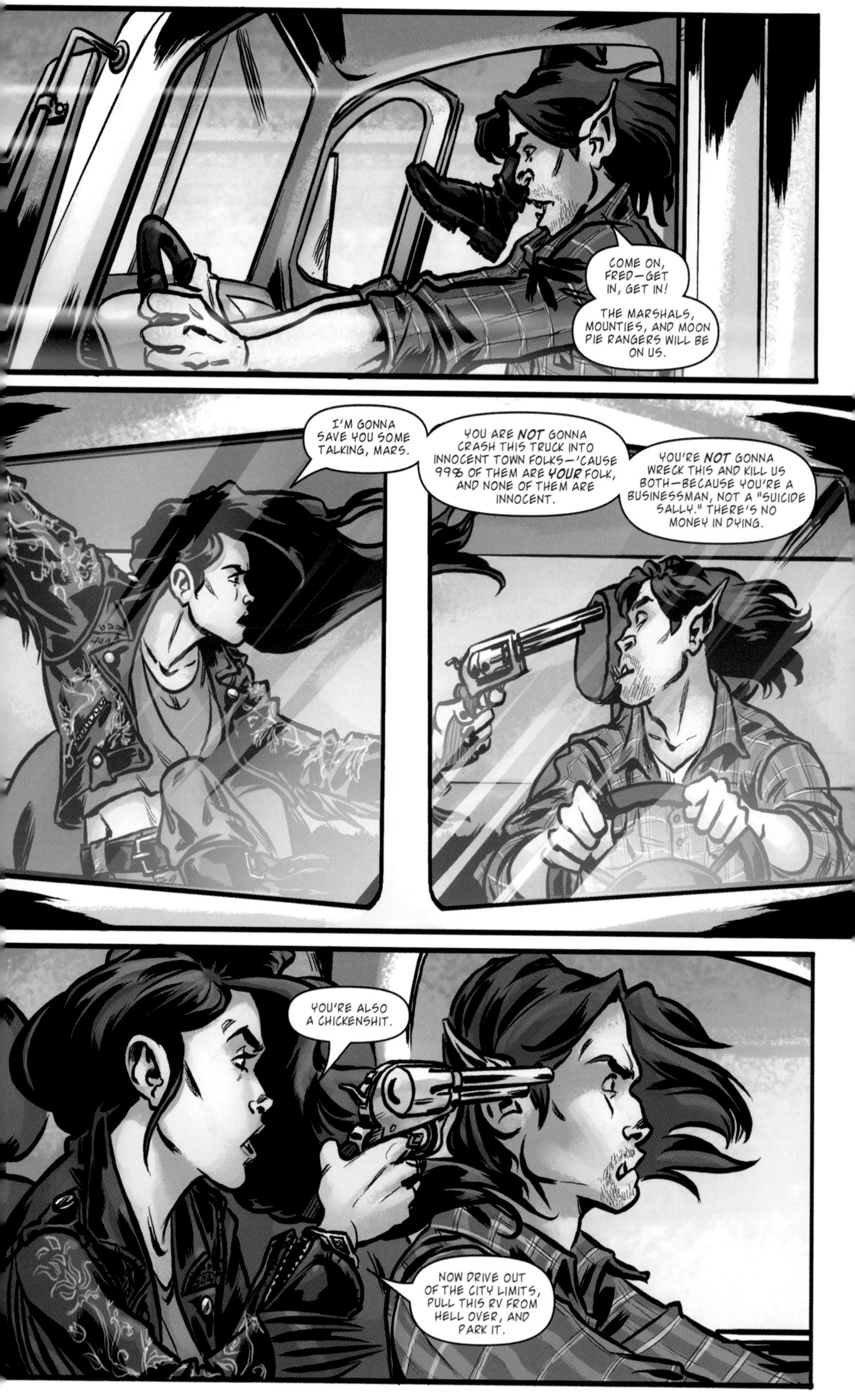
COME ON, FRED—GET IN, GET IN!
THE MARSHALS, MOUNTIES, AND MOON PIE RANGERS WILL BE ON US.
I'M GONNA SAVE YOU SOME TALKING, MARS.
YOU ARE NOT GONNA CRASH THIS TRUCK INTO INNOCENT TOWN FOLKS—'CAUSE 99% OF THEM ARE YOUR FOLK, AND NONE OF THEM ARE INNOCENT.
YOU'RE NOT GONNA WRECK THIS AND KILL US BOTH—BECAUSE YOU'RE A BUSINESSMAN, NOT A "SUICIDE SALLY." THERE'S NO MONEY IN DYING.
YOU'RE ALSO A CHICKENSHIT.
NOW DRIVE OUT OF THE CITY LIMITS, PULL THIS RV FROM HELL OVER, AND PARK IT.

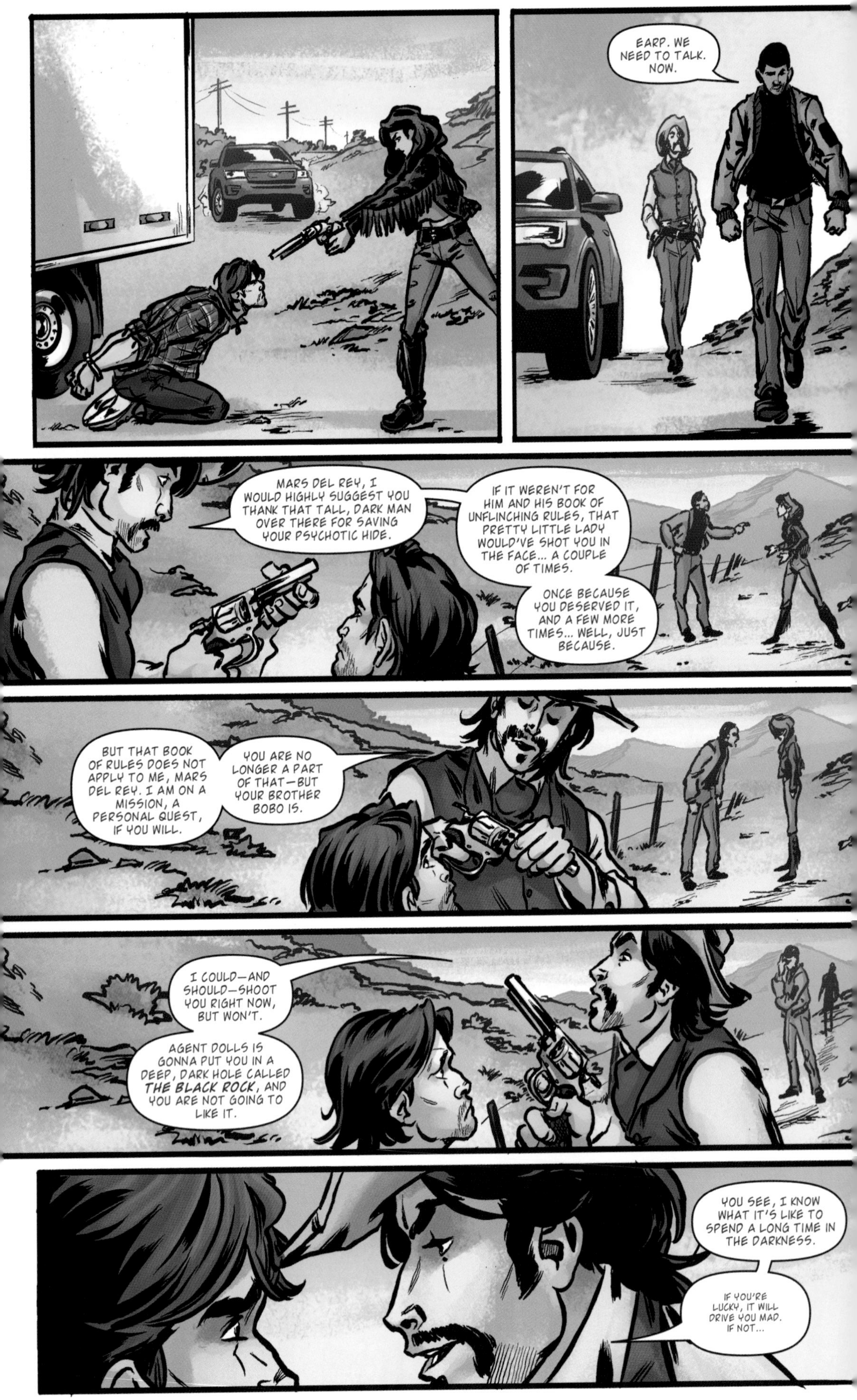
EARP. WE NEED TO TALK. NOW.
MARS DEL REY, I WOULD HIGHLY SUGGEST YOU THANK THAT TALL, DARK MAN OVER THERE FOR SAVING YOUR PSYCHOTIC HIDE.
IF IT WEREN'T FOR HIM AND HIS BOOK OF UNFLINCHING RULES, THAT PRETTY LITTLE LADY WOULD'VE SHOT YOU IN THE FACE... A COUPLE OF TIMES.
ONCE BECAUSE YOU DESERVED IT, AND A FEW MORE TIMES... WELL, JUST BECAUSE.
BUT THAT BOOK OF RULES DOES NOT APPLY TO ME, MARS DEL REY. I AM ON A MISSION, A PERSONAL QUEST, IF YOU WILL.
YOU ARE NO LONGER A PART OF THAT—BUT YOUR BROTHER BOBO IS.
I COULD—AND SHOULD—SHOOT YOU RIGHT NOW, BUT WON'T.
AGENT DOLLS IS GONNA PUT YOU IN A DEEP, DARK HOLE CALLED ***THE BLACK ROCK***, AND YOU ARE NOT GOING TO LIKE IT.
YOU SEE, I KNOW WHAT IT'S LIKE TO SPEND A LONG TIME IN THE DARKNESS.
IF YOU'RE LUCKY, IT WILL DRIVE YOU MAD. IF NOT...

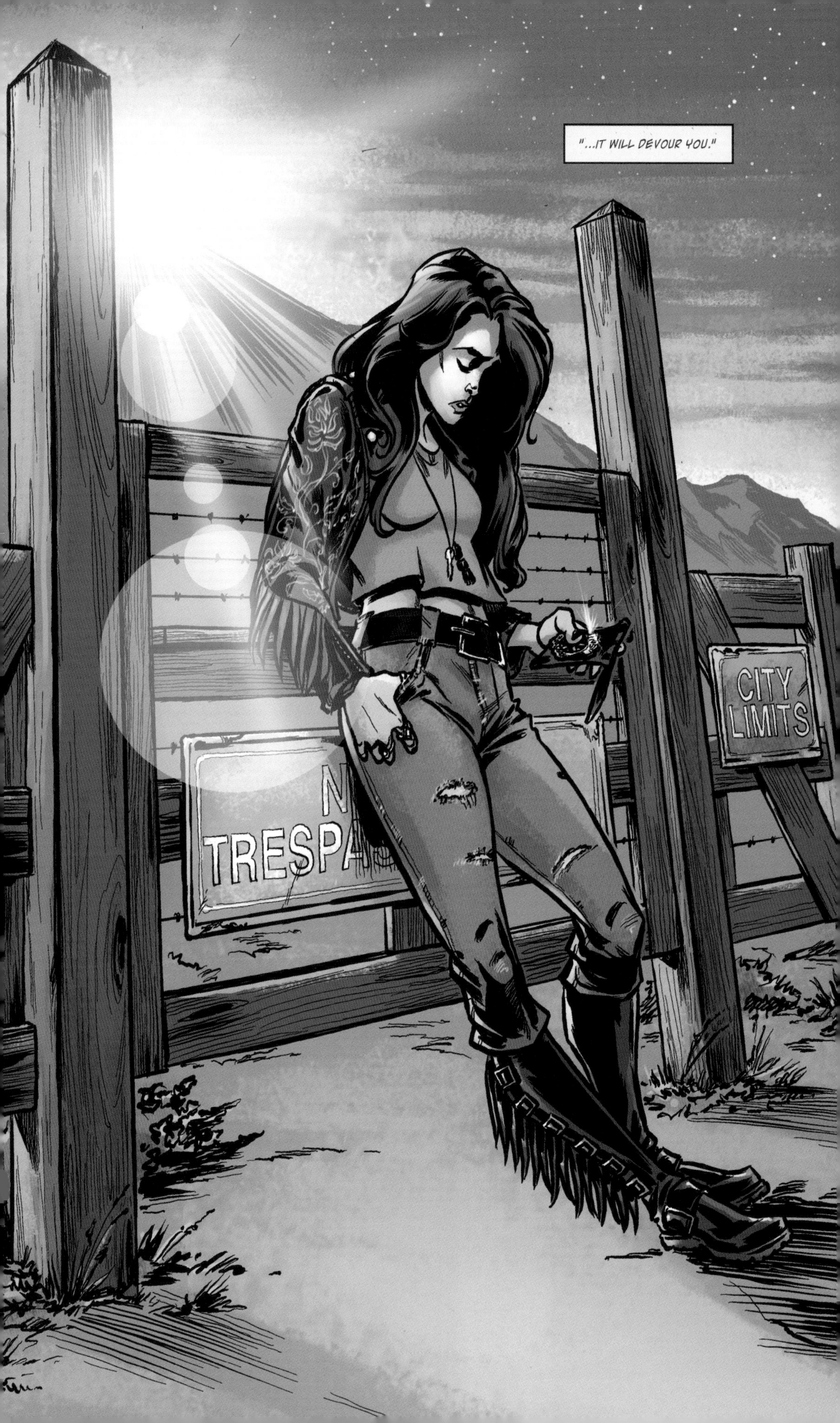
"...IT WILL DEVOUR YOU."
N
TRESPA
CITY LIMITS

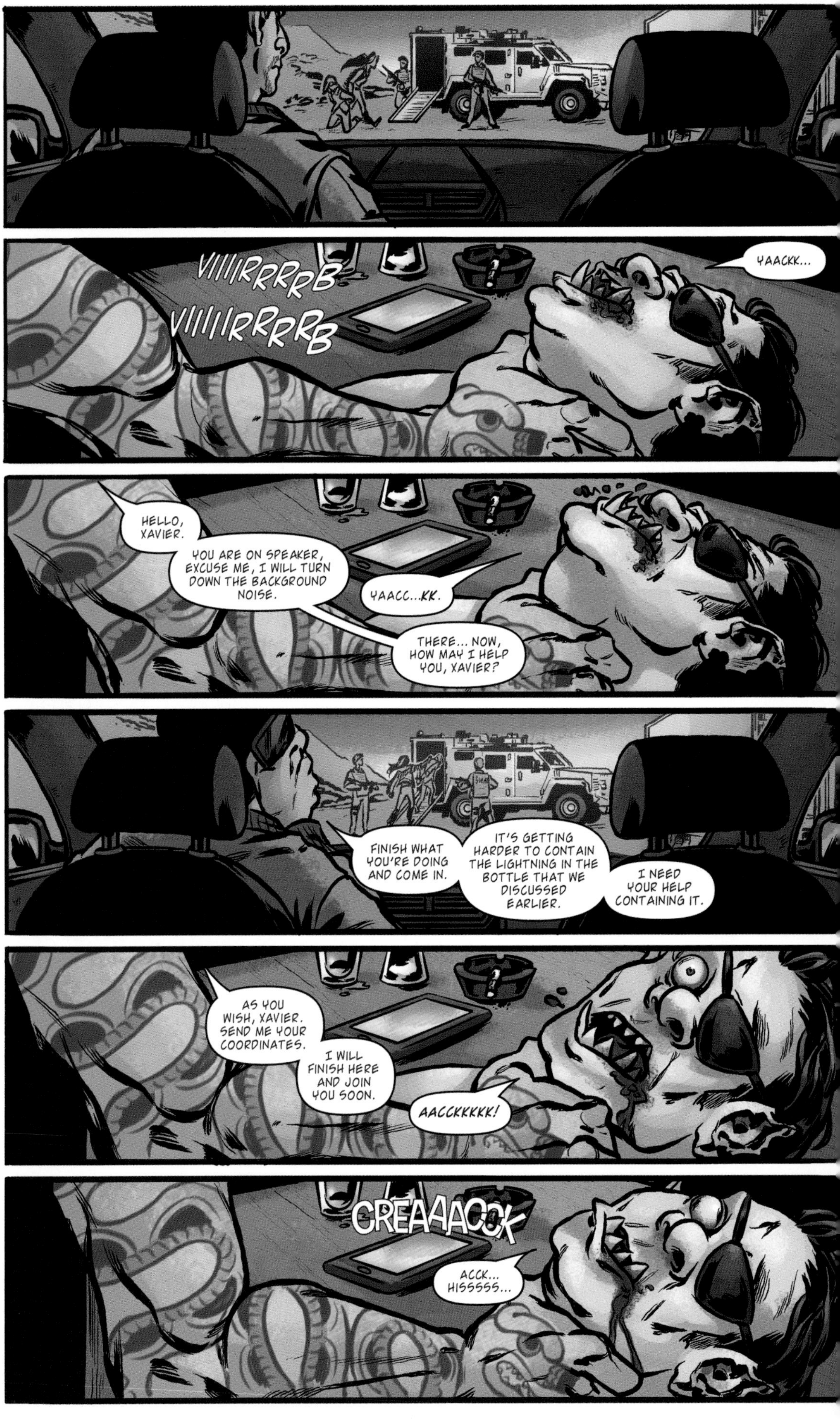
VIIIIRRRRB
VIIIIRRRRB
YAACKK...
HELLO, XAVIER.
YOU ARE ON SPEAKER, EXCUSE ME, I WILL TURN DOWN THE BACKGROUND NOISE.
YAACC...KK.
THERE... NOW, HOW MAY I HELP YOU, XAVIER?
FINISH WHAT YOU'RE DOING AND COME IN.
IT'S GETTING HARDER TO CONTAIN THE LIGHTNING IN THE BOTTLE THAT WE DISCUSSED EARLIER.
I NEED YOUR HELP CONTAINING IT.
AS YOU WISH, XAVIER. SEND ME YOUR COORDINATES.
I WILL FINISH HERE AND JOIN YOU SOON.
AACCKKKKK!
CREAAACCK
ACCK... HISSSSS...

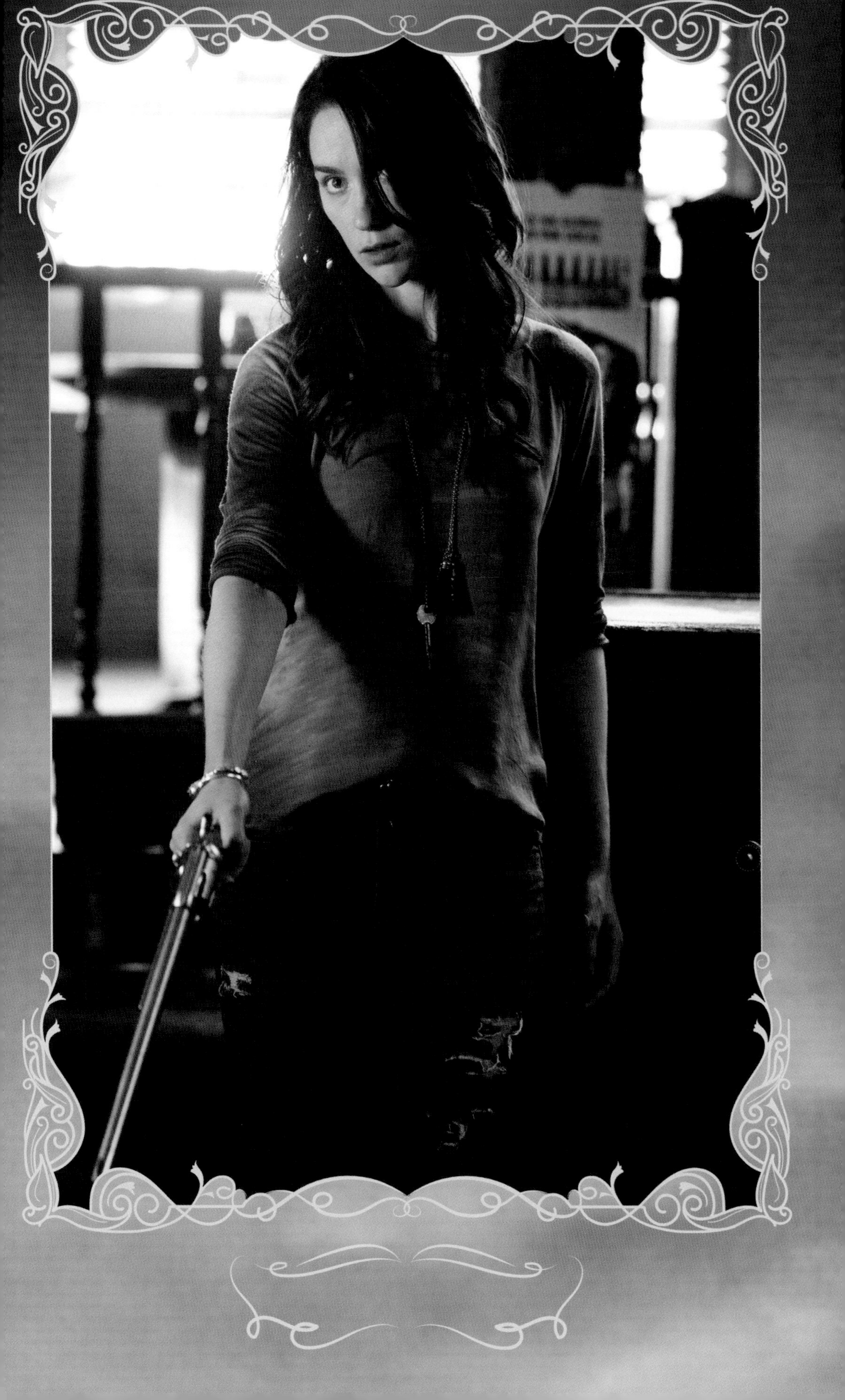

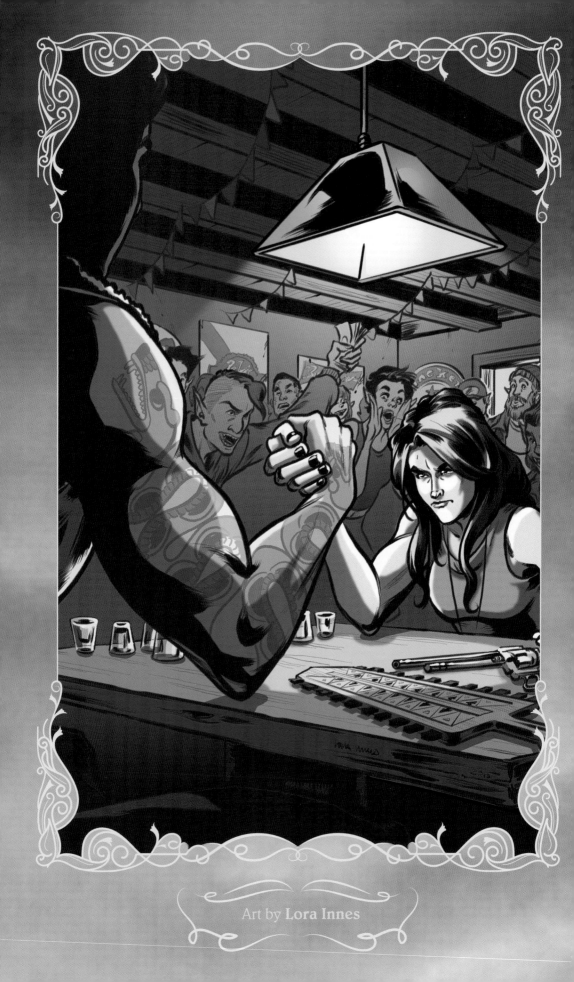

Art by **Lora Innes**

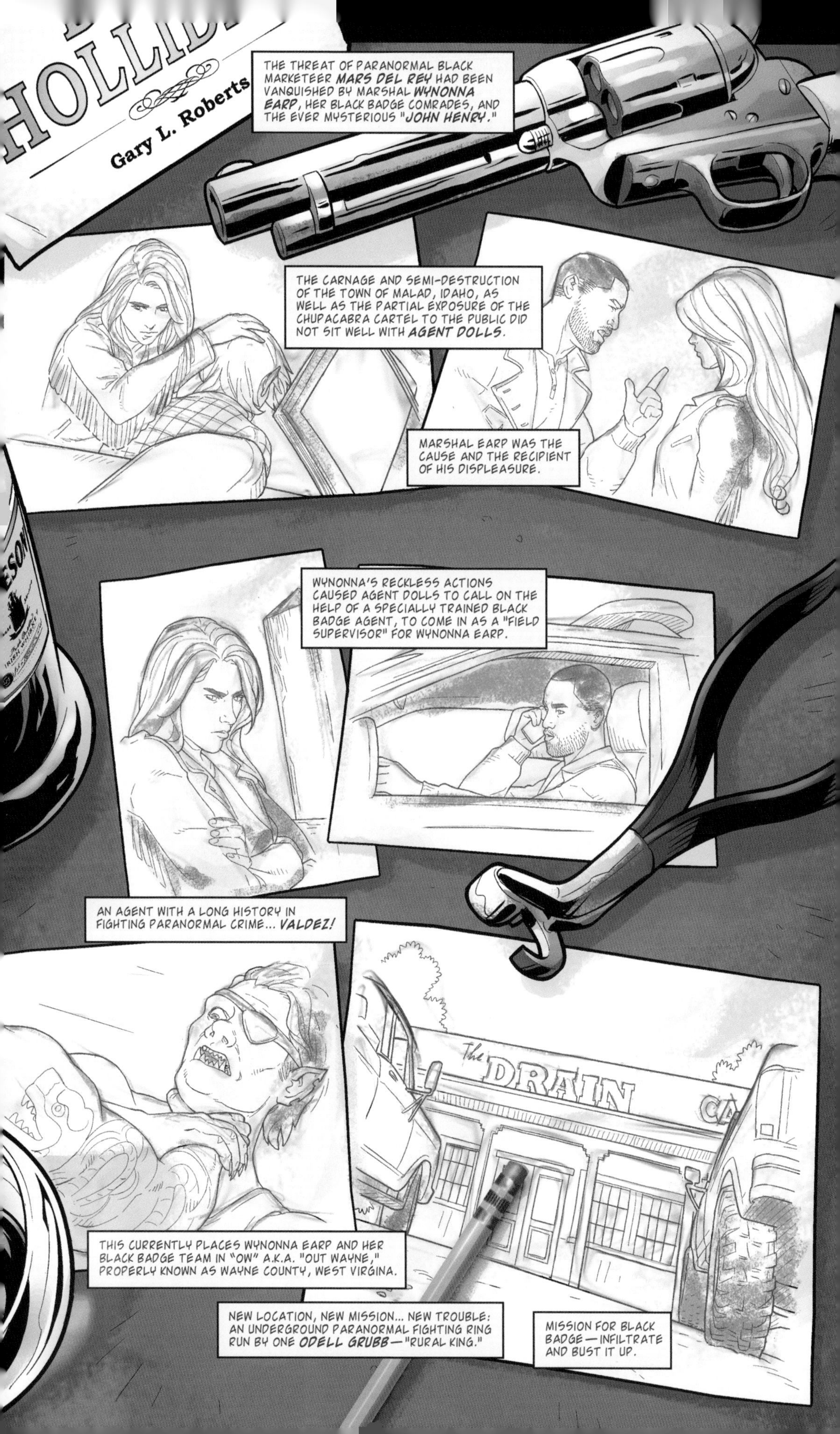

Gary L. Roberts
THE THREAT OF PARANORMAL BLACK MARKETEER MARS DEL REY HAD BEEN VANQUISHED BY MARSHAL WYNONNA EARP, HER BLACK BADGE COMRADES, AND THE EVER MYSTERIOUS "JOHN HENRY."
THE CARNAGE AND SEMI-DESTRUCTION OF THE TOWN OF MALAD, IDAHO, AS WELL AS THE PARTIAL EXPOSURE OF THE CHUPACABRA CARTEL TO THE PUBLIC DID NOT SIT WELL WITH AGENT DOLLS.
MARSHAL EARP WAS THE CAUSE AND THE RECIPIENT OF HIS DISPLEASURE.
WYNONNA'S RECKLESS ACTIONS CAUSED AGENT DOLLS TO CALL ON THE HELP OF A SPECIALLY TRAINED BLACK BADGE AGENT, TO COME IN AS A "FIELD SUPERVISOR" FOR WYNONNA EARP.
AN AGENT WITH A LONG HISTORY IN FIGHTING PARANORMAL CRIME... VALDEZ!
The DRAIN
THIS CURRENTLY PLACES WYNONNA EARP AND HER BLACK BADGE TEAM IN "OW" A.K.A. "OUT WAYNE," PROPERLY KNOWN AS WAYNE COUNTY, WEST VIRGINIA.
NEW LOCATION, NEW MISSION... NEW TROUBLE: AN UNDERGROUND PARANORMAL FIGHTING RING RUN BY ONE ODELL GRUBB — "RURAL KING."
MISSION FOR BLACK BADGE — INFILTRATE AND BUST IT UP.

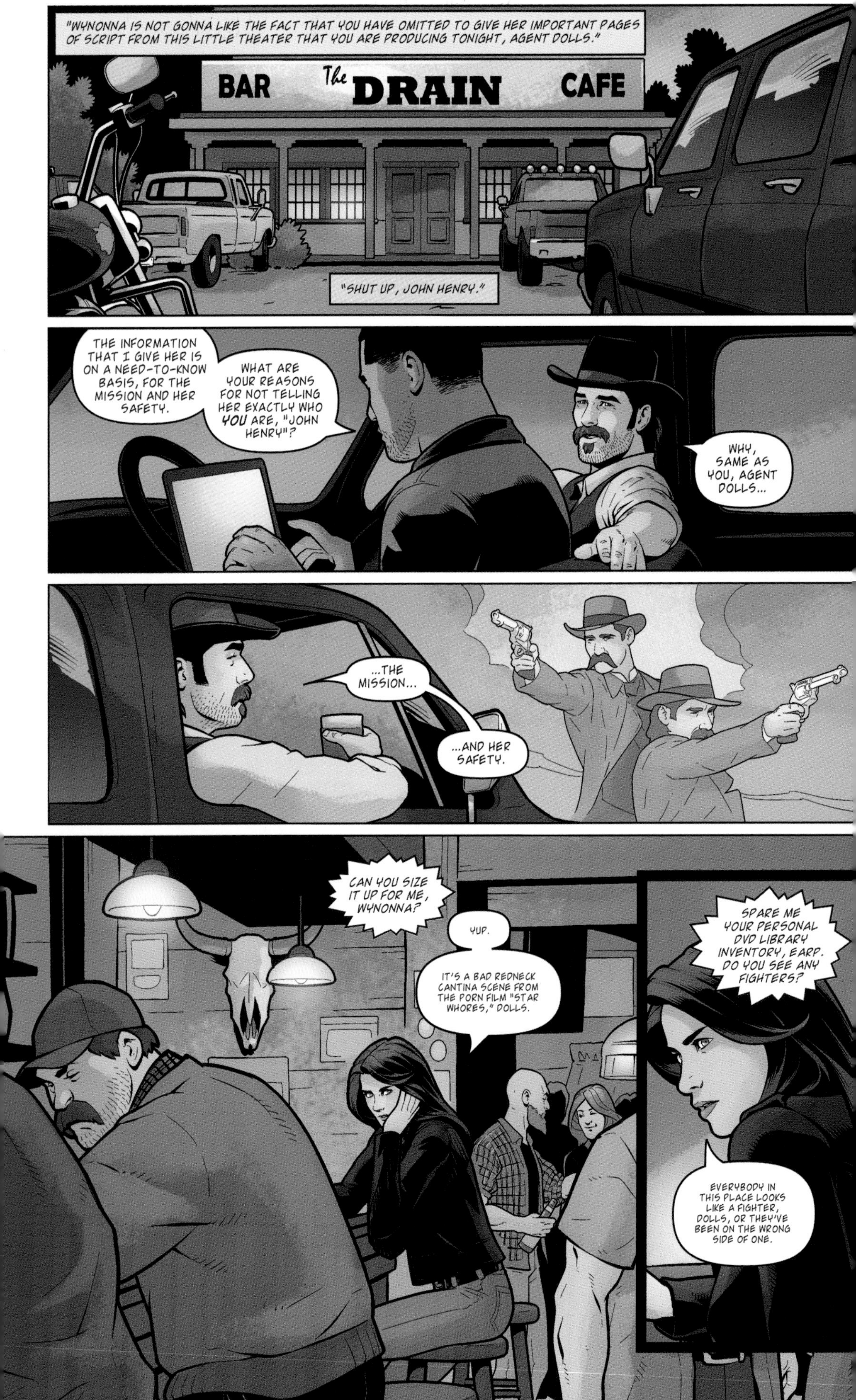
"WYNONNA IS NOT GONNA LIKE THE FACT THAT YOU HAVE OMITTED TO GIVE HER IMPORTANT PAGES OF SCRIPT FROM THIS LITTLE THEATER THAT YOU ARE PRODUCING TONIGHT, AGENT DOLLS."
BAR The DRAIN CAFE
"SHUT UP, JOHN HENRY."
THE INFORMATION THAT I GIVE HER IS ON A NEED-TO-KNOW BASIS, FOR THE MISSION AND HER SAFETY.
WHAT ARE YOUR REASONS FOR NOT TELLING HER EXACTLY WHO YOU ARE, "JOHN HENRY"?
WHY, SAME AS YOU, AGENT DOLLS...
...THE MISSION...
...AND HER SAFETY.
CAN YOU SIZE IT UP FOR ME, WYNONNA?
YUP.
IT'S A BAD REDNECK CANTINA SCENE FROM THE PORN FILM "STAR WHORES," DOLLS.
SPARE ME YOUR PERSONAL DVD LIBRARY INVENTORY, EARP. DO YOU SEE ANY FIGHTERS?
EVERYBODY IN THIS PLACE LOOKS LIKE A FIGHTER, DOLLS, OR THEY'VE BEEN ON THE WRONG SIDE OF ONE.

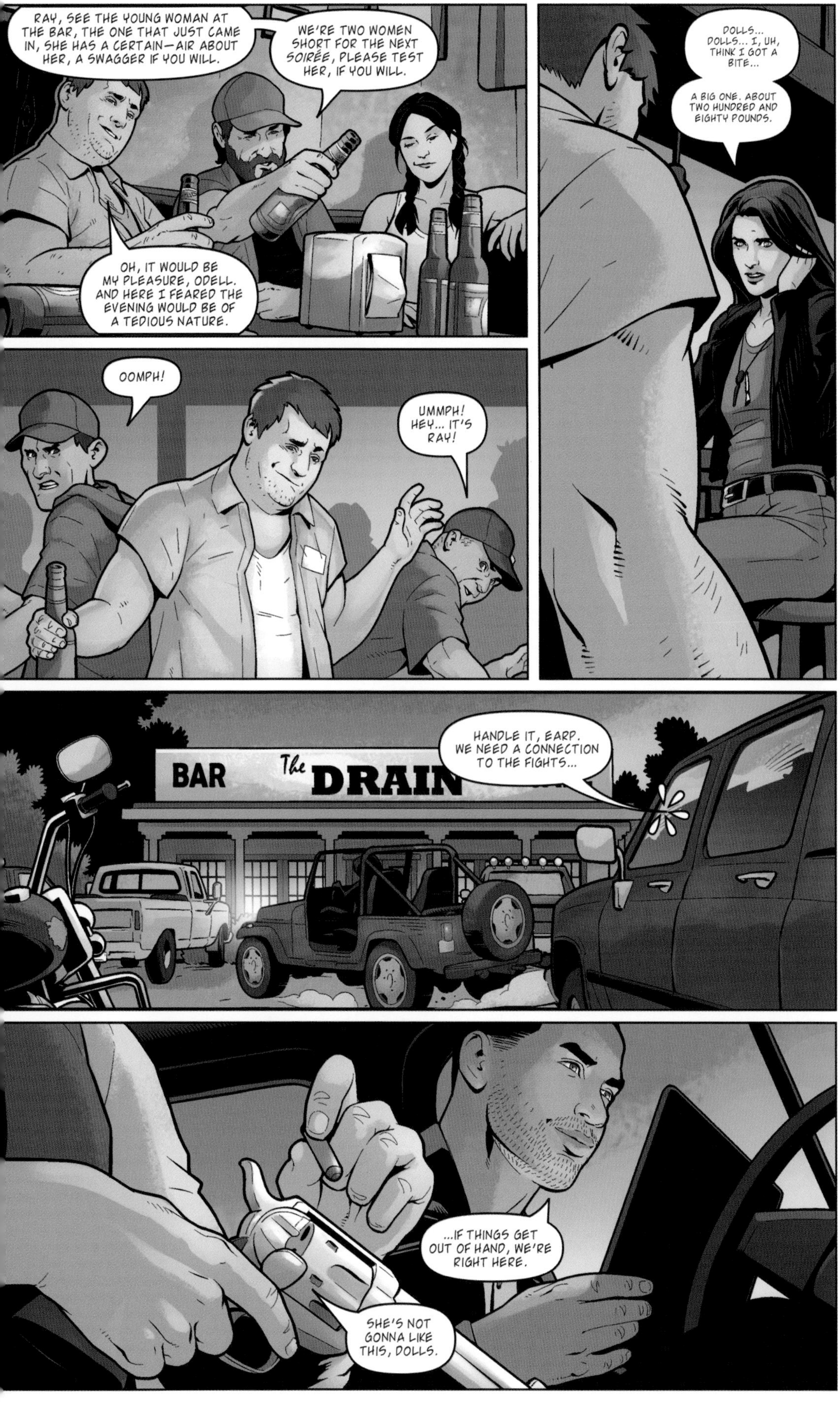
RAY, SEE THE YOUNG WOMAN AT THE BAR, THE ONE THAT JUST CAME IN, SHE HAS A CERTAIN—AIR ABOUT HER, A SWAGGER IF YOU WILL.
WE'RE TWO WOMEN SHORT FOR THE NEXT SOIRÉE, PLEASE TEST HER, IF YOU WILL.
OH, IT WOULD BE MY PLEASURE, ODELL. AND HERE I FEARED THE EVENING WOULD BE OF A TEDIOUS NATURE.
OOMPH!
UMMPH! HEY... IT'S RAY!
DOLLS... DOLLS... I, UH, THINK I GOT A BITE...
A BIG ONE. ABOUT TWO HUNDRED AND EIGHTY POUNDS.
BAR
The DRAIN
HANDLE IT, EARP. WE NEED A CONNECTION TO THE FIGHTS...
...IF THINGS GET OUT OF HAND, WE'RE RIGHT HERE.
SHE'S NOT GONNA LIKE THIS, DOLLS.

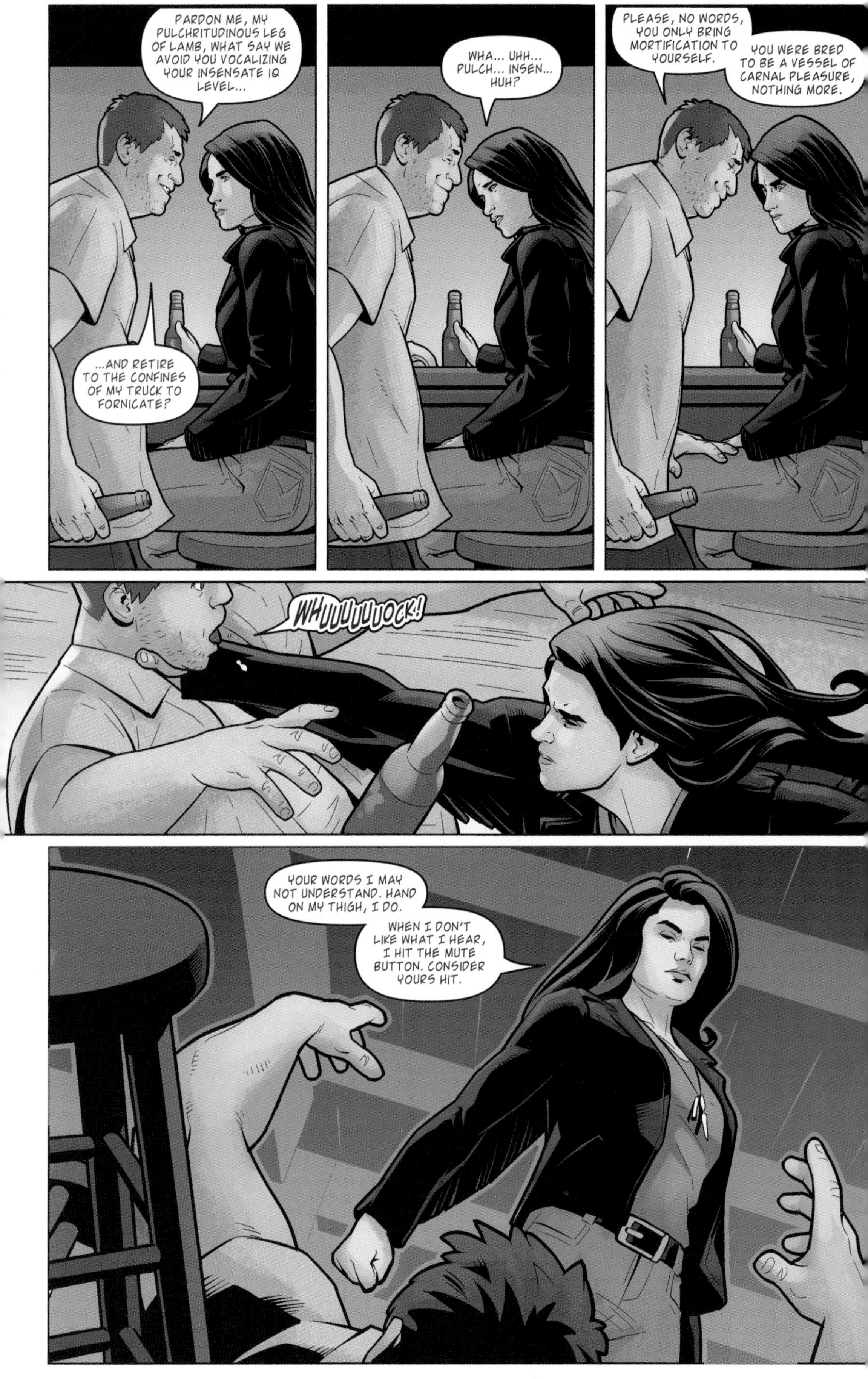
PARDON ME, MY PULCHRITUDINOUS LEG OF LAMB, WHAT SAY WE AVOID YOU VOCALIZING YOUR INSENSATE IQ LEVEL...
...AND RETIRE TO THE CONFINES OF MY TRUCK TO FORNICATE?
WHA... UHH... PULCH... INSEN... HUH?
PLEASE, NO WORDS, YOU ONLY BRING MORTIFICATION TO YOURSELF.
YOU WERE BRED TO BE A VESSEL OF CARNAL PLEASURE, NOTHING MORE.
WHUUUUUOCK!
YOUR WORDS I MAY NOT UNDERSTAND. HAND ON MY THIGH, I DO.
WHEN I DON'T LIKE WHAT I HEAR, I HIT THE MUTE BUTTON. CONSIDER YOURS HIT.

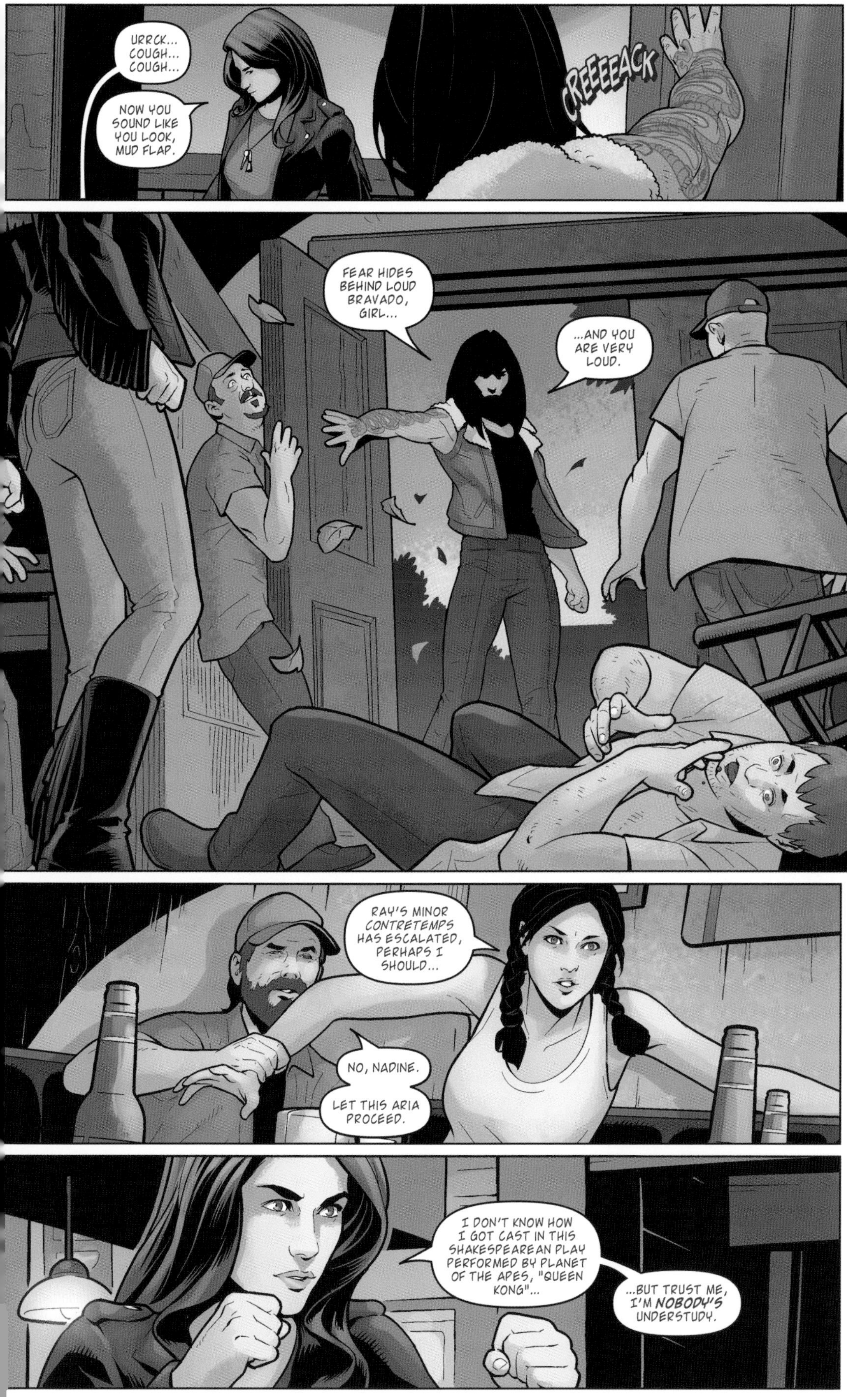
URRCK... COUGH... COUGH...
NOW YOU SOUND LIKE YOU LOOK, MUD FLAP.
CREEEEACK
FEAR HIDES BEHIND LOUD BRAVADO, GIRL...
...AND YOU ARE VERY LOUD.
RAY'S MINOR CONTRETEMPS HAS ESCALATED, PERHAPS I SHOULD...
NO, NADINE.
LET THIS ARIA PROCEED.
I DON'T KNOW HOW I GOT CAST IN THIS SHAKESPEAREAN PLAY PERFORMED BY PLANET OF THE APES, "QUEEN KONG"...
...BUT TRUST ME, I'M NOBODY'S UNDERSTUDY.

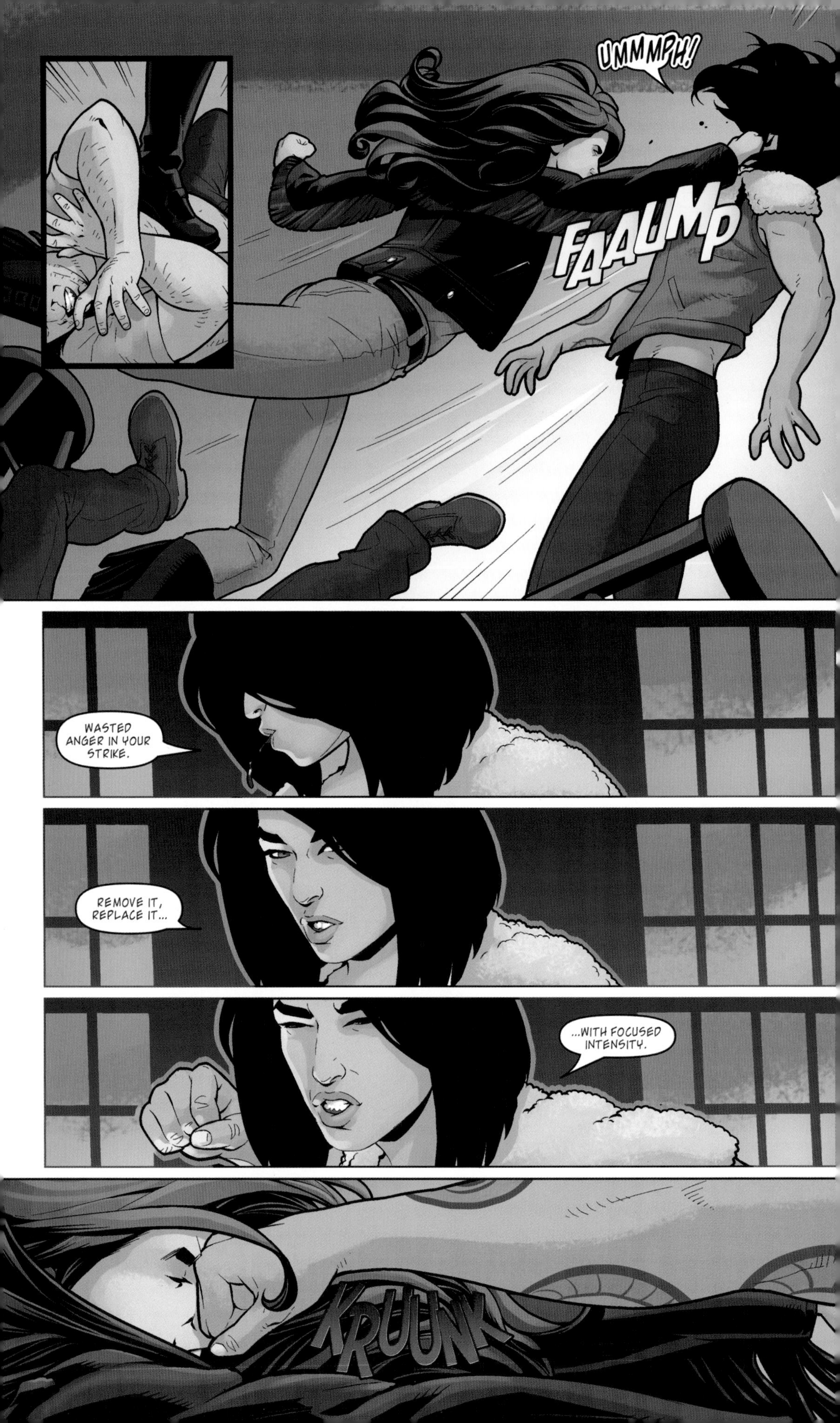
UMMMPH!
FAAUMP
WASTED ANGER IN YOUR STRIKE.
REMOVE IT, REPLACE IT...
...WITH FOCUSED INTENSITY.
KRUUNK

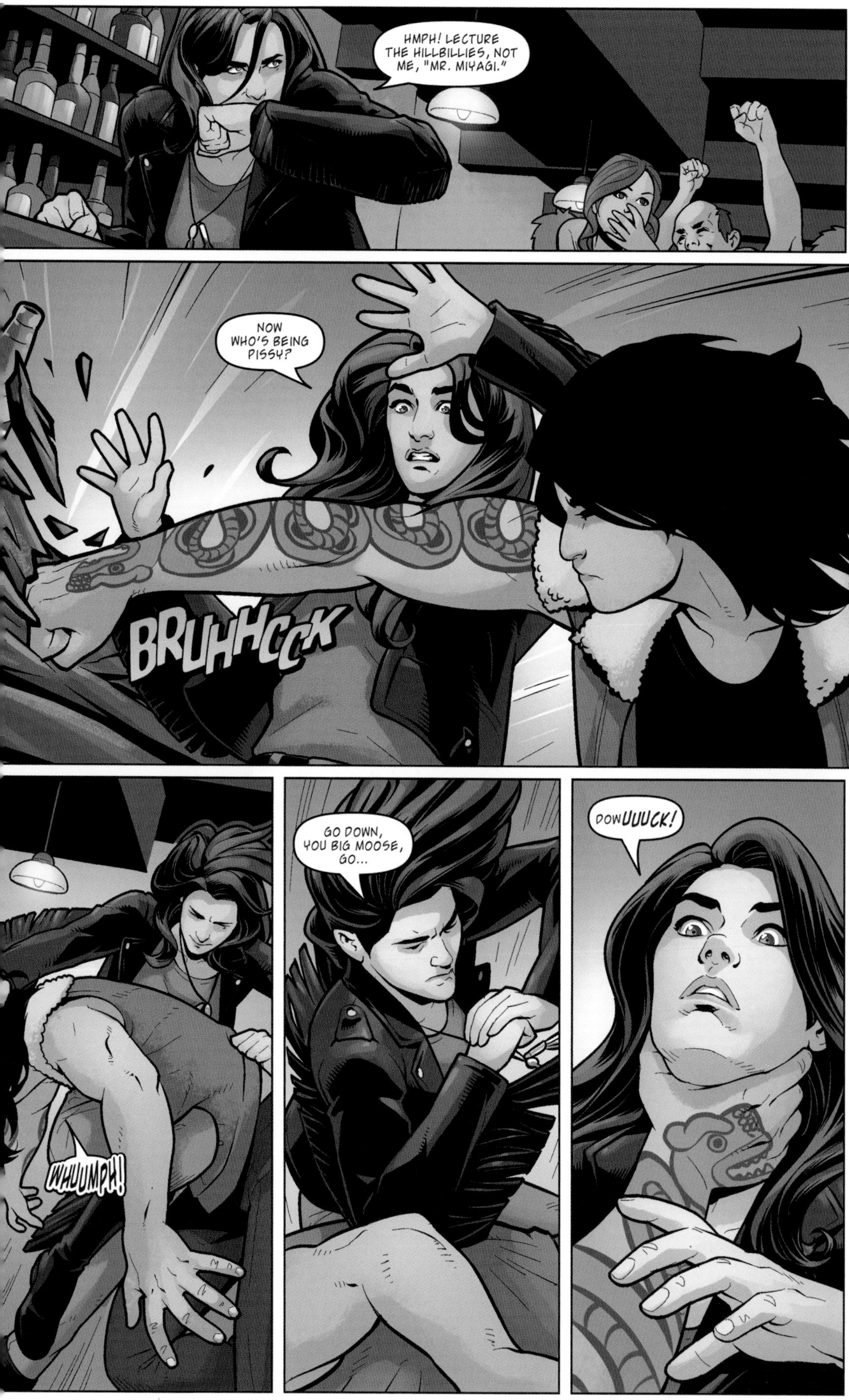
HMPH! LECTURE THE HILLBILLIES, NOT ME, "MR. MIYAGI."
NOW WHO'S BEING PISSY?
BRUHHCCCK
WHUUMPH!
GO DOWN, YOU BIG MOOSE, GO...
DOWUUUCK!

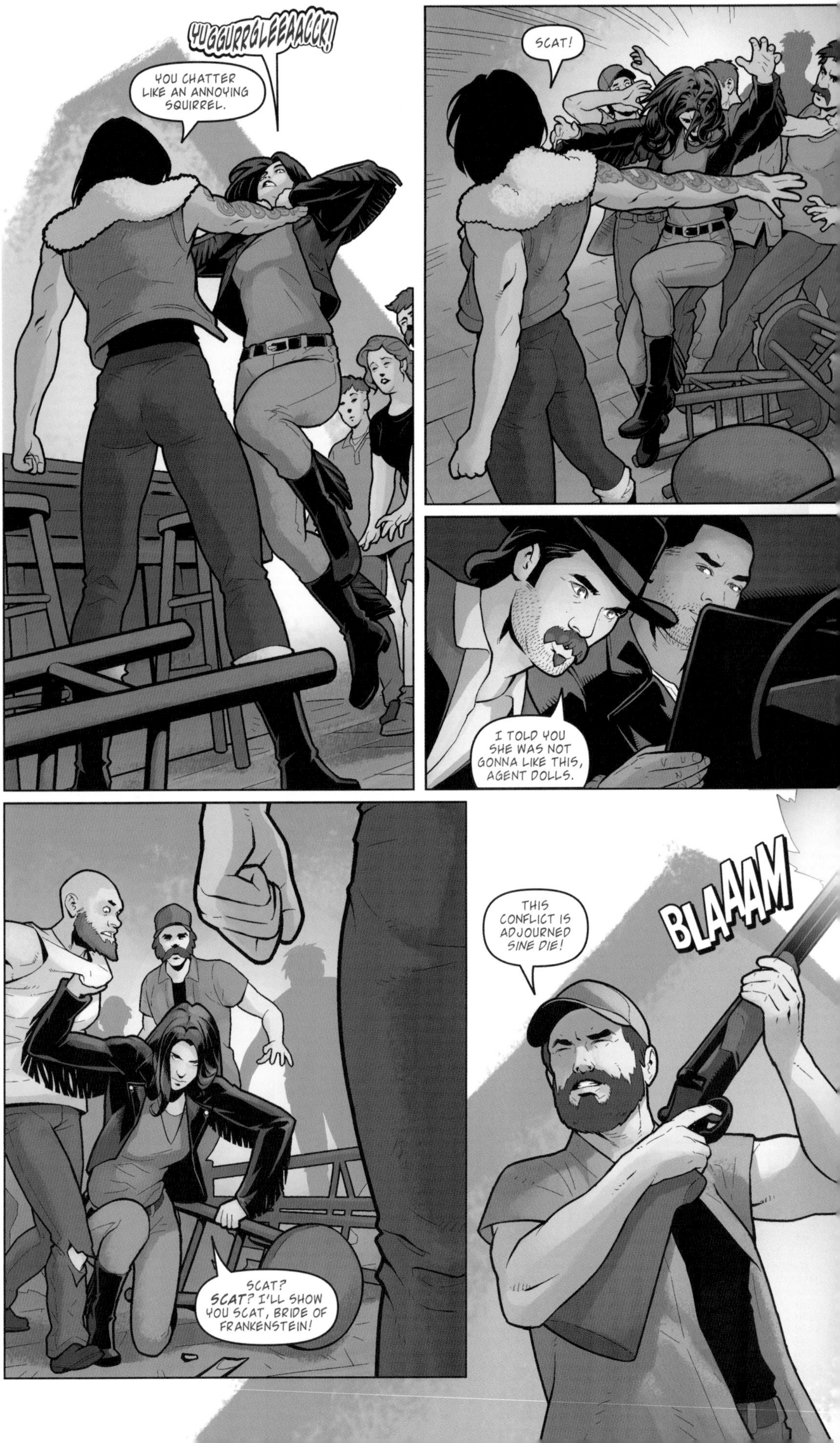
YUGGURRGLEEAACCK!
YOU CHATTER LIKE AN ANNOYING SQUIRREL.
SCAT!
I TOLD YOU SHE WAS NOT GONNA LIKE THIS, AGENT DOLLS.
SCAT? SCAT? I'LL SHOW YOU SCAT, BRIDE OF FRANKENSTEIN!
THIS CONFLICT IS ADJOURNED SINE DIE!
BLAAAM

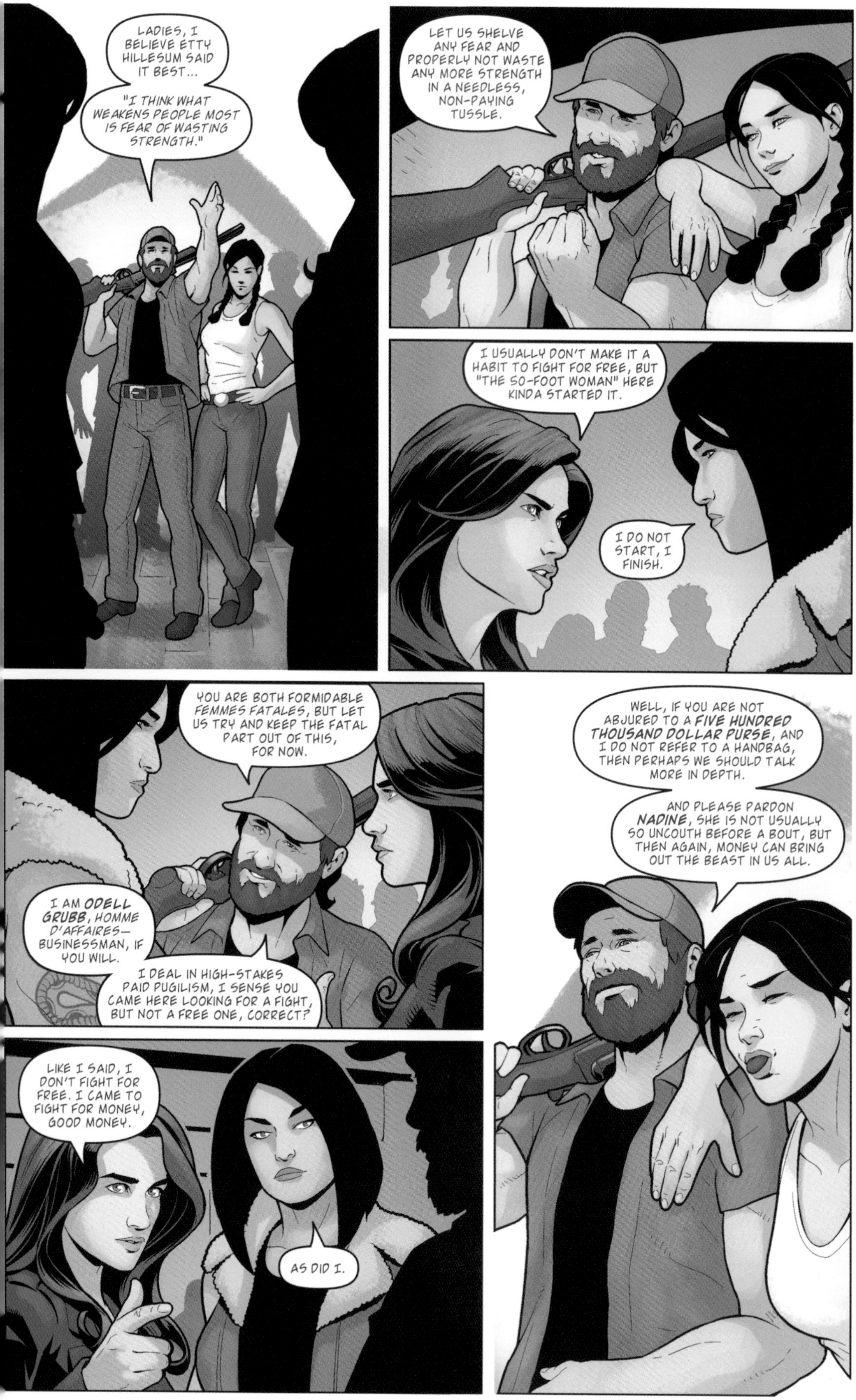
LADIES, I BELIEVE ETTY HILLESUM SAID IT BEST...
"I THINK WHAT WEAKENS PEOPLE MOST IS FEAR OF WASTING STRENGTH."
LET US SHELVE ANY FEAR AND PROPERLY NOT WASTE ANY MORE STRENGTH IN A NEEDLESS, NON-PAYING TUSSLE.
I USUALLY DON'T MAKE IT A HABIT TO FIGHT FOR FREE, BUT "THE 50-FOOT WOMAN" HERE KINDA STARTED IT.
I DO NOT START, I FINISH.
YOU ARE BOTH FORMIDABLE FEMMES FATALES, BUT LET US TRY AND KEEP THE FATAL PART OUT OF THIS, FOR NOW.
I AM ODELL GRUBB, HOMME D'AFFAIRES—BUSINESSMAN, IF YOU WILL.
I DEAL IN HIGH-STAKES PAID PUGILISM, I SENSE YOU CAME HERE LOOKING FOR A FIGHT, BUT NOT A FREE ONE, CORRECT?
LIKE I SAID, I DON'T FIGHT FOR FREE. I CAME TO FIGHT FOR MONEY, GOOD MONEY.
AS DID I.
WELL, IF YOU ARE NOT ABJURED TO A FIVE HUNDRED THOUSAND DOLLAR PURSE, AND I DO NOT REFER TO A HANDBAG, THEN PERHAPS WE SHOULD TALK MORE IN DEPTH.
AND PLEASE PARDON NADINE, SHE IS NOT USUALLY SO UNCOUTH BEFORE A BOUT, BUT THEN AGAIN, MONEY CAN BRING OUT THE BEAST IN US ALL.

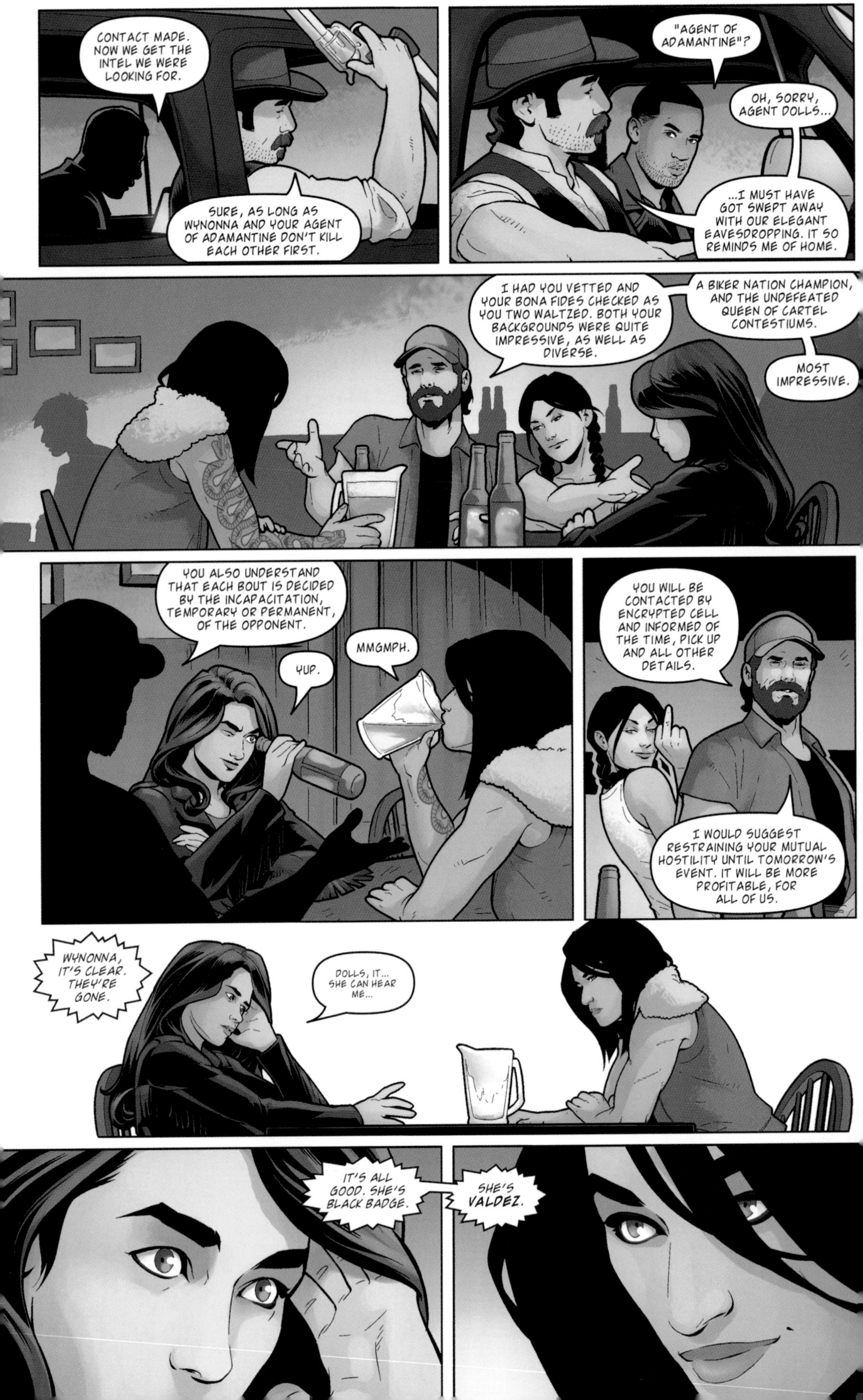
CONTACT MADE. NOW WE GET THE INTEL WE WERE LOOKING FOR.
SURE, AS LONG AS WYNONNA AND YOUR AGENT OF ADAMANTINE DON'T KILL EACH OTHER FIRST.
"AGENT OF ADAMANTINE"?
OH, SORRY, AGENT DOLLS...
...I MUST HAVE GOT SWEPT AWAY WITH OUR ELEGANT EAVESDROPPING. IT SO REMINDS ME OF HOME.
I HAD YOU VETTED AND YOUR BONA FIDES CHECKED AS YOU TWO WALTZED. BOTH YOUR BACKGROUNDS WERE QUITE IMPRESSIVE, AS WELL AS DIVERSE.
A BIKER NATION CHAMPION, AND THE UNDEFEATED QUEEN OF CARTEL CONTESTIUMS.
MOST IMPRESSIVE.
YOU ALSO UNDERSTAND THAT EACH BOUT IS DECIDED BY THE INCAPACITATION, TEMPORARY OR PERMANENT, OF THE OPPONENT.
YUP.
MMGMPH.
YOU WILL BE CONTACTED BY ENCRYPTED CELL AND INFORMED OF THE TIME, PICK UP AND ALL OTHER DETAILS.
I WOULD SUGGEST RESTRAINING YOUR MUTUAL HOSTILITY UNTIL TOMORROW'S EVENT. IT WILL BE MORE PROFITABLE, FOR ALL OF US.
WYNONNA, IT'S CLEAR. THEY'RE GONE.
DOLLS, IT... SHE CAN HEAR ME...
IT'S ALL GOOD. SHE'S BLACK BADGE.
SHE'S VALDEZ.

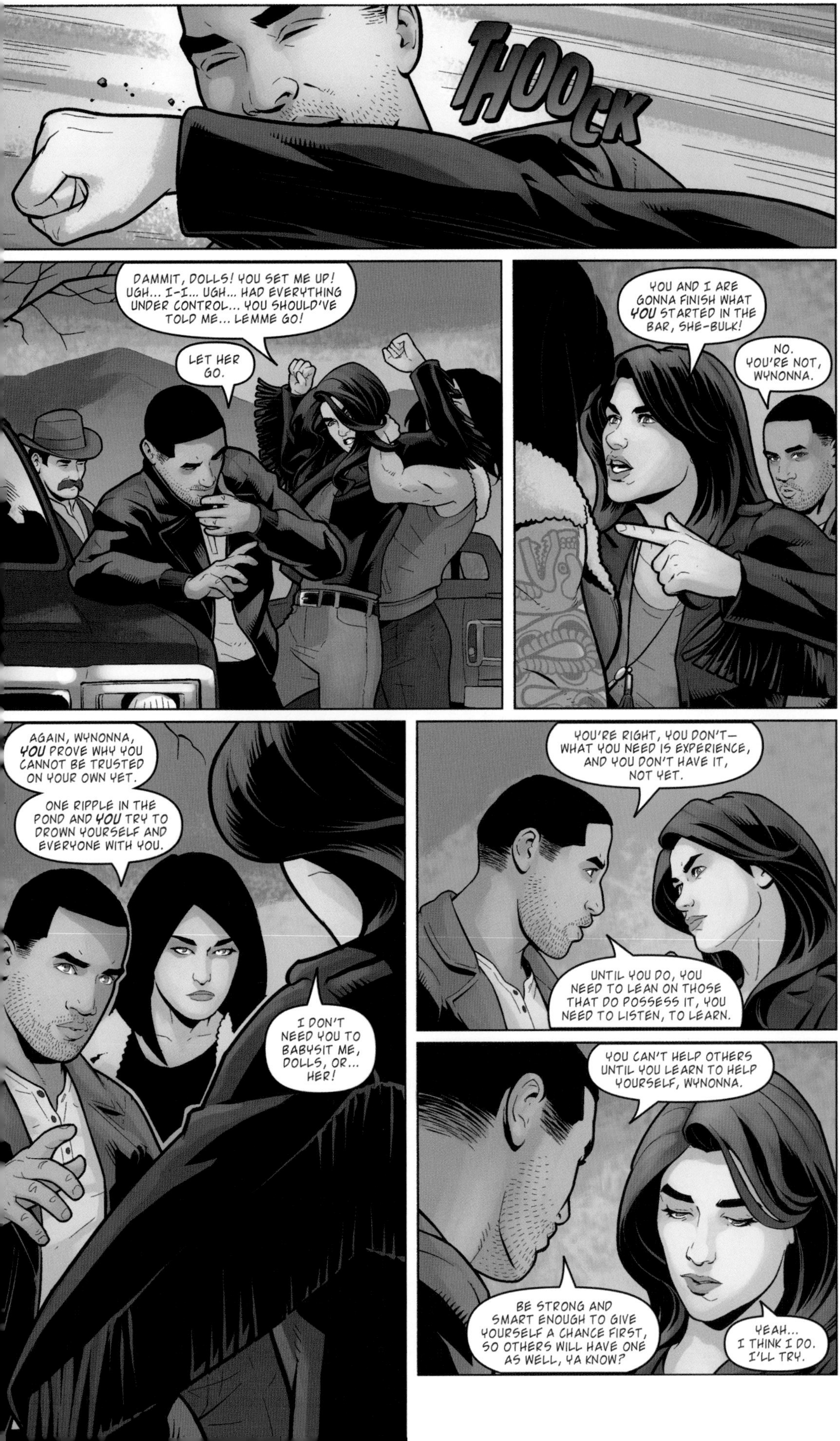
THOOCK
DAMMIT, DOLLS! YOU SET ME UP! UGH... I-I... UGH... HAD EVERYTHING UNDER CONTROL... YOU SHOULD'VE TOLD ME... LEMME GO!
LET HER GO.
YOU AND I ARE GONNA FINISH WHAT YOU STARTED IN THE BAR, SHE-BULK!
NO. YOU'RE NOT, WYNONNA.
AGAIN, WYNONNA, YOU PROVE WHY YOU CANNOT BE TRUSTED ON YOUR OWN YET.
ONE RIPPLE IN THE POND AND YOU TRY TO DROWN YOURSELF AND EVERYONE WITH YOU.
I DON'T NEED YOU TO BABYSIT ME, DOLLS, OR... HER!
YOU'RE RIGHT, YOU DON'T— WHAT YOU NEED IS EXPERIENCE, AND YOU DON'T HAVE IT, NOT YET.
UNTIL YOU DO, YOU NEED TO LEAN ON THOSE THAT DO POSSESS IT, YOU NEED TO LISTEN, TO LEARN.
YOU CAN'T HELP OTHERS UNTIL YOU LEARN TO HELP YOURSELF, WYNONNA.
BE STRONG AND SMART ENOUGH TO GIVE YOURSELF A CHANCE FIRST, SO OTHERS WILL HAVE ONE AS WELL, YA KNOW?
YEAH... I THINK I DO. I'LL TRY.

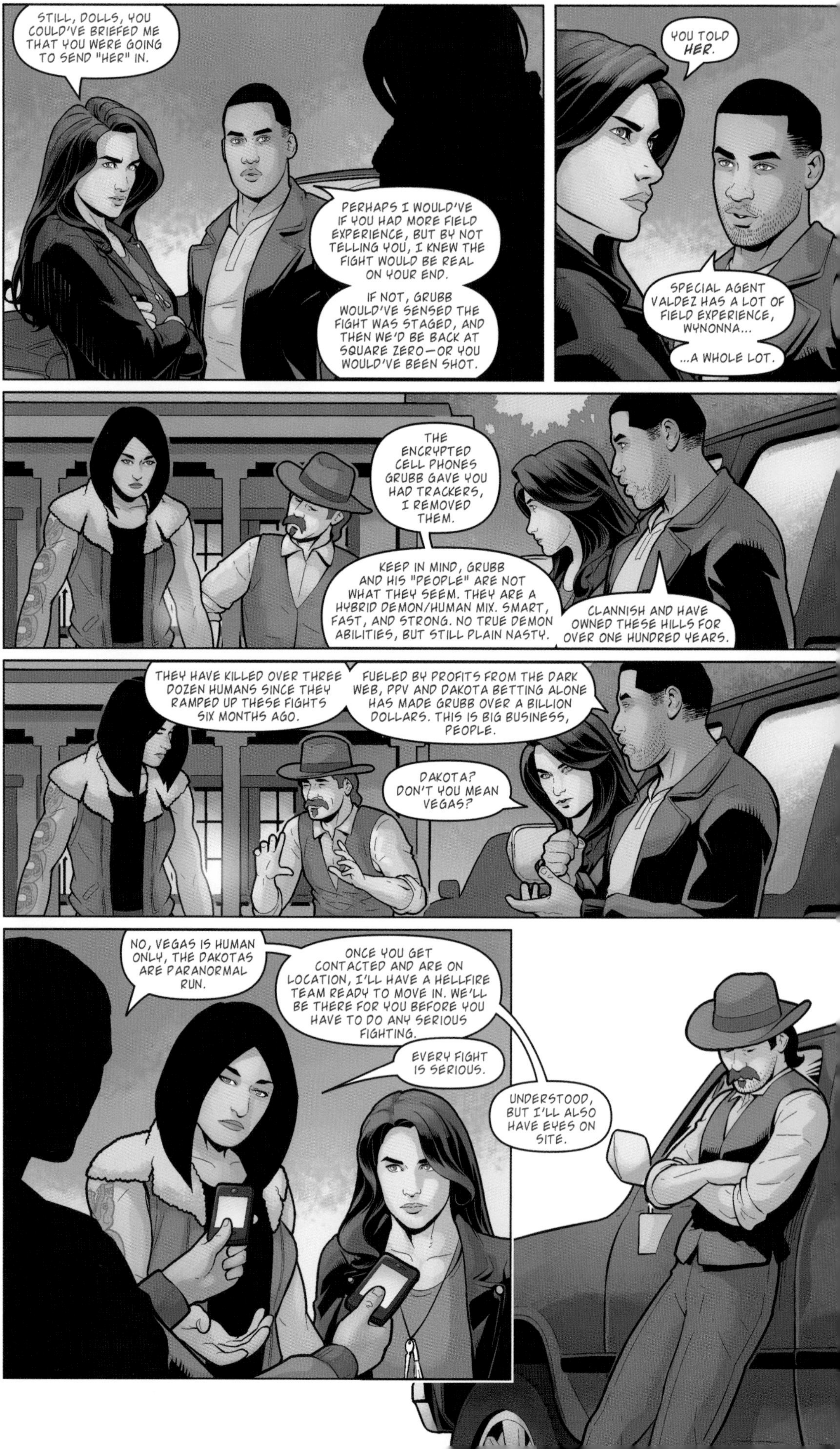

STILL, DOLLS, YOU COULD'VE BRIEFED ME THAT YOU WERE GOING TO SEND "HER" IN.
PERHAPS I WOULD'VE IF YOU HAD MORE FIELD EXPERIENCE, BUT BY NOT TELLING YOU, I KNEW THE FIGHT WOULD BE REAL ON YOUR END.
IF NOT, GRUBB WOULD'VE SENSED THE FIGHT WAS STAGED, AND THEN WE'D BE BACK AT SQUARE ZERO—OR YOU WOULD'VE BEEN SHOT.
YOU TOLD HER.
SPECIAL AGENT VALDEZ HAS A LOT OF FIELD EXPERIENCE, WYNONNA...
...A WHOLE LOT.
THE ENCRYPTED CELL PHONES GRUBB GAVE YOU HAD TRACKERS, I REMOVED THEM.
KEEP IN MIND, GRUBB AND HIS "PEOPLE" ARE NOT WHAT THEY SEEM. THEY ARE A HYBRID DEMON/HUMAN MIX. SMART, FAST, AND STRONG. NO TRUE DEMON ABILITIES, BUT STILL PLAIN NASTY.
CLANNISH AND HAVE OWNED THESE HILLS FOR OVER ONE HUNDRED YEARS.
THEY HAVE KILLED OVER THREE DOZEN HUMANS SINCE THEY RAMPED UP THESE FIGHTS SIX MONTHS AGO.
FUELED BY PROFITS FROM THE DARK WEB, PPV AND DAKOTA BETTING ALONE HAS MADE GRUBB OVER A BILLION DOLLARS. THIS IS BIG BUSINESS, PEOPLE.
DAKOTA? DON'T YOU MEAN VEGAS?
NO, VEGAS IS HUMAN ONLY, THE DAKOTAS ARE PARANORMAL RUN.
ONCE YOU GET CONTACTED AND ARE ON LOCATION, I'LL HAVE A HELLFIRE TEAM READY TO MOVE IN. WE'LL BE THERE FOR YOU BEFORE YOU HAVE TO DO ANY SERIOUS FIGHTING.
EVERY FIGHT IS SERIOUS.
UNDERSTOOD, BUT I'LL ALSO HAVE EYES ON SITE.

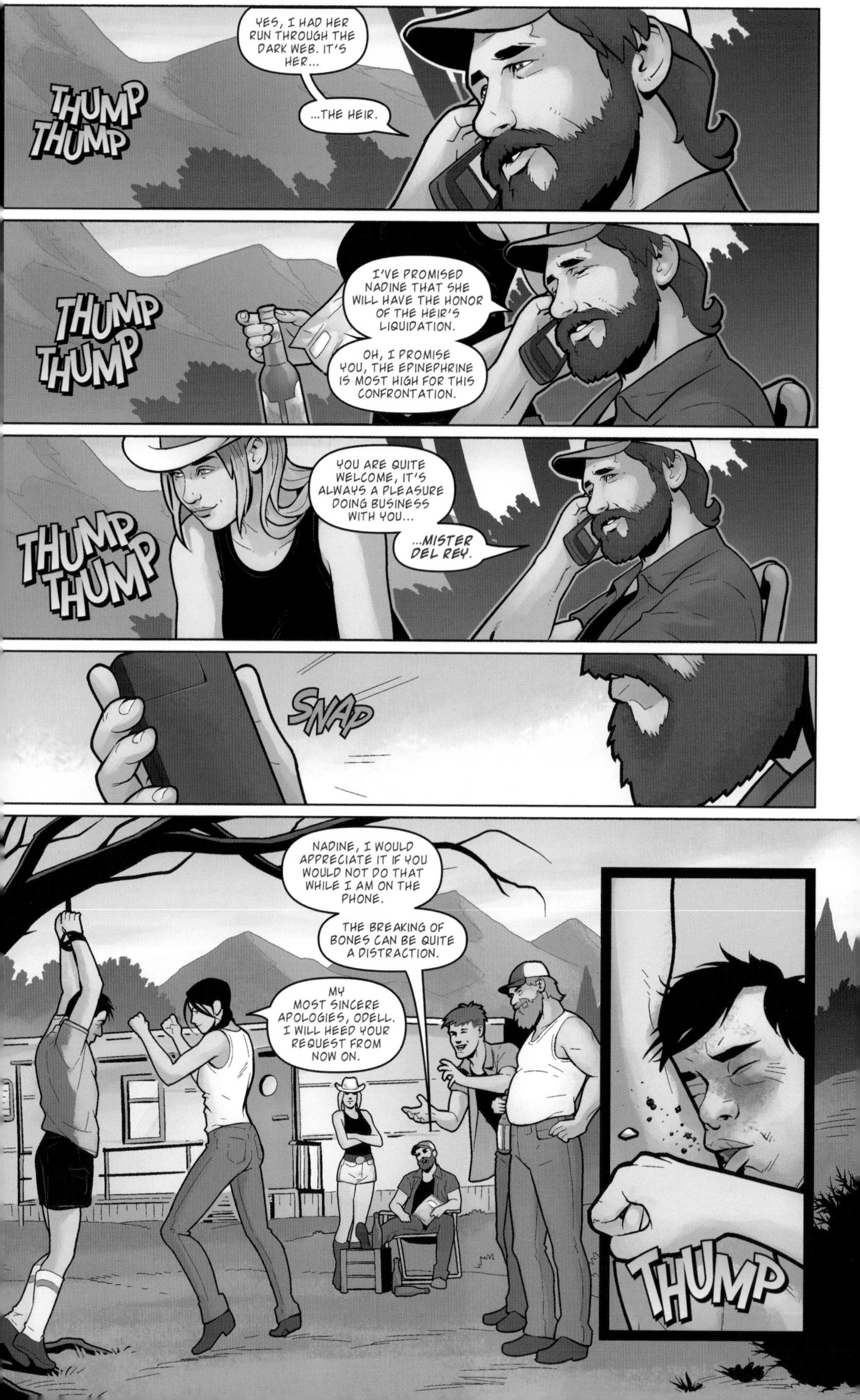
YES, I HAD HER RUN THROUGH THE DARK WEB. IT'S HER...
...THE HEIR.
THUMP THUMP
I'VE PROMISED NADINE THAT SHE WILL HAVE THE HONOR OF THE HEIR'S LIQUIDATION.
OH, I PROMISE YOU, THE EPINEPHRINE IS MOST HIGH FOR THIS CONFRONTATION.
THUMP THUMP
YOU ARE QUITE WELCOME, IT'S ALWAYS A PLEASURE DOING BUSINESS WITH YOU...
...MISTER DEL REY.
THUMP THUMP
SNAP
NADINE, I WOULD APPRECIATE IT IF YOU WOULD NOT DO THAT WHILE I AM ON THE PHONE.
THE BREAKING OF BONES CAN BE QUITE A DISTRACTION.
MY MOST SINCERE APOLOGIES, ODELL. I WILL HEED YOUR REQUEST FROM NOW ON.
THUMP

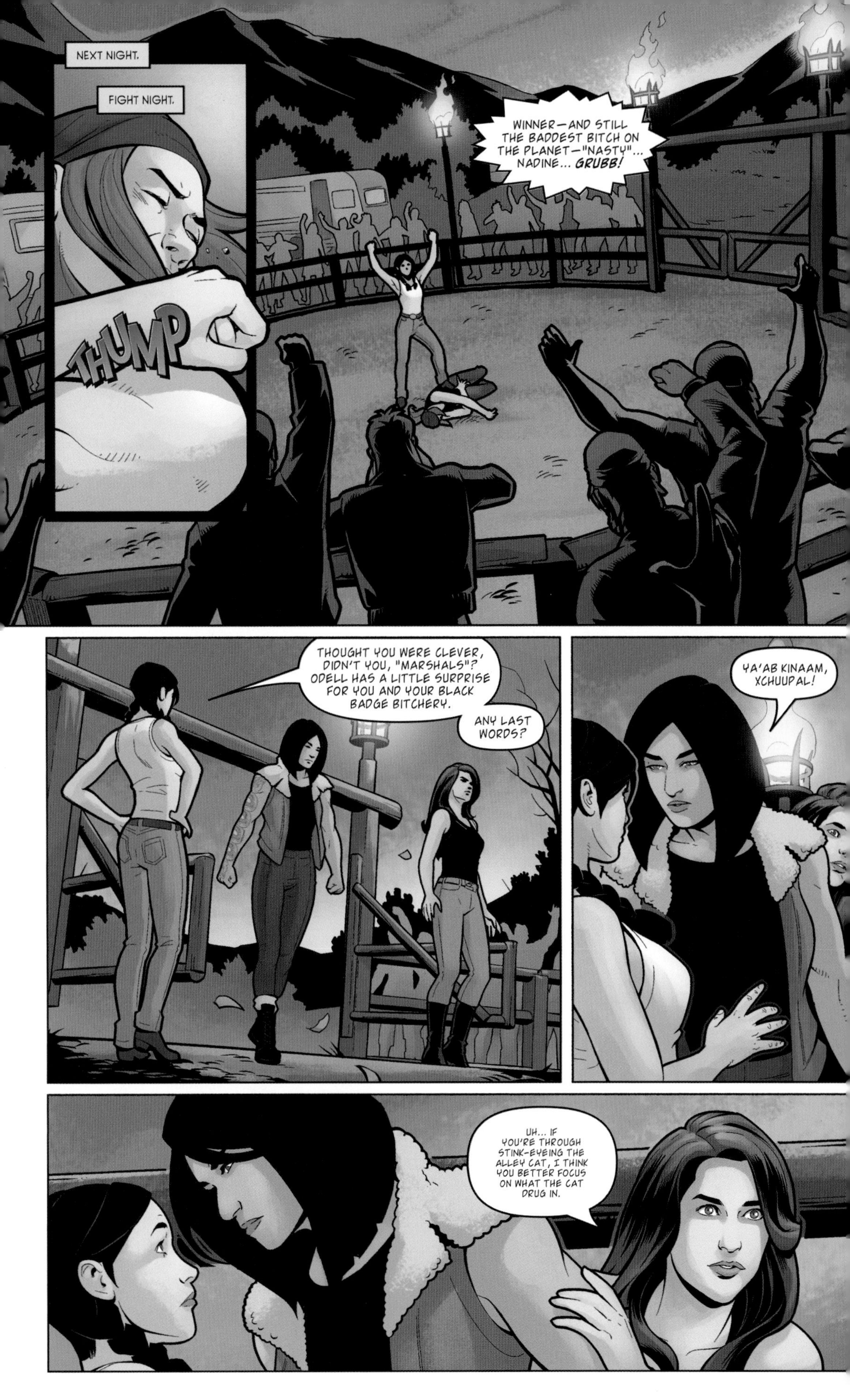
NEXT NIGHT.
FIGHT NIGHT.
THUMP
WINNER—AND STILL THE BADDEST BITCH ON THE PLANET—"NASTY"... NADINE... GRUBB!
THOUGHT YOU WERE CLEVER, DIDN'T YOU, "MARSHALS"? ODELL HAS A LITTLE SURPRISE FOR YOU AND YOUR BLACK BADGE BITCHERY.
ANY LAST WORDS?
YA'AB KINAAM, XCHUUPAL!
UH... IF YOU'RE THROUGH STINK-EYEING THE ALLEY CAT, I THINK YOU BETTER FOCUS ON WHAT THE CAT DRUG IN.

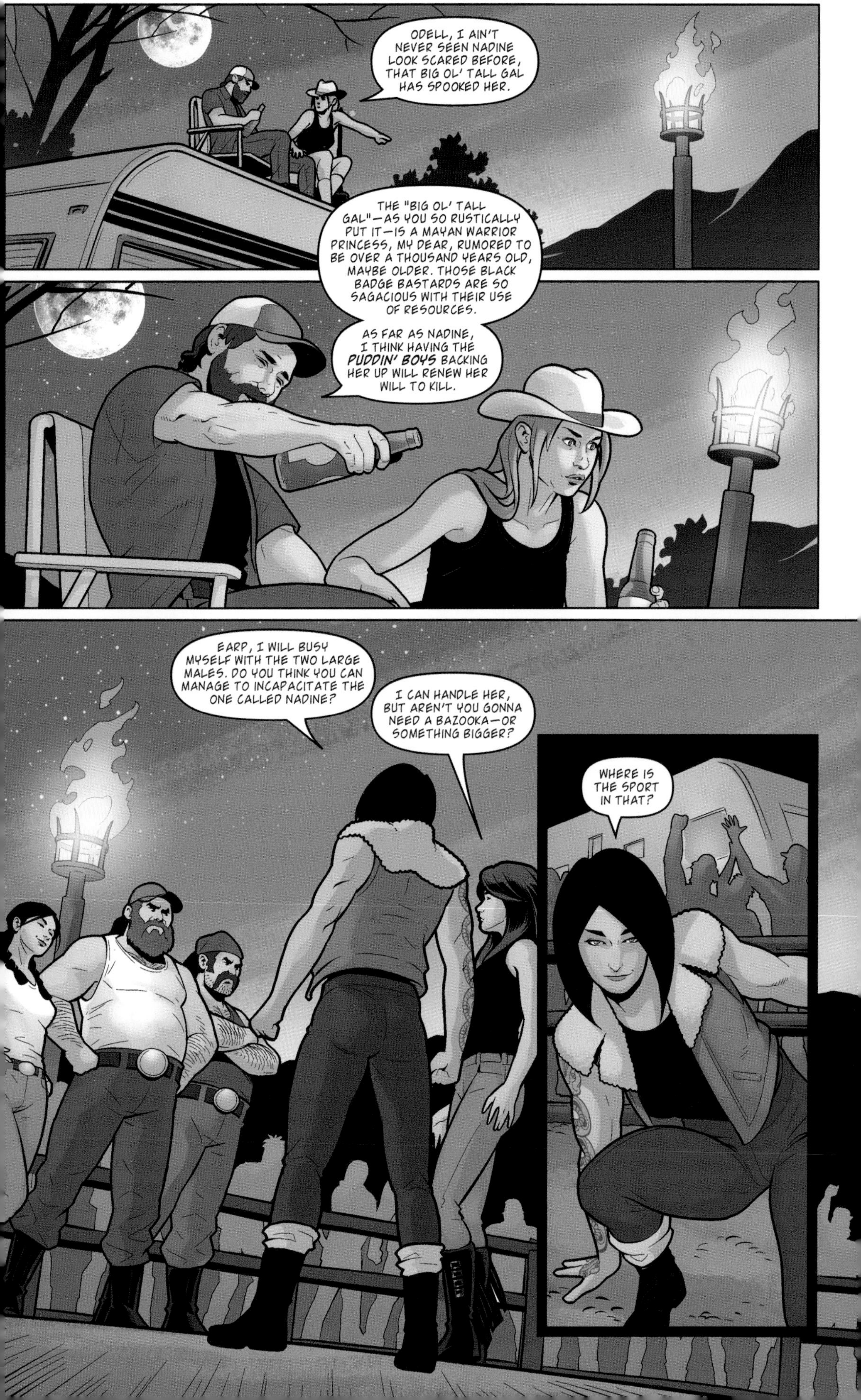
ODELL, I AIN'T NEVER SEEN NADINE LOOK SCARED BEFORE, THAT BIG OL' TALL GAL HAS SPOOKED HER.
THE "BIG OL' TALL GAL"—AS YOU SO RUSTICALLY PUT IT—IS A MAYAN WARRIOR PRINCESS, MY DEAR, RUMORED TO BE OVER A THOUSAND YEARS OLD, MAYBE OLDER. THOSE BLACK BADGE BASTARDS ARE SO SAGACIOUS WITH THEIR USE OF RESOURCES.
AS FAR AS NADINE, I THINK HAVING THE PUDDIN' BOYS BACKING HER UP WILL RENEW HER WILL TO KILL.
EARP, I WILL BUSY MYSELF WITH THE TWO LARGE MALES. DO YOU THINK YOU CAN MANAGE TO INCAPACITATE THE ONE CALLED NADINE?
I CAN HANDLE HER, BUT AREN'T YOU GONNA NEED A BAZOOKA—OR SOMETHING BIGGER?
WHERE IS THE SPORT IN THAT?

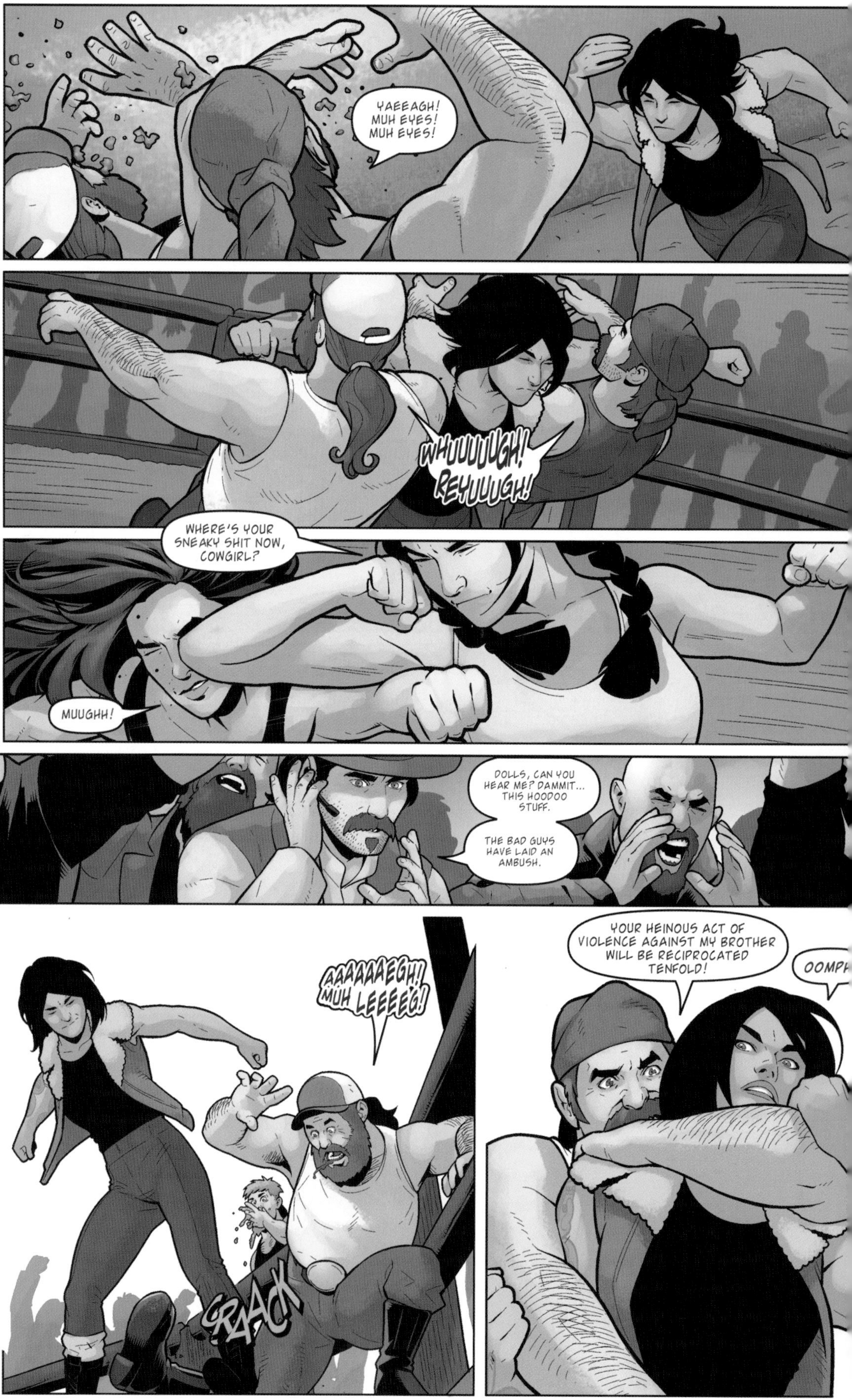
YAEEAGH! MUH EYES! MUH EYES!
WHUUUUGH! REYUUUGH!
WHERE'S YOUR SNEAKY SHIT NOW, COWGIRL?
MUUGHH!
DOLLS, CAN YOU HEAR ME? DAMMIT... THIS HOODOO STUFF.
THE BAD GUYS HAVE LAID AN AMBUSH.
AAAAAAEGH! MUH LEEEEG!
CRAACK
YOUR HEINOUS ACT OF VIOLENCE AGAINST MY BROTHER WILL BE RECIPROCATED TENFOLD!
OOMPH

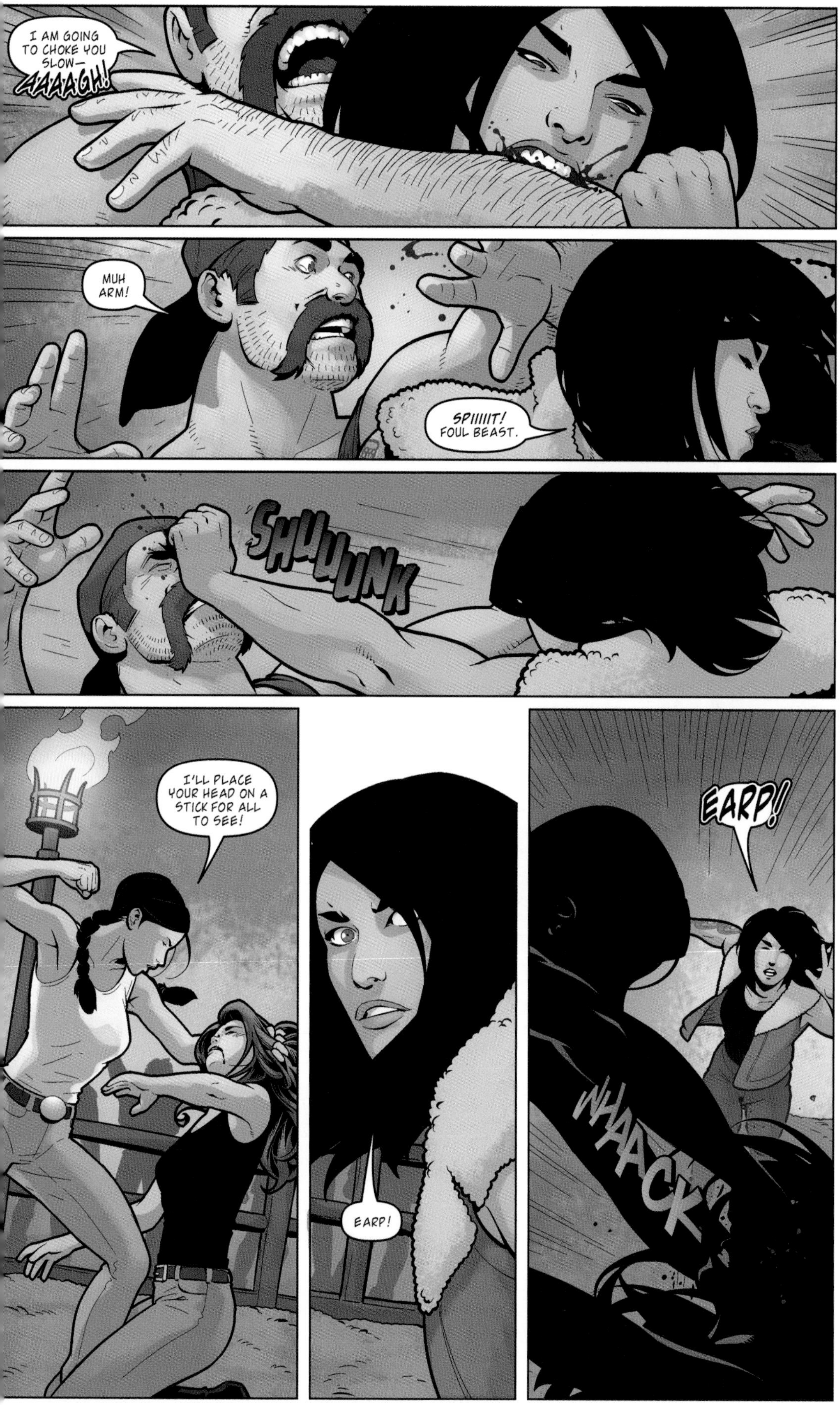
I AM GOING TO CHOKE YOU SLOW—
AAAAGH!
MUH ARM!
SPIIIIIT! FOUL BEAST.
SHUUUNK
I'LL PLACE YOUR HEAD ON A STICK FOR ALL TO SEE!
EARP!
EARP!
WHAACK

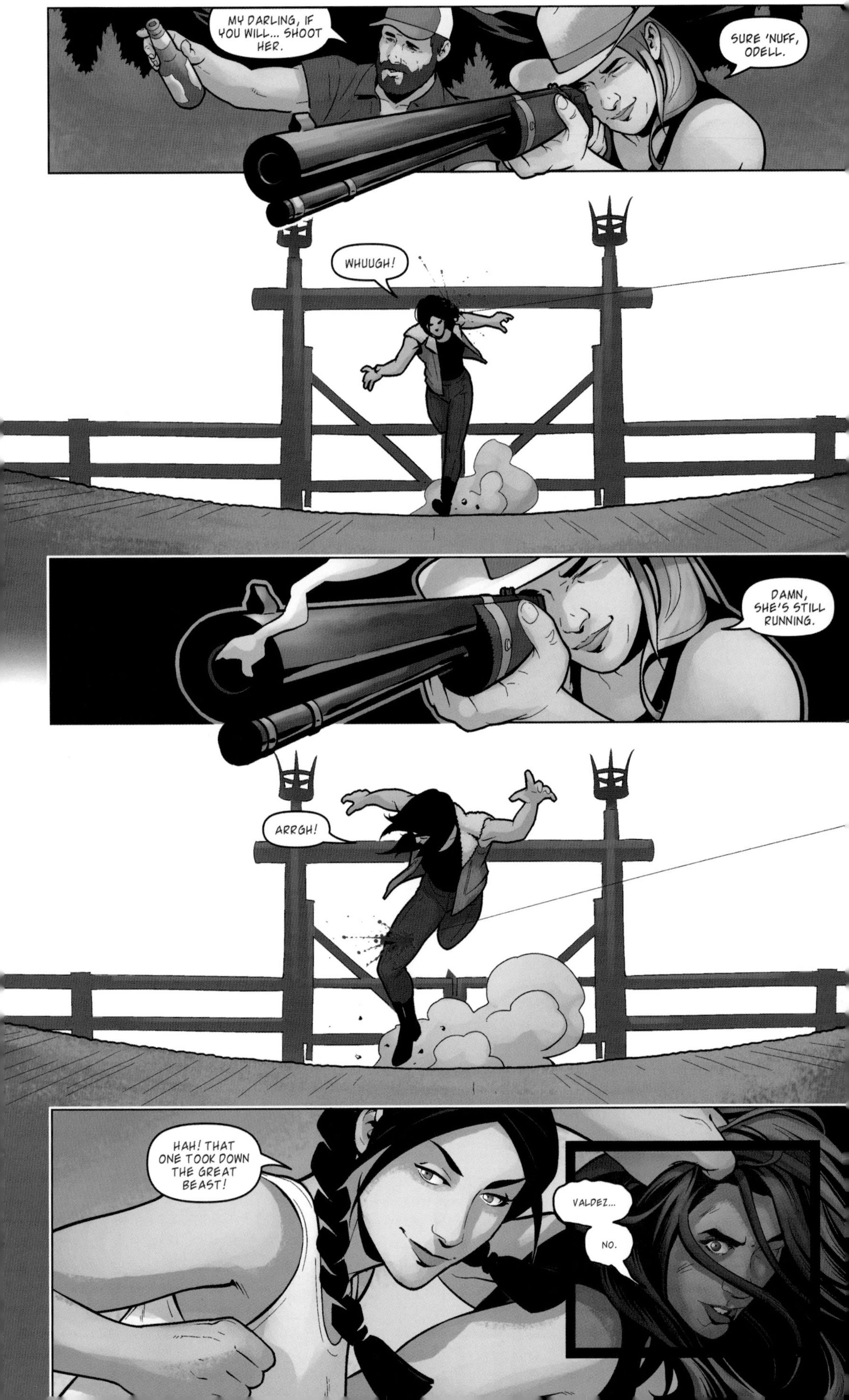
MY DARLING, IF YOU WILL... SHOOT HER.
SURE 'NUFF, ODELL.
WHUUGH!
DAMN, SHE'S STILL RUNNING.
ARRGH!
HAH! THAT ONE TOOK DOWN THE GREAT BEAST!
VALDEZ...
NO.

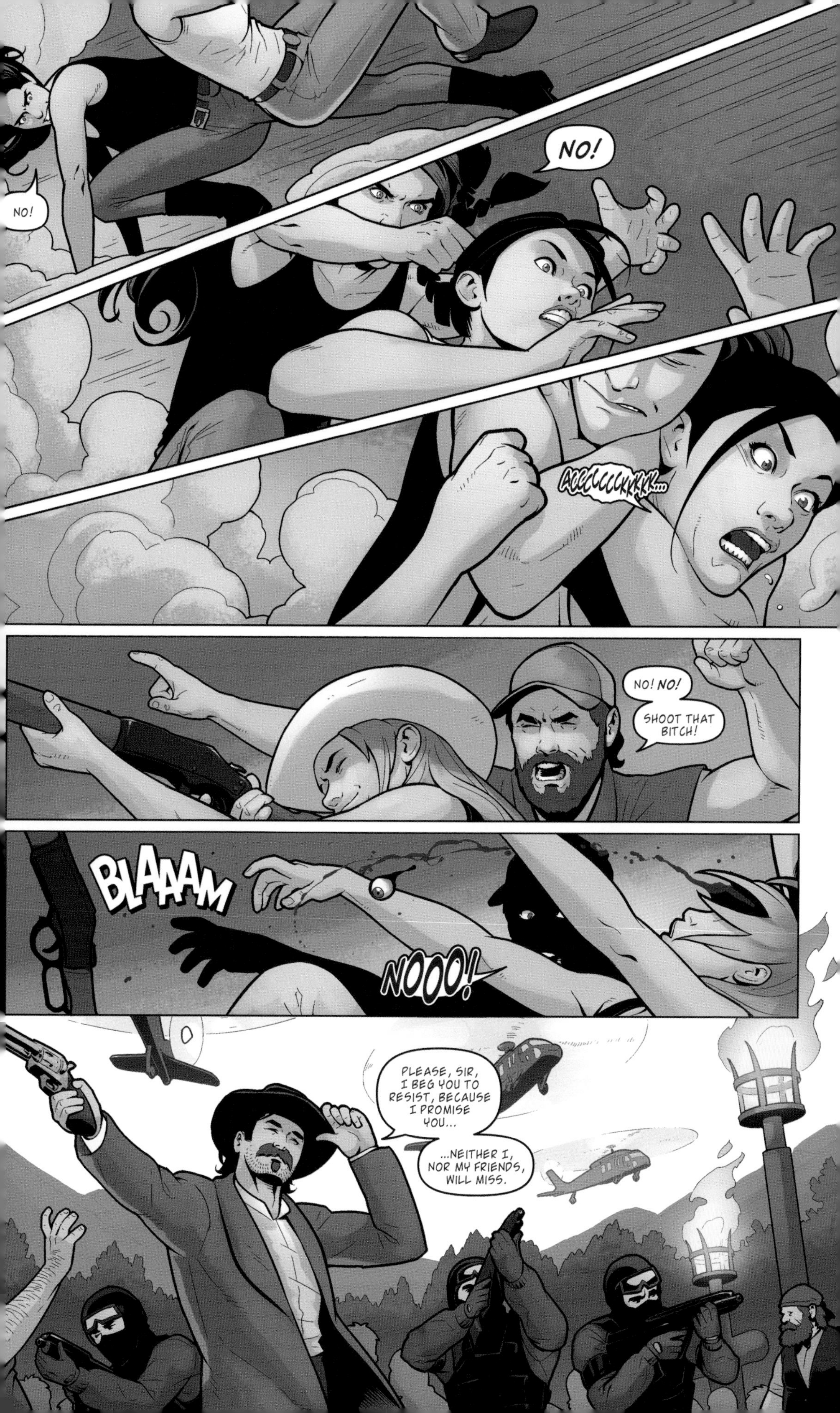
NO!
NO!
AOCCCCCCKKKKK...
NO! NO!
SHOOT THAT BITCH!
BLAAAM
NOOO!
PLEASE, SIR, I BEG YOU TO RESIST, BECAUSE I PROMISE YOU...
...NEITHER I, NOR MY FRIENDS, WILL MISS.

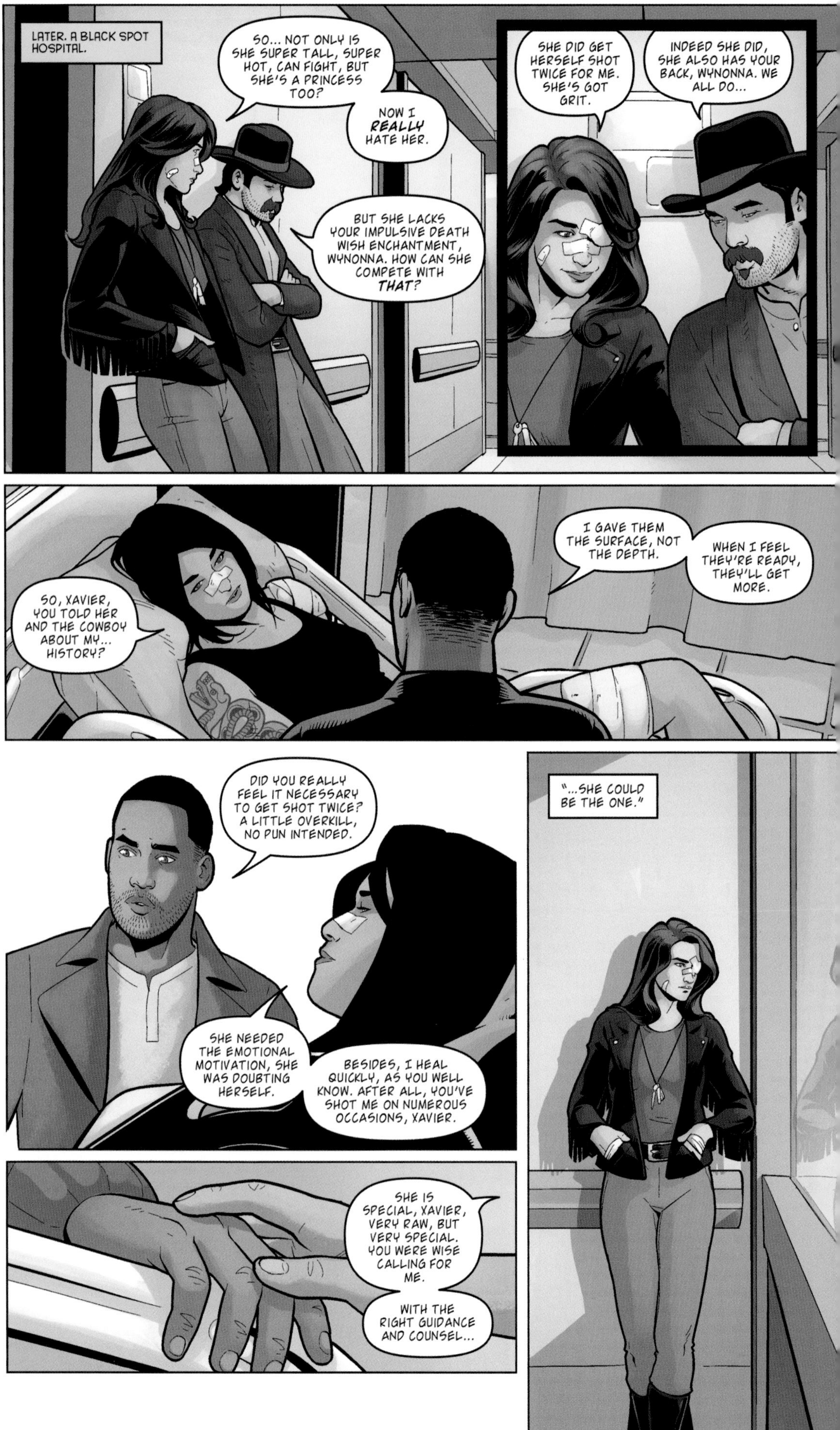

LATER. A BLACK SPOT HOSPITAL.
SO... NOT ONLY IS SHE SUPER TALL, SUPER HOT, CAN FIGHT, BUT SHE'S A PRINCESS TOO?
NOW I REALLY HATE HER.
BUT SHE LACKS YOUR IMPULSIVE DEATH WISH ENCHANTMENT, WYNONNA. HOW CAN SHE COMPETE WITH THAT?
SHE DID GET HERSELF SHOT TWICE FOR ME. SHE'S GOT GRIT.
INDEED SHE DID, SHE ALSO HAS YOUR BACK, WYNONNA. WE ALL DO...
SO, XAVIER, YOU TOLD HER AND THE COWBOY ABOUT MY... HISTORY?
I GAVE THEM THE SURFACE, NOT THE DEPTH.
WHEN I FEEL THEY'RE READY, THEY'LL GET MORE.
DID YOU REALLY FEEL IT NECESSARY TO GET SHOT TWICE? A LITTLE OVERKILL, NO PUN INTENDED.
SHE NEEDED THE EMOTIONAL MOTIVATION, SHE WAS DOUBTING HERSELF.
BESIDES, I HEAL QUICKLY, AS YOU WELL KNOW. AFTER ALL, YOU'VE SHOT ME ON NUMEROUS OCCASIONS, XAVIER.
SHE IS SPECIAL, XAVIER, VERY RAW, BUT VERY SPECIAL. YOU WERE WISE CALLING FOR ME.
WITH THE RIGHT GUIDANCE AND COUNSEL...
"...SHE COULD BE THE ONE."

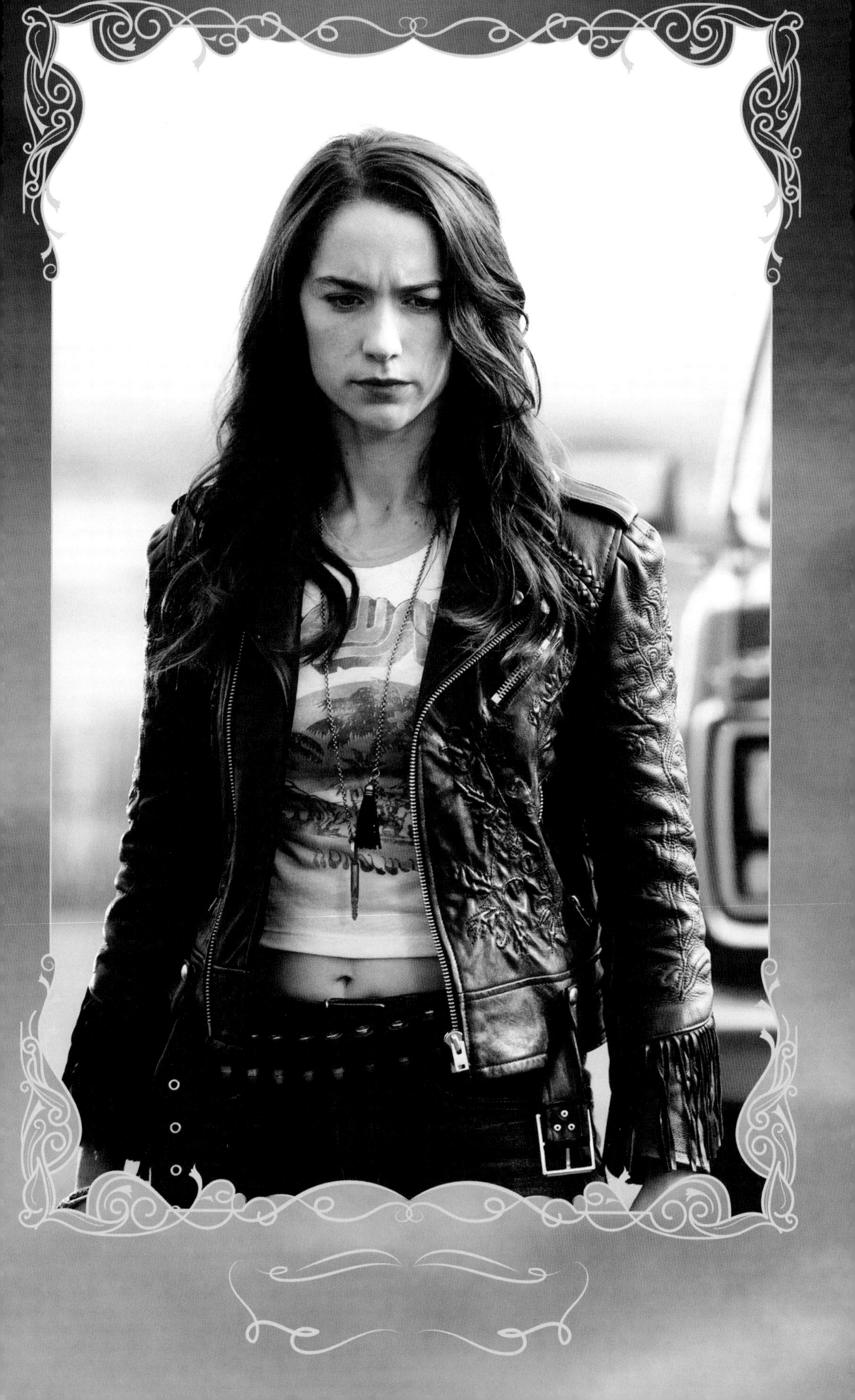

OOD COURT

Art by **Lora Innes**

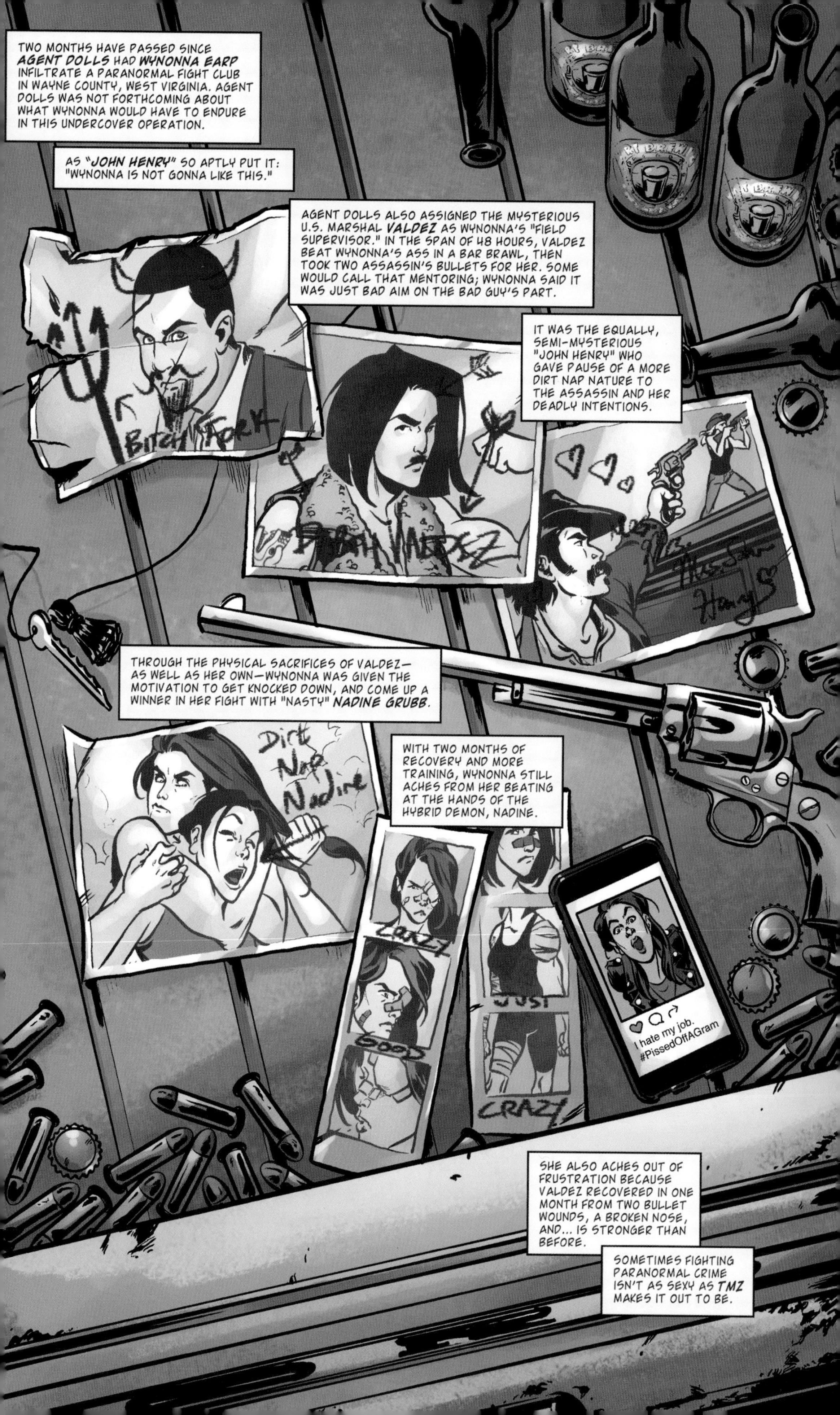

TWO MONTHS HAVE PASSED SINCE **AGENT DOLLS** HAD **WYNONNA EARP** INFILTRATE A PARANORMAL FIGHT CLUB IN WAYNE COUNTY, WEST VIRGINIA. AGENT DOLLS WAS NOT FORTHCOMING ABOUT WHAT WYNONNA WOULD HAVE TO ENDURE IN THIS UNDERCOVER OPERATION.
AS "**JOHN HENRY**" SO APTLY PUT IT: "WYNONNA IS NOT GONNA LIKE THIS."
AGENT DOLLS ALSO ASSIGNED THE MYSTERIOUS U.S. MARSHAL **VALDEZ** AS WYNONNA'S "FIELD SUPERVISOR." IN THE SPAN OF 48 HOURS, VALDEZ BEAT WYNONNA'S ASS IN A BAR BRAWL, THEN TOOK TWO ASSASSIN'S BULLETS FOR HER. SOME WOULD CALL THAT MENTORING; WYNONNA SAID IT WAS JUST BAD AIM ON THE BAD GUY'S PART.
BITCH FORK
IT WAS THE EQUALLY, SEMI-MYSTERIOUS "JOHN HENRY" WHO GAVE PAUSE OF A MORE DIRT NAP NATURE TO THE ASSASSIN AND HER DEADLY INTENTIONS.
THROUGH THE PHYSICAL SACRIFICES OF VALDEZ—AS WELL AS HER OWN—WYNONNA WAS GIVEN THE MOTIVATION TO GET KNOCKED DOWN, AND COME UP A WINNER IN HER FIGHT WITH "NASTY" **NADINE GRUBB**.
Dirt Nap Nadine
WITH TWO MONTHS OF RECOVERY AND MORE TRAINING, WYNONNA STILL ACHES FROM HER BEATING AT THE HANDS OF THE HYBRID DEMON, NADINE.
CRAZY
GOOD
JUST
CRAZY
I hate my job.
#PissedOffAGram
SHE ALSO ACHES OUT OF FRUSTRATION BECAUSE VALDEZ RECOVERED IN ONE MONTH FROM TWO BULLET WOUNDS, A BROKEN NOSE, AND... IS STRONGER THAN BEFORE.
SOMETIMES FIGHTING PARANORMAL CRIME ISN'T AS SEXY AS **TMZ** MAKES IT OUT TO BE.

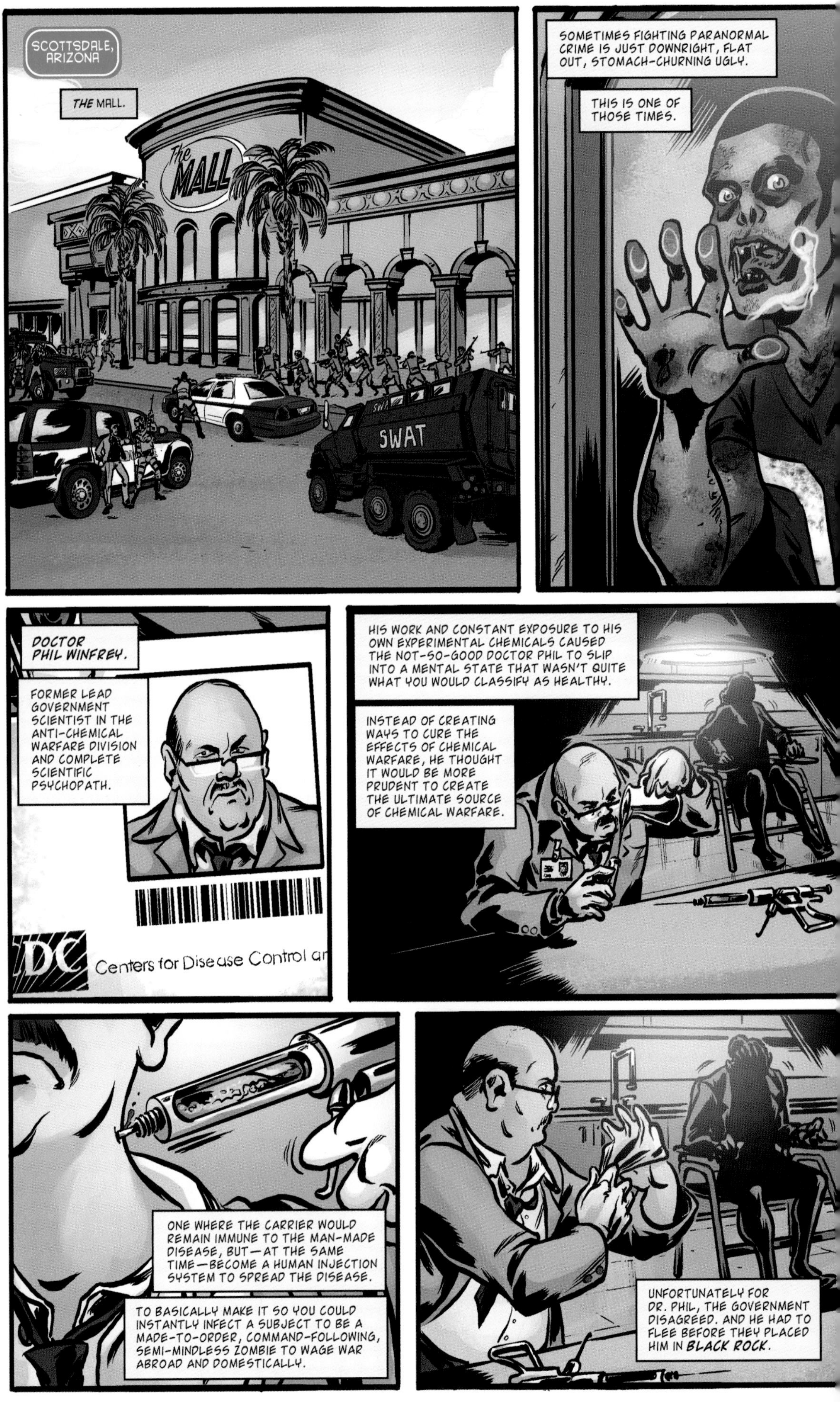
SCOTTSDALE, ARIZONA
THE MALL.
The MALL
SWAT
SOMETIMES FIGHTING PARANORMAL CRIME IS JUST DOWNRIGHT, FLAT OUT, STOMACH-CHURNING UGLY.
THIS IS ONE OF THOSE TIMES.
DOCTOR PHIL WINFREY.
FORMER LEAD GOVERNMENT SCIENTIST IN THE ANTI-CHEMICAL WARFARE DIVISION AND COMPLETE SCIENTIFIC PSYCHOPATH.
Centers for Disease Control ar
HIS WORK AND CONSTANT EXPOSURE TO HIS OWN EXPERIMENTAL CHEMICALS CAUSED THE NOT-SO-GOOD DOCTOR PHIL TO SLIP INTO A MENTAL STATE THAT WASN'T QUITE WHAT YOU WOULD CLASSIFY AS HEALTHY.
INSTEAD OF CREATING WAYS TO CURE THE EFFECTS OF CHEMICAL WARFARE, HE THOUGHT IT WOULD BE MORE PRUDENT TO CREATE THE ULTIMATE SOURCE OF CHEMICAL WARFARE.
ONE WHERE THE CARRIER WOULD REMAIN IMMUNE TO THE MAN-MADE DISEASE, BUT—AT THE SAME TIME—BECOME A HUMAN INJECTION SYSTEM TO SPREAD THE DISEASE.
TO BASICALLY MAKE IT SO YOU COULD INSTANTLY INFECT A SUBJECT TO BE A MADE-TO-ORDER, COMMAND-FOLLOWING, SEMI-MINDLESS ZOMBIE TO WAGE WAR ABROAD AND DOMESTICALLY.
UNFORTUNATELY FOR DR. PHIL, THE GOVERNMENT DISAGREED. AND HE HAD TO FLEE BEFORE THEY PLACED HIM IN *BLACK ROCK*.

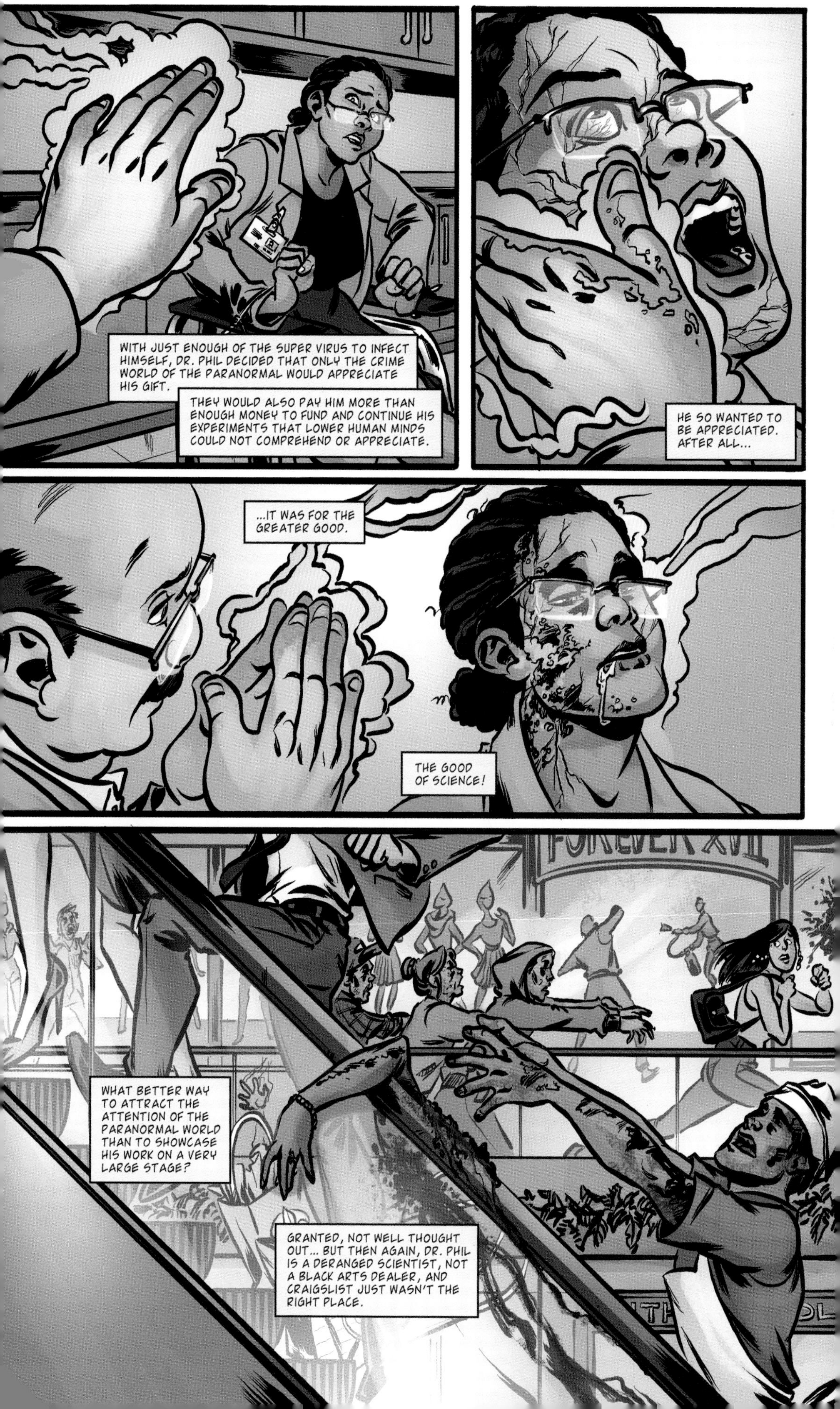

WITH JUST ENOUGH OF THE SUPER VIRUS TO INFECT HIMSELF, DR. PHIL DECIDED THAT ONLY THE CRIME WORLD OF THE PARANORMAL WOULD APPRECIATE HIS GIFT.
THEY WOULD ALSO PAY HIM MORE THAN ENOUGH MONEY TO FUND AND CONTINUE HIS EXPERIMENTS THAT LOWER HUMAN MINDS COULD NOT COMPREHEND OR APPRECIATE.
HE SO WANTED TO BE APPRECIATED. AFTER ALL...
...IT WAS FOR THE GREATER GOOD.
THE GOOD OF SCIENCE!
WHAT BETTER WAY TO ATTRACT THE ATTENTION OF THE PARANORMAL WORLD THAN TO SHOWCASE HIS WORK ON A VERY LARGE STAGE?
GRANTED, NOT WELL THOUGHT OUT... BUT THEN AGAIN, DR. PHIL IS A DERANGED SCIENTIST, NOT A BLACK ARTS DEALER, AND CRAIGSLIST JUST WASN'T THE RIGHT PLACE.

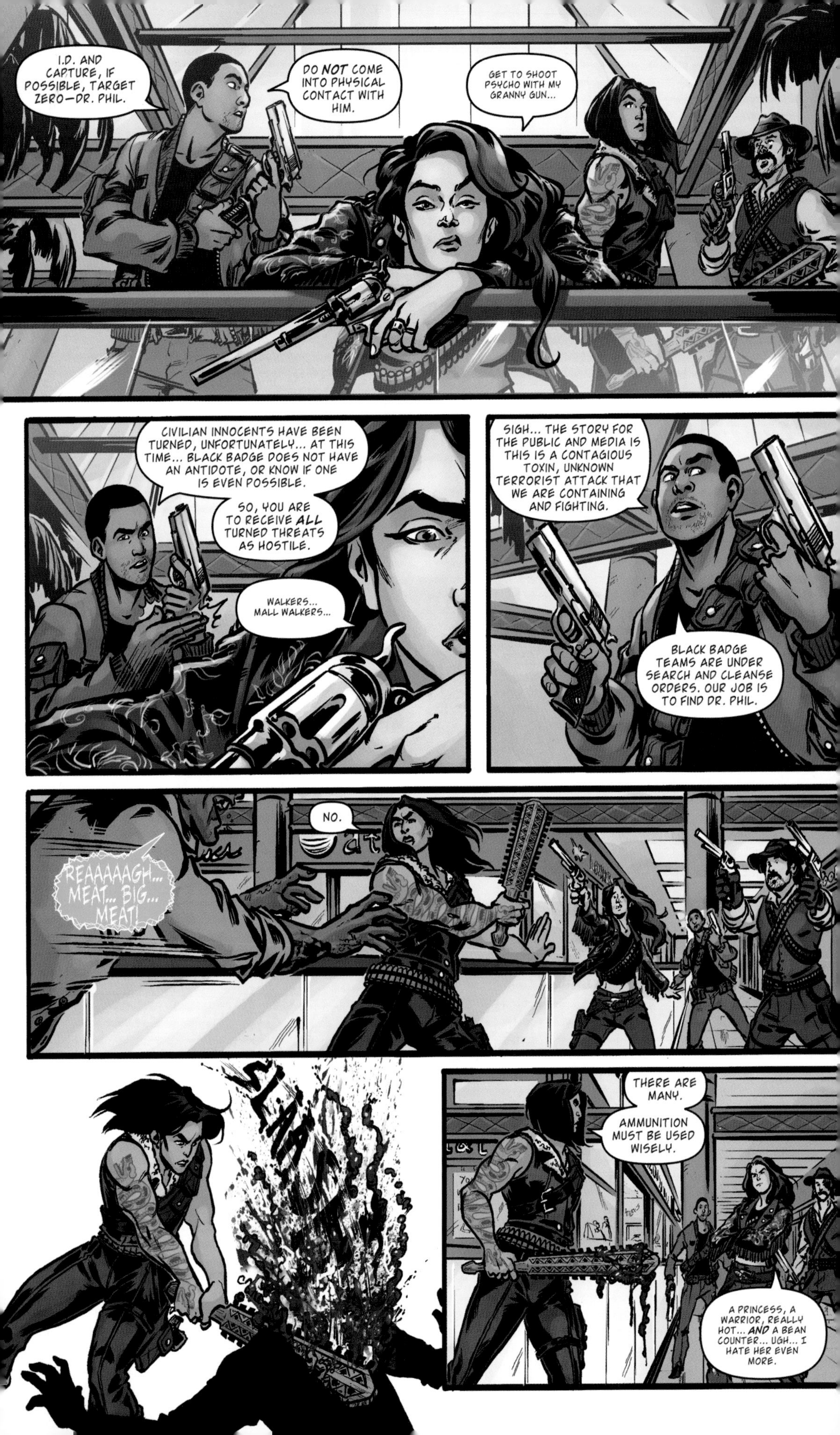
I.D. AND CAPTURE, IF POSSIBLE, TARGET ZERO—DR. PHIL.
DO **NOT** COME INTO PHYSICAL CONTACT WITH HIM.
GET TO SHOOT PSYCHO WITH MY GRANNY GUN...
CIVILIAN INNOCENTS HAVE BEEN TURNED, UNFORTUNATELY... AT THIS TIME... BLACK BADGE DOES NOT HAVE AN ANTIDOTE, OR KNOW IF ONE IS EVEN POSSIBLE.
SO, YOU ARE TO RECEIVE **ALL** TURNED THREATS AS HOSTILE.
WALKERS... MALL WALKERS...
SIGH... THE STORY FOR THE PUBLIC AND MEDIA IS THIS IS A CONTAGIOUS TOXIN, UNKNOWN TERRORIST ATTACK THAT WE ARE CONTAINING AND FIGHTING.
BLACK BADGE TEAMS ARE UNDER SEARCH AND CLEANSE ORDERS. OUR JOB IS TO FIND DR. PHIL.
REAAAAAGH... MEAT... BIG... MEAT!
NO.
THERE ARE MANY.
AMMUNITION MUST BE USED WISELY.
A PRINCESS, A WARRIOR, REALLY HOT... **AND** A BEAN COUNTER... UGH... I HATE HER EVEN MORE.

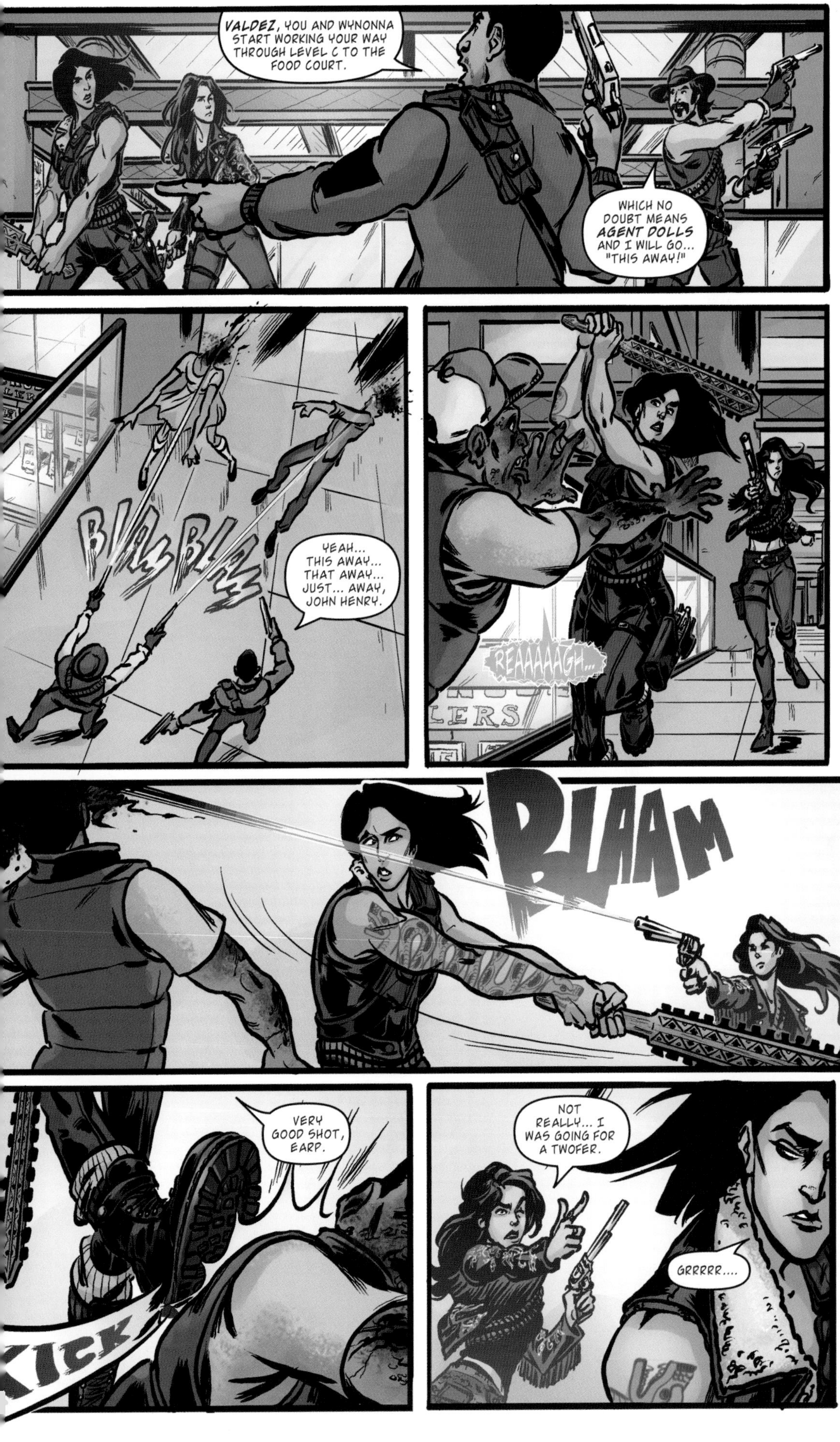
VALDEZ, YOU AND WYNONNA START WORKING YOUR WAY THROUGH LEVEL C TO THE FOOD COURT.
WHICH NO DOUBT MEANS AGENT DOLLS AND I WILL GO... "THIS AWAY!"
BLAM BLAM
YEAH... THIS AWAY... THAT AWAY... JUST... AWAY, JOHN HENRY.
REAAAAAGH...
BLAAM
VERY GOOD SHOT, EARP.
KICK
NOT REALLY... I WAS GOING FOR A TWOFER.
GRRRRR....

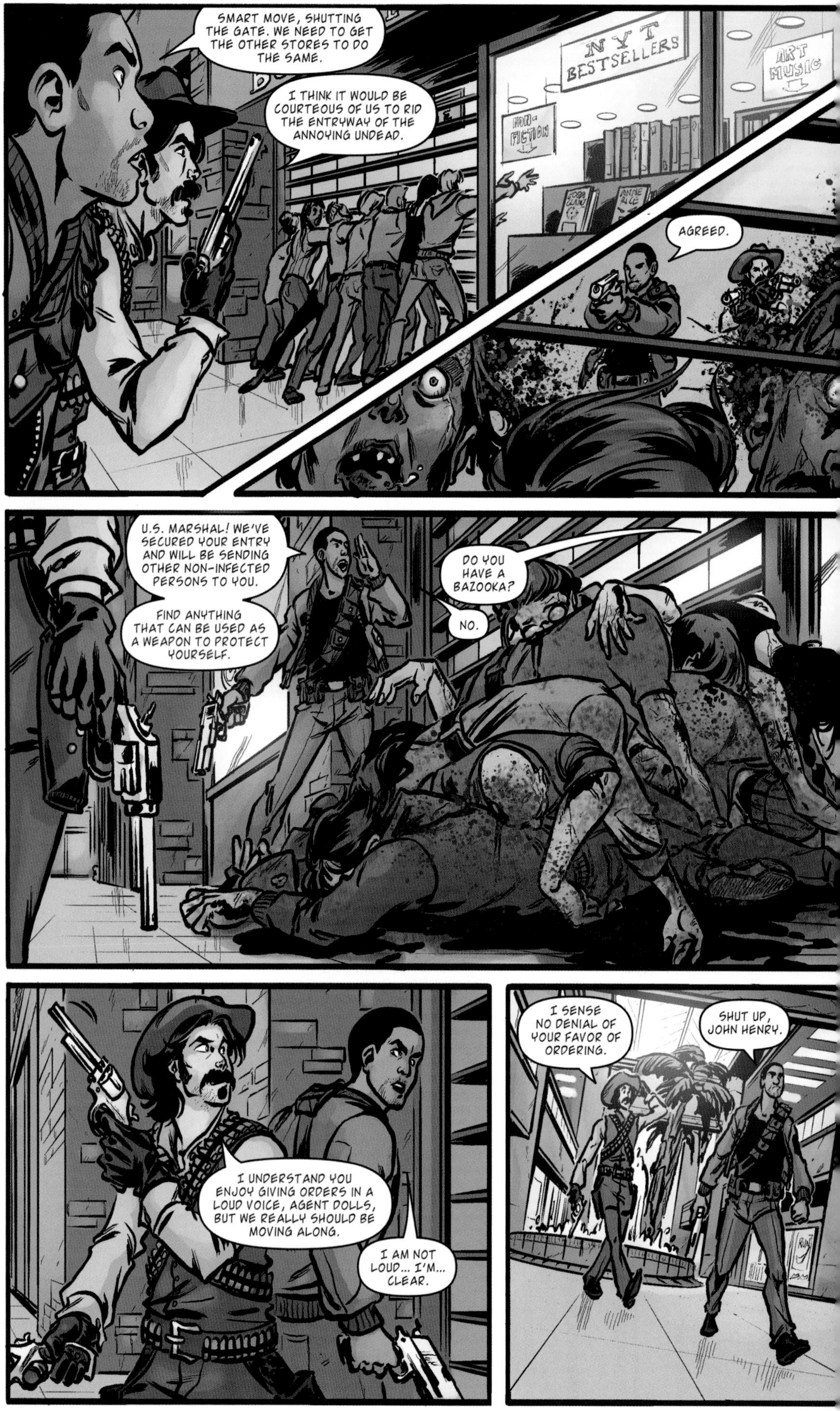

SMART MOVE, SHUTTING THE GATE. WE NEED TO GET THE OTHER STORES TO DO THE SAME.
I THINK IT WOULD BE COURTEOUS OF US TO RID THE ENTRYWAY OF THE ANNOYING UNDEAD.
NYT BESTSELLERS
NON-FICTION
ART MUSIC
AGREED.
U.S. MARSHAL! WE'VE SECURED YOUR ENTRY AND WILL BE SENDING OTHER NON-INFECTED PERSONS TO YOU.
FIND ANYTHING THAT CAN BE USED AS A WEAPON TO PROTECT YOURSELF.
DO YOU HAVE A BAZOOKA?
NO.
I UNDERSTAND YOU ENJOY GIVING ORDERS IN A LOUD VOICE, AGENT DOLLS, BUT WE REALLY SHOULD BE MOVING ALONG.
I AM NOT LOUD... I'M... CLEAR.
I SENSE NO DENIAL OF YOUR FAVOR OF ORDERING.
SHUT UP, JOHN HENRY.

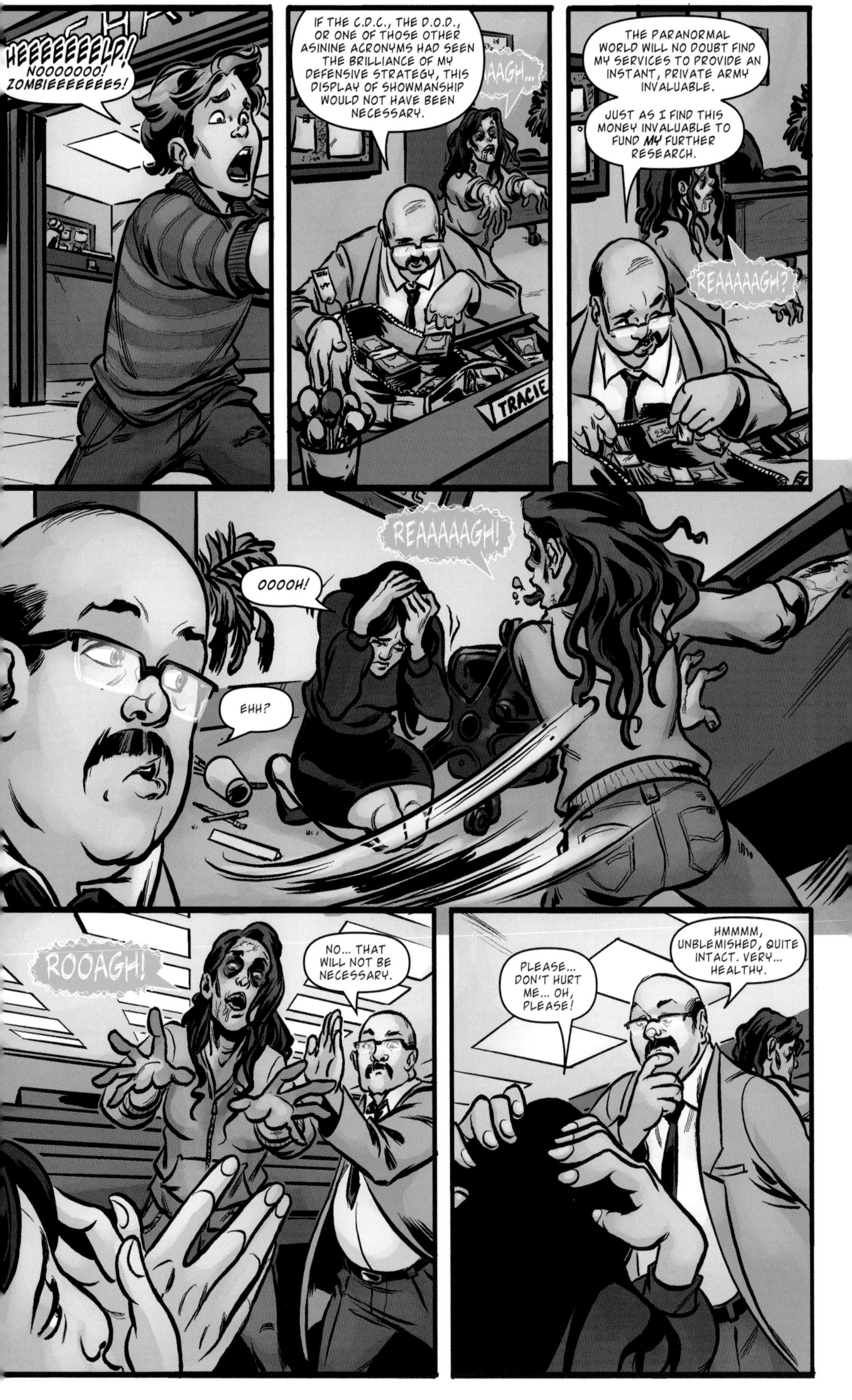
HEEEEEEEELP!! NOOOOOOO! ZOMBIEEEEEEES!
IF THE C.D.C., THE D.O.D., OR ONE OF THOSE OTHER ASININE ACRONYMS HAD SEEN THE BRILLIANCE OF MY DEFENSIVE STRATEGY, THIS DISPLAY OF SHOWMANSHIP WOULD NOT HAVE BEEN NECESSARY.
...AAGH...
TRACIE
THE PARANORMAL WORLD WILL NO DOUBT FIND MY SERVICES TO PROVIDE AN INSTANT, PRIVATE ARMY INVALUABLE.
JUST AS I FIND THIS MONEY INVALUABLE TO FUND MY FURTHER RESEARCH.
REAAAAAGH?
REAAAAAGH!
OOOOH!
EHH?
ROOAGH!
NO... THAT WILL NOT BE NECESSARY.
PLEASE... DON'T HURT ME... OH, PLEASE!
HMMMM, UNBLEMISHED, QUITE INTACT. VERY... HEALTHY.

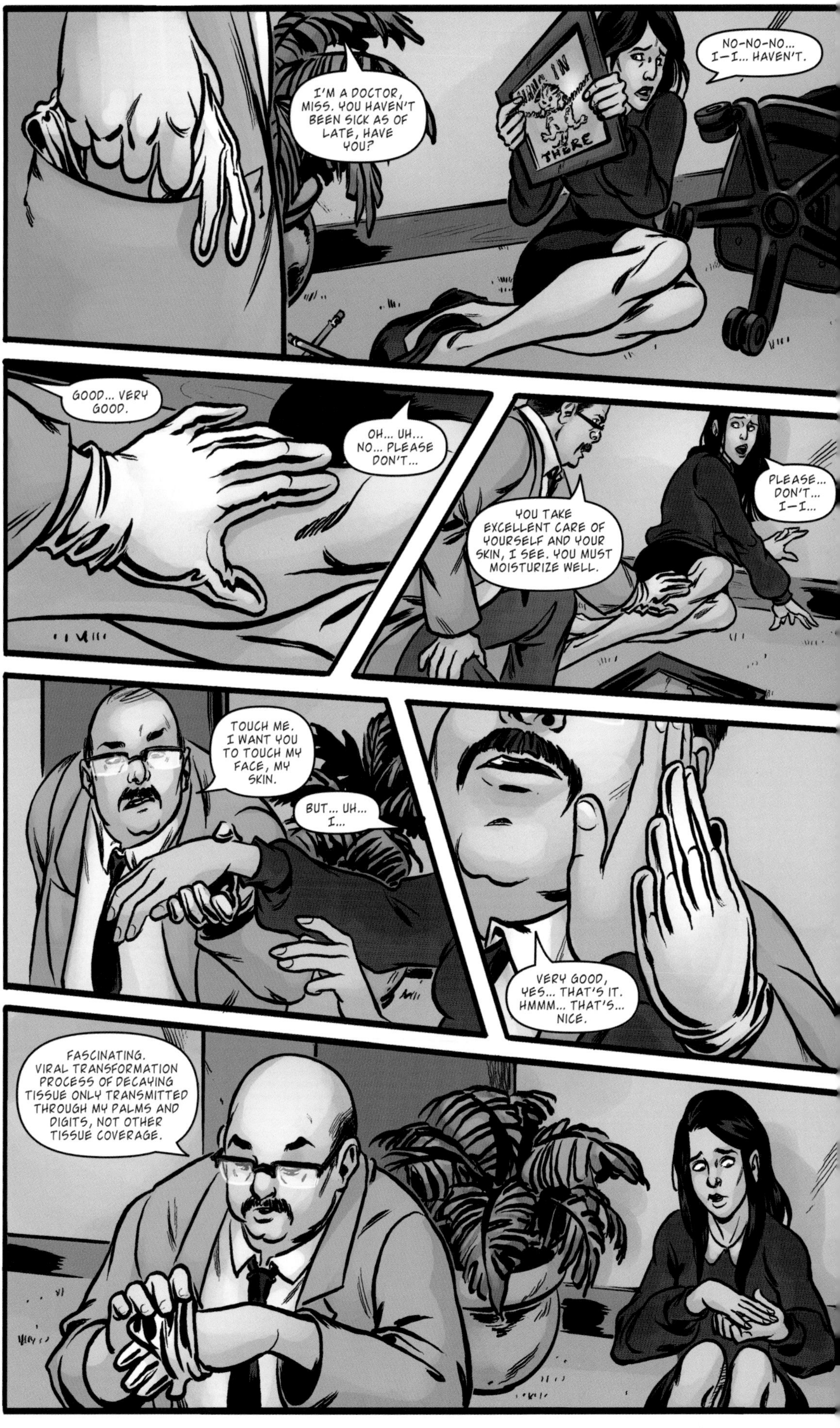

I'M A DOCTOR, MISS. YOU HAVEN'T BEEN SICK AS OF LATE, HAVE YOU?
NO-NO-NO... I—I... HAVEN'T.
IN THERE
GOOD... VERY GOOD.
OH... UH... NO... PLEASE DON'T...
YOU TAKE EXCELLENT CARE OF YOURSELF AND YOUR SKIN, I SEE. YOU MUST MOISTURIZE WELL.
PLEASE... DON'T... I—I...
TOUCH ME. I WANT YOU TO TOUCH MY FACE, MY SKIN.
BUT... UH... I...
VERY GOOD, YES... THAT'S IT. HMMM... THAT'S... NICE.
FASCINATING. VIRAL TRANSFORMATION PROCESS OF DECAYING TISSUE ONLY TRANSMITTED THROUGH MY PALMS AND DIGITS, NOT OTHER TISSUE COVERAGE.

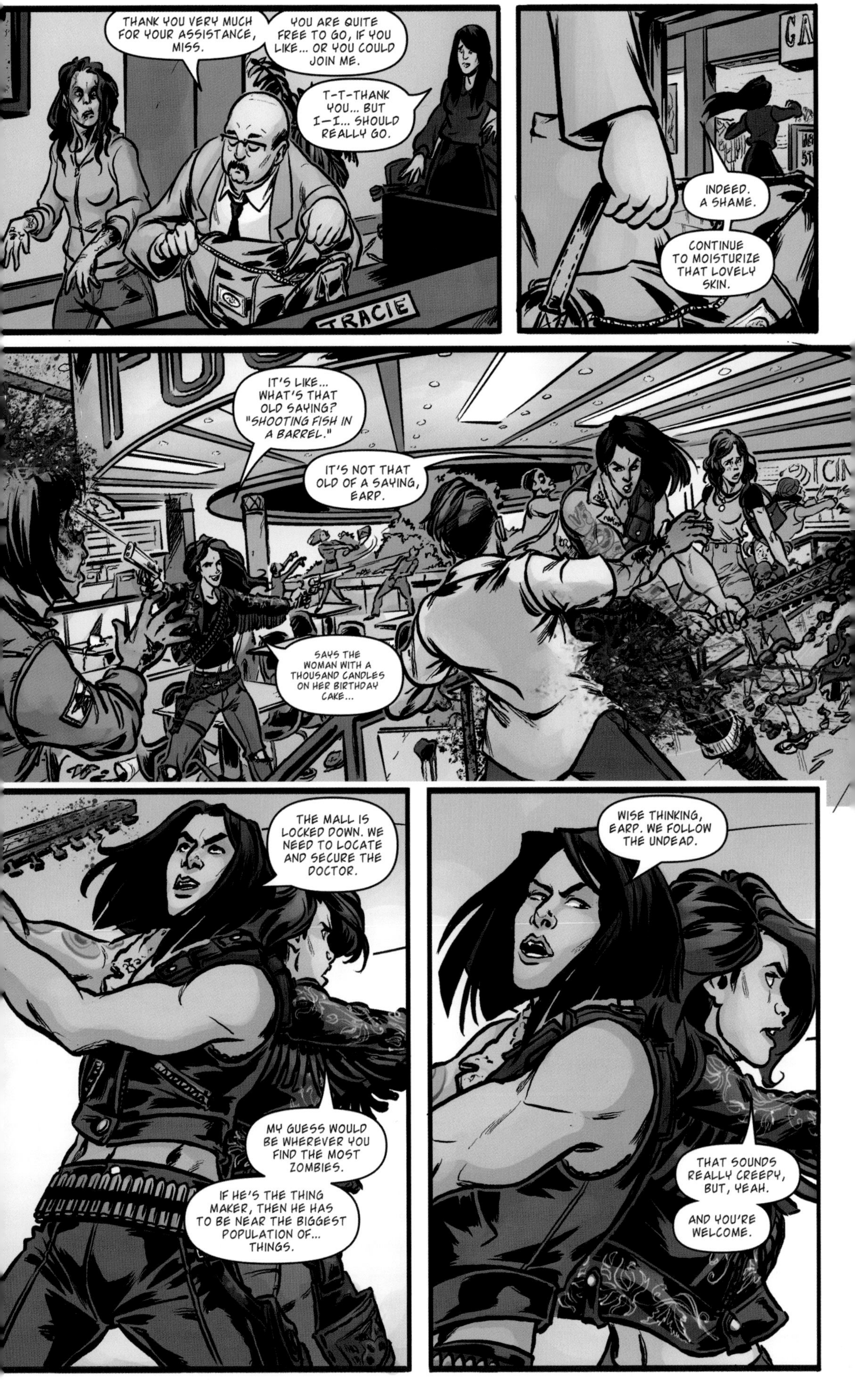
THANK YOU VERY MUCH FOR YOUR ASSISTANCE, MISS.
YOU ARE QUITE FREE TO GO, IF YOU LIKE... OR YOU COULD JOIN ME.
T-T-THANK YOU... BUT I—I... SHOULD REALLY GO.
TRACIE
INDEED. A SHAME.
CONTINUE TO MOISTURIZE THAT LOVELY SKIN.
IT'S LIKE... WHAT'S THAT OLD SAYING? "SHOOTING FISH IN A BARREL."
IT'S NOT THAT OLD OF A SAYING, EARP.
SAYS THE WOMAN WITH A THOUSAND CANDLES ON HER BIRTHDAY CAKE...
THE MALL IS LOCKED DOWN. WE NEED TO LOCATE AND SECURE THE DOCTOR.
MY GUESS WOULD BE WHEREVER YOU FIND THE MOST ZOMBIES.
IF HE'S THE THING MAKER, THEN HE HAS TO BE NEAR THE BIGGEST POPULATION OF... THINGS.
WISE THINKING, EARP. WE FOLLOW THE UNDEAD.
THAT SOUNDS REALLY CREEPY, BUT, YEAH.
AND YOU'RE WELCOME.

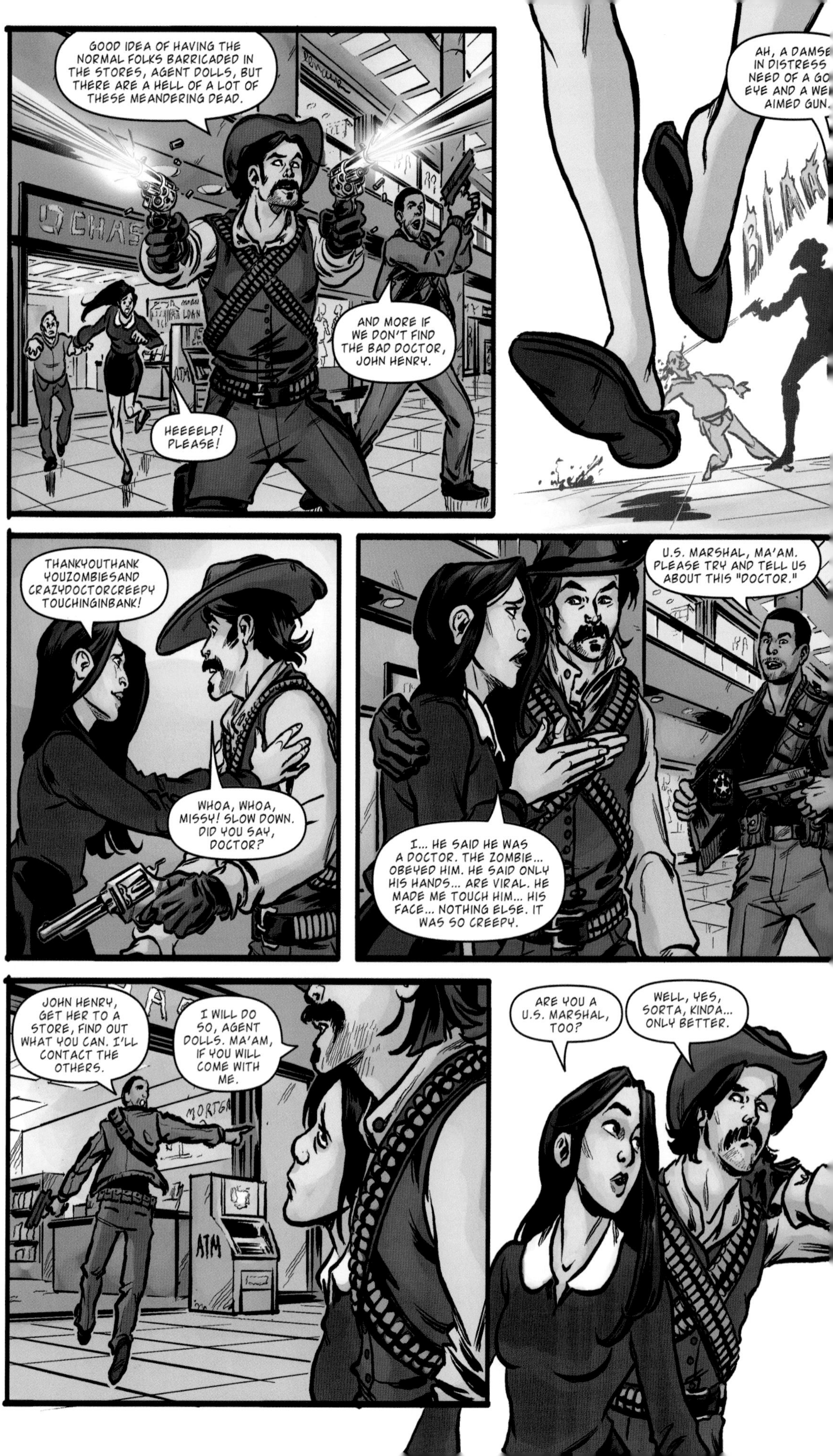
GOOD IDEA OF HAVING THE NORMAL FOLKS BARRICADED IN THE STORES, AGENT DOLLS, BUT THERE ARE A HELL OF A LOT OF THESE MEANDERING DEAD.
AND MORE IF WE DON'T FIND THE BAD DOCTOR, JOHN HENRY.
HEEEELP! PLEASE!
AH, A DAMSE IN DISTRESS NEED OF A GO EYE AND A WE AIMED GUN.
THANKYOUTHANK YOUZOMBIESAND CRAZYDOCTORCREEPY TOUCHINGINBANK!
WHOA, WHOA, MISSY! SLOW DOWN. DID YOU SAY, DOCTOR?
U.S. MARSHAL, MA'AM. PLEASE TRY AND TELL US ABOUT THIS "DOCTOR."
I... HE SAID HE WAS A DOCTOR. THE ZOMBIE... OBEYED HIM. HE SAID ONLY HIS HANDS... ARE VIRAL. HE MADE ME TOUCH HIM... HIS FACE... NOTHING ELSE. IT WAS SO CREEPY.
JOHN HENRY, GET HER TO A STORE, FIND OUT WHAT YOU CAN. I'LL CONTACT THE OTHERS.
I WILL DO SO, AGENT DOLLS. MA'AM, IF YOU WILL COME WITH ME.
ARE YOU A U.S. MARSHAL, TOO?
WELL, YES, SORTA, KINDA... ONLY BETTER.

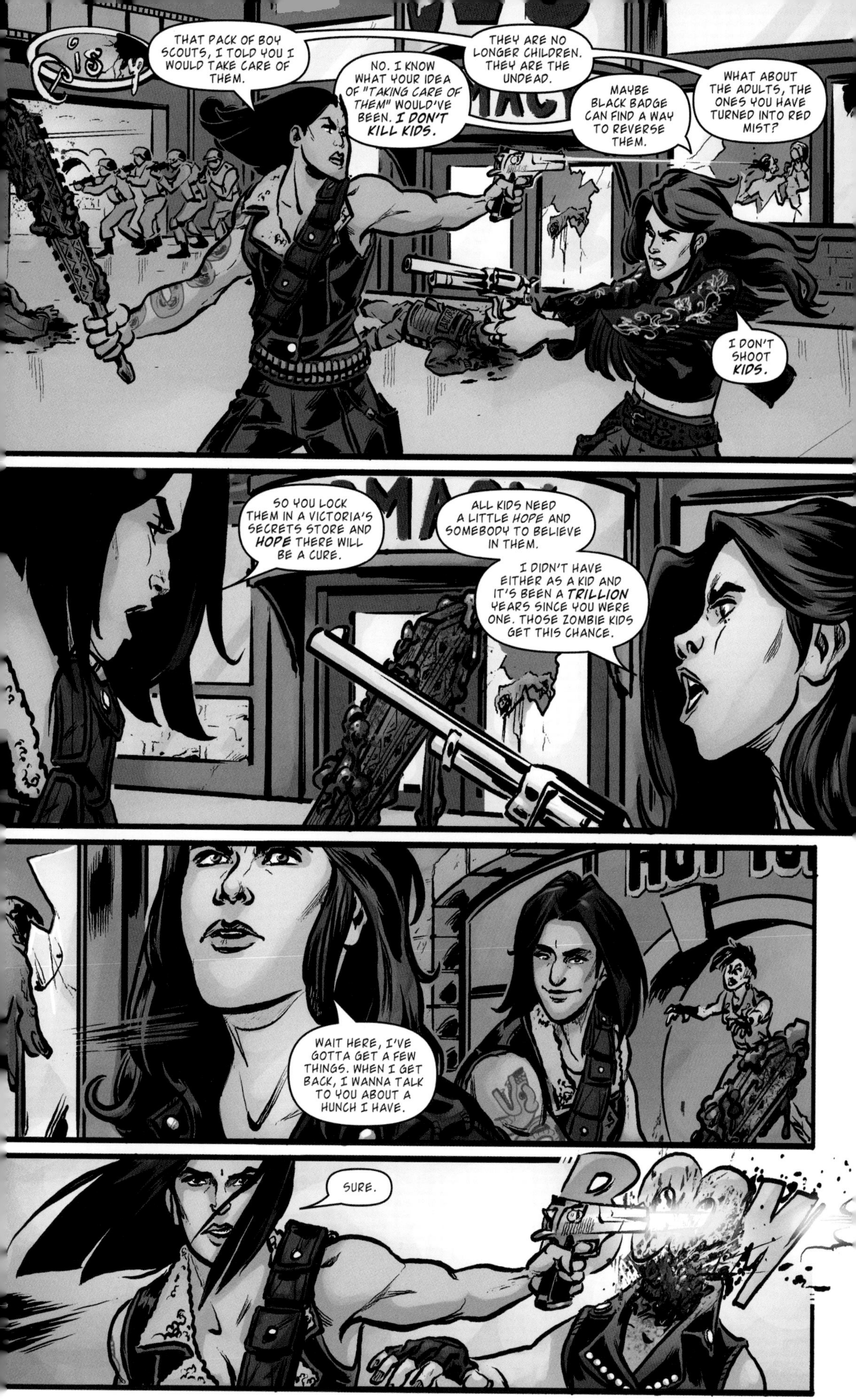
THAT PACK OF BOY SCOUTS, I TOLD YOU I WOULD TAKE CARE OF THEM.
NO. I KNOW WHAT YOUR IDEA OF "TAKING CARE OF THEM" WOULD'VE BEEN. I DON'T KILL KIDS.
THEY ARE NO LONGER CHILDREN. THEY ARE THE UNDEAD.
MAYBE BLACK BADGE CAN FIND A WAY TO REVERSE THEM.
WHAT ABOUT THE ADULTS, THE ONES YOU HAVE TURNED INTO RED MIST?
I DON'T SHOOT KIDS.
SO YOU LOCK THEM IN A VICTORIA'S SECRETS STORE AND HOPE THERE WILL BE A CURE.
ALL KIDS NEED A LITTLE HOPE AND SOMEBODY TO BELIEVE IN THEM.
I DIDN'T HAVE EITHER AS A KID AND IT'S BEEN A TRILLION YEARS SINCE YOU WERE ONE. THOSE ZOMBIE KIDS GET THIS CHANCE.
WAIT HERE, I'VE GOTTA GET A FEW THINGS. WHEN I GET BACK, I WANNA TALK TO YOU ABOUT A HUNCH I HAVE.
SURE.

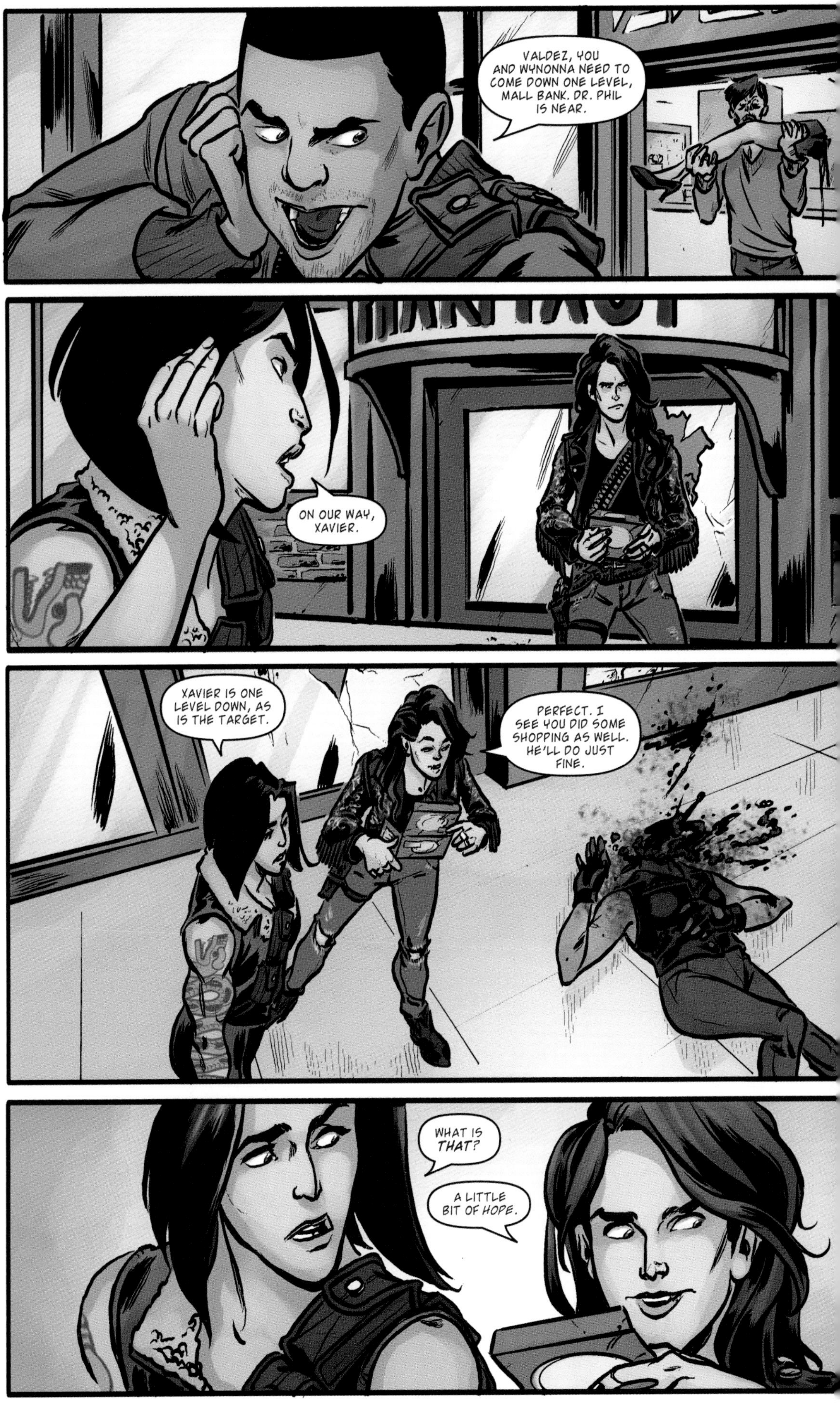
VALDEZ, YOU AND WYNONNA NEED TO COME DOWN ONE LEVEL, MALL BANK. DR. PHIL IS NEAR.
ON OUR WAY, XAVIER.
XAVIER IS ONE LEVEL DOWN, AS IS THE TARGET.
PERFECT. I SEE YOU DID SOME SHOPPING AS WELL. HE'LL DO JUST FINE.
WHAT IS *THAT?*
A LITTLE BIT OF *HOPE.*

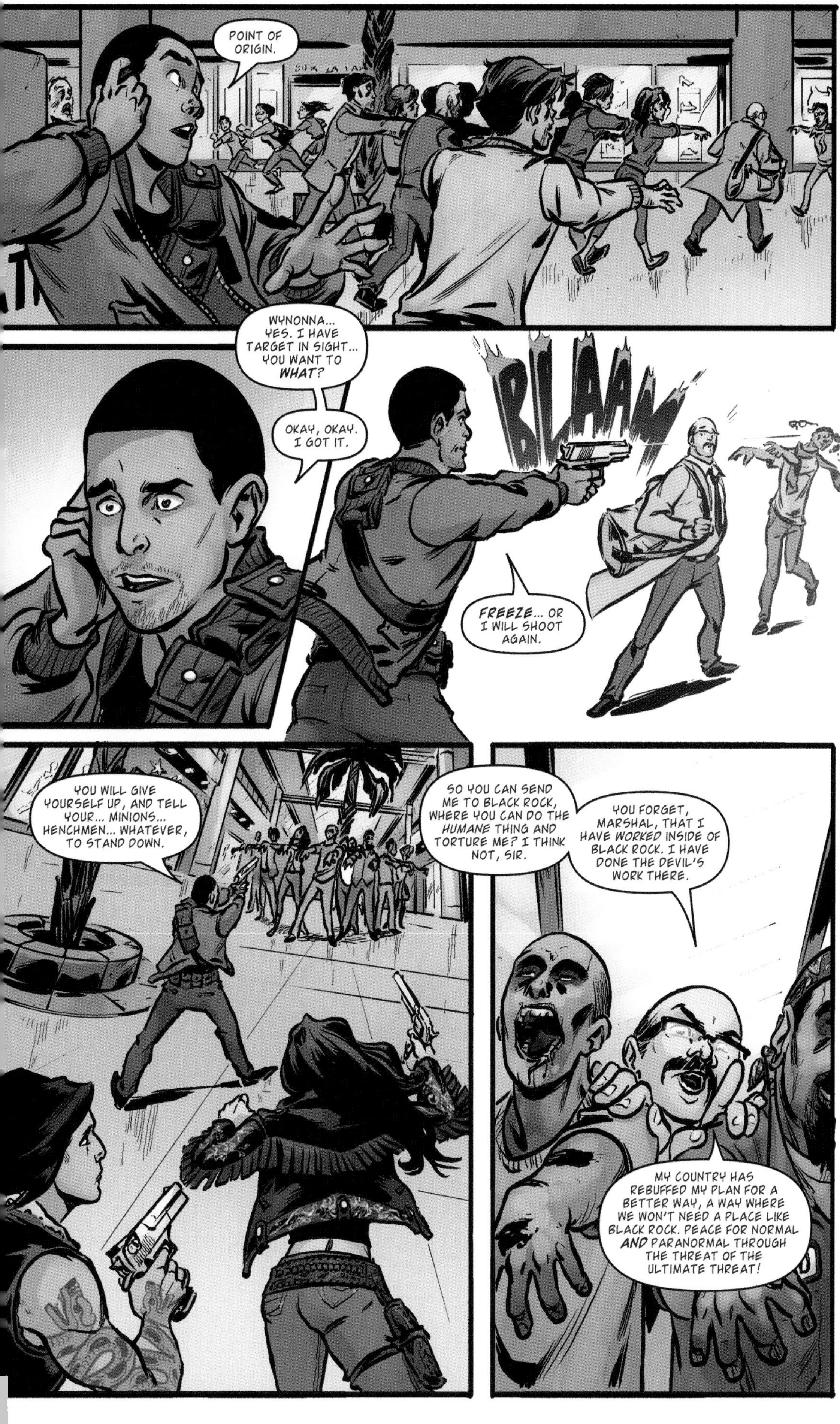
POINT OF ORIGIN.
WYNONNA... YES. I HAVE TARGET IN SIGHT... YOU WANT TO *WHAT*?
OKAY, OKAY. I GOT IT.
BLAAM
FREEZE... OR I WILL SHOOT AGAIN.
YOU WILL GIVE YOURSELF UP, AND TELL YOUR... MINIONS... HENCHMEN... WHATEVER, TO STAND DOWN.
SO YOU CAN SEND ME TO BLACK ROCK, WHERE YOU CAN DO THE *HUMANE* THING AND TORTURE ME? I THINK NOT, SIR.
YOU FORGET, MARSHAL, THAT I HAVE *WORKED* INSIDE OF BLACK ROCK. I HAVE DONE THE DEVIL'S WORK THERE.
MY COUNTRY HAS REBUFFED MY PLAN FOR A BETTER WAY, A WAY WHERE WE WON'T NEED A PLACE LIKE BLACK ROCK. PEACE FOR NORMAL ***AND*** PARANORMAL THROUGH THE THREAT OF THE ULTIMATE THREAT!

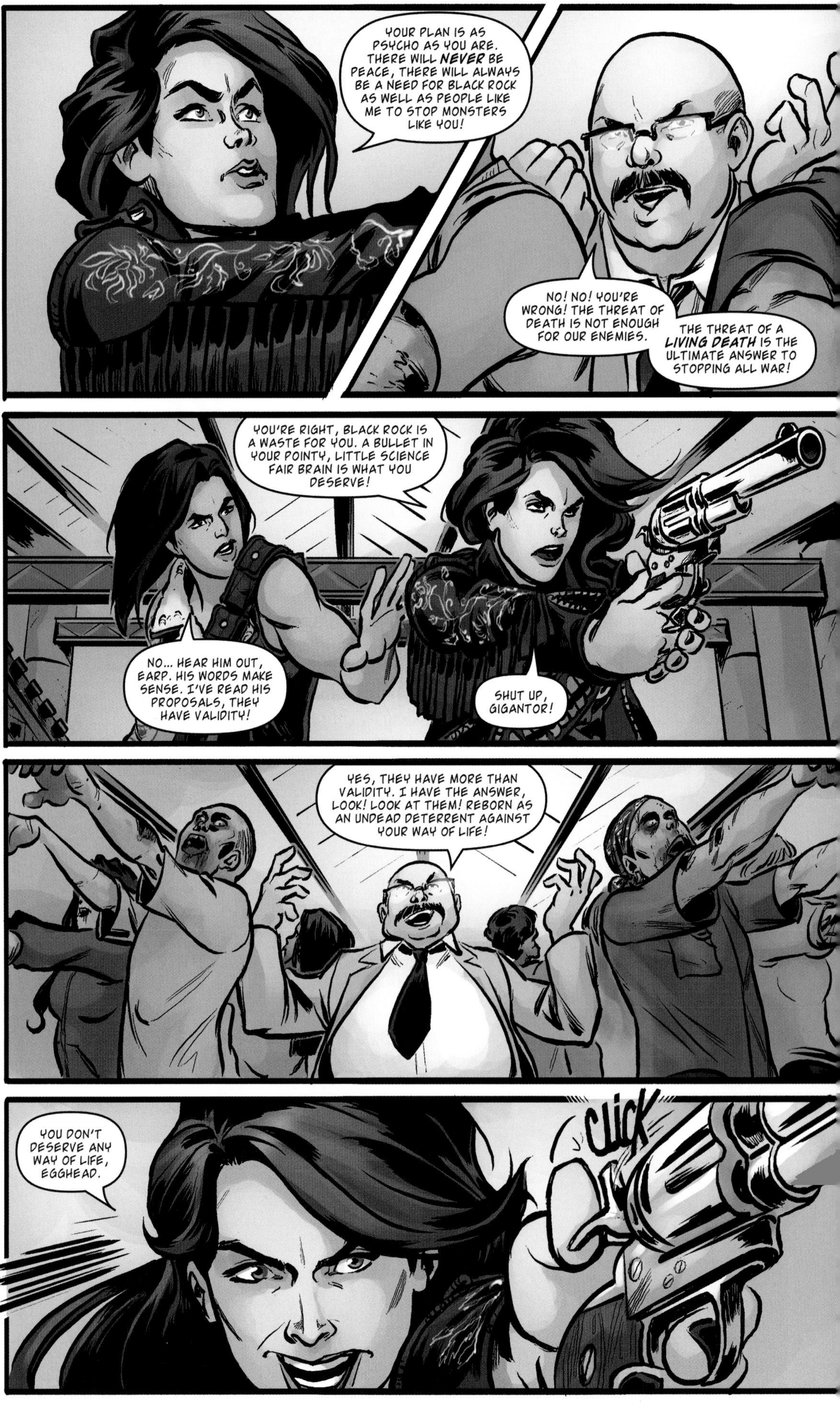
YOUR PLAN IS AS PSYCHO AS YOU ARE. THERE WILL NEVER BE PEACE, THERE WILL ALWAYS BE A NEED FOR BLACK ROCK AS WELL AS PEOPLE LIKE ME TO STOP MONSTERS LIKE YOU!
NO! NO! YOU'RE WRONG! THE THREAT OF DEATH IS NOT ENOUGH FOR OUR ENEMIES.
THE THREAT OF A LIVING DEATH IS THE ULTIMATE ANSWER TO STOPPING ALL WAR!
YOU'RE RIGHT, BLACK ROCK IS A WASTE FOR YOU. A BULLET IN YOUR POINTY, LITTLE SCIENCE FAIR BRAIN IS WHAT YOU DESERVE!
NO... HEAR HIM OUT, EARP. HIS WORDS MAKE SENSE. I'VE READ HIS PROPOSALS, THEY HAVE VALIDITY!
SHUT UP, GIGANTOR!
YES, THEY HAVE MORE THAN VALIDITY. I HAVE THE ANSWER, LOOK! LOOK AT THEM! REBORN AS AN UNDEAD DETERRENT AGAINST YOUR WAY OF LIFE!
YOU DON'T DESERVE ANY WAY OF LIFE, EGGHEAD.
CLICK

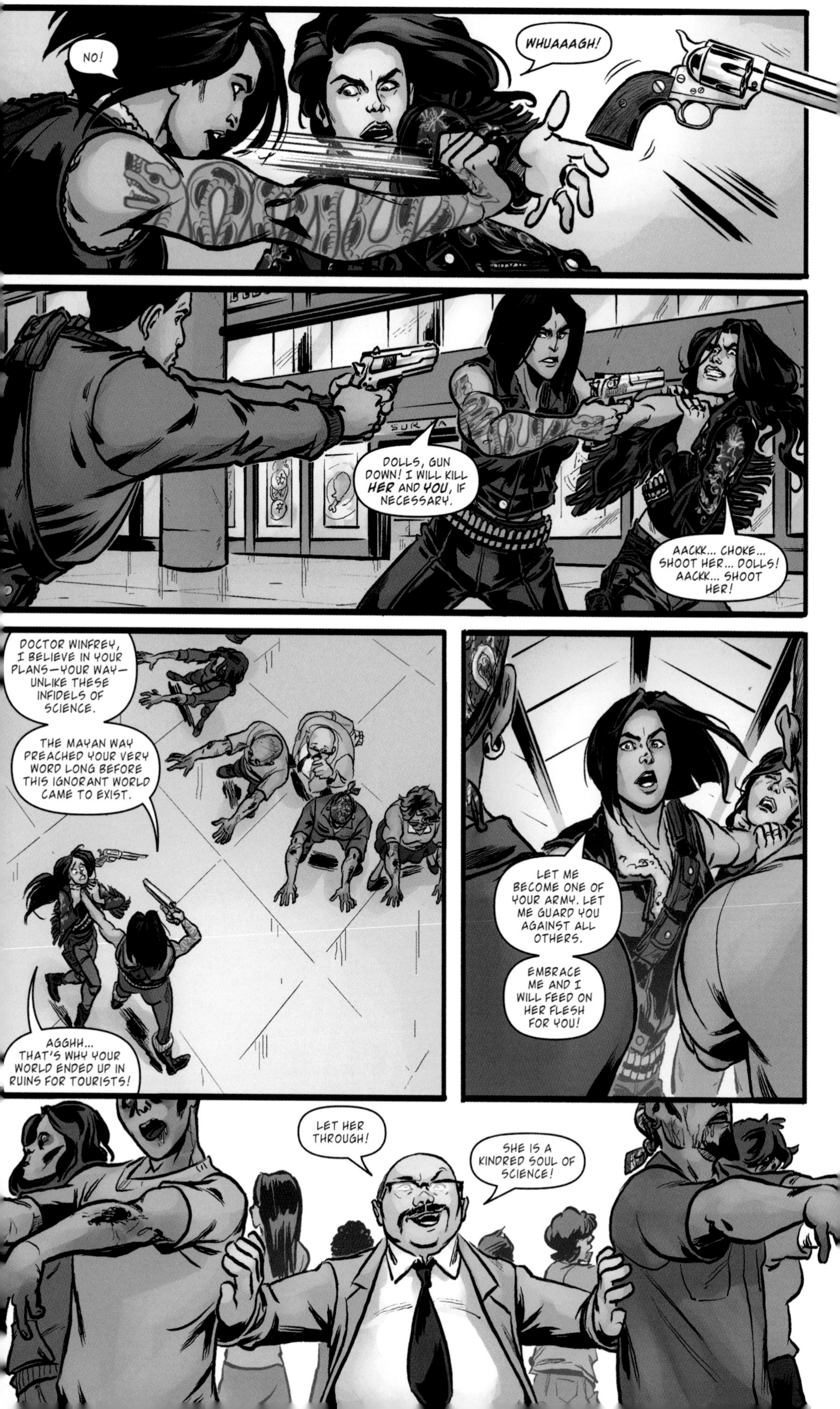
NO!
WHUAAAGH!
DOLLS, GUN DOWN! I WILL KILL HER AND YOU, IF NECESSARY.
AACKK... CHOKE... SHOOT HER... DOLLS! AACKK... SHOOT HER!
DOCTOR WINFREY, I BELIEVE IN YOUR PLANS—YOUR WAY—UNLIKE THESE INFIDELS OF SCIENCE.
THE MAYAN WAY PREACHED YOUR VERY WORD LONG BEFORE THIS IGNORANT WORLD CAME TO EXIST.
AGGHH... THAT'S WHY YOUR WORLD ENDED UP IN RUINS FOR TOURISTS!
LET ME BECOME ONE OF YOUR ARMY. LET ME GUARD YOU AGAINST ALL OTHERS.
EMBRACE ME AND I WILL FEED ON HER FLESH FOR YOU!
LET HER THROUGH!
SHE IS A KINDRED SOUL OF SCIENCE!

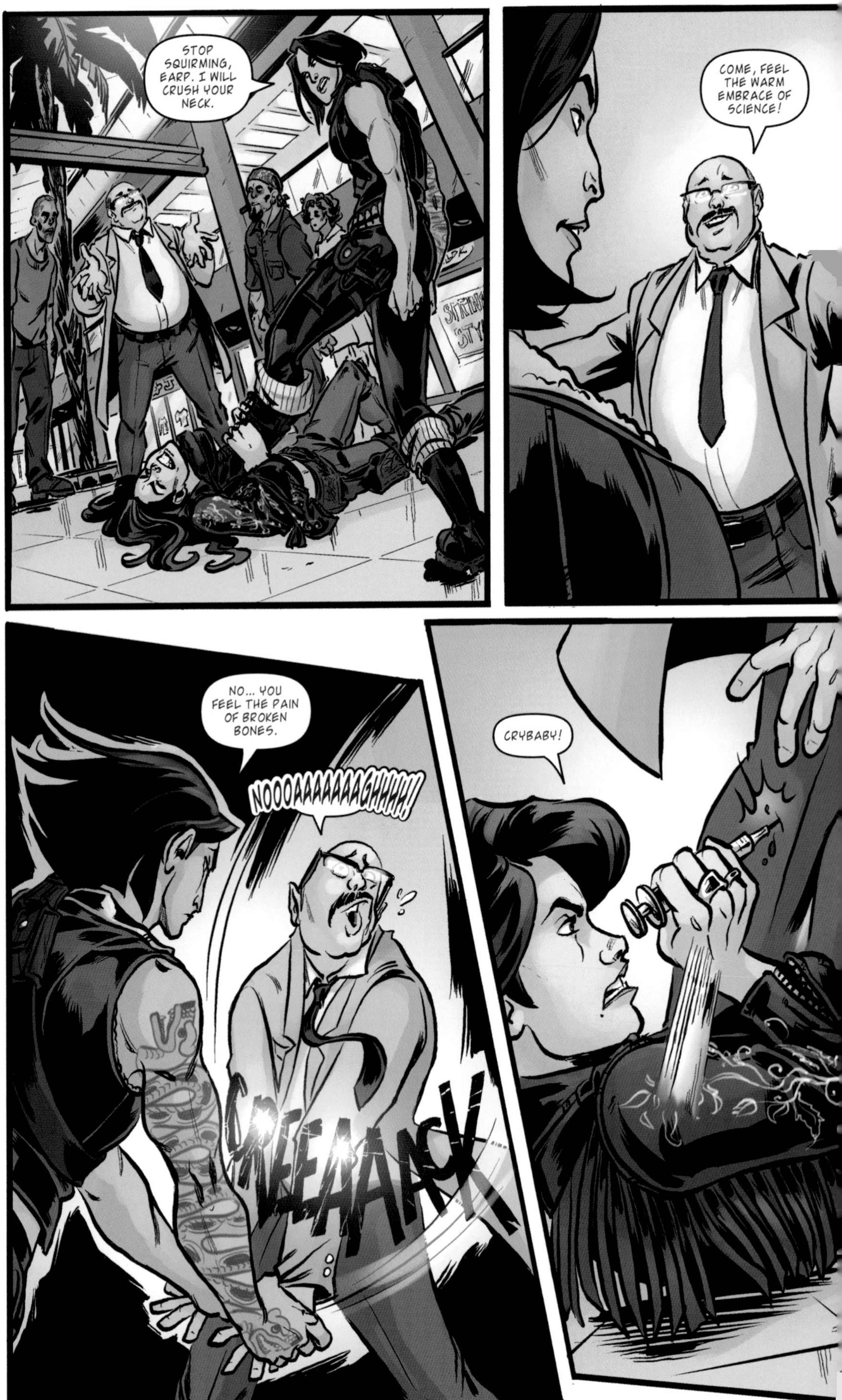
STOP SQUIRMING, EARP. I WILL CRUSH YOUR NECK.
COME, FEEL THE WARM EMBRACE OF SCIENCE!
NO... YOU FEEL THE PAIN OF BROKEN BONES.
NOOOAAAAAAGHHHH!
CREEAACK
CRYBABY!

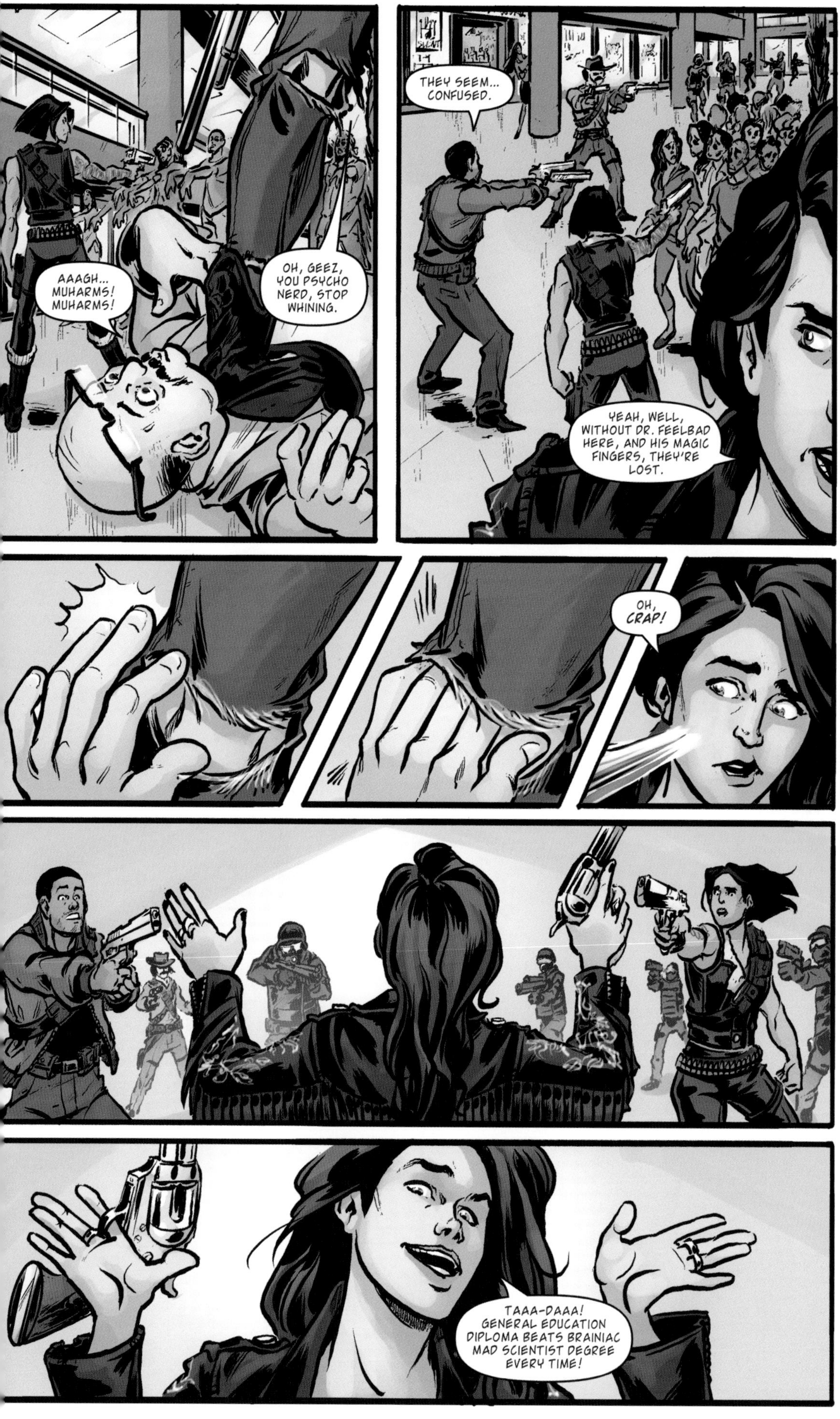
AAAGH... MUHARMS! MUHARMS!
OH, GEEZ, YOU PSYCHO NERD, STOP WHINING.
THEY SEEM... CONFUSED.
YEAH, WELL, WITHOUT DR. FEELBAD HERE, AND HIS MAGIC FINGERS, THEY'RE LOST.
OH, CRAP!
TAAA-DAAA! GENERAL EDUCATION DIPLOMA BEATS BRAINIAC MAD SCIENTIST DEGREE EVERY TIME!

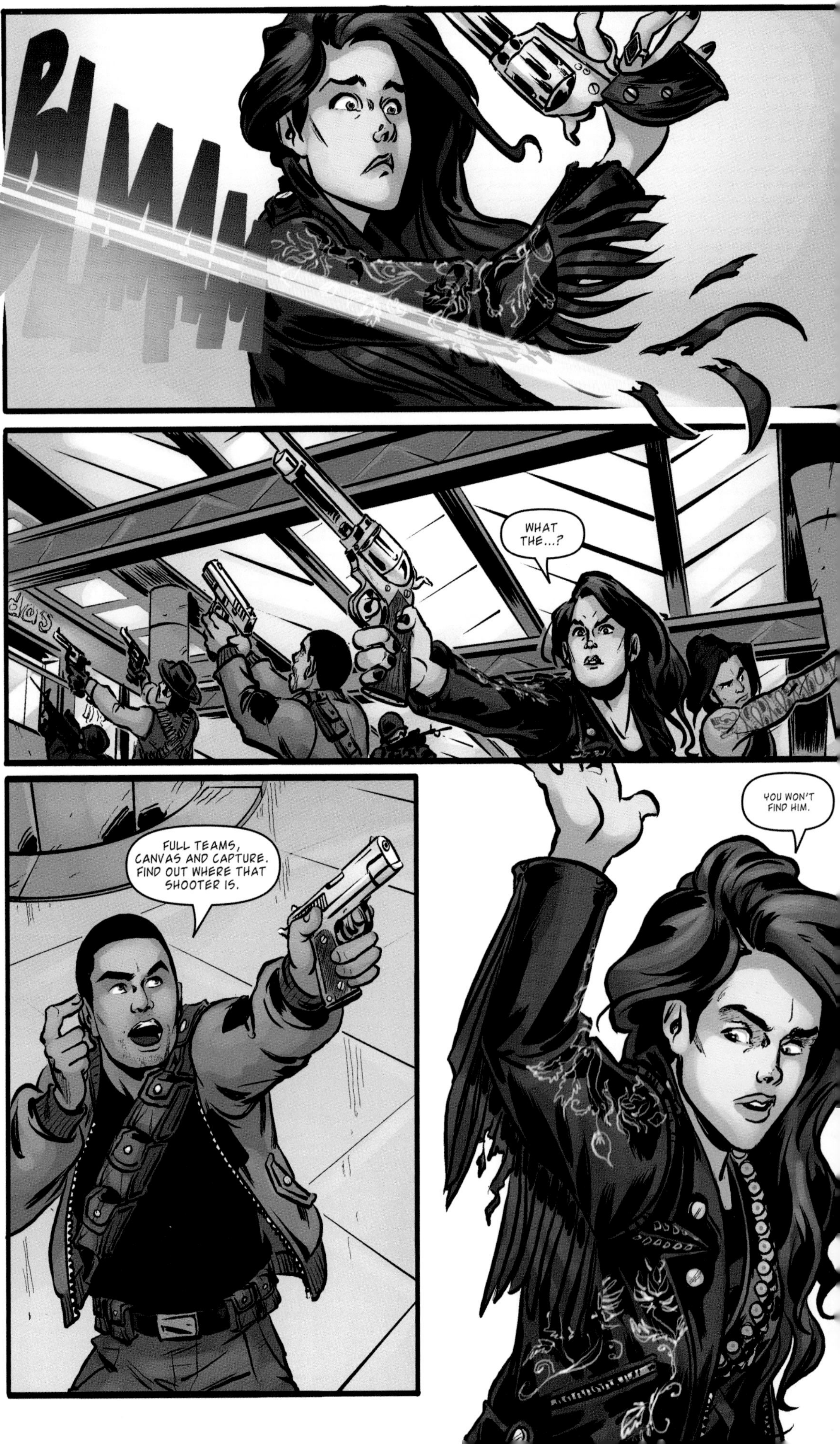
WHAT THE...?
FULL TEAMS, CANVAS AND CAPTURE. FIND OUT WHERE THAT SHOOTER IS.
YOU WON'T FIND HIM.

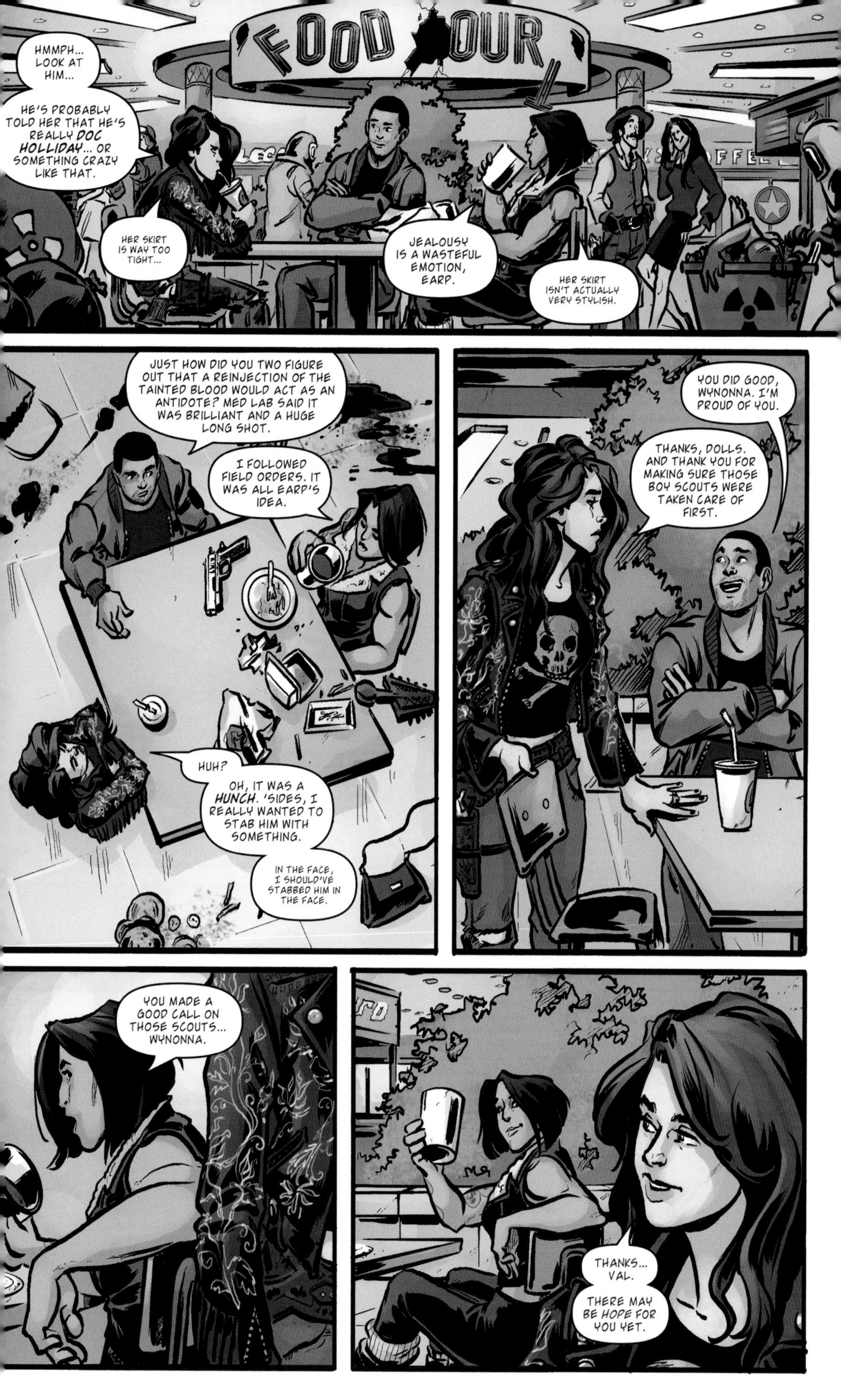
FOOD COUR
HMMPH... LOOK AT HIM...
HE'S PROBABLY TOLD HER THAT HE'S REALLY DOC HOLLIDAY... OR SOMETHING CRAZY LIKE THAT.
HER SKIRT IS WAY TOO TIGHT...
JEALOUSY IS A WASTEFUL EMOTION, EARP.
HER SKIRT ISN'T ACTUALLY VERY STYLISH.
JUST HOW DID YOU TWO FIGURE OUT THAT A REINJECTION OF THE TAINTED BLOOD WOULD ACT AS AN ANTIDOTE? MED LAB SAID IT WAS BRILLIANT AND A HUGE LONG SHOT.
I FOLLOWED FIELD ORDERS. IT WAS ALL EARP'S IDEA.
HUH?
OH, IT WAS A HUNCH. 'SIDES, I REALLY WANTED TO STAB HIM WITH SOMETHING.
IN THE FACE, I SHOULD'VE STABBED HIM IN THE FACE.
YOU DID GOOD, WYNONNA. I'M PROUD OF YOU.
THANKS, DOLLS. AND THANK YOU FOR MAKING SURE THOSE BOY SCOUTS WERE TAKEN CARE OF FIRST.
YOU MADE A GOOD CALL ON THOSE SCOUTS... WYNONNA.
THANKS... VAL.
THERE MAY BE HOPE FOR YOU YET.

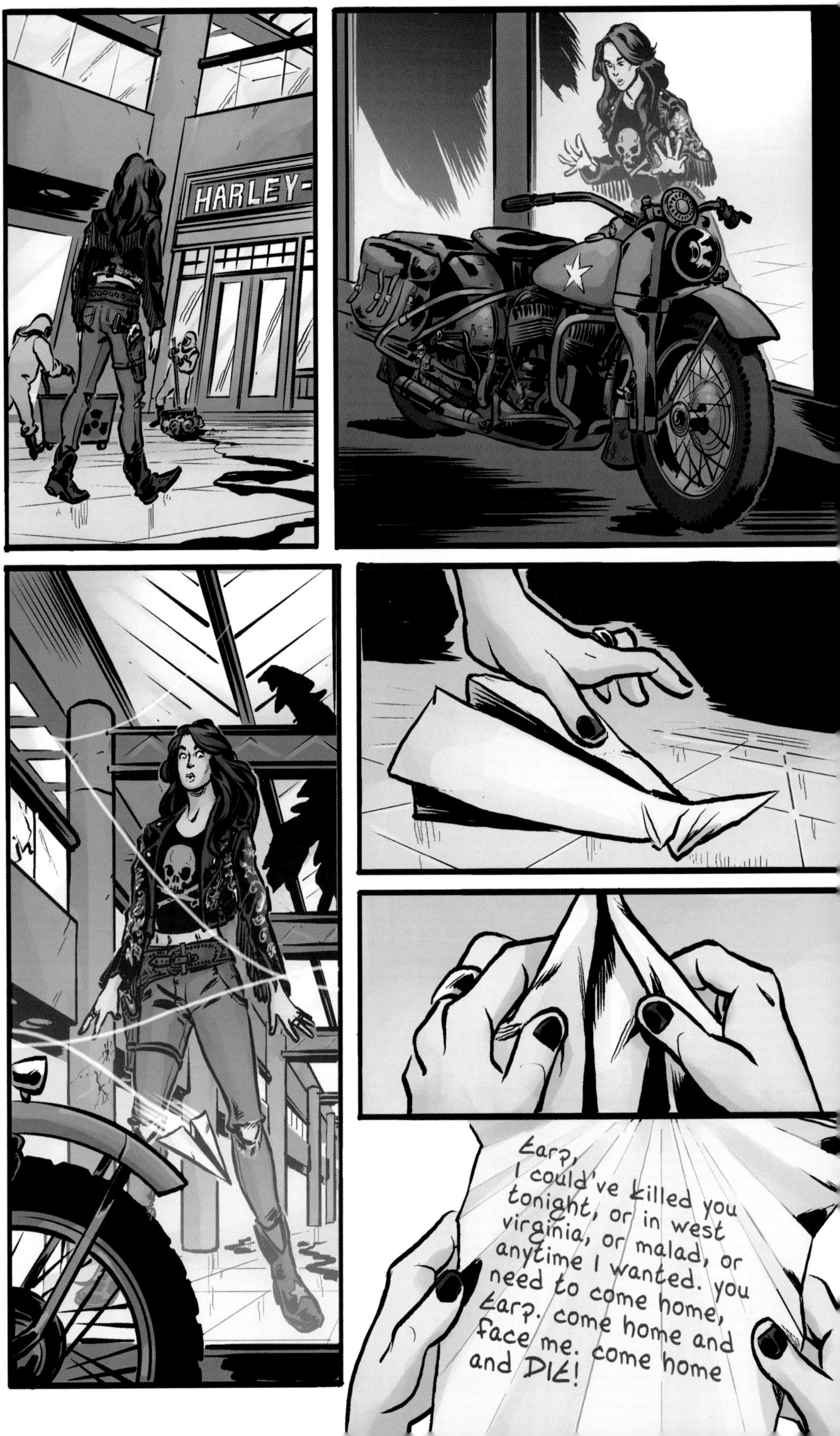
HARLEY-
Earp,
I could've killed you tonight, or in west virginia, or malad, or anytime I wanted. you need to come home, Earp. come home and face me. come home and DIE!

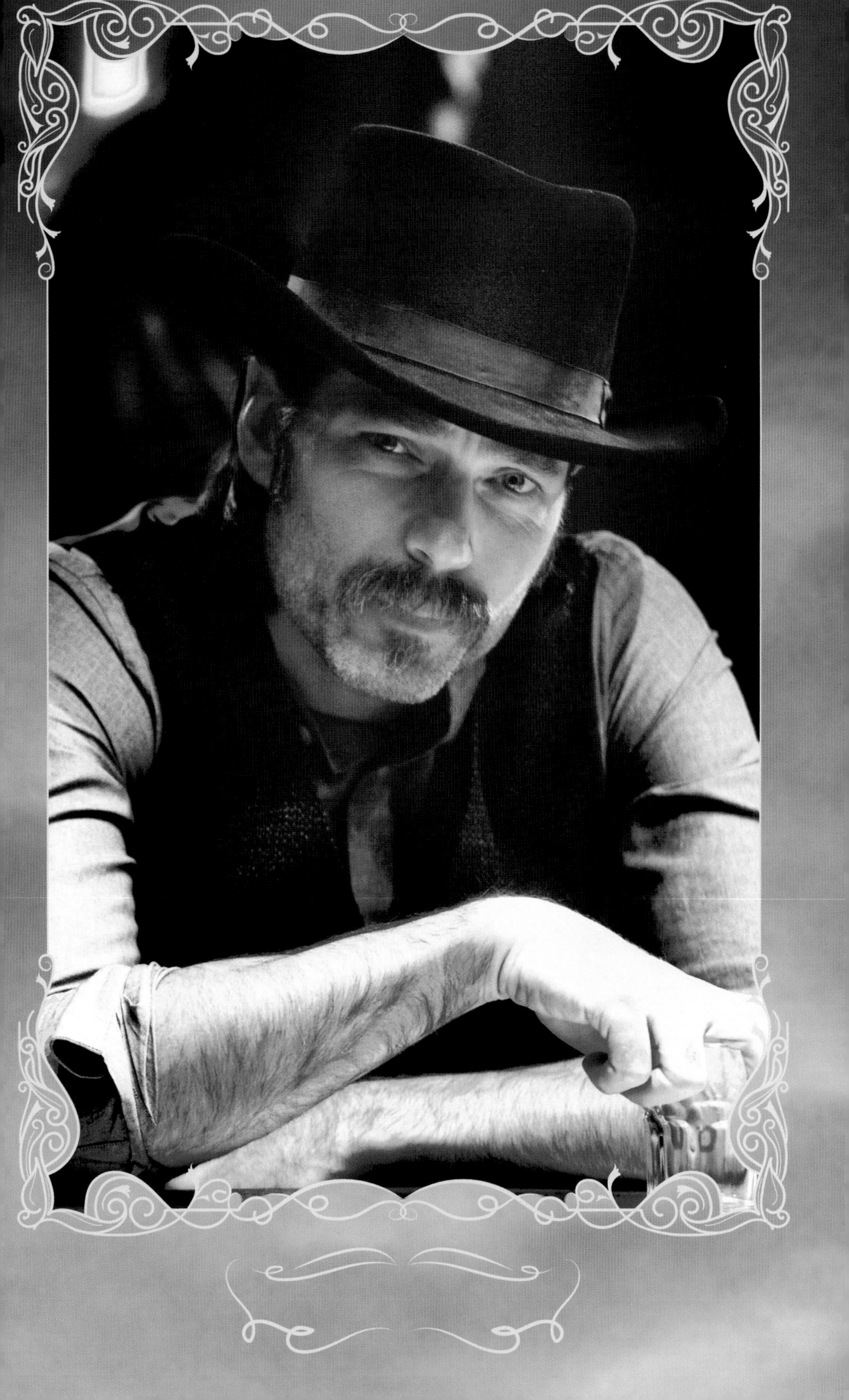

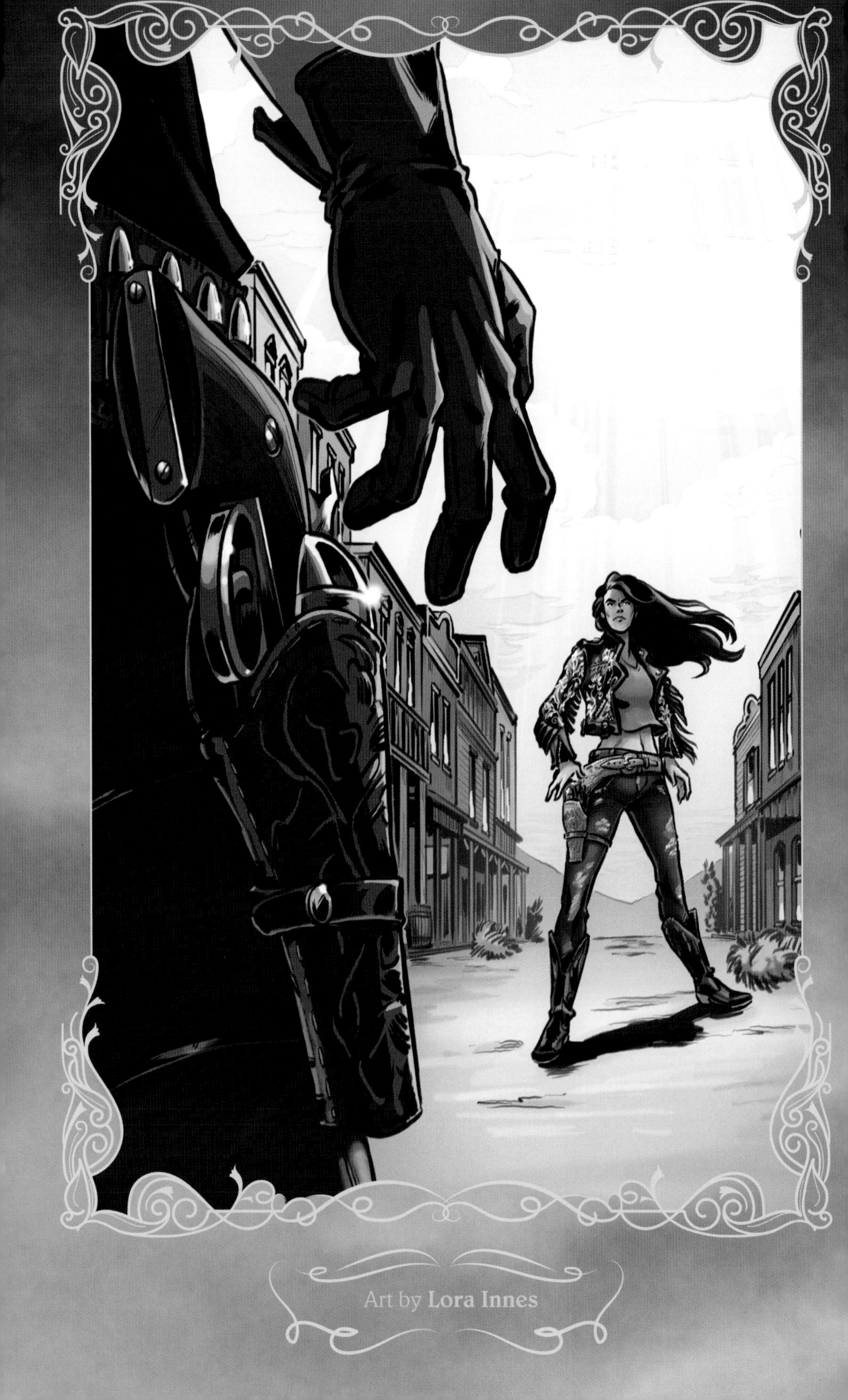

Art by **Lora Innes**

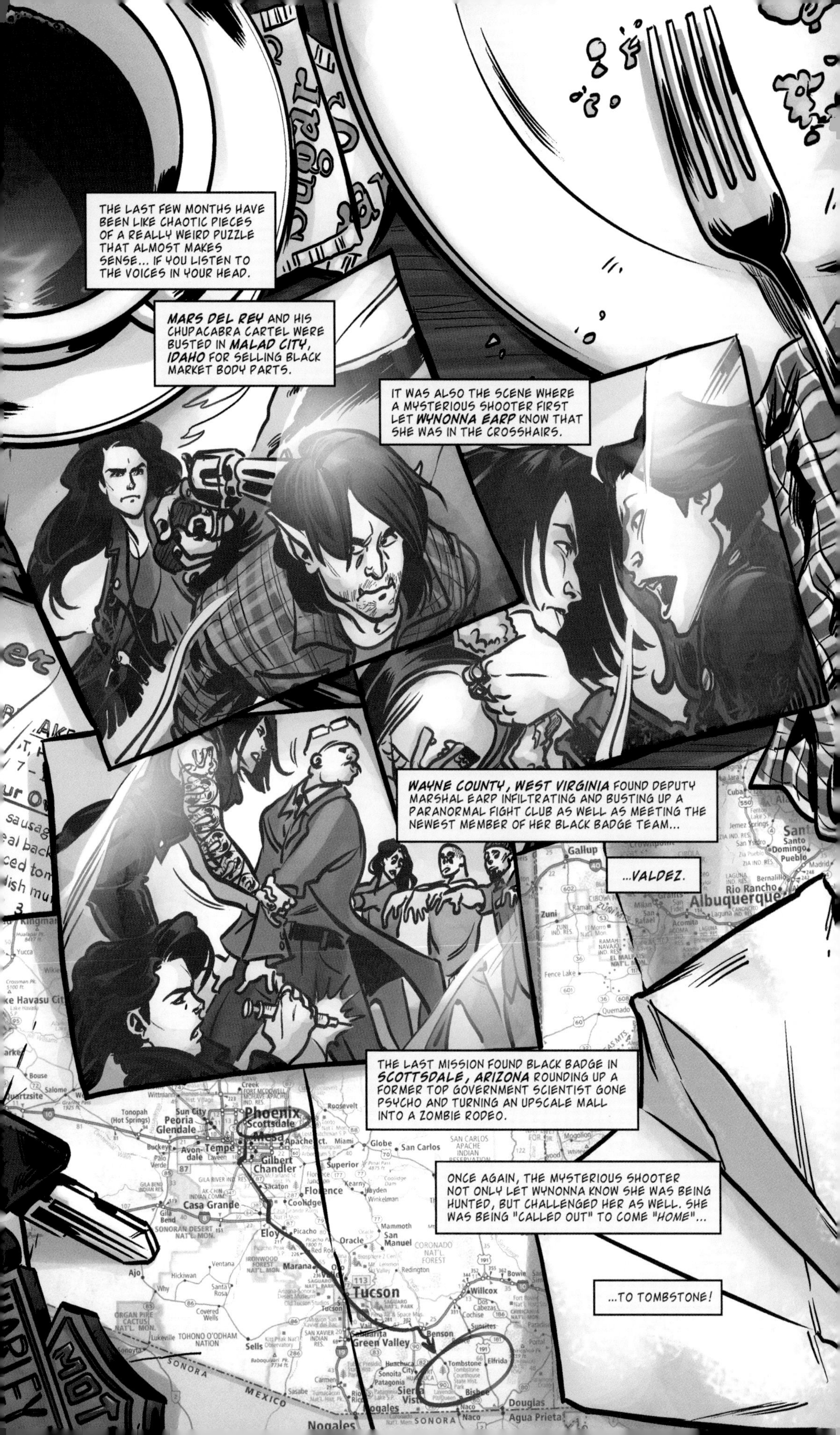
THE LAST FEW MONTHS HAVE BEEN LIKE CHAOTIC PIECES OF A REALLY WEIRD PUZZLE THAT ALMOST MAKES SENSE... IF YOU LISTEN TO THE VOICES IN YOUR HEAD.
MARS DEL REY AND HIS CHUPACABRA CARTEL WERE BUSTED IN MALAD CITY, IDAHO FOR SELLING BLACK MARKET BODY PARTS.
IT WAS ALSO THE SCENE WHERE A MYSTERIOUS SHOOTER FIRST LET WYNONNA EARP KNOW THAT SHE WAS IN THE CROSSHAIRS.
WAYNE COUNTY, WEST VIRGINIA FOUND DEPUTY MARSHAL EARP INFILTRATING AND BUSTING UP A PARANORMAL FIGHT CLUB AS WELL AS MEETING THE NEWEST MEMBER OF HER BLACK BADGE TEAM...
...VALDEZ.
THE LAST MISSION FOUND BLACK BADGE IN SCOTTSDALE, ARIZONA ROUNDING UP A FORMER TOP GOVERNMENT SCIENTIST GONE PSYCHO AND TURNING AN UPSCALE MALL INTO A ZOMBIE RODEO.
ONCE AGAIN, THE MYSTERIOUS SHOOTER NOT ONLY LET WYNONNA KNOW SHE WAS BEING HUNTED, BUT CHALLENGED HER AS WELL. SHE WAS BEING "CALLED OUT" TO COME "HOME"...
...TO TOMBSTONE!

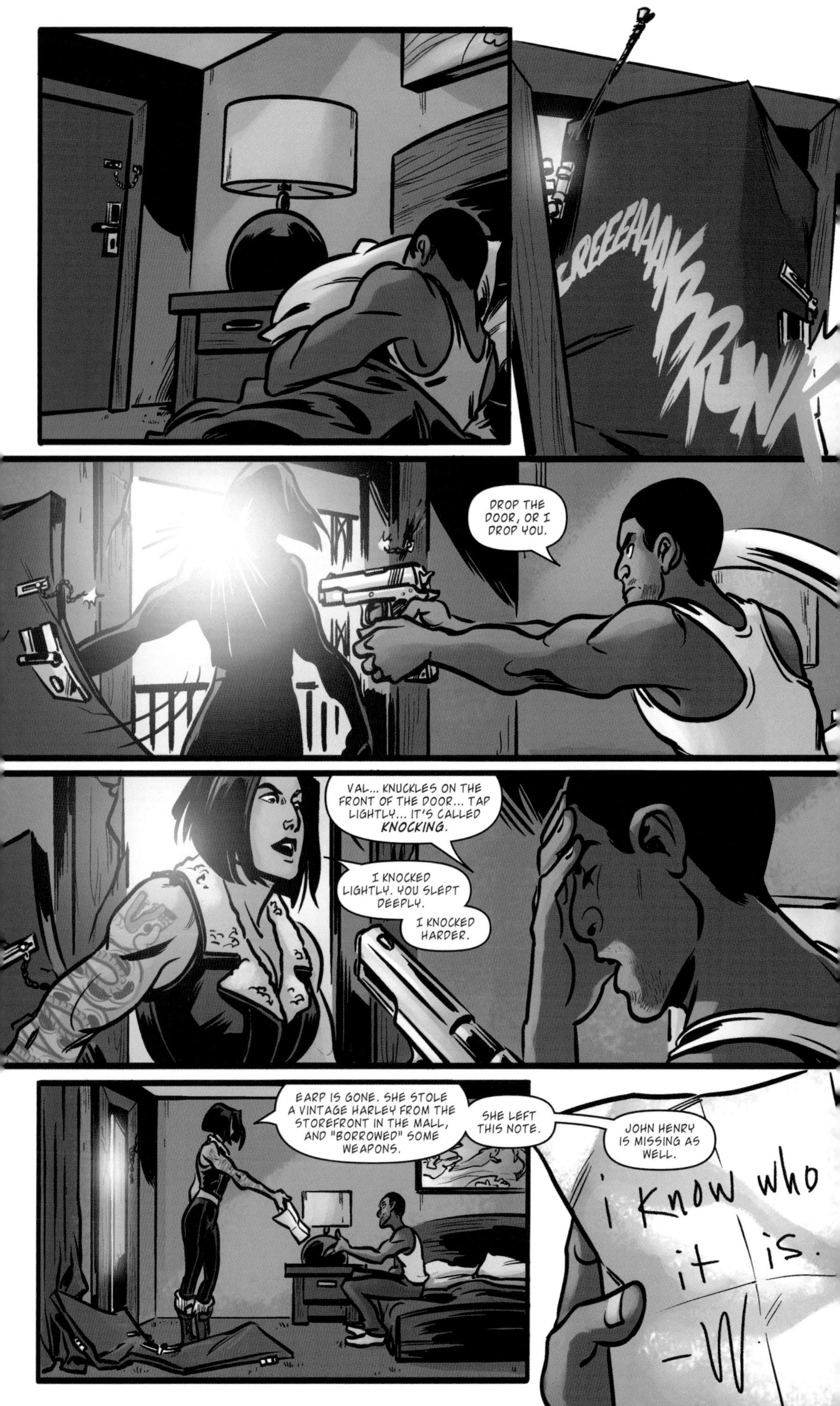

DROP THE DOOR, OR I DROP YOU.
VAL... KNUCKLES ON THE FRONT OF THE DOOR... TAP LIGHTLY... IT'S CALLED **KNOCKING**.
I KNOCKED LIGHTLY. YOU SLEPT DEEPLY.
I KNOCKED HARDER.
EARP IS GONE. SHE STOLE A VINTAGE HARLEY FROM THE STOREFRONT IN THE MALL, AND "BORROWED" SOME WEAPONS.
SHE LEFT THIS NOTE.
JOHN HENRY IS MISSING AS WELL.
i know who it is.
-W

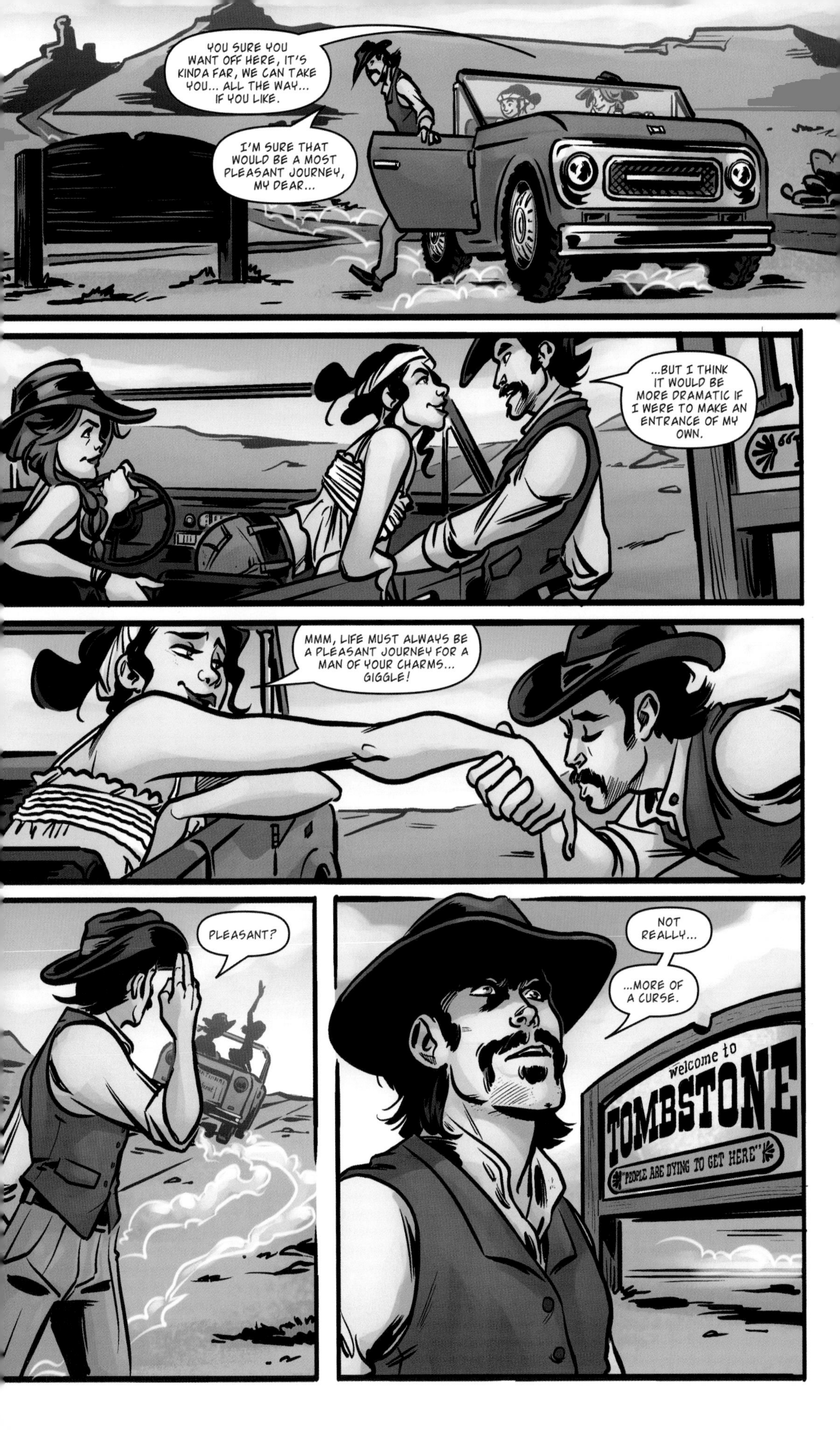
YOU SURE YOU WANT OFF HERE, IT'S KINDA FAR, WE CAN TAKE YOU... ALL THE WAY... IF YOU LIKE.
I'M SURE THAT WOULD BE A MOST PLEASANT JOURNEY, MY DEAR...
...BUT I THINK IT WOULD BE MORE DRAMATIC IF I WERE TO MAKE AN ENTRANCE OF MY OWN.
MMM, LIFE MUST ALWAYS BE A PLEASANT JOURNEY FOR A MAN OF YOUR CHARMS... GIGGLE!
PLEASANT?
NOT REALLY...
...MORE OF A CURSE.
welcome to
TOMBSTONE
"PEOPLE ARE DYING TO GET HERE"

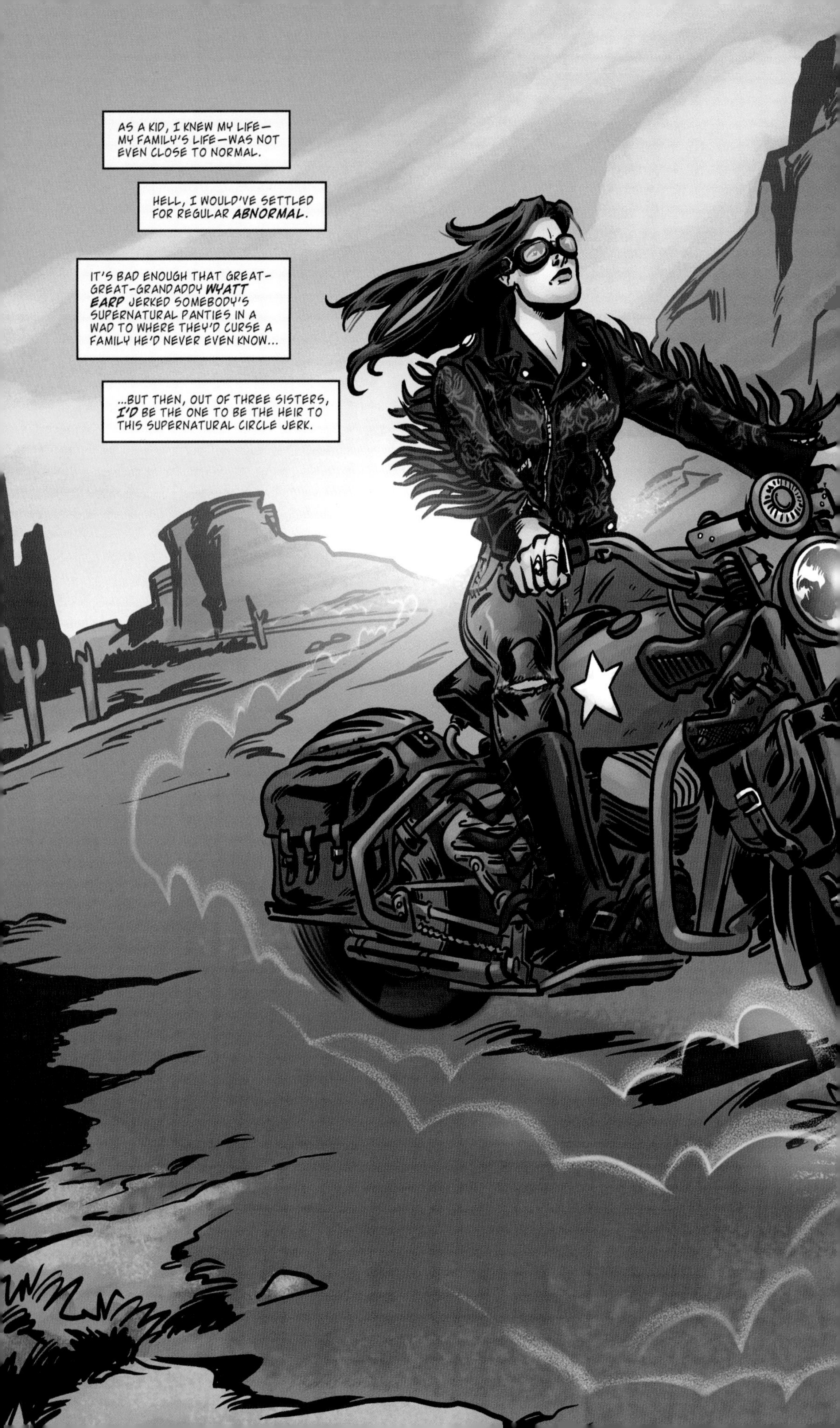

AS A KID, I KNEW MY LIFE—MY FAMILY'S LIFE—WAS NOT EVEN CLOSE TO NORMAL.
HELL, I WOULD'VE SETTLED FOR REGULAR ***ABNORMAL***.
IT'S BAD ENOUGH THAT GREAT-GREAT-GRANDADDY ***WYATT EARP*** JERKED SOMEBODY'S SUPERNATURAL PANTIES IN A WAD TO WHERE THEY'D CURSE A FAMILY HE'D NEVER EVEN KNOW...
...BUT THEN, OUT OF THREE SISTERS, ***I'D*** BE THE ONE TO BE THE HEIR TO THIS SUPERNATURAL CIRCLE JERK.

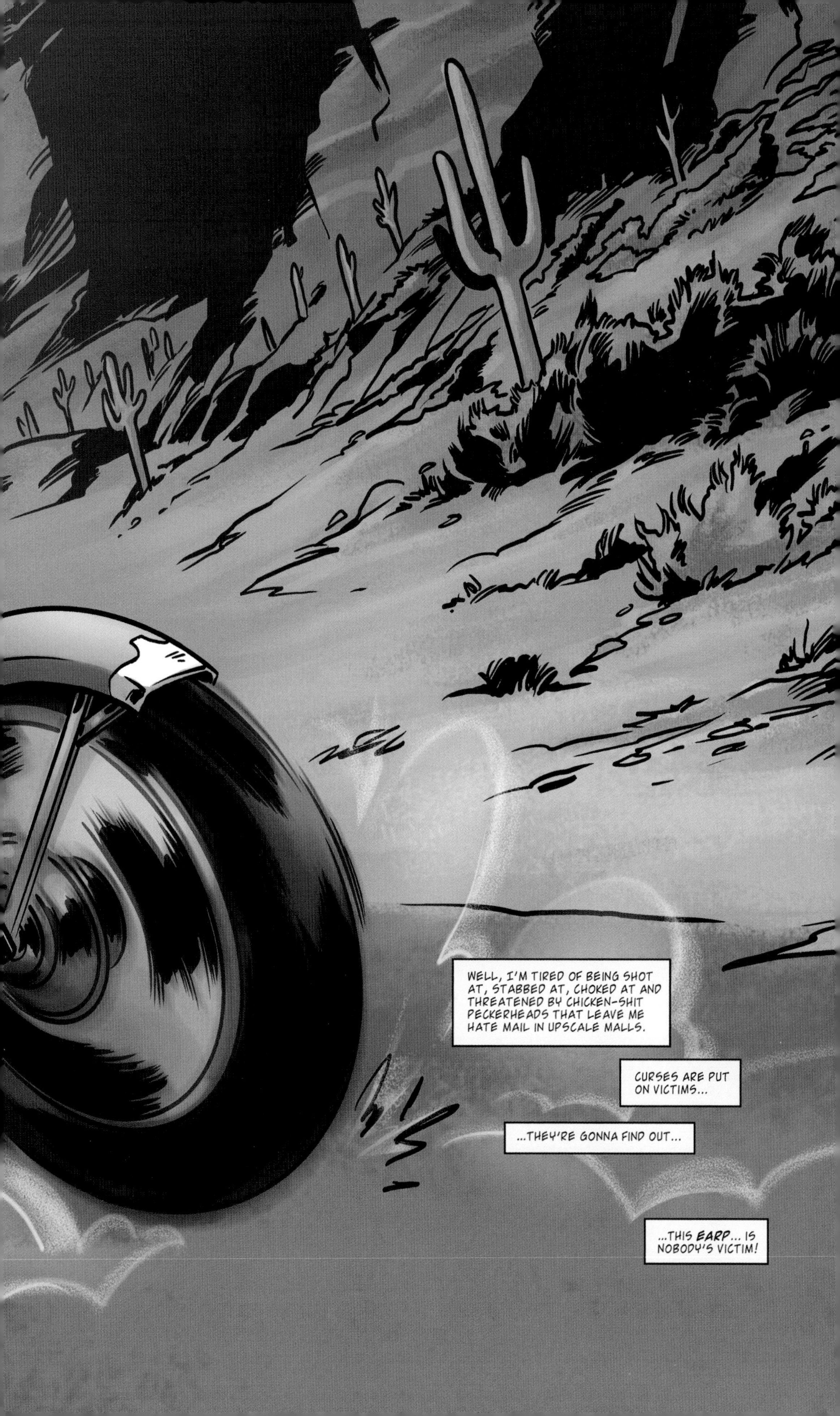
WELL, I'M TIRED OF BEING SHOT AT, STABBED AT, CHOKED AT AND THREATENED BY CHICKEN-SHIT PECKERHEADS THAT LEAVE ME HATE MAIL IN UPSCALE MALLS.
CURSES ARE PUT ON VICTIMS...
...THEY'RE GONNA FIND OUT...
...THIS EARP... IS NOBODY'S VICTIM!

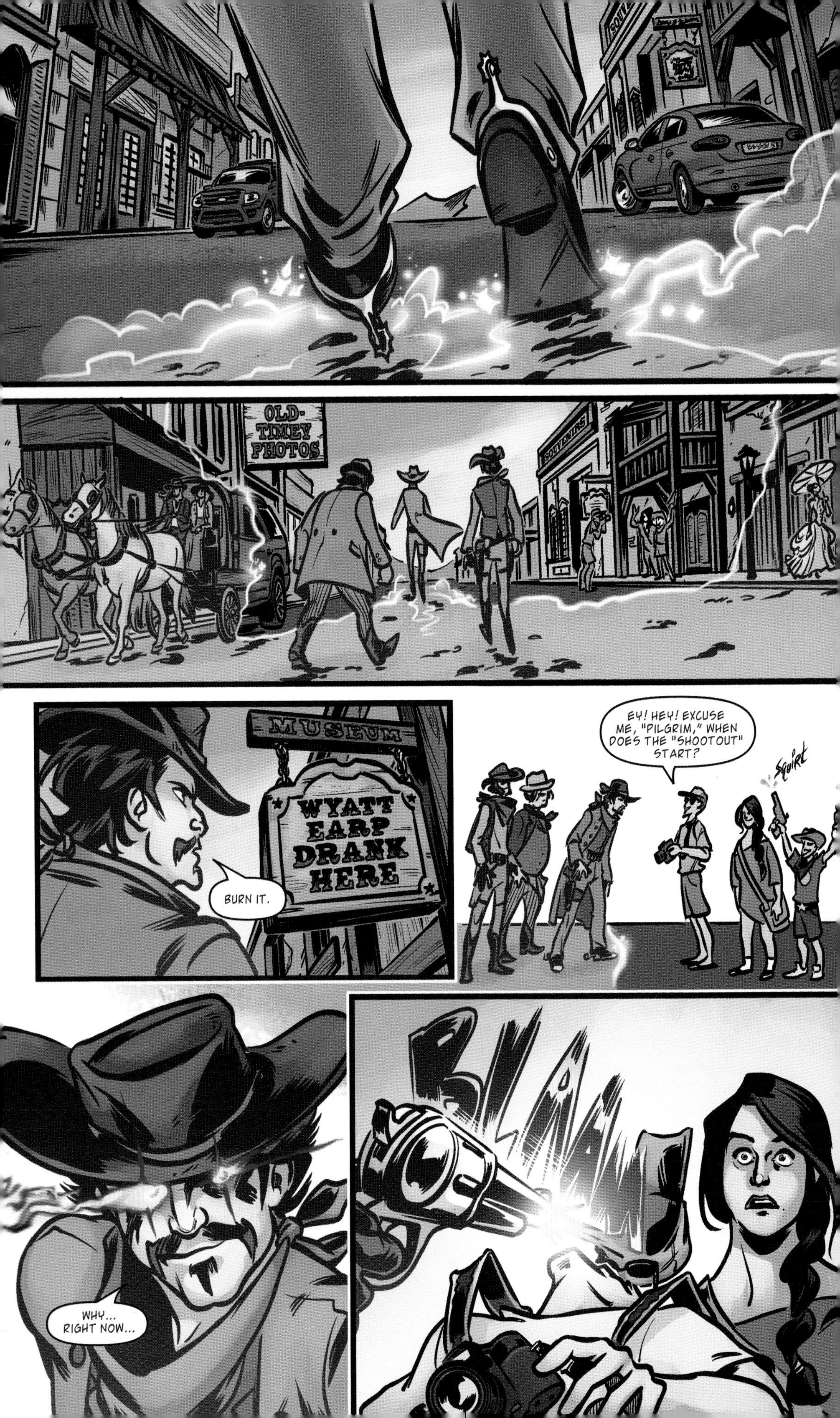
OLD-TIMEY PHOTOS
SOUVENIRS
MUSEUM
WYATT EARP DRANK HERE
BURN IT.
EY! HEY! EXCUSE ME, "PILGRIM," WHEN DOES THE "SHOOTOUT" START?
SQUIRT
WHY... RIGHT NOW...
BLAM

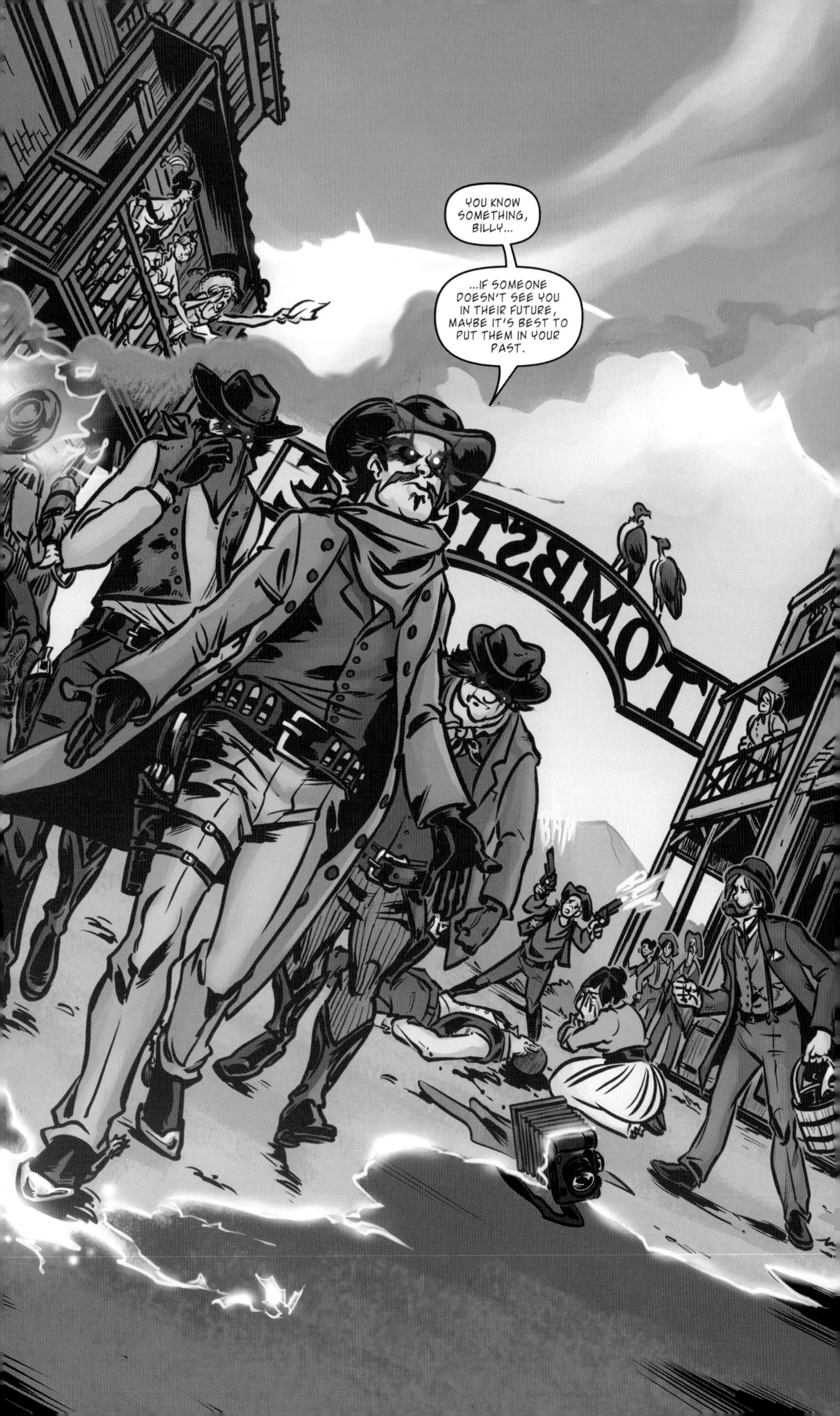
YOU KNOW SOMETHING, BILLY...
...IF SOMEONE DOESN'T SEE YOU IN THEIR FUTURE, MAYBE IT'S BEST TO PUT THEM IN YOUR PAST.

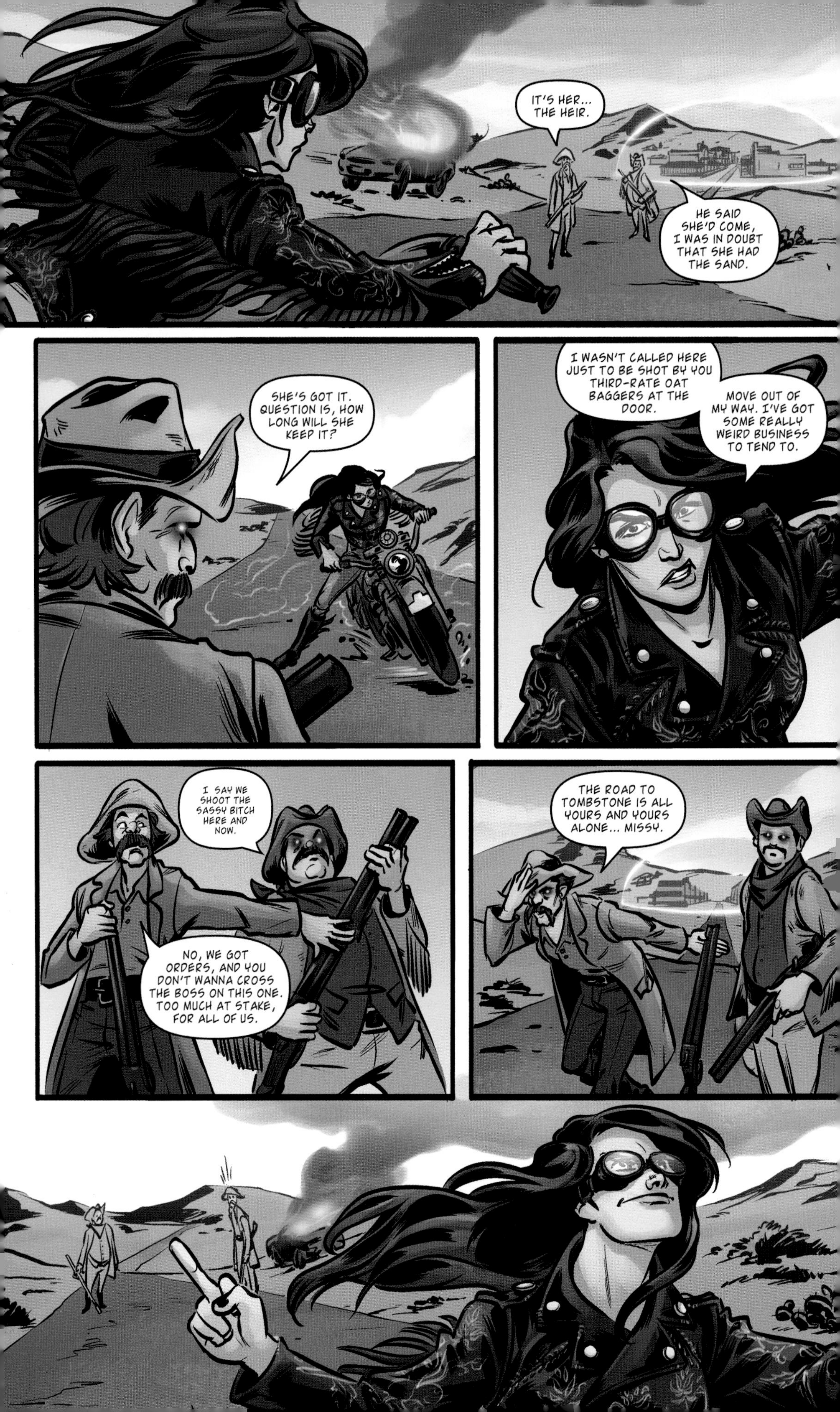

IT'S HER... THE HEIR.
HE SAID SHE'D COME, I WAS IN DOUBT THAT SHE HAD THE SAND.
SHE'S GOT IT. QUESTION IS, HOW LONG WILL SHE KEEP IT?
I WASN'T CALLED HERE JUST TO BE SHOT BY YOU THIRD-RATE OAT BAGGERS AT THE DOOR.
MOVE OUT OF MY WAY. I'VE GOT SOME REALLY WEIRD BUSINESS TO TEND TO.
I SAY WE SHOOT THE SASSY BITCH HERE AND NOW.
NO, WE GOT ORDERS, AND YOU DON'T WANNA CROSS THE BOSS ON THIS ONE. TOO MUCH AT STAKE, FOR ALL OF US.
THE ROAD TO TOMBSTONE IS ALL YOURS AND YOURS ALONE... MISSY.

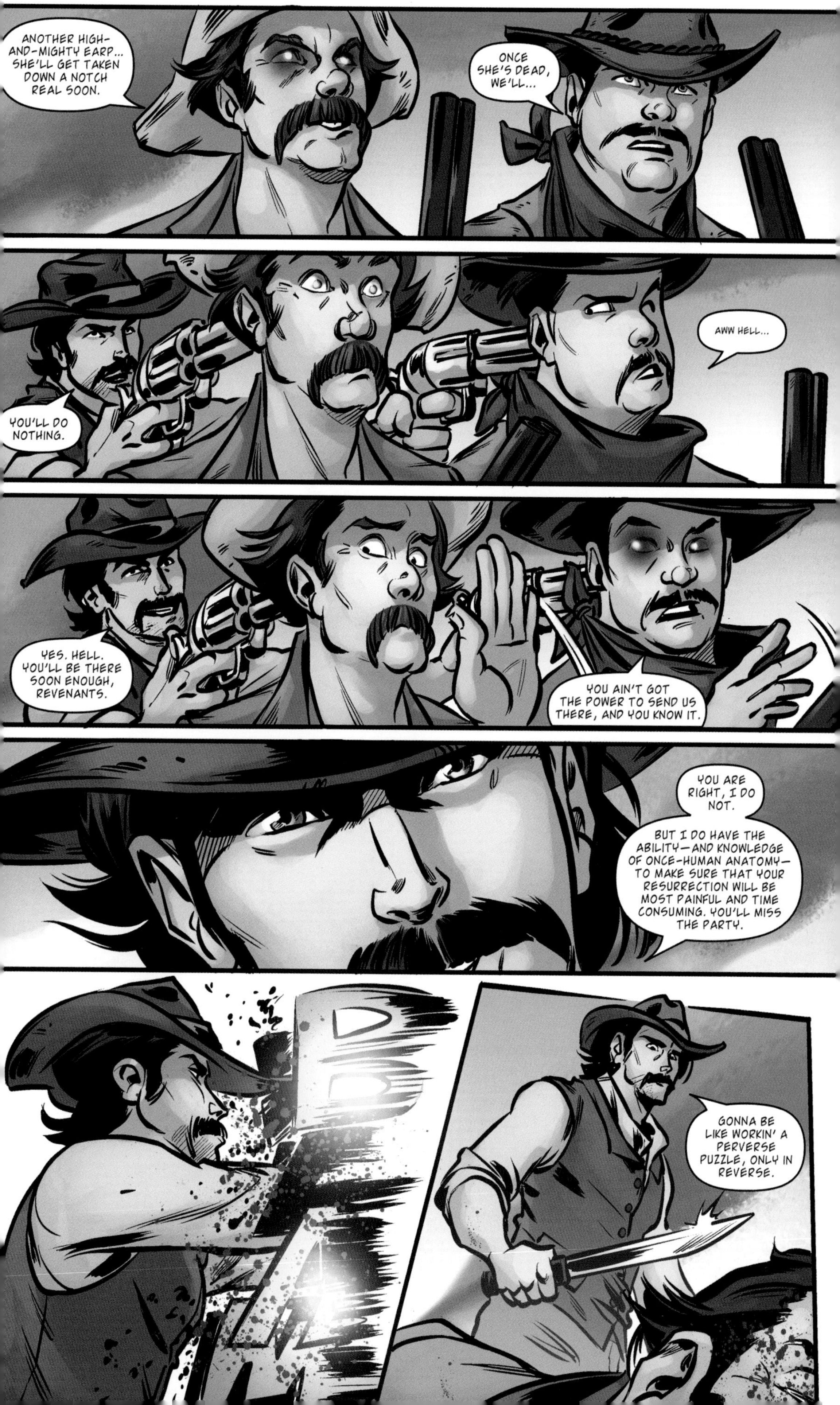
ANOTHER HIGH-AND-MIGHTY EARP... SHE'LL GET TAKEN DOWN A NOTCH REAL SOON.
ONCE SHE'S DEAD, WE'LL...
AWW HELL...
YOU'LL DO NOTHING.
YES. HELL. YOU'LL BE THERE SOON ENOUGH, REVENANTS.
YOU AIN'T GOT THE POWER TO SEND US THERE, AND YOU KNOW IT.
YOU ARE RIGHT, I DO NOT.
BUT I DO HAVE THE ABILITY—AND KNOWLEDGE OF ONCE-HUMAN ANATOMY—TO MAKE SURE THAT YOUR RESURRECTION WILL BE MOST PAINFUL AND TIME CONSUMING. YOU'LL MISS THE PARTY.
GONNA BE LIKE WORKIN' A PERVERSE PUZZLE, ONLY IN REVERSE.

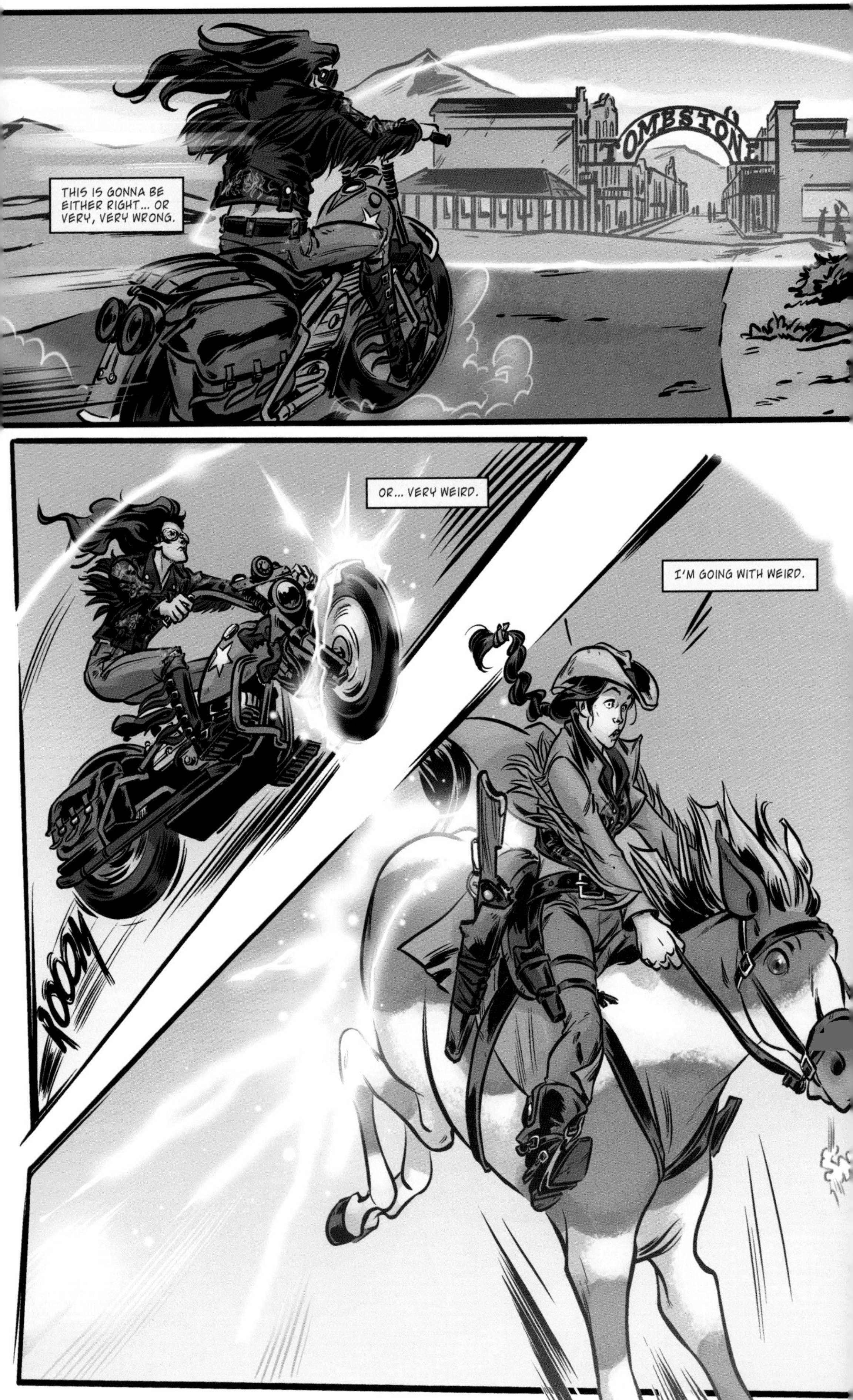
THIS IS GONNA BE EITHER RIGHT... OR VERY, VERY WRONG.
TOMBSTONE
OR... VERY WEIRD.
I'M GOING WITH WEIRD.

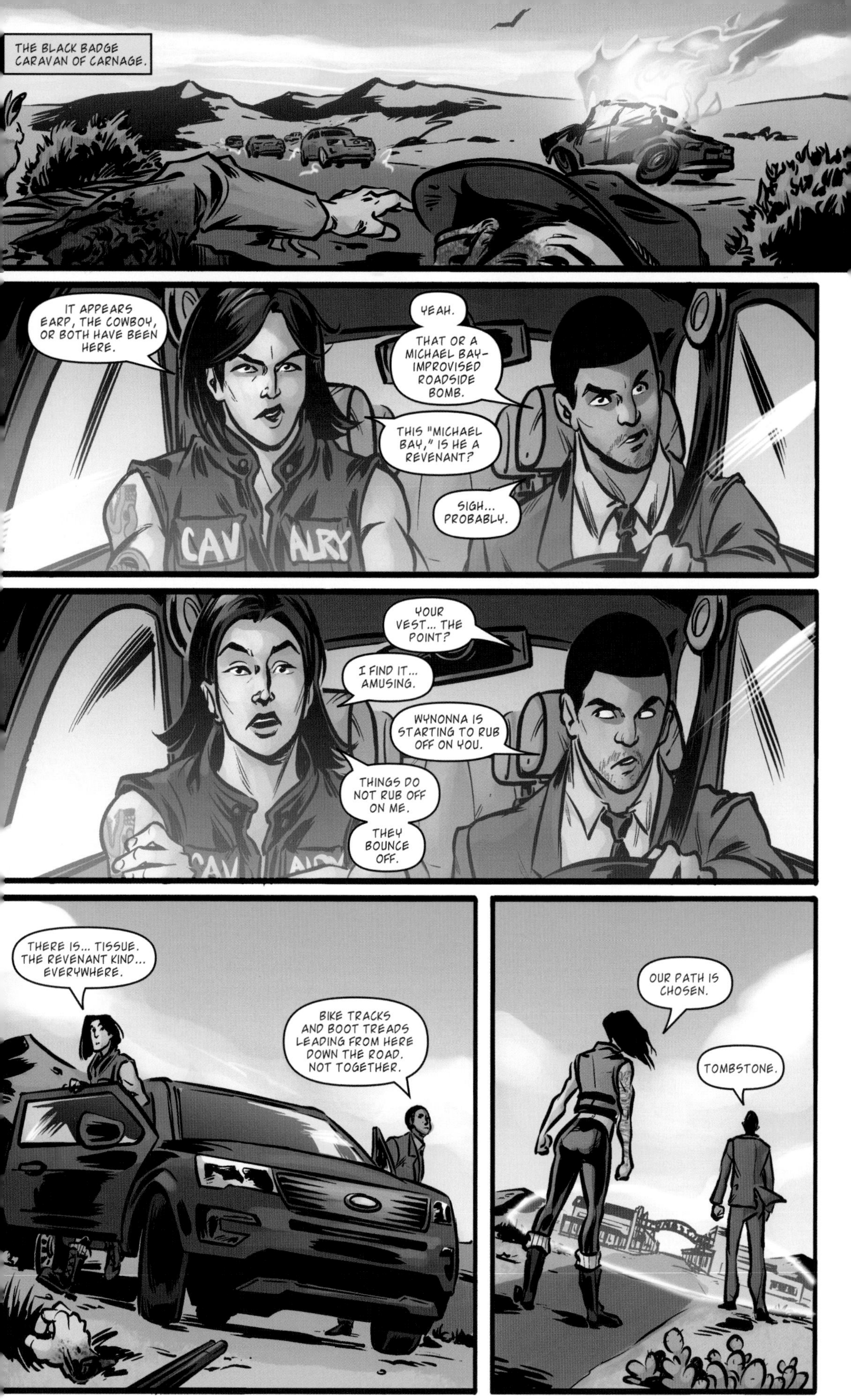
THE BLACK BADGE CARAVAN OF CARNAGE.
IT APPEARS EARP, THE COWBOY, OR BOTH HAVE BEEN HERE.
YEAH.
THAT OR A MICHAEL BAY-IMPROVISED ROADSIDE BOMB.
THIS "MICHAEL BAY," IS HE A REVENANT?
SIGH... PROBABLY.
CAVALRY
YOUR VEST... THE POINT?
I FIND IT... AMUSING.
WYNONNA IS STARTING TO RUB OFF ON YOU.
THINGS DO NOT RUB OFF ON ME.
THEY BOUNCE OFF.
THERE IS... TISSUE. THE REVENANT KIND... EVERYWHERE.
BIKE TRACKS AND BOOT TREADS LEADING FROM HERE DOWN THE ROAD. NOT TOGETHER.
OUR PATH IS CHOSEN.
TOMBSTONE.

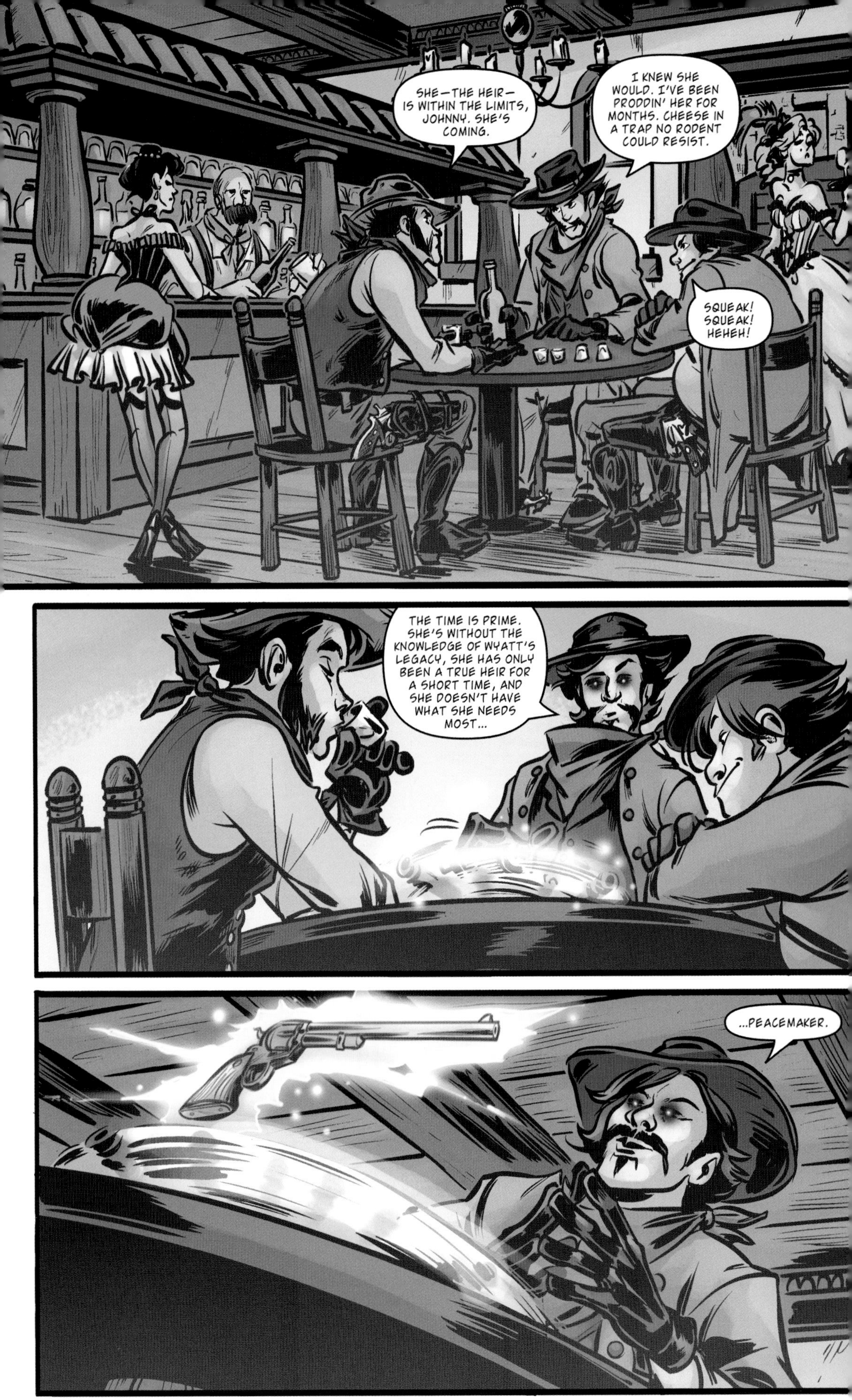
SHE—THE HEIR—IS WITHIN THE LIMITS, JOHNNY. SHE'S COMING.
I KNEW SHE WOULD. I'VE BEEN PRODDIN' HER FOR MONTHS. CHEESE IN A TRAP NO RODENT COULD RESIST.
SQUEAK! SQUEAK! HEHEH!
THE TIME IS PRIME. SHE'S WITHOUT THE KNOWLEDGE OF WYATT'S LEGACY, SHE HAS ONLY BEEN A TRUE HEIR FOR A SHORT TIME, AND SHE DOESN'T HAVE WHAT SHE NEEDS MOST...
...PEACEMAKER.

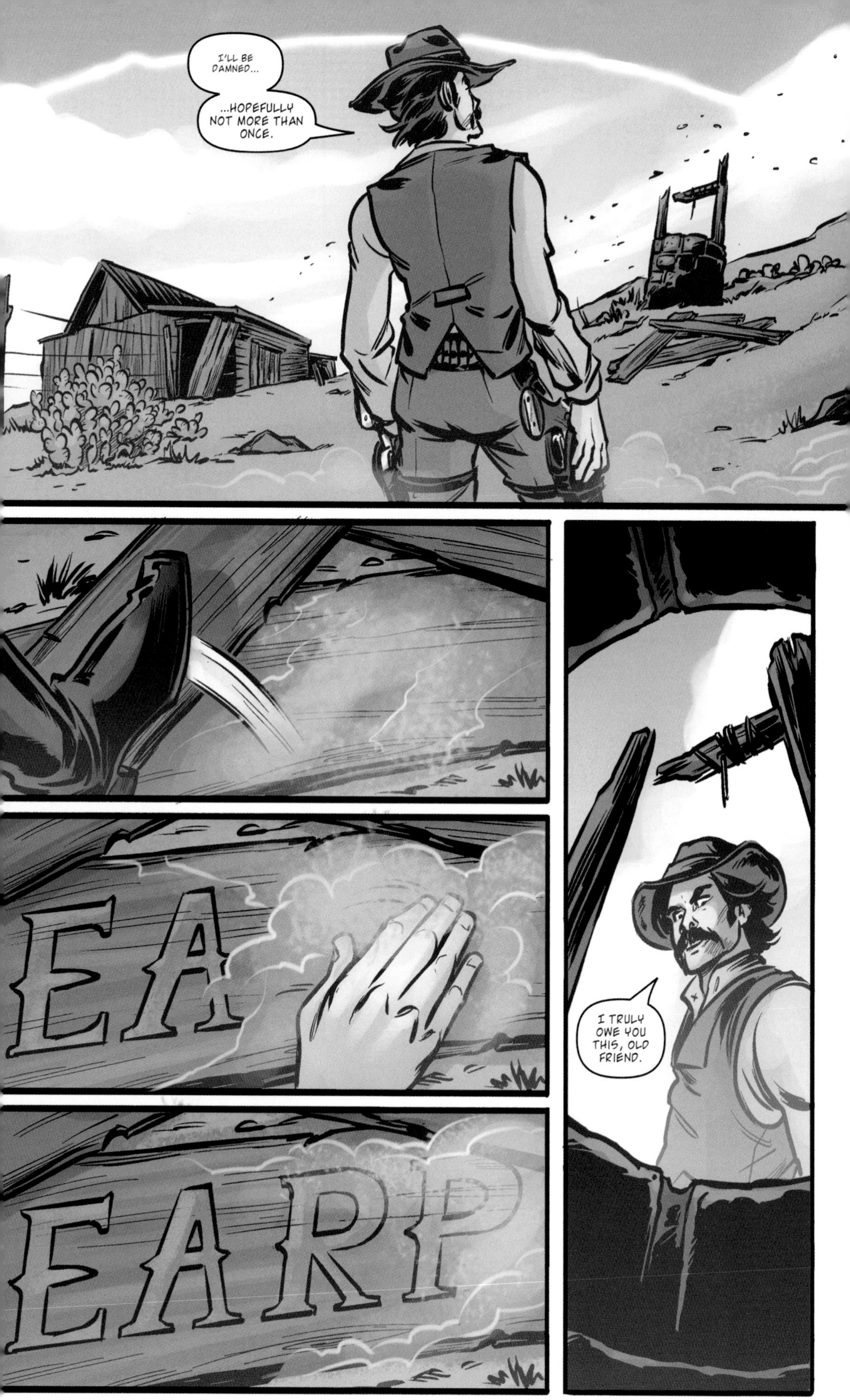
I'LL BE DAMNED...
...HOPEFULLY NOT MORE THAN ONCE.
EA
EARP
I TRULY OWE YOU THIS, OLD FRIEND.

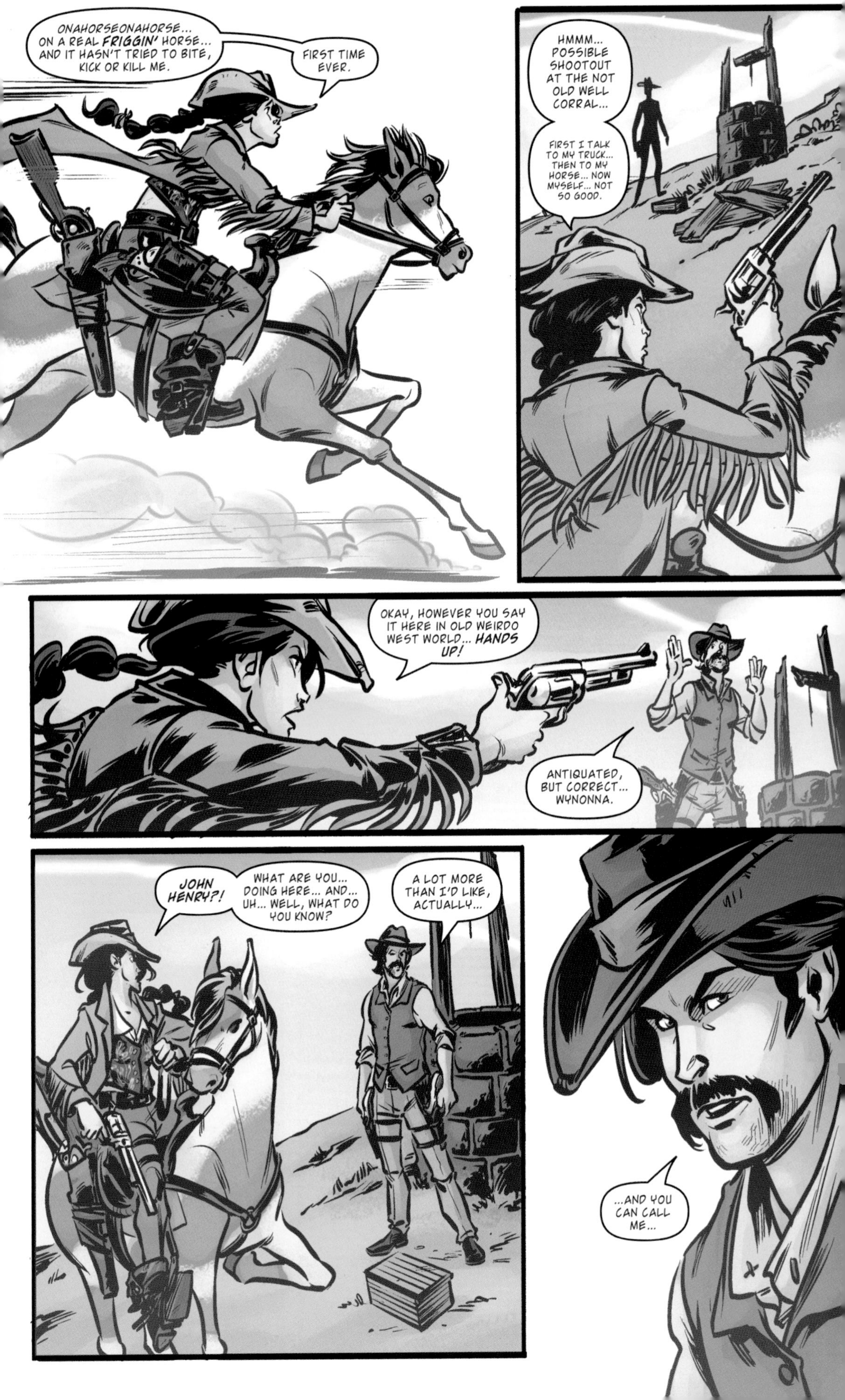
ONAHORSEONAHORSE... ON A REAL FRIGGIN' HORSE... AND IT HASN'T TRIED TO BITE, KICK OR KILL ME.
FIRST TIME EVER.
HMMM... POSSIBLE SHOOTOUT AT THE NOT OLD WELL CORRAL...
FIRST I TALK TO MY TRUCK... THEN TO MY HORSE... NOW MYSELF... NOT SO GOOD.
OKAY, HOWEVER YOU SAY IT HERE IN OLD WEIRDO WEST WORLD... HANDS UP!
ANTIQUATED, BUT CORRECT... WYNONNA.
JOHN HENRY?!
WHAT ARE YOU... DOING HERE... AND... UH... WELL, WHAT DO YOU KNOW?
A LOT MORE THAN I'D LIKE, ACTUALLY...
...AND YOU CAN CALL ME...

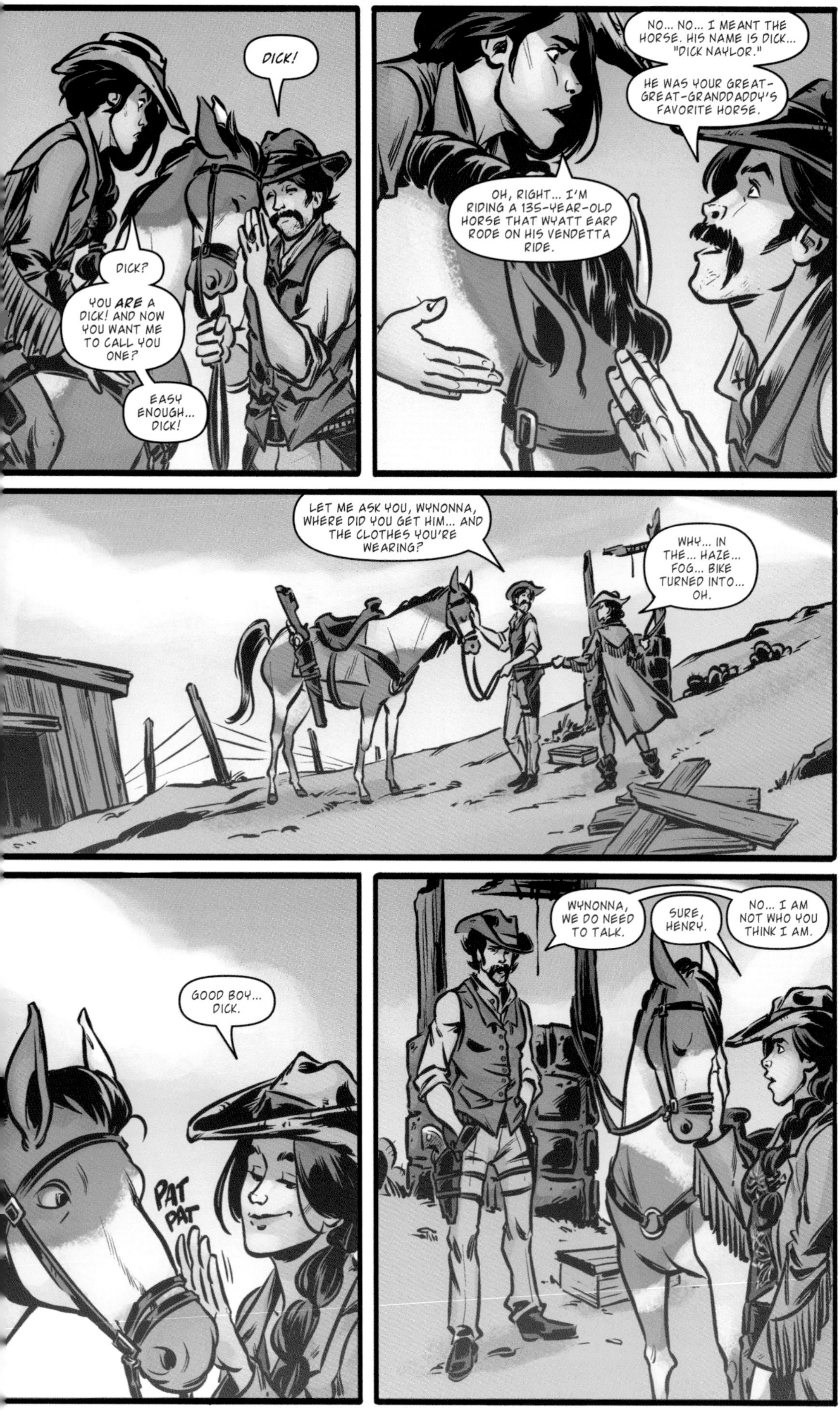
DICK!
DICK?
YOU ARE A DICK! AND NOW YOU WANT ME TO CALL YOU ONE?
EASY ENOUGH... DICK!
NO... NO... I MEANT THE HORSE. HIS NAME IS DICK... "DICK NAYLOR."
HE WAS YOUR GREAT-GREAT-GRANDDADDY'S FAVORITE HORSE.
OH, RIGHT... I'M RIDING A 135-YEAR-OLD HORSE THAT WYATT EARP RODE ON HIS VENDETTA RIDE.
LET ME ASK YOU, WYNONNA, WHERE DID YOU GET HIM... AND THE CLOTHES YOU'RE WEARING?
WHY... IN THE... HAZE... FOG... BIKE TURNED INTO... OH.
GOOD BOY... DICK.
PAT PAT
WYNONNA, WE DO NEED TO TALK.
SURE, HENRY.
NO... I AM NOT WHO YOU THINK I AM.

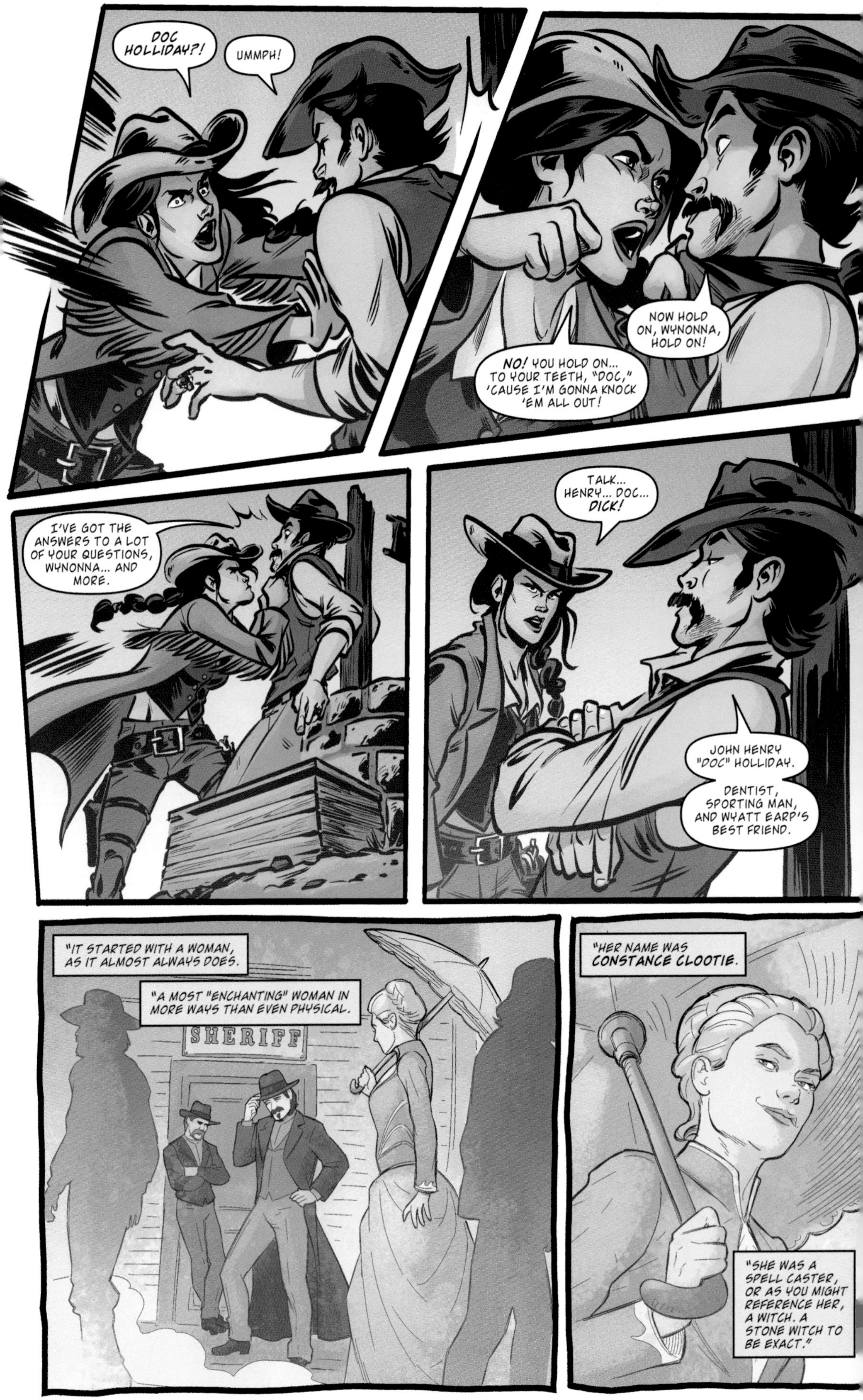
DOC HOLLIDAY?!
UMMPH!
NOW HOLD ON, WYNONNA, HOLD ON!
NO! YOU HOLD ON... TO YOUR TEETH, "DOC," 'CAUSE I'M GONNA KNOCK 'EM ALL OUT!
I'VE GOT THE ANSWERS TO A LOT OF YOUR QUESTIONS, WYNONNA... AND MORE.
TALK... HENRY... DOC... DICK!
JOHN HENRY "DOC" HOLLIDAY.
DENTIST, SPORTING MAN, AND WYATT EARP'S BEST FRIEND.
"IT STARTED WITH A WOMAN, AS IT ALMOST ALWAYS DOES.
"A MOST "ENCHANTING" WOMAN IN MORE WAYS THAN EVEN PHYSICAL.
SHERIFF
"HER NAME WAS CONSTANCE CLOOTIE.
"SHE WAS A SPELL CASTER, OR AS YOU MIGHT REFERENCE HER, A WITCH. A STONE WITCH TO BE EXACT."

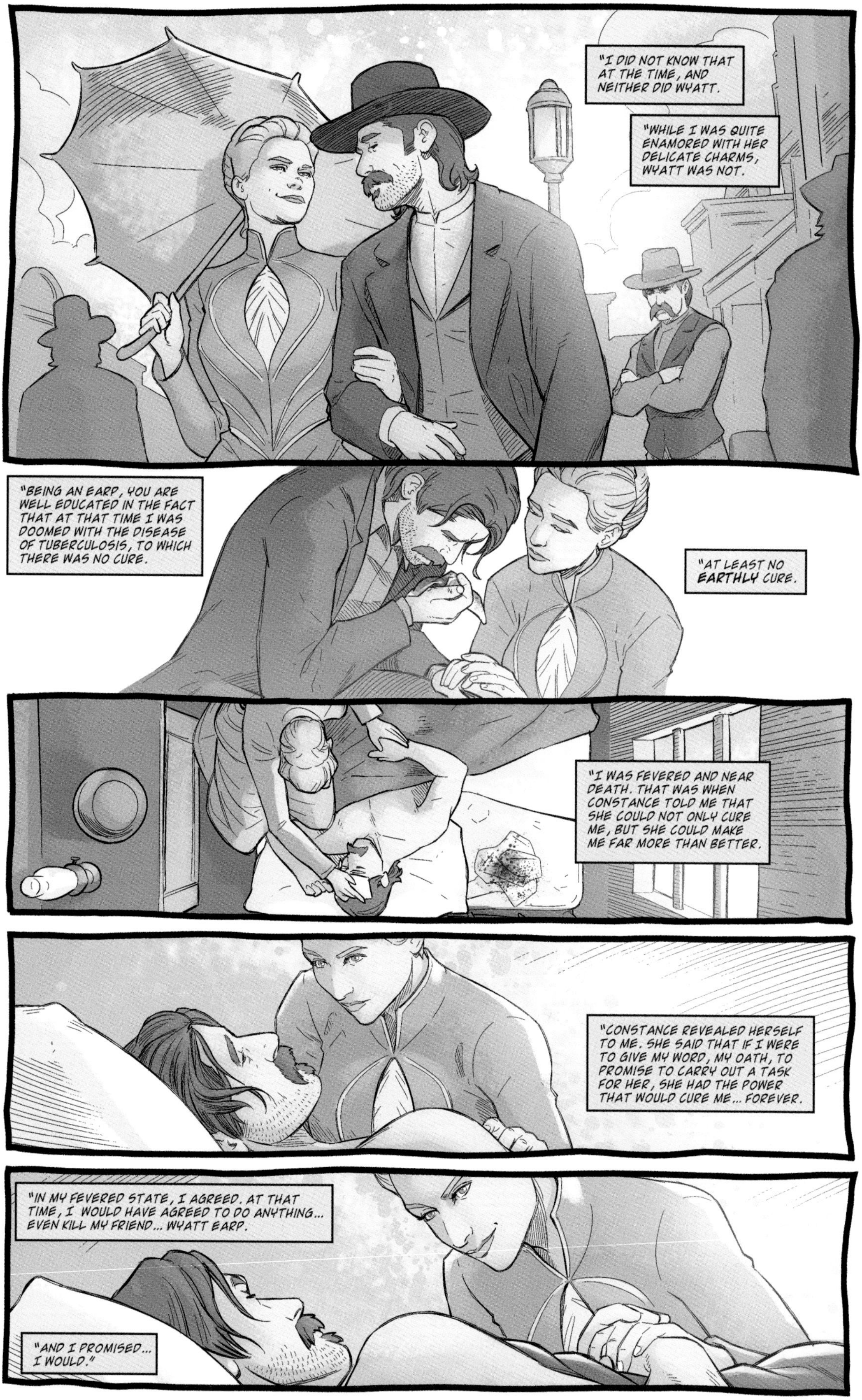
"I DID NOT KNOW THAT AT THE TIME, AND NEITHER DID WYATT.
"WHILE I WAS QUITE ENAMORED WITH HER DELICATE CHARMS, WYATT WAS NOT.
"BEING AN EARP, YOU ARE WELL EDUCATED IN THE FACT THAT AT THAT TIME I WAS DOOMED WITH THE DISEASE OF TUBERCULOSIS, TO WHICH THERE WAS NO CURE.
"AT LEAST NO **EARTHLY** CURE.
"I WAS FEVERED AND NEAR DEATH. THAT WAS WHEN CONSTANCE TOLD ME THAT SHE COULD NOT ONLY CURE ME, BUT SHE COULD MAKE ME FAR MORE THAN BETTER.
"CONSTANCE REVEALED HERSELF TO ME. SHE SAID THAT IF I WERE TO GIVE MY WORD, MY OATH, TO PROMISE TO CARRY OUT A TASK FOR HER, SHE HAD THE POWER THAT WOULD CURE ME... FOREVER.
"IN MY FEVERED STATE, I AGREED. AT THAT TIME, I WOULD HAVE AGREED TO DO ANYTHING... EVEN KILL MY FRIEND... WYATT EARP.
"AND I PROMISED... I WOULD."

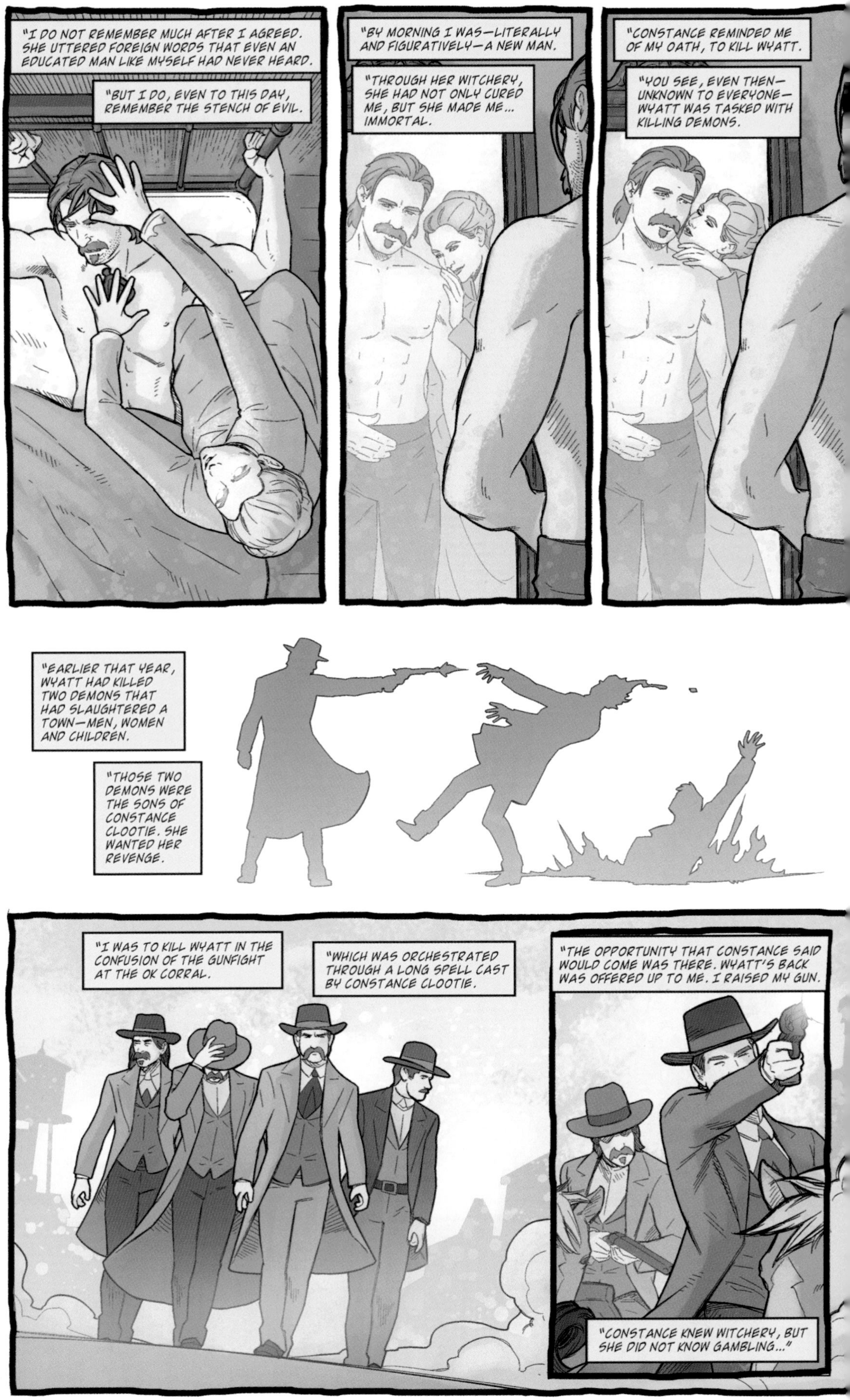
"I DO NOT REMEMBER MUCH AFTER I AGREED. SHE UTTERED FOREIGN WORDS THAT EVEN AN EDUCATED MAN LIKE MYSELF HAD NEVER HEARD.
"BUT I DO, EVEN TO THIS DAY, REMEMBER THE STENCH OF EVIL.
"BY MORNING I WAS—LITERALLY AND FIGURATIVELY—A NEW MAN.
"THROUGH HER WITCHERY, SHE HAD NOT ONLY CURED ME, BUT SHE MADE ME... IMMORTAL.
"CONSTANCE REMINDED ME OF MY OATH, TO KILL WYATT.
"YOU SEE, EVEN THEN—UNKNOWN TO EVERYONE—WYATT WAS TASKED WITH KILLING DEMONS.
"EARLIER THAT YEAR, WYATT HAD KILLED TWO DEMONS THAT HAD SLAUGHTERED A TOWN—MEN, WOMEN AND CHILDREN.
"THOSE TWO DEMONS WERE THE SONS OF CONSTANCE CLOOTIE. SHE WANTED HER REVENGE.
"I WAS TO KILL WYATT IN THE CONFUSION OF THE GUNFIGHT AT THE OK CORRAL.
"WHICH WAS ORCHESTRATED THROUGH A LONG SPELL CAST BY CONSTANCE CLOOTIE.
"THE OPPORTUNITY THAT CONSTANCE SAID WOULD COME WAS THERE. WYATT'S BACK WAS OFFERED UP TO ME. I RAISED MY GUN.
"CONSTANCE KNEW WITCHERY, BUT SHE DID NOT KNOW GAMBLING..."

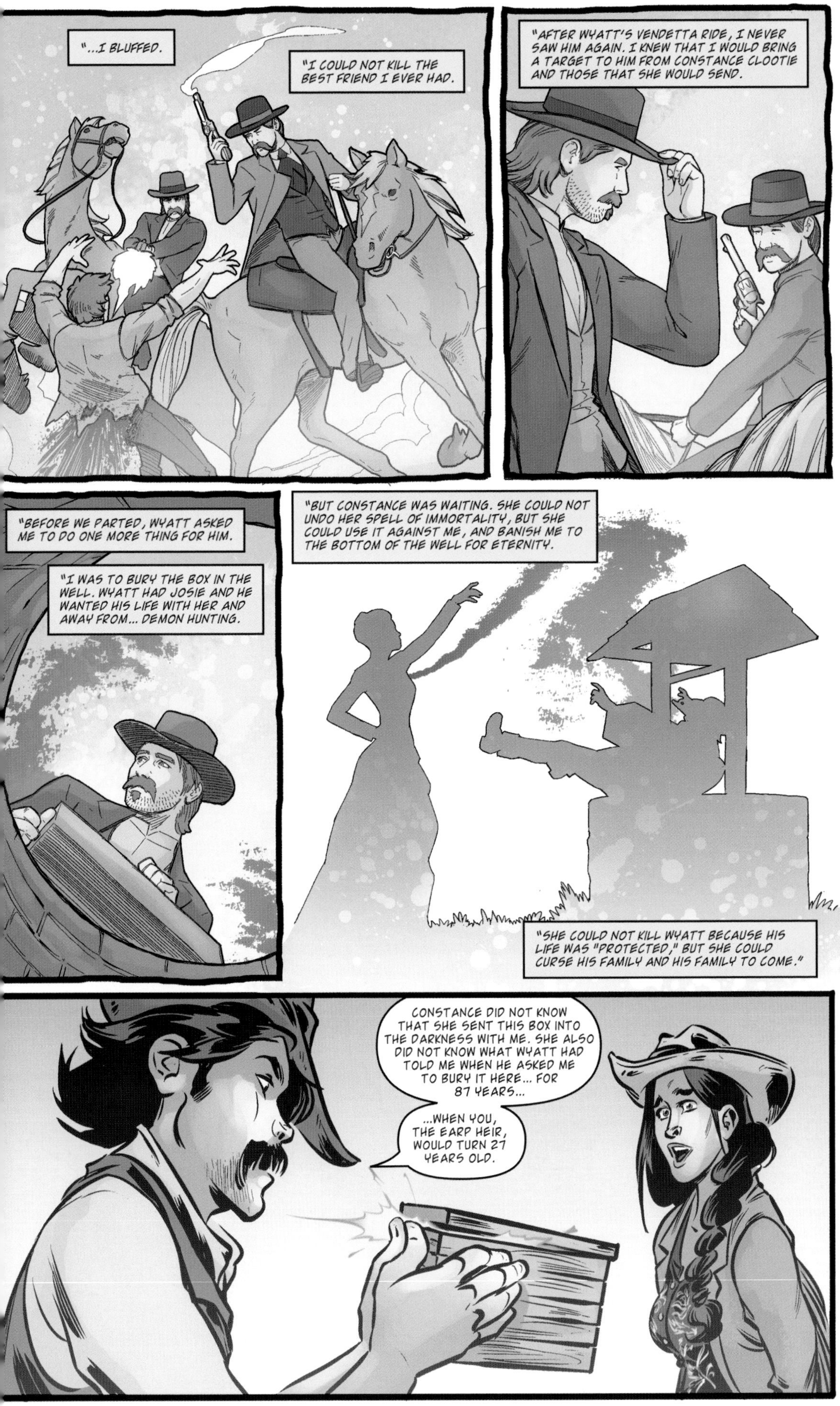
"...I BLUFFED.
"I COULD NOT KILL THE BEST FRIEND I EVER HAD.
"AFTER WYATT'S VENDETTA RIDE, I NEVER SAW HIM AGAIN. I KNEW THAT I WOULD BRING A TARGET TO HIM FROM CONSTANCE CLOOTIE AND THOSE THAT SHE WOULD SEND.
"BEFORE WE PARTED, WYATT ASKED ME TO DO ONE MORE THING FOR HIM.
"I WAS TO BURY THE BOX IN THE WELL. WYATT HAD JOSIE AND HE WANTED HIS LIFE WITH HER AND AWAY FROM... DEMON HUNTING.
"BUT CONSTANCE WAS WAITING. SHE COULD NOT UNDO HER SPELL OF IMMORTALITY, BUT SHE COULD USE IT AGAINST ME, AND BANISH ME TO THE BOTTOM OF THE WELL FOR ETERNITY.
"SHE COULD NOT KILL WYATT BECAUSE HIS LIFE WAS "PROTECTED," BUT SHE COULD CURSE HIS FAMILY AND HIS FAMILY TO COME."
CONSTANCE DID NOT KNOW THAT SHE SENT THIS BOX INTO THE DARKNESS WITH ME. SHE ALSO DID NOT KNOW WHAT WYATT HAD TOLD ME WHEN HE ASKED ME TO BURY IT HERE... FOR 87 YEARS...
...WHEN YOU, THE EARP HEIR, WOULD TURN 27 YEARS OLD.

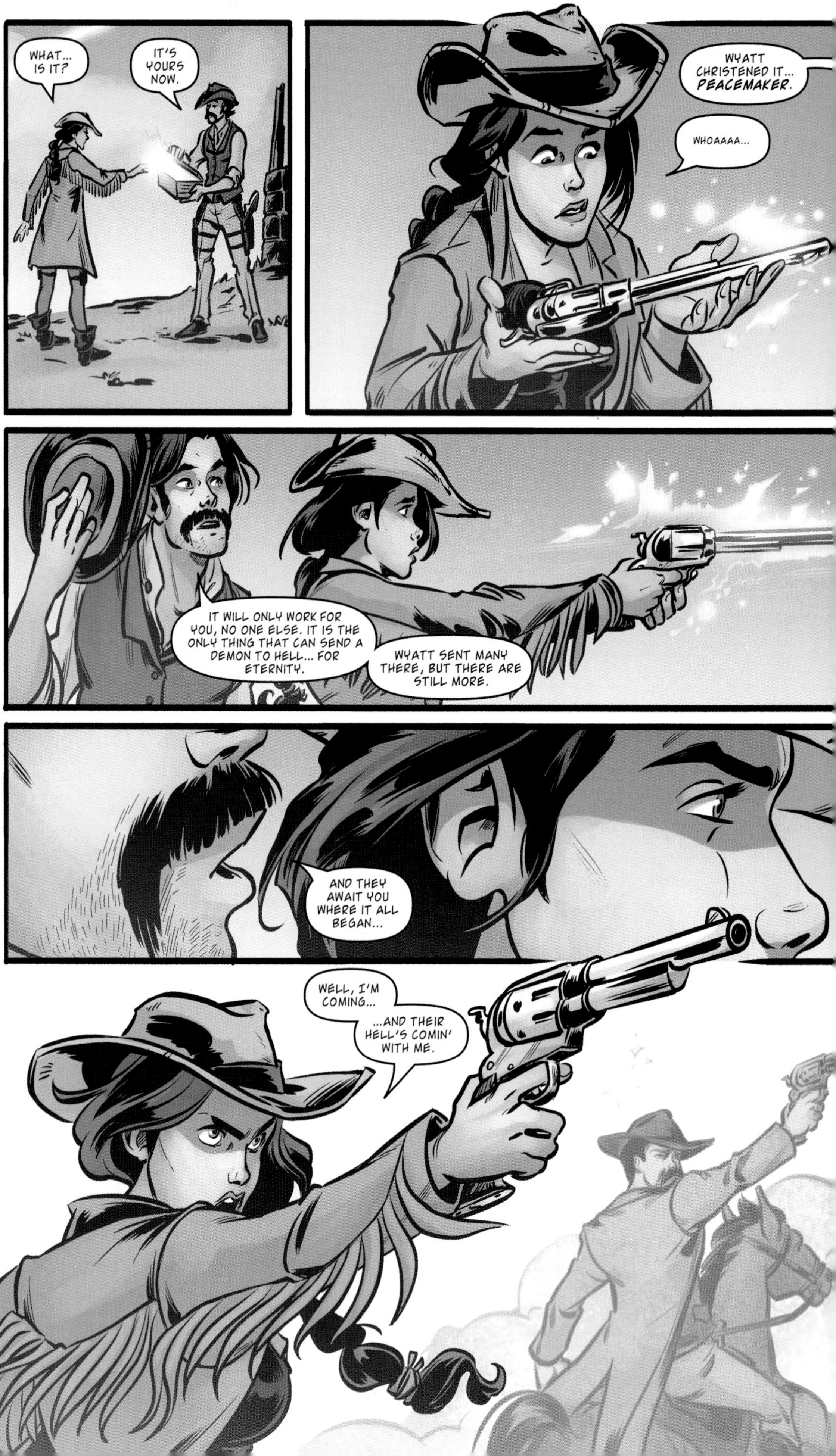
WHAT... IS IT?
IT'S YOURS NOW.
WYATT CHRISTENED IT... PEACEMAKER.
WHOAAAA...
IT WILL ONLY WORK FOR YOU, NO ONE ELSE. IT IS THE ONLY THING THAT CAN SEND A DEMON TO HELL... FOR ETERNITY.
WYATT SENT MANY THERE, BUT THERE ARE STILL MORE.
AND THEY AWAIT YOU WHERE IT ALL BEGAN...
WELL, I'M COMING...
...AND THEIR HELL'S COMIN' WITH ME.

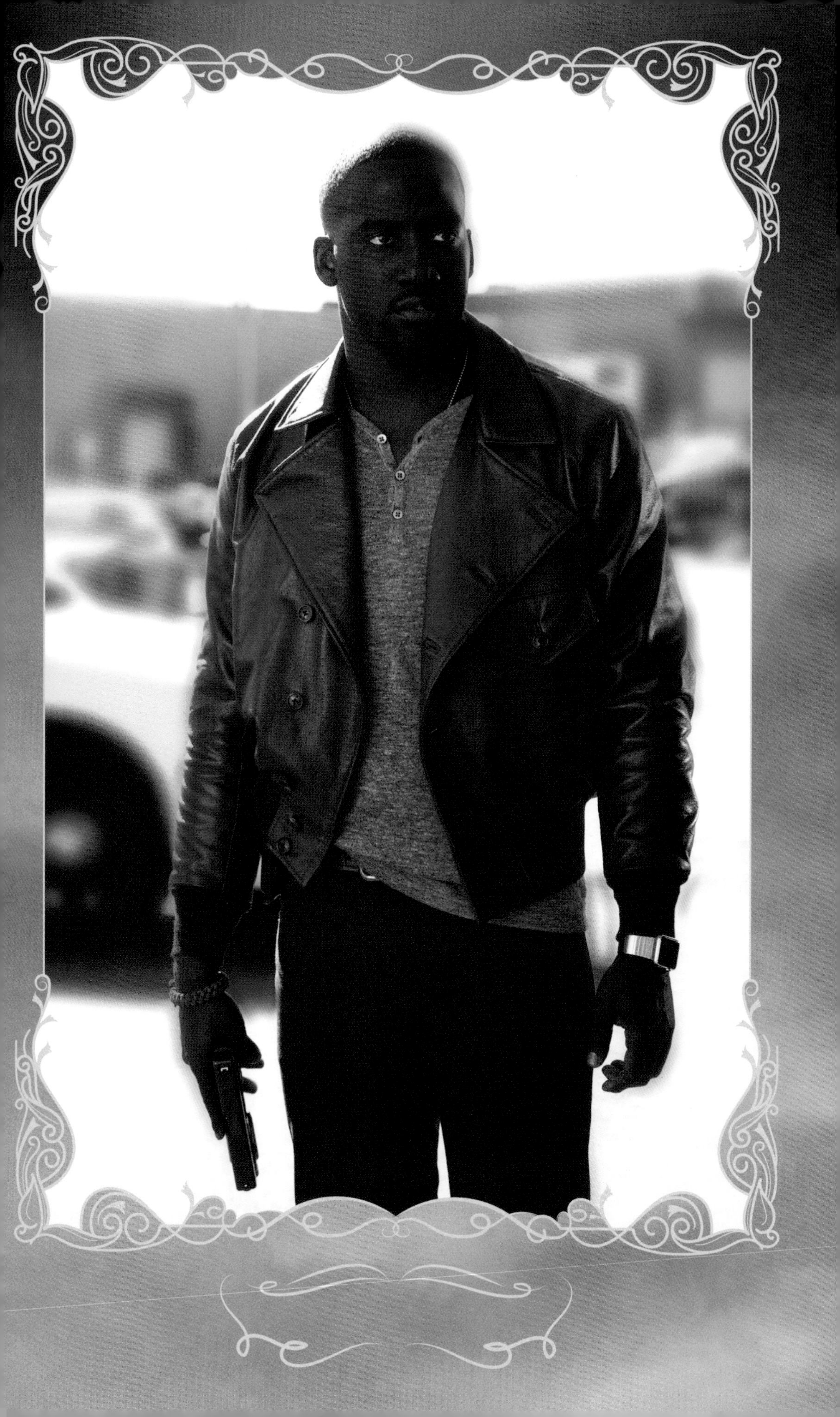

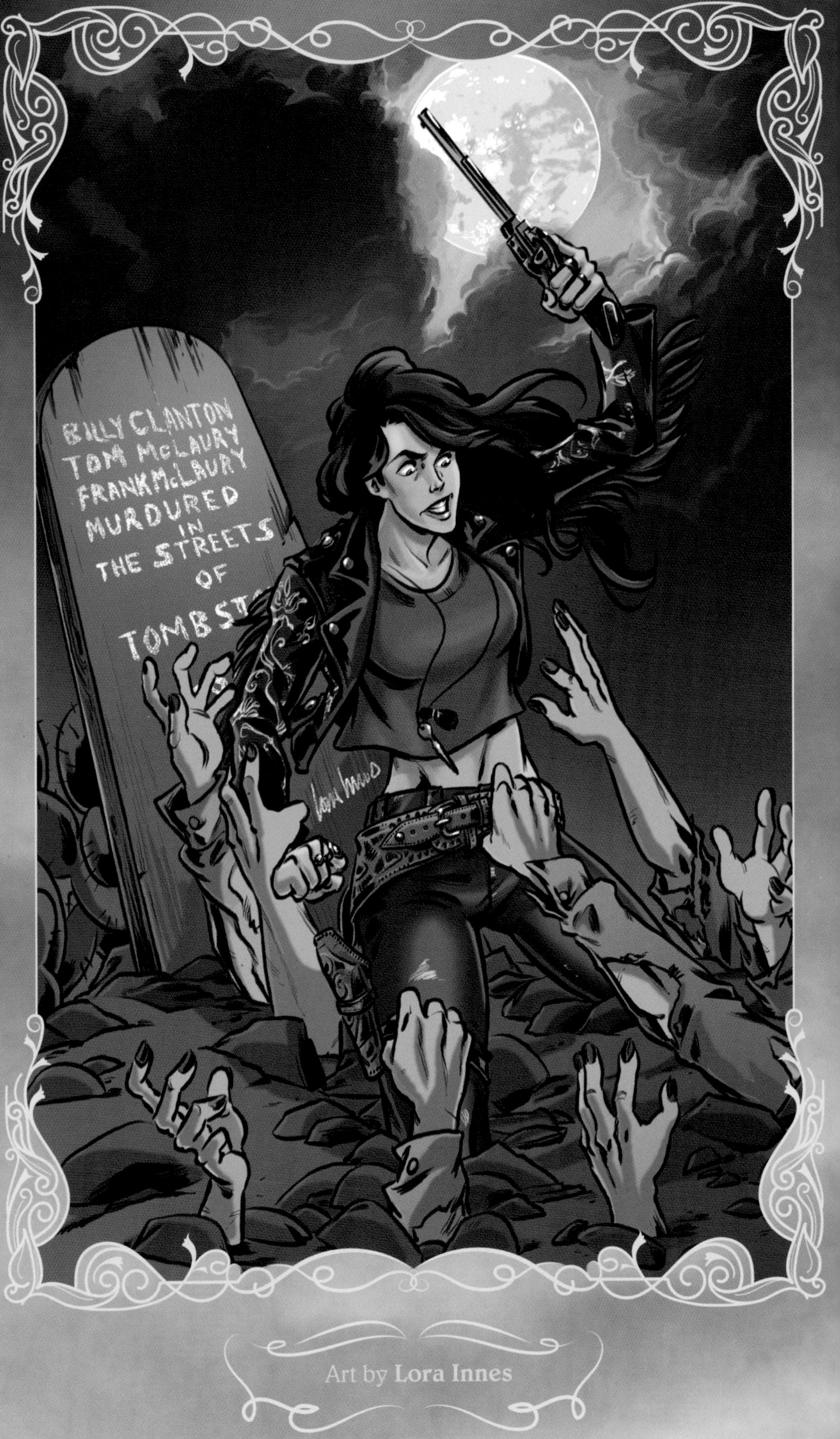
BILLY CLANTON
TOM McLAURY
FRANK McLAURY
MURDURED
IN
THE STREETS
OF
TOMBST

Art by **Lora Innes**

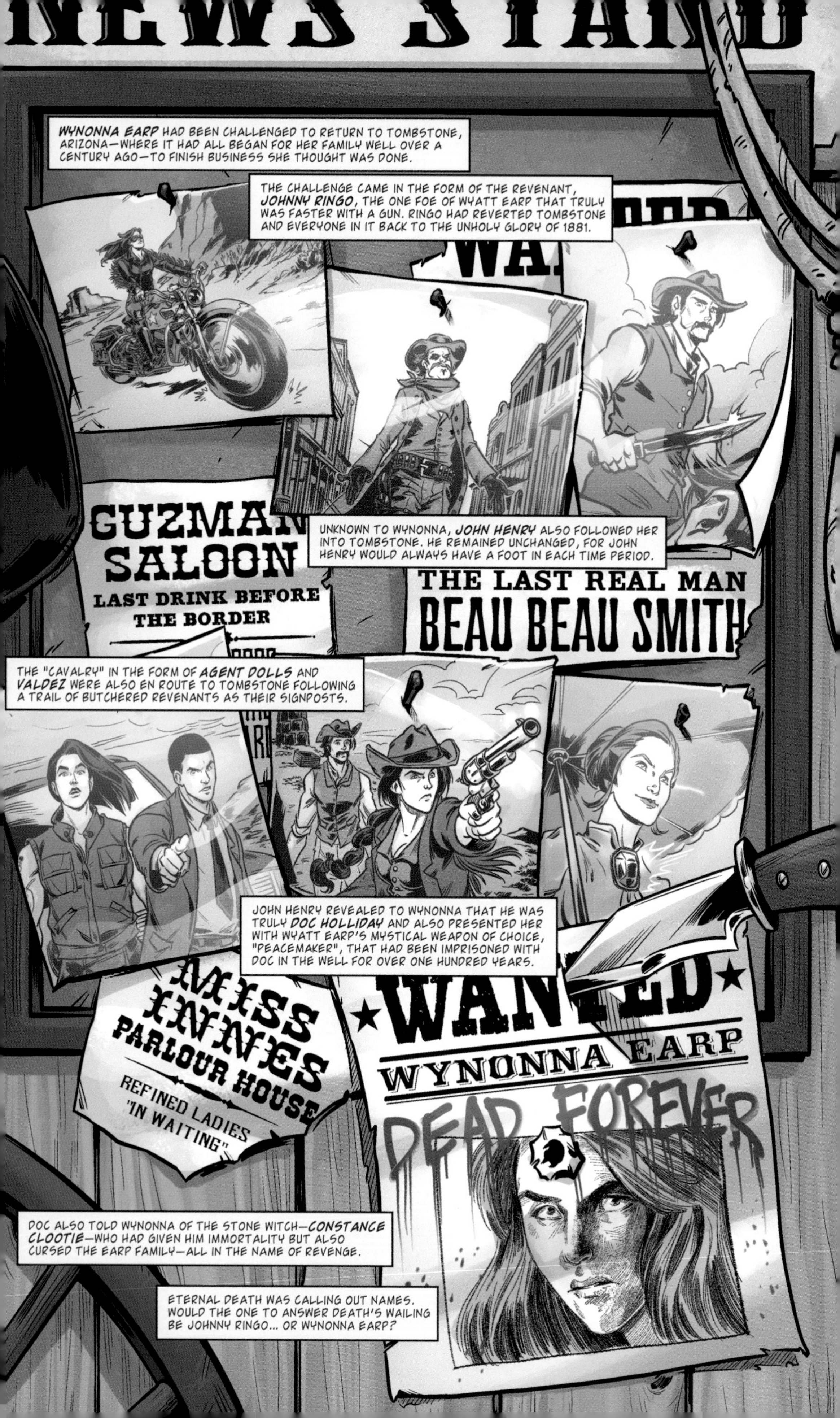
NEWS STAND
WYNONNA EARP HAD BEEN CHALLENGED TO RETURN TO TOMBSTONE, ARIZONA—WHERE IT HAD ALL BEGAN FOR HER FAMILY WELL OVER A CENTURY AGO—TO FINISH BUSINESS SHE THOUGHT WAS DONE.
THE CHALLENGE CAME IN THE FORM OF THE REVENANT, JOHNNY RINGO, THE ONE FOE OF WYATT EARP THAT TRULY WAS FASTER WITH A GUN. RINGO HAD REVERTED TOMBSTONE AND EVERYONE IN IT BACK TO THE UNHOLY GLORY OF 1881.
GUZMAN SALOON
LAST DRINK BEFORE THE BORDER
UNKNOWN TO WYNONNA, JOHN HENRY ALSO FOLLOWED HER INTO TOMBSTONE. HE REMAINED UNCHANGED, FOR JOHN HENRY WOULD ALWAYS HAVE A FOOT IN EACH TIME PERIOD.
THE LAST REAL MAN
BEAU BEAU SMITH
THE "CAVALRY" IN THE FORM OF AGENT DOLLS AND VALDEZ WERE ALSO EN ROUTE TO TOMBSTONE FOLLOWING A TRAIL OF BUTCHERED REVENANTS AS THEIR SIGNPOSTS.
JOHN HENRY REVEALED TO WYNONNA THAT HE WAS TRULY DOC HOLLIDAY AND ALSO PRESENTED HER WITH WYATT EARP'S MYSTICAL WEAPON OF CHOICE, "PEACEMAKER", THAT HAD BEEN IMPRISONED WITH DOC IN THE WELL FOR OVER ONE HUNDRED YEARS.
MISS INNES PARLOUR HOUSE
REFINED LADIES "IN WAITING"
WYNONNA EARP
DEAD FOREVER
DOC ALSO TOLD WYNONNA OF THE STONE WITCH—CONSTANCE CLOOTIE—WHO HAD GIVEN HIM IMMORTALITY BUT ALSO CURSED THE EARP FAMILY—ALL IN THE NAME OF REVENGE.
ETERNAL DEATH WAS CALLING OUT NAMES. WOULD THE ONE TO ANSWER DEATH'S WAILING BE JOHNNY RINGO... OR WYNONNA EARP?

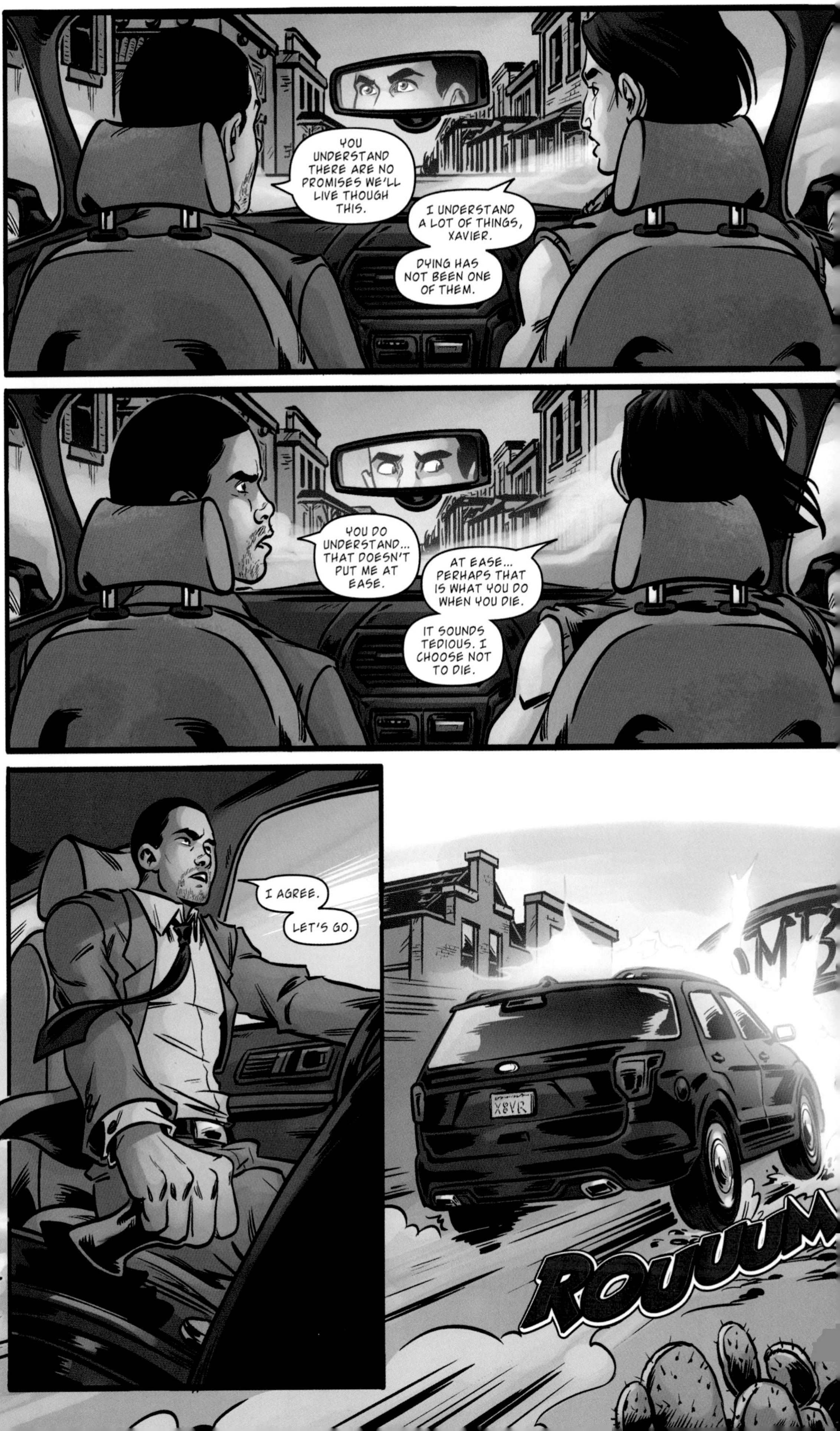
YOU UNDERSTAND THERE ARE NO PROMISES WE'LL LIVE THOUGH THIS.
I UNDERSTAND A LOT OF THINGS, XAVIER.
DYING HAS NOT BEEN ONE OF THEM.
YOU DO UNDERSTAND... THAT DOESN'T PUT ME AT EASE.
AT EASE... PERHAPS THAT IS WHAT YOU DO WHEN YOU DIE.
IT SOUNDS TEDIOUS. I CHOOSE NOT TO DIE.
I AGREE.
LET'S GO.
X8VR
ROUUUM

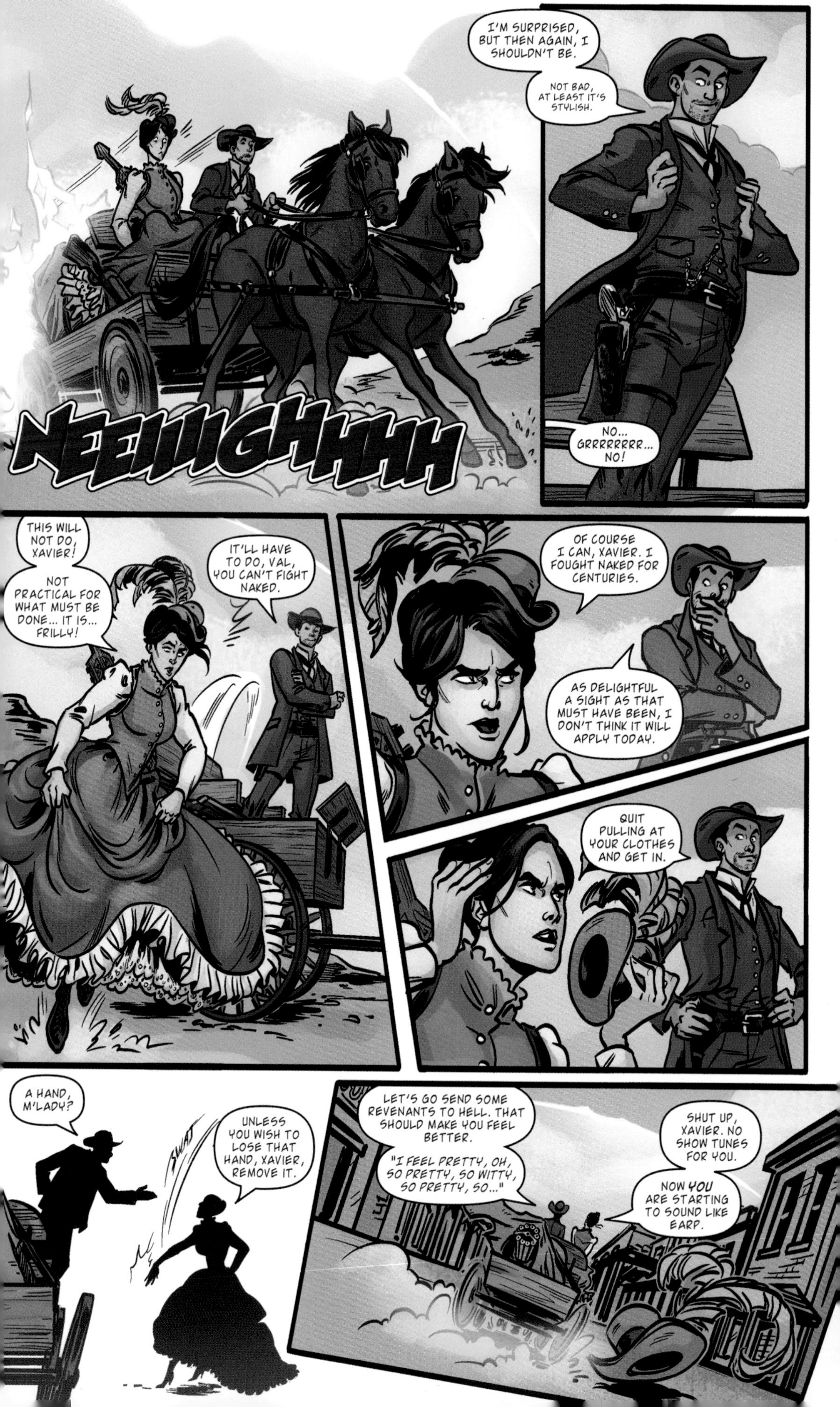
NEEIIIIGHHHH
I'M SURPRISED, BUT THEN AGAIN, I SHOULDN'T BE.
NOT BAD, AT LEAST IT'S STYLISH.
NO... GRRRRRRR... NO!
THIS WILL NOT DO, XAVIER!
NOT PRACTICAL FOR WHAT MUST BE DONE... IT IS... FRILLY!
IT'LL HAVE TO DO, VAL, YOU CAN'T FIGHT NAKED.
OF COURSE I CAN, XAVIER. I FOUGHT NAKED FOR CENTURIES.
AS DELIGHTFUL A SIGHT AS THAT MUST HAVE BEEN, I DON'T THINK IT WILL APPLY TODAY.
QUIT PULLING AT YOUR CLOTHES AND GET IN.
A HAND, M'LADY?
UNLESS YOU WISH TO LOSE THAT HAND, XAVIER, REMOVE IT.
SWAT
LET'S GO SEND SOME REVENANTS TO HELL. THAT SHOULD MAKE YOU FEEL BETTER.
"I FEEL PRETTY, OH, SO PRETTY, SO WITTY, SO PRETTY, SO..."
SHUT UP, XAVIER. NO SHOW TUNES FOR YOU.
NOW YOU ARE STARTING TO SOUND LIKE EARP.

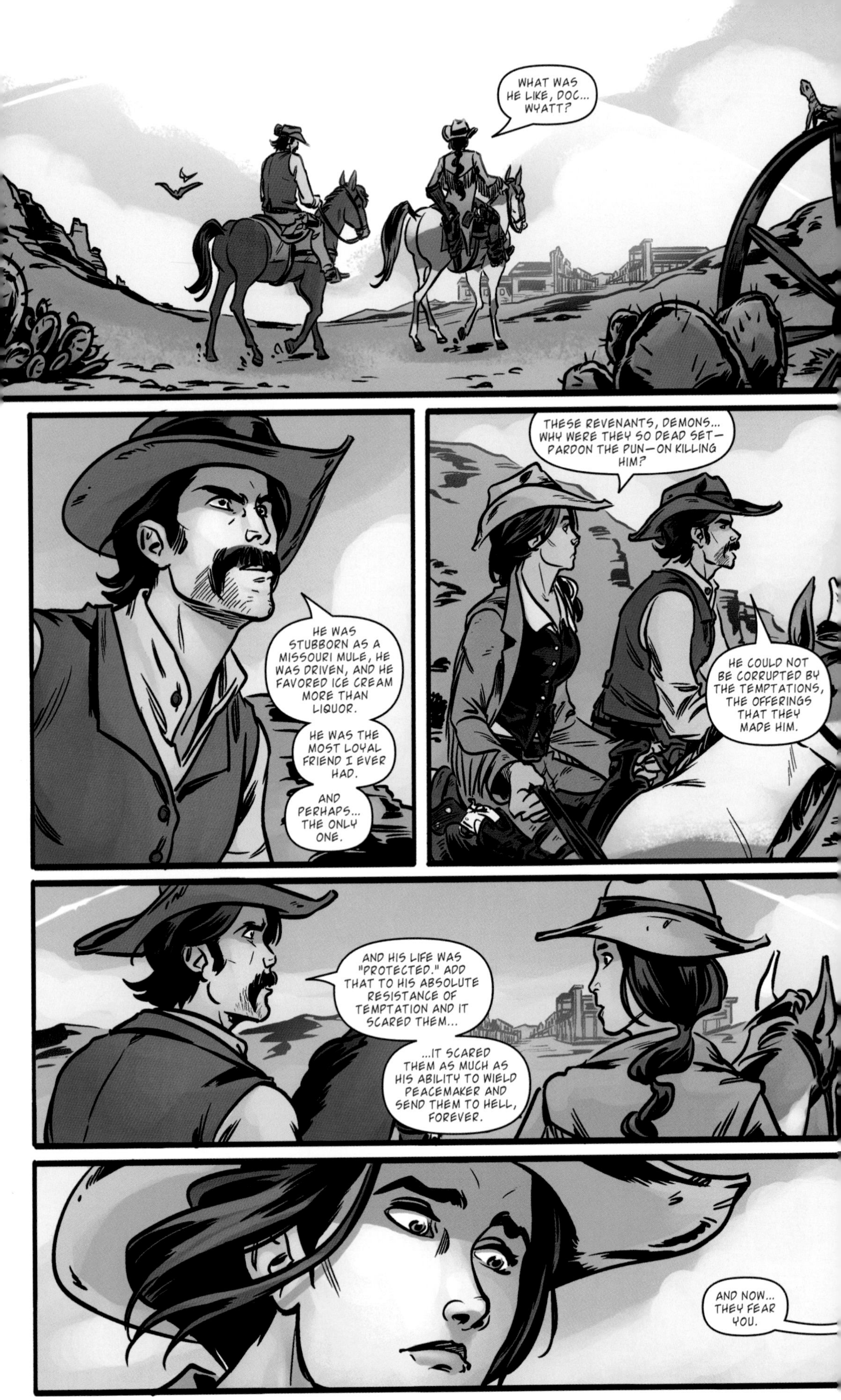
WHAT WAS HE LIKE, DOC... WYATT?
HE WAS STUBBORN AS A MISSOURI MULE, HE WAS DRIVEN, AND HE FAVORED ICE CREAM MORE THAN LIQUOR.
HE WAS THE MOST LOYAL FRIEND I EVER HAD.
AND PERHAPS... THE ONLY ONE.
THESE REVENANTS, DEMONS... WHY WERE THEY SO DEAD SET—PARDON THE PUN—ON KILLING HIM?
HE COULD NOT BE CORRUPTED BY THE TEMPTATIONS, THE OFFERINGS THAT THEY MADE HIM.
AND HIS LIFE WAS "PROTECTED." ADD THAT TO HIS ABSOLUTE RESISTANCE OF TEMPTATION AND IT SCARED THEM...
...IT SCARED THEM AS MUCH AS HIS ABILITY TO WIELD PEACEMAKER AND SEND THEM TO HELL, FOREVER.
AND NOW... THEY FEAR YOU.

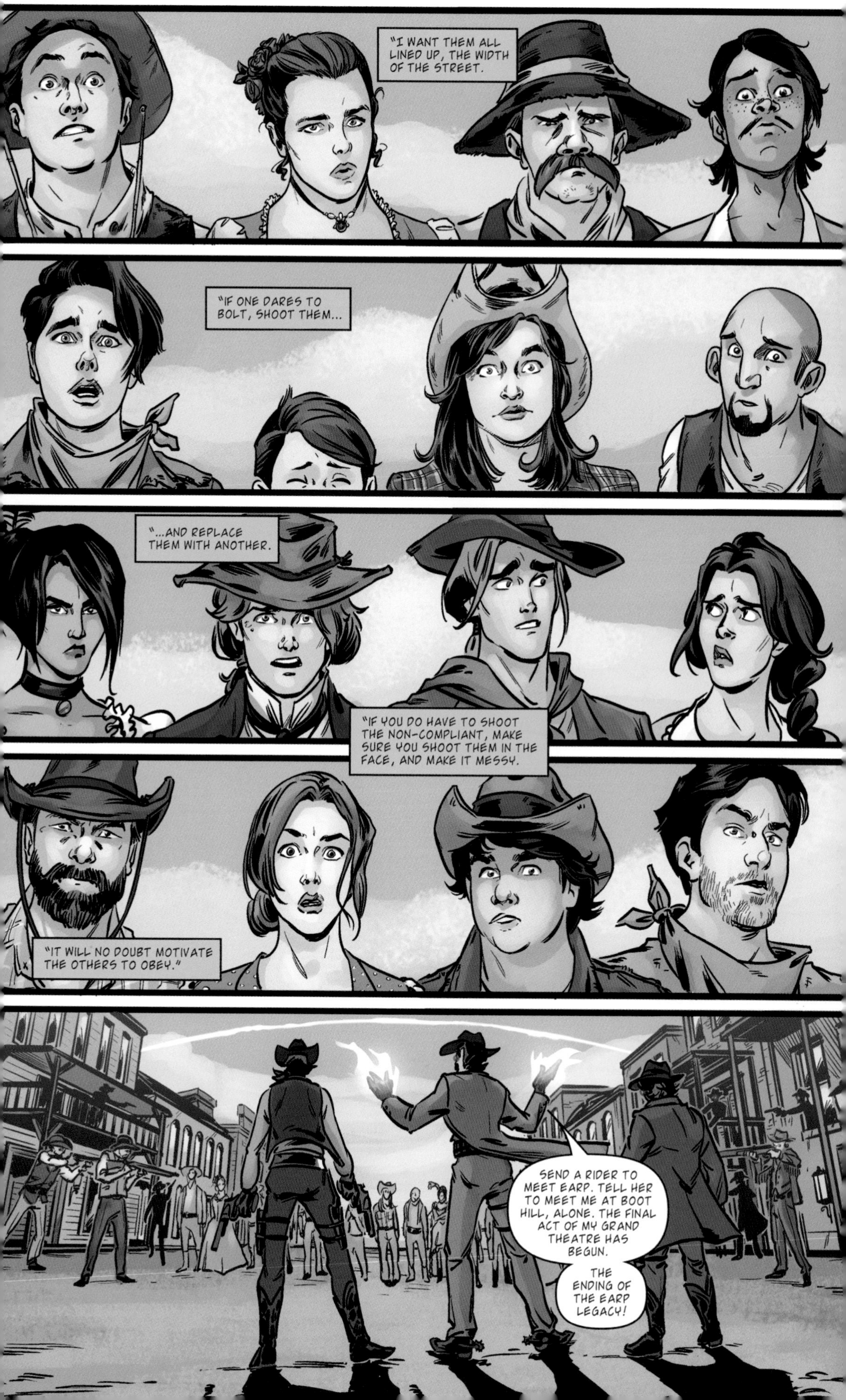
"I WANT THEM ALL LINED UP, THE WIDTH OF THE STREET.
"IF ONE DARES TO BOLT, SHOOT THEM...
"...AND REPLACE THEM WITH ANOTHER.
"IF YOU DO HAVE TO SHOOT THE NON-COMPLIANT, MAKE SURE YOU SHOOT THEM IN THE FACE, AND MAKE IT MESSY.
"IT WILL NO DOUBT MOTIVATE THE OTHERS TO OBEY."
SEND A RIDER TO MEET EARP. TELL HER TO MEET ME AT BOOT HILL, ALONE. THE FINAL ACT OF MY GRAND THEATRE HAS BEGUN.
THE ENDING OF THE EARP LEGACY!

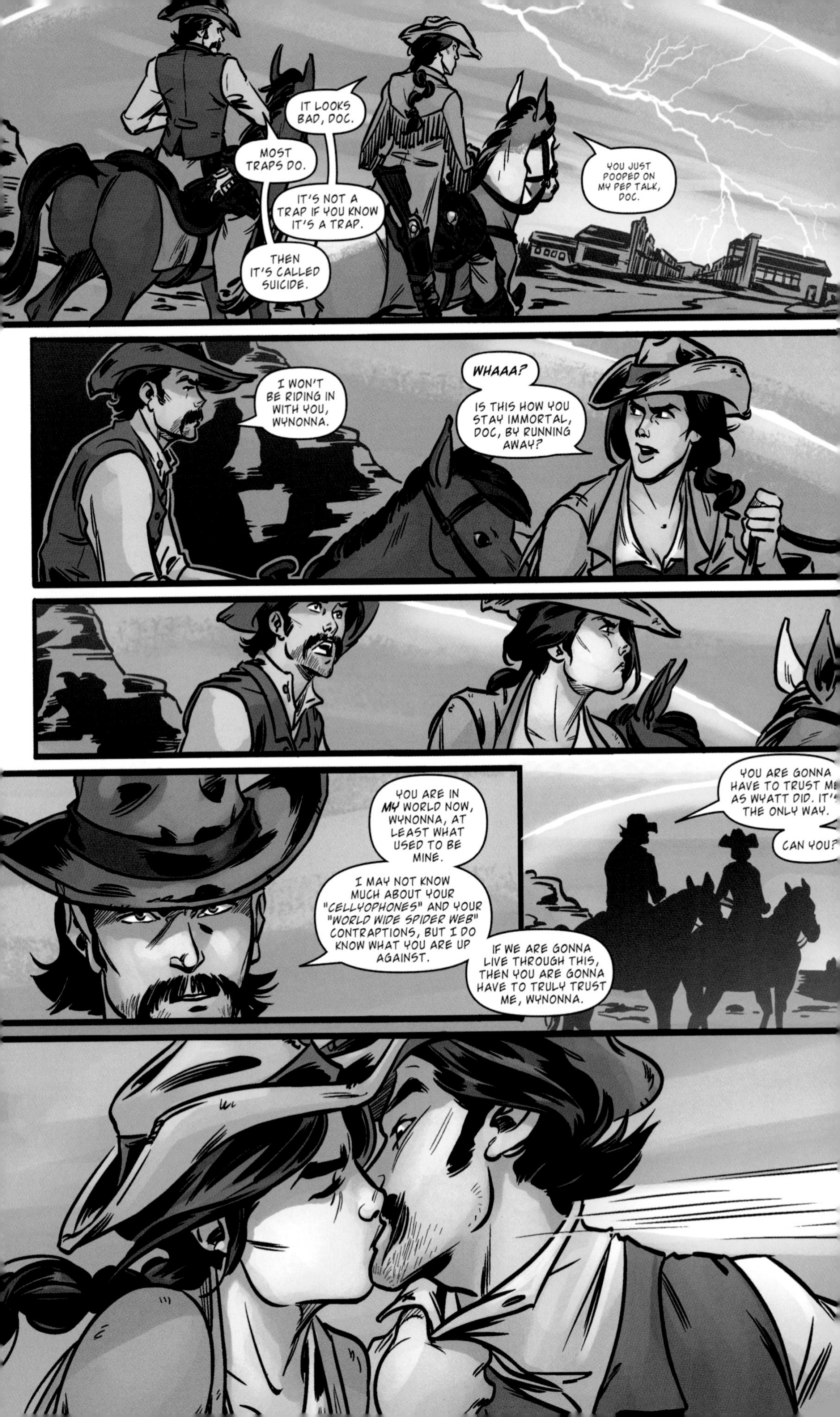

IT LOOKS BAD, DOC.
MOST TRAPS DO.
IT'S NOT A TRAP IF YOU KNOW IT'S A TRAP.
THEN IT'S CALLED SUICIDE.
YOU JUST POOPED ON MY PEP TALK, DOC.
I WON'T BE RIDING IN WITH YOU, WYNONNA.
WHAAA?
IS THIS HOW YOU STAY IMMORTAL, DOC, BY RUNNING AWAY?
YOU ARE IN MY WORLD NOW, WYNONNA, AT LEAST WHAT USED TO BE MINE.
I MAY NOT KNOW MUCH ABOUT YOUR "CELLYOPHONES" AND YOUR "WORLD WIDE SPIDER WEB" CONTRAPTIONS, BUT I DO KNOW WHAT YOU ARE UP AGAINST.
IF WE ARE GONNA LIVE THROUGH THIS, THEN YOU ARE GONNA HAVE TO TRULY TRUST ME, WYNONNA.
YOU ARE GONNA HAVE TO TRUST ME AS WYATT DID. IT'S THE ONLY WAY.
CAN YOU?

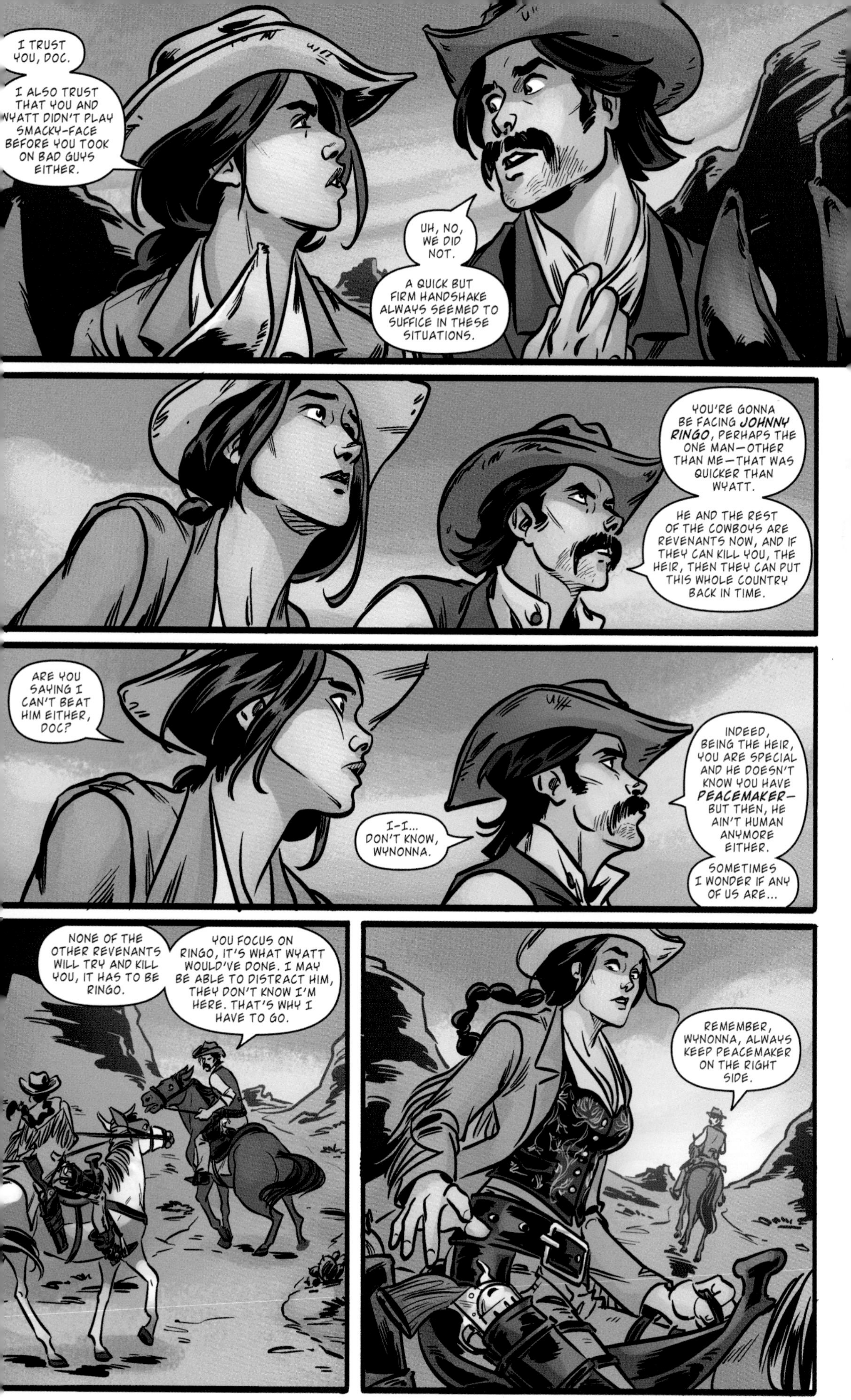
I TRUST YOU, DOC.
I ALSO TRUST THAT YOU AND WYATT DIDN'T PLAY SMACKY-FACE BEFORE YOU TOOK ON BAD GUYS EITHER.
UH, NO, WE DID NOT.
A QUICK BUT FIRM HANDSHAKE ALWAYS SEEMED TO SUFFICE IN THESE SITUATIONS.
YOU'RE GONNA BE FACING JOHNNY RINGO, PERHAPS THE ONE MAN—OTHER THAN ME—THAT WAS QUICKER THAN WYATT.
HE AND THE REST OF THE COWBOYS ARE REVENANTS NOW, AND IF THEY CAN KILL YOU, THE HEIR, THEN THEY CAN PUT THIS WHOLE COUNTRY BACK IN TIME.
ARE YOU SAYING I CAN'T BEAT HIM EITHER, DOC?
I-I... DON'T KNOW, WYNONNA.
INDEED, BEING THE HEIR, YOU ARE SPECIAL AND HE DOESN'T KNOW YOU HAVE PEACEMAKER—BUT THEN, HE AIN'T HUMAN ANYMORE EITHER.
SOMETIMES I WONDER IF ANY OF US ARE...
NONE OF THE OTHER REVENANTS WILL TRY AND KILL YOU, IT HAS TO BE RINGO.
YOU FOCUS ON RINGO, IT'S WHAT WYATT WOULD'VE DONE. I MAY BE ABLE TO DISTRACT HIM, THEY DON'T KNOW I'M HERE. THAT'S WHY I HAVE TO GO.
REMEMBER, WYNONNA, ALWAYS KEEP PEACEMAKER ON THE RIGHT SIDE.

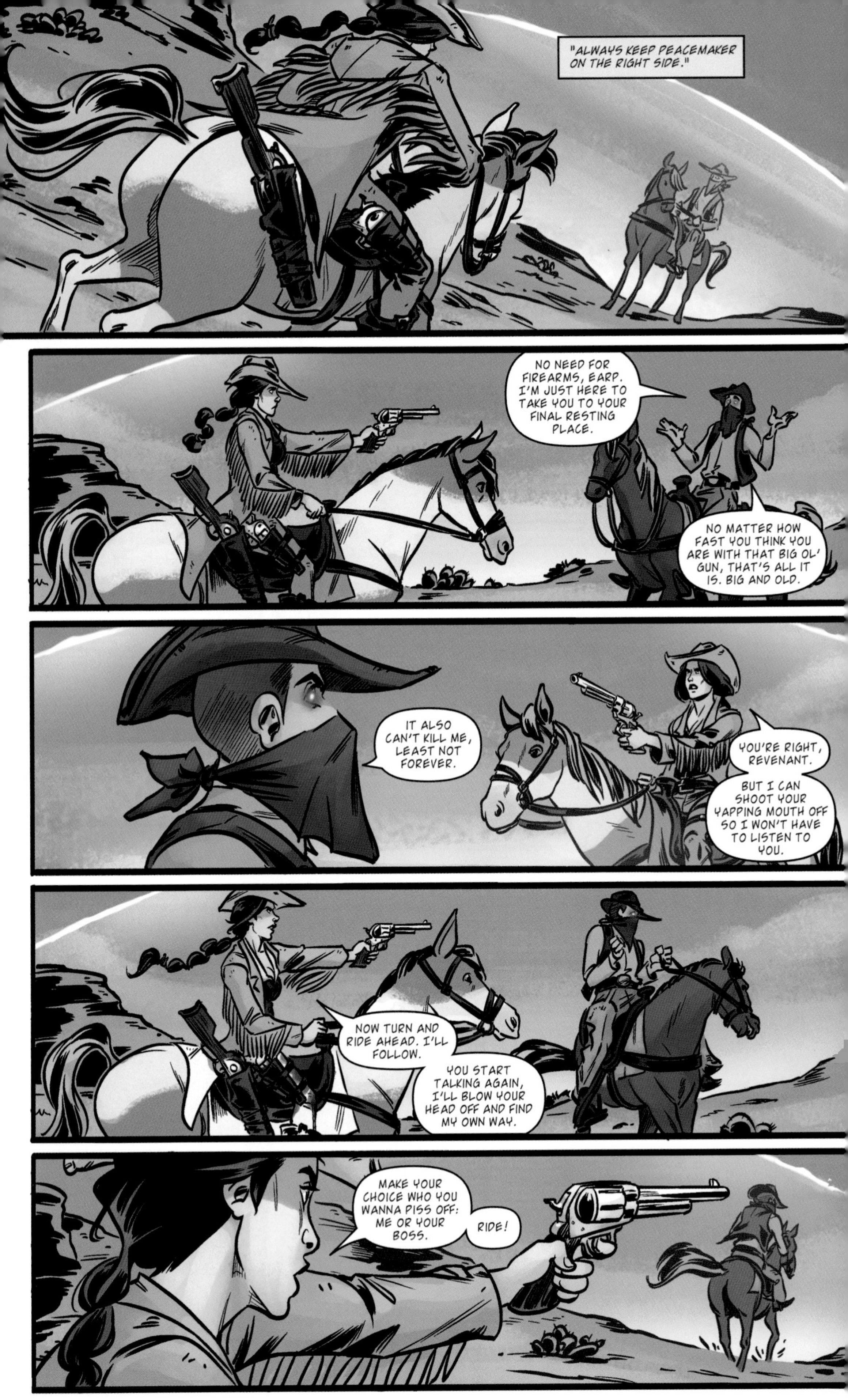
"ALWAYS KEEP PEACEMAKER ON THE RIGHT SIDE."
NO NEED FOR FIREARMS, EARP. I'M JUST HERE TO TAKE YOU TO YOUR FINAL RESTING PLACE.
NO MATTER HOW FAST YOU THINK YOU ARE WITH THAT BIG OL' GUN, THAT'S ALL IT IS. BIG AND OLD.
IT ALSO CAN'T KILL ME, LEAST NOT FOREVER.
YOU'RE RIGHT, REVENANT.
BUT I CAN SHOOT YOUR YAPPING MOUTH OFF SO I WON'T HAVE TO LISTEN TO YOU.
NOW TURN AND RIDE AHEAD. I'LL FOLLOW.
YOU START TALKING AGAIN, I'LL BLOW YOUR HEAD OFF AND FIND MY OWN WAY.
MAKE YOUR CHOICE WHO YOU WANNA PISS OFF: ME OR YOUR BOSS.
RIDE!

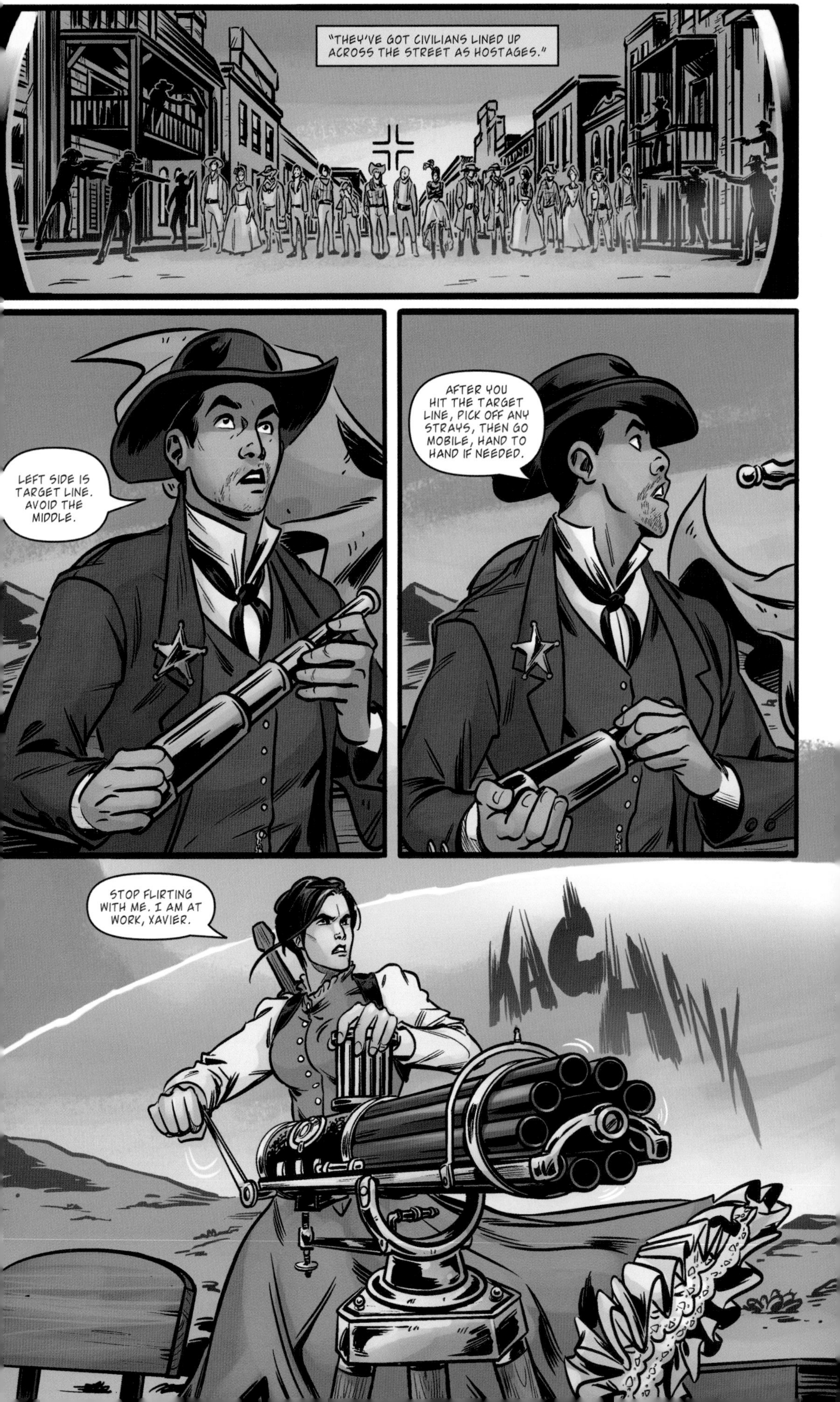
"THEY'VE GOT CIVILIANS LINED UP ACROSS THE STREET AS HOSTAGES."
LEFT SIDE IS TARGET LINE. AVOID THE MIDDLE.
AFTER YOU HIT THE TARGET LINE, PICK OFF ANY STRAYS, THEN GO MOBILE, HAND TO HAND IF NEEDED.
STOP FLIRTING WITH ME. I AM AT WORK, XAVIER.
KACHANK

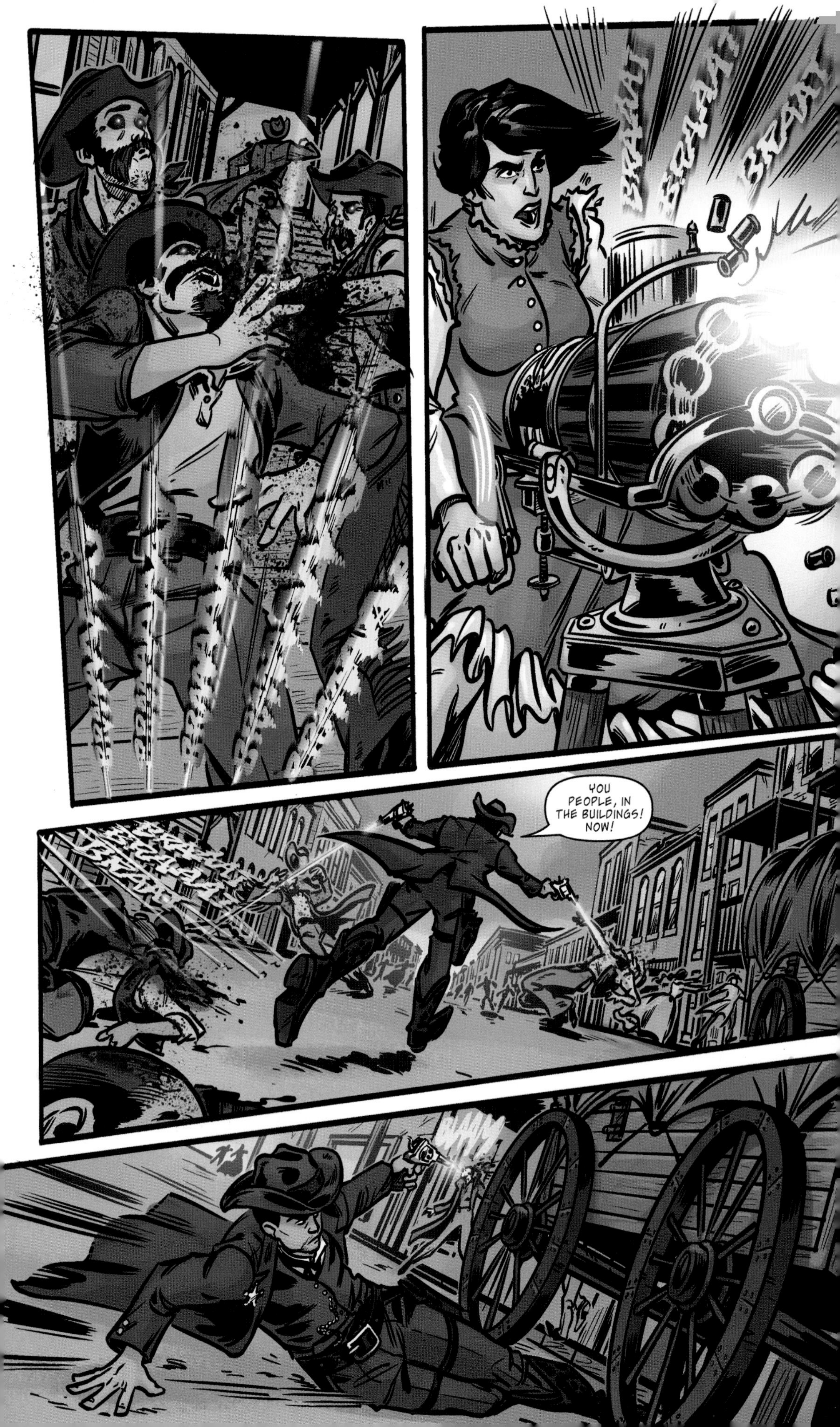
BRAAAT BRAAAT BRAAAT
YOU PEOPLE, IN THE BUILDINGS! NOW!
BLAAM

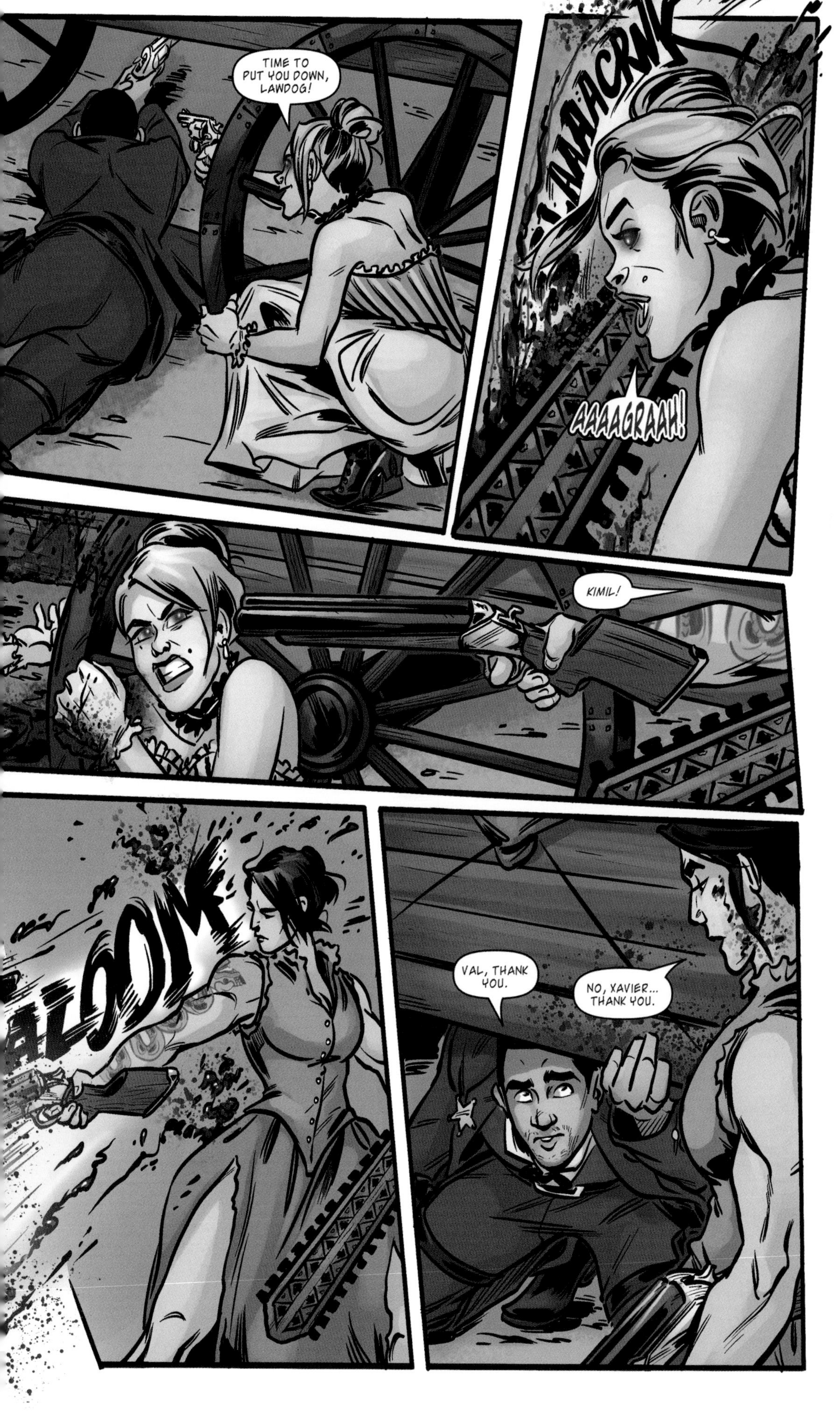
TIME TO PUT YOU DOWN, LAWDOG!
AAAACRNK
AAAAGRAAH!
KIMIL!
AZOOM
VAL, THANK YOU.
NO, XAVIER... THANK YOU.

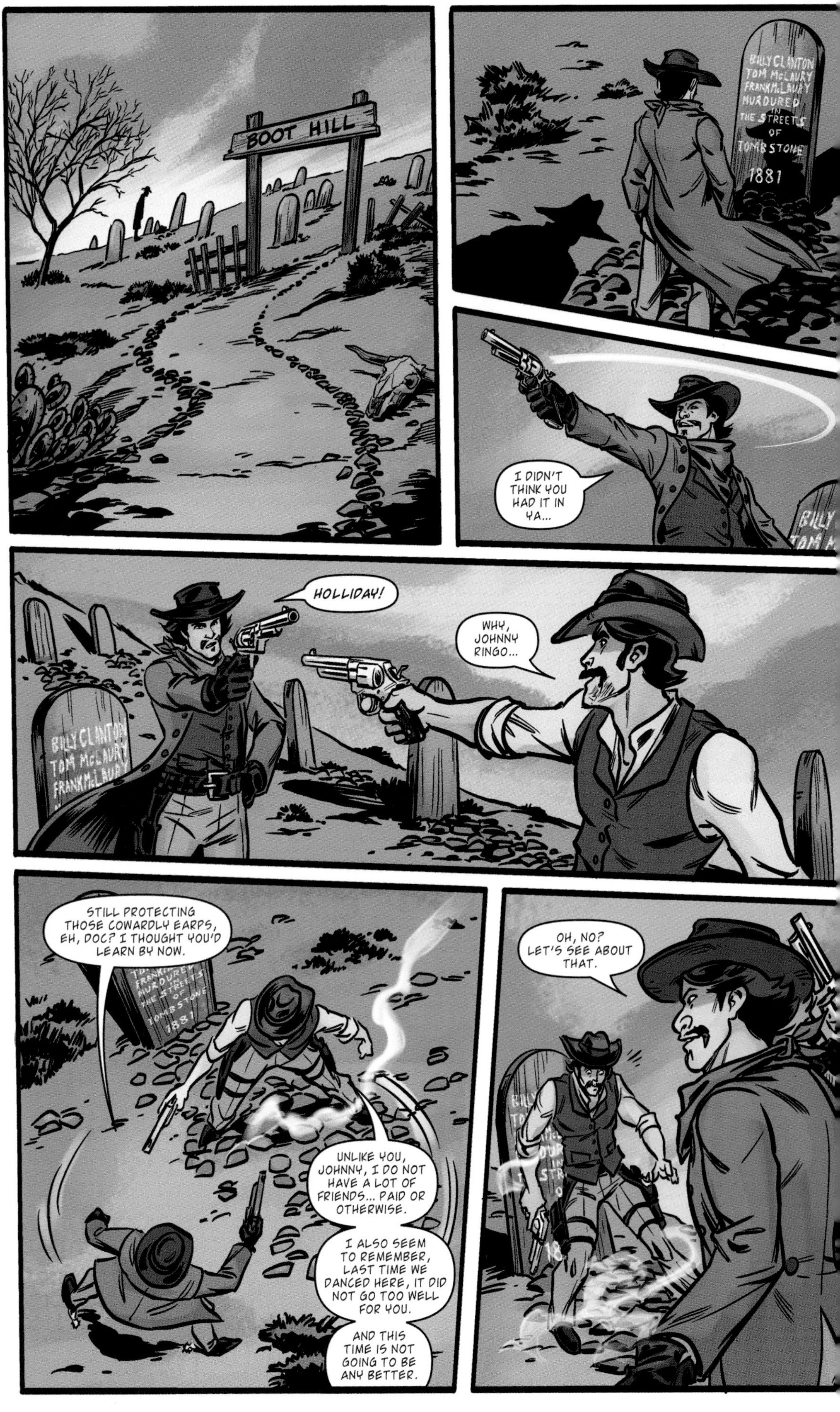
BOOT HILL
BILLY CLANTON TOM McLAURY FRANK McLAURY MURDURED IN THE STREETS OF TOMBSTONE 1881
I DIDN'T THINK YOU HAD IT IN YA...
HOLLIDAY!
WHY, JOHNNY RINGO...
STILL PROTECTING THOSE COWARDLY EARPS, EH, DOC? I THOUGHT YOU'D LEARN BY NOW.
UNLIKE YOU, JOHNNY, I DO NOT HAVE A LOT OF FRIENDS... PAID OR OTHERWISE.
I ALSO SEEM TO REMEMBER, LAST TIME WE DANCED HERE, IT DID NOT GO TOO WELL FOR YOU.
AND THIS TIME IS NOT GOING TO BE ANY BETTER.
OH, NO? LET'S SEE ABOUT THAT.

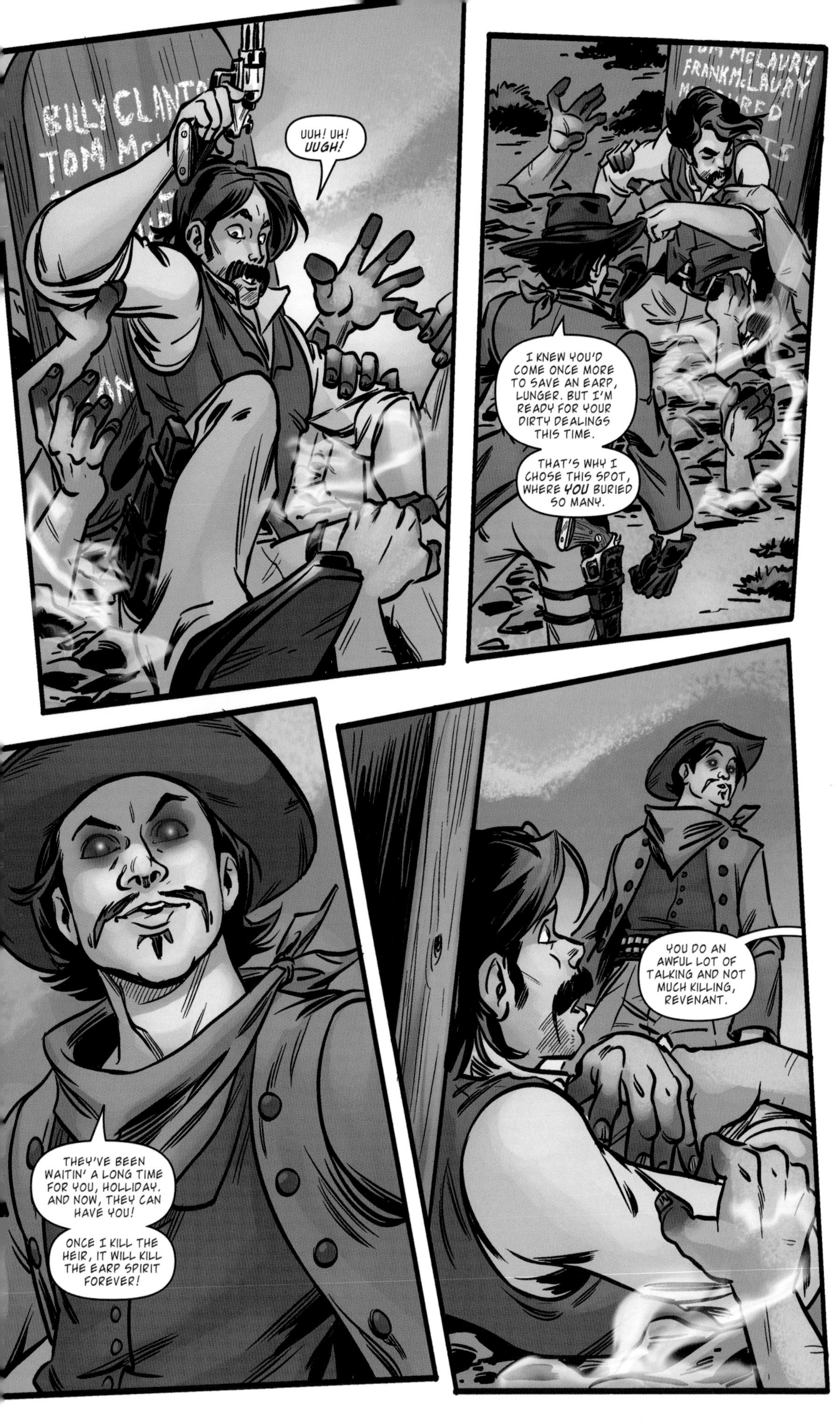
BILLY CLANTON
TOM McLAURY
UUH! UH! UUGH!
TOM McLAURY
FRANK McLAURY
I KNEW YOU'D COME ONCE MORE TO SAVE AN EARP, LUNGER. BUT I'M READY FOR YOUR DIRTY DEALINGS THIS TIME.
THAT'S WHY I CHOSE THIS SPOT, WHERE YOU BURIED SO MANY.
THEY'VE BEEN WAITIN' A LONG TIME FOR YOU, HOLLIDAY. AND NOW, THEY CAN HAVE YOU!
ONCE I KILL THE HEIR, IT WILL KILL THE EARP SPIRIT FOREVER!
YOU DO AN AWFUL LOT OF TALKING AND NOT MUCH KILLING, REVENANT.

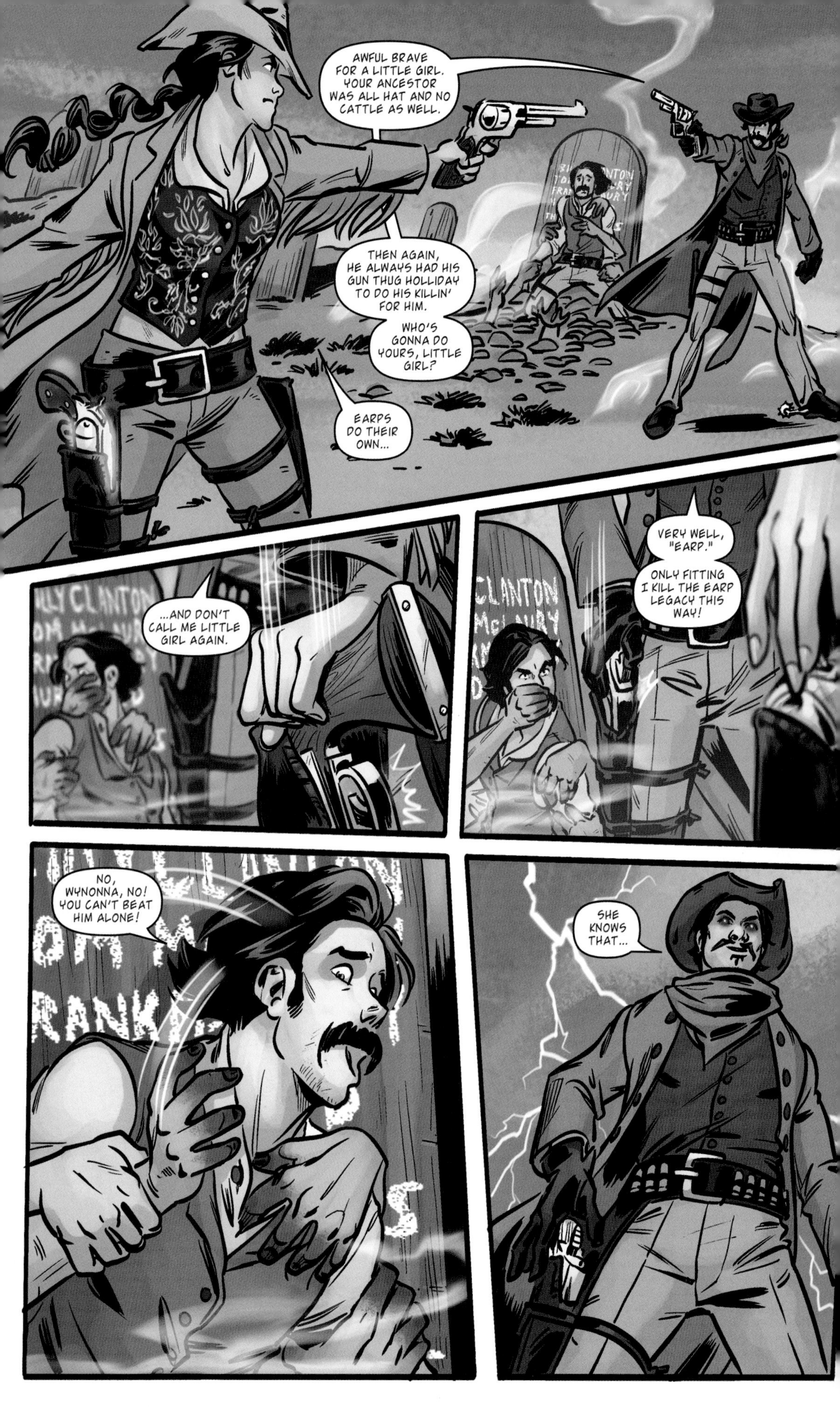
AWFUL BRAVE FOR A LITTLE GIRL. YOUR ANCESTOR WAS ALL HAT AND NO CATTLE AS WELL.
THEN AGAIN, HE ALWAYS HAD HIS GUN THUG HOLLIDAY TO DO HIS KILLIN' FOR HIM.
WHO'S GONNA DO YOURS, LITTLE GIRL?
EARPS DO THEIR OWN...
...AND DON'T CALL ME LITTLE GIRL AGAIN.
VERY WELL, "EARP."
ONLY FITTING I KILL THE EARP LEGACY THIS WAY!
NO, WYNONNA, NO! YOU CAN'T BEAT HIM ALONE!
SHE KNOWS THAT...

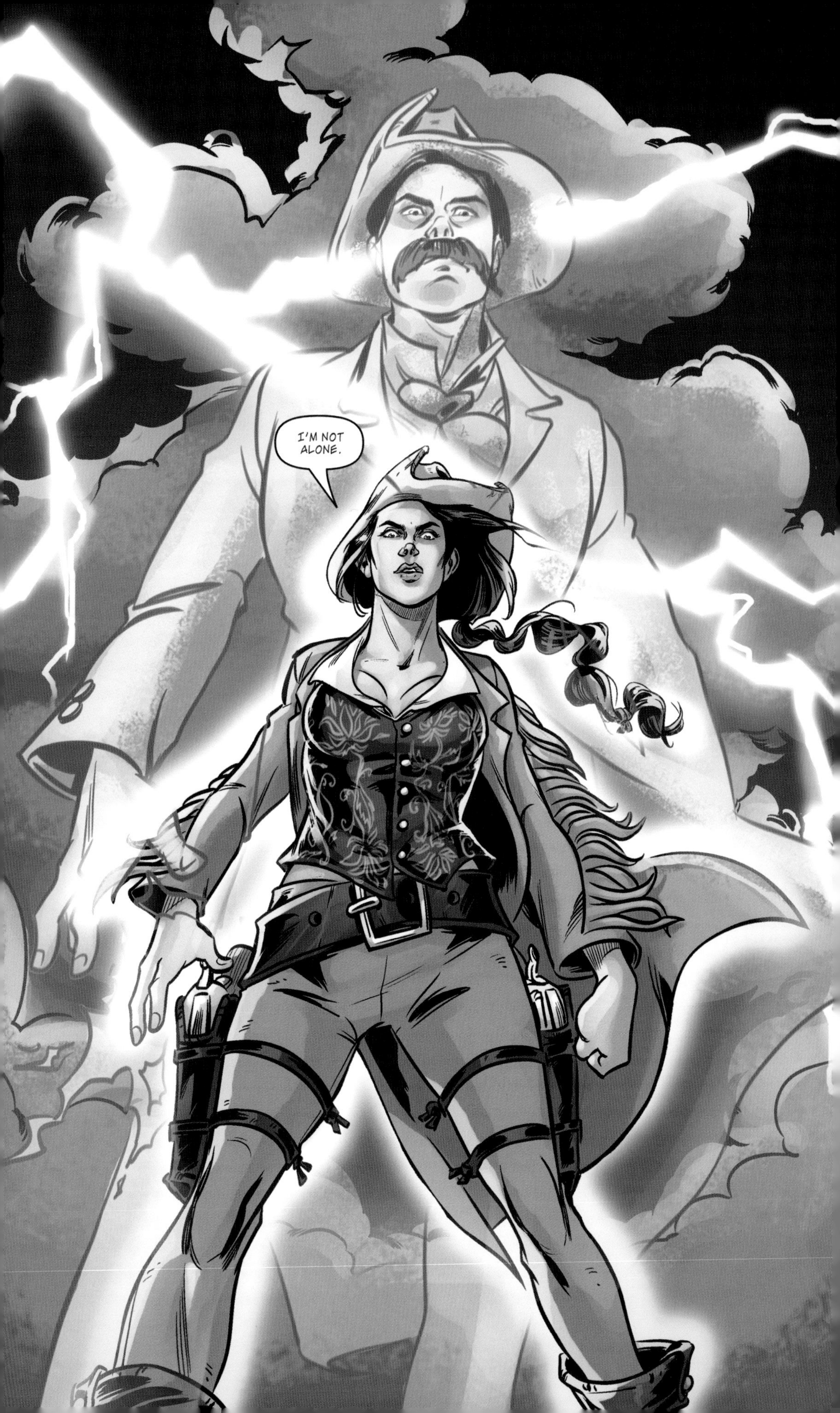
I'M NOT ALONE.

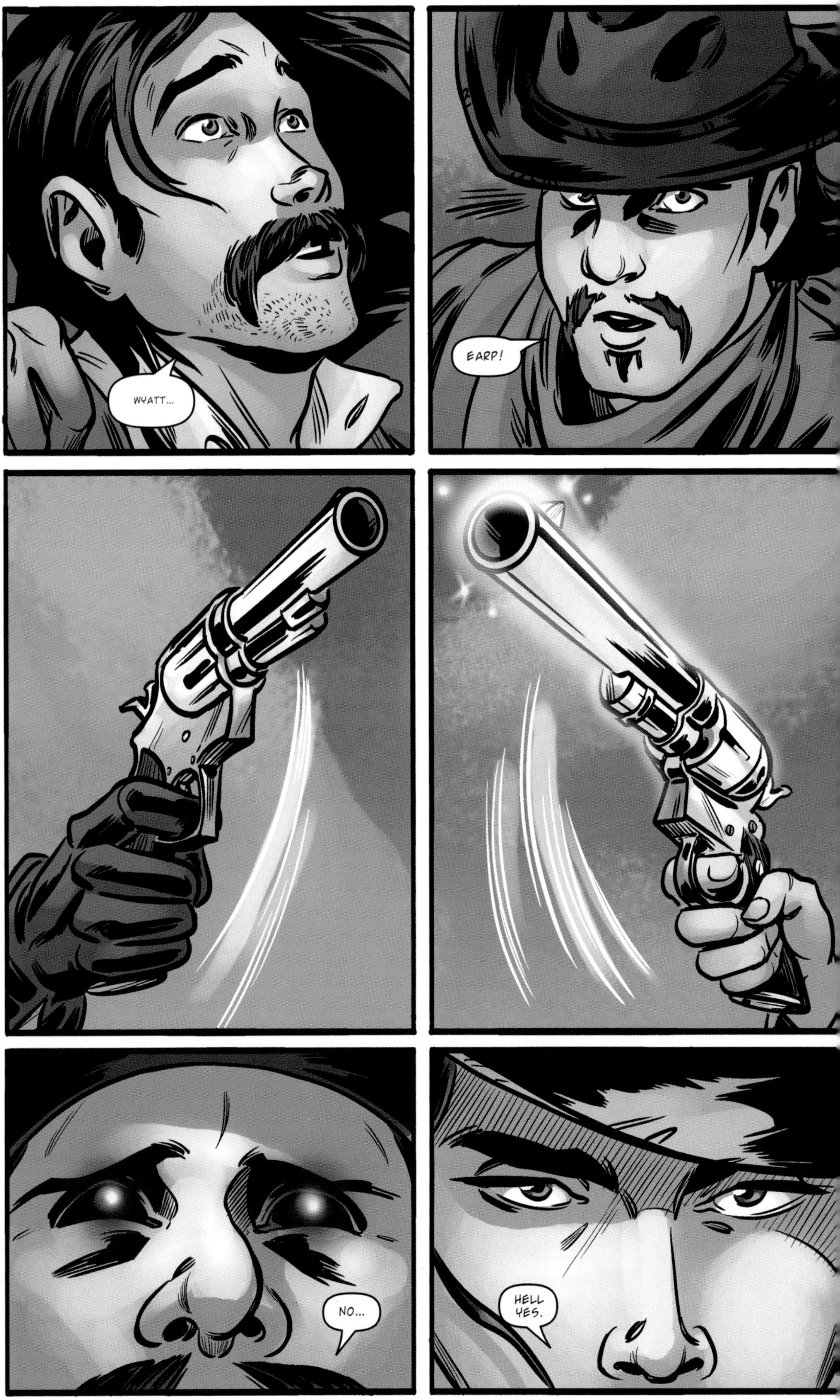
WYATT...
EARP!
NO...
HELL YES.

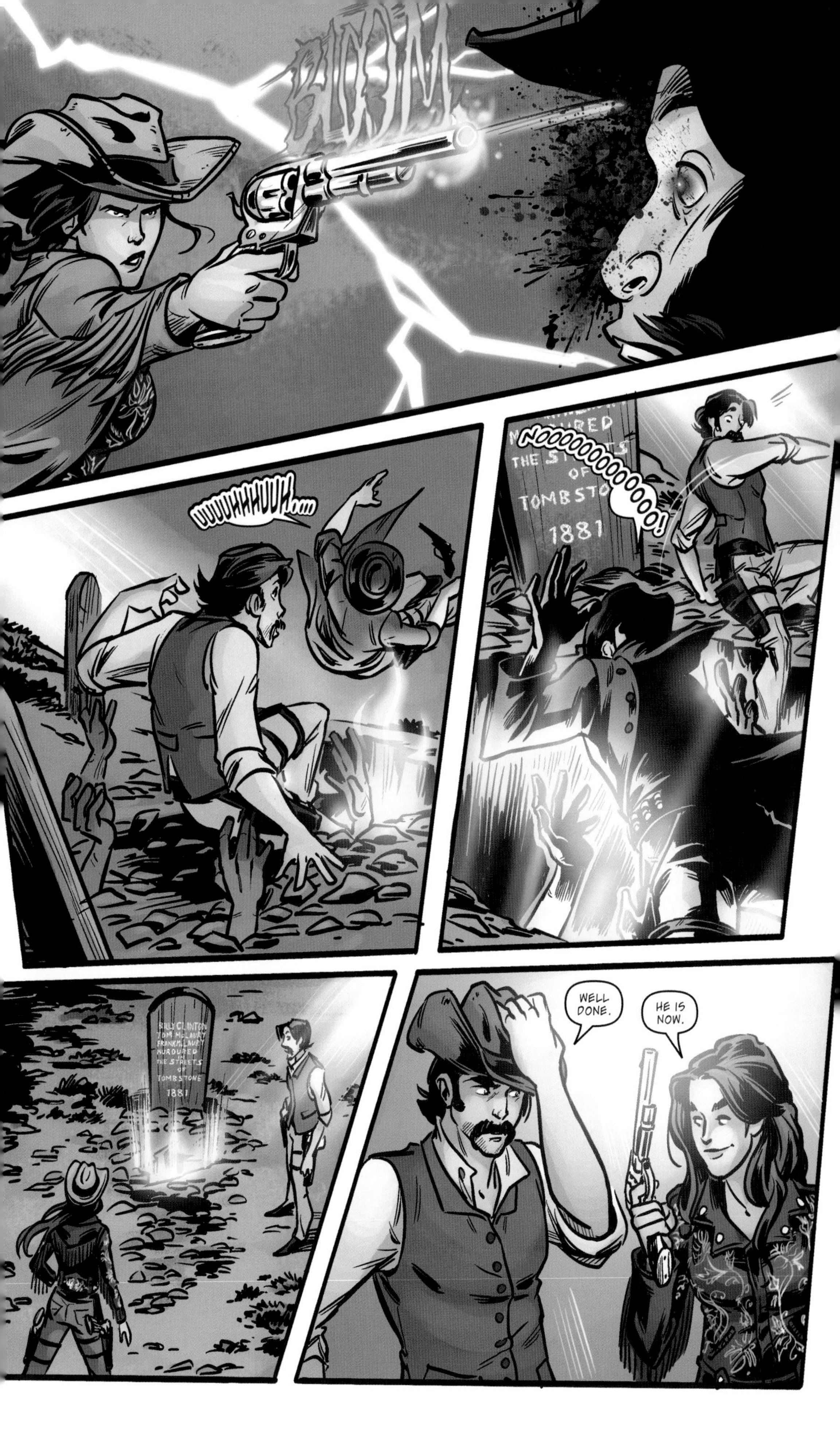
BOOM
UUUUHHHUUH....
NOOOOOOOOOOOOO!
BILLY CLANTON
TOM McLAURY
FRANK McLAURY
MURDURED
IN
THE STREETS
OF
TOMBSTONE
1881
WELL DONE.
HE IS NOW.

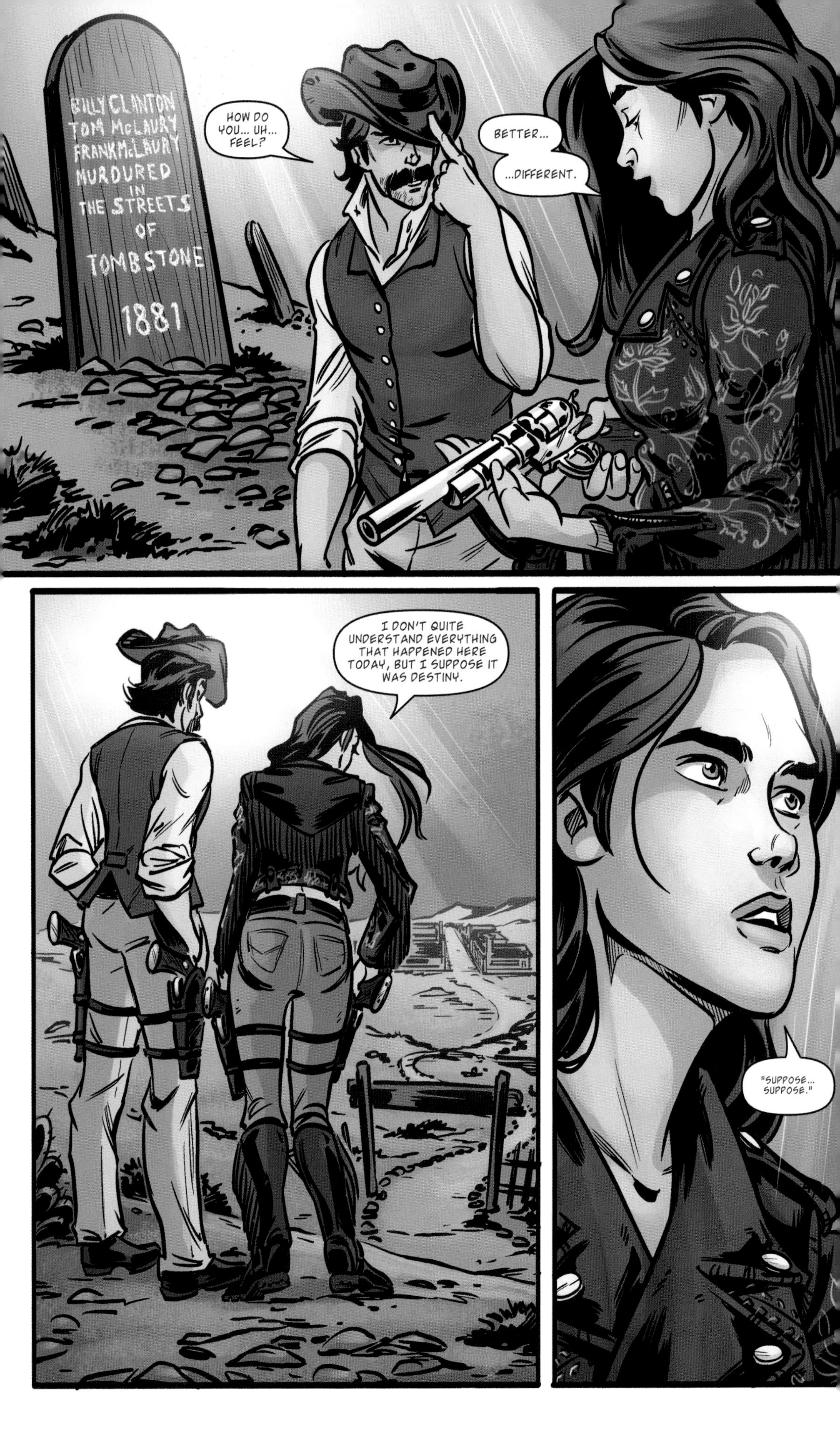
BILLY CLANTON
TOM McLAURY
FRANK McLAURY
MURDURED IN THE STREETS OF TOMBSTONE
1881
HOW DO YOU... UH... FEEL?
BETTER...
...DIFFERENT.
I DON'T QUITE UNDERSTAND EVERYTHING THAT HAPPENED HERE TODAY, BUT I SUPPOSE IT WAS DESTINY.
"SUPPOSE... SUPPOSE."

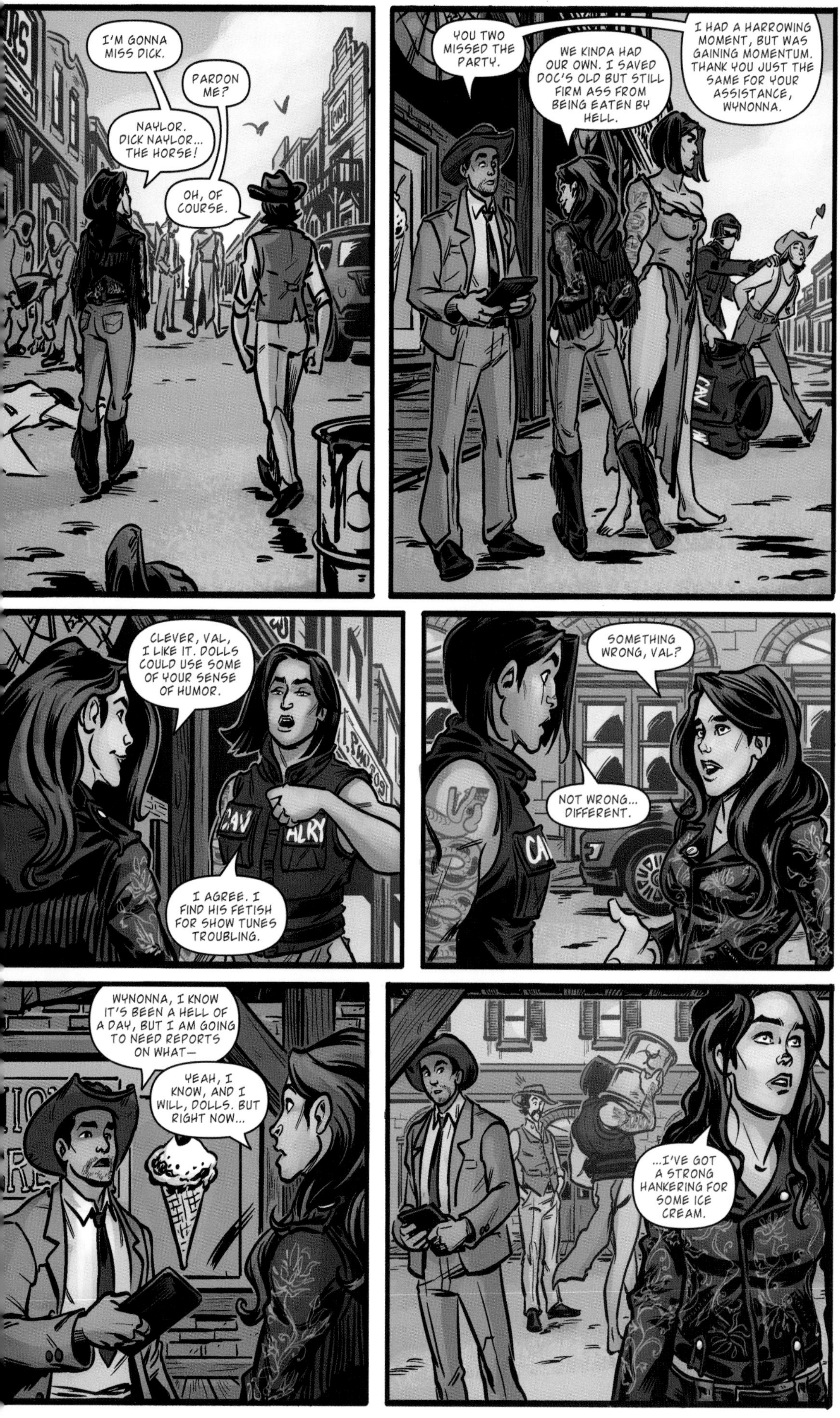
I'M GONNA MISS DICK.
PARDON ME?
NAYLOR. DICK NAYLOR... THE HORSE!
OH, OF COURSE.
YOU TWO MISSED THE PARTY.
WE KINDA HAD OUR OWN. I SAVED DOC'S OLD BUT STILL FIRM ASS FROM BEING EATEN BY HELL.
I HAD A HARROWING MOMENT, BUT WAS GAINING MOMENTUM. THANK YOU JUST THE SAME FOR YOUR ASSISTANCE, WYNONNA.
CLEVER, VAL, I LIKE IT. DOLLS COULD USE SOME OF YOUR SENSE OF HUMOR.
I AGREE. I FIND HIS FETISH FOR SHOW TUNES TROUBLING.
SOMETHING WRONG, VAL?
NOT WRONG... DIFFERENT.
WYNONNA, I KNOW IT'S BEEN A HELL OF A DAY, BUT I AM GOING TO NEED REPORTS ON WHAT—
YEAH, I KNOW, AND I WILL, DOLLS. BUT RIGHT NOW...
...I'VE GOT A STRONG HANKERING FOR SOME ICE CREAM.

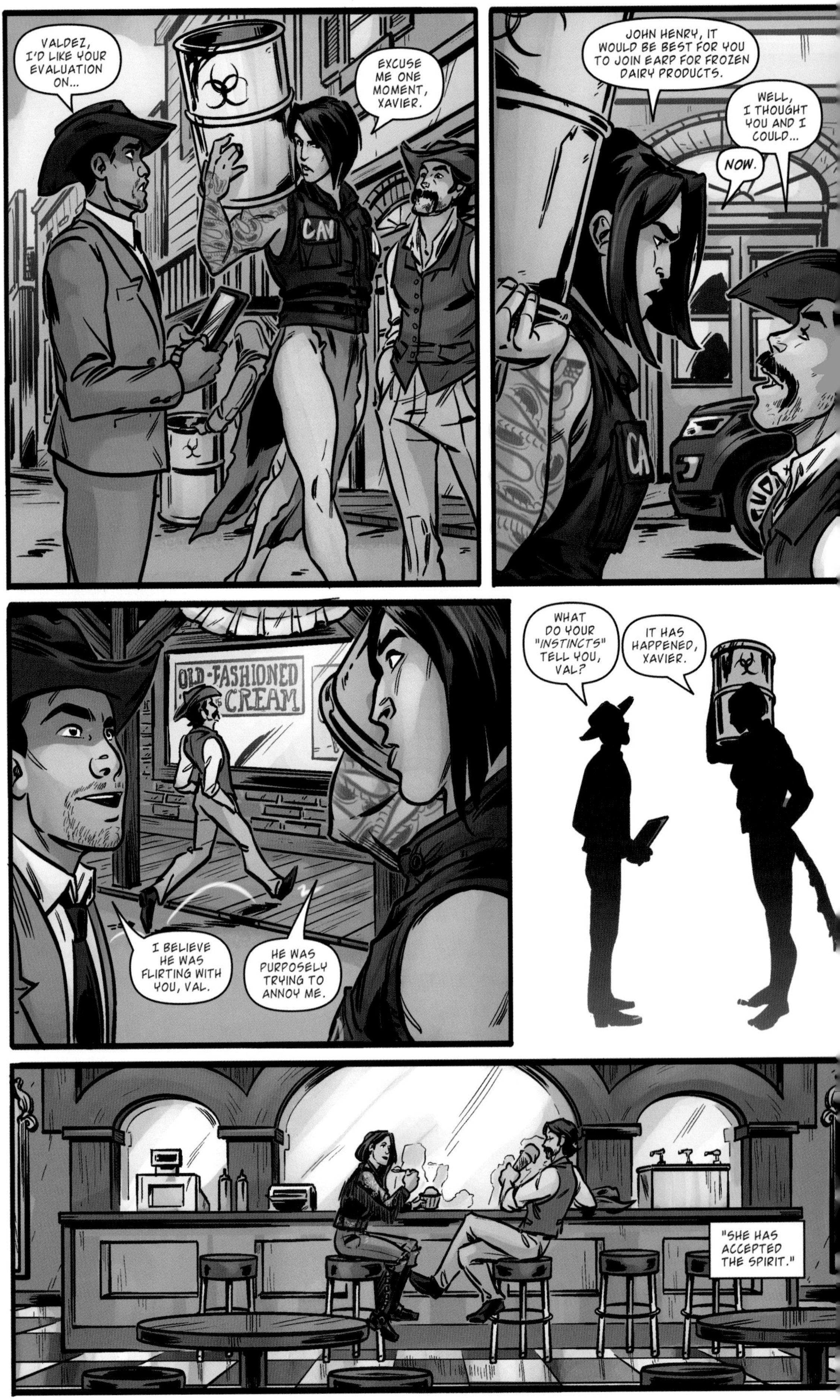
VALDEZ, I'D LIKE YOUR EVALUATION ON...
EXCUSE ME ONE MOMENT, XAVIER.
JOHN HENRY, IT WOULD BE BEST FOR YOU TO JOIN EARP FOR FROZEN DAIRY PRODUCTS.
WELL, I THOUGHT YOU AND I COULD...
NOW.
OLD-FASHIONED CREAM
I BELIEVE HE WAS FLIRTING WITH YOU, VAL.
HE WAS PURPOSELY TRYING TO ANNOY ME.
WHAT DO YOUR "INSTINCTS" TELL YOU, VAL?
IT HAS HAPPENED, XAVIER.
"SHE HAS ACCEPTED THE SPIRIT."

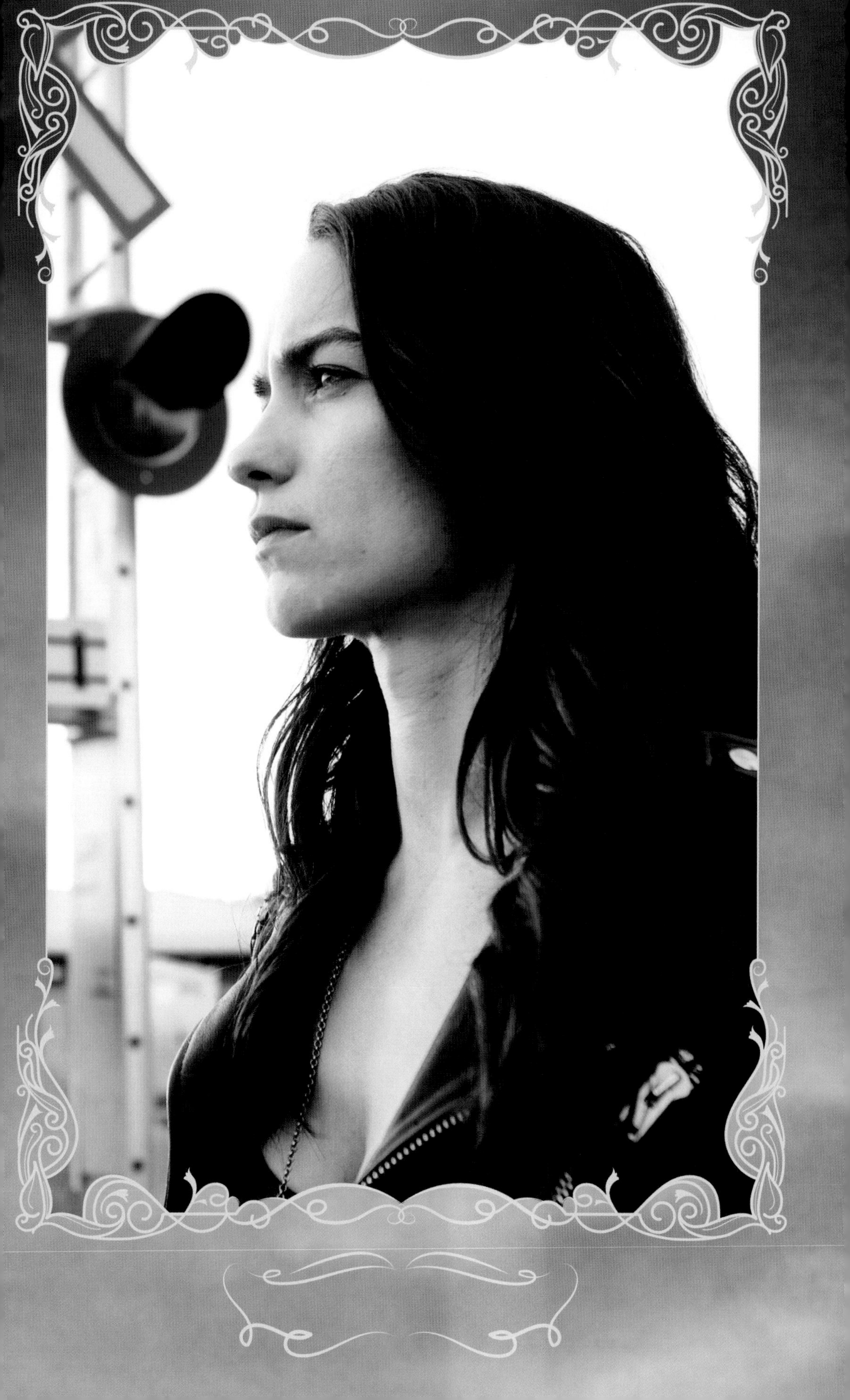

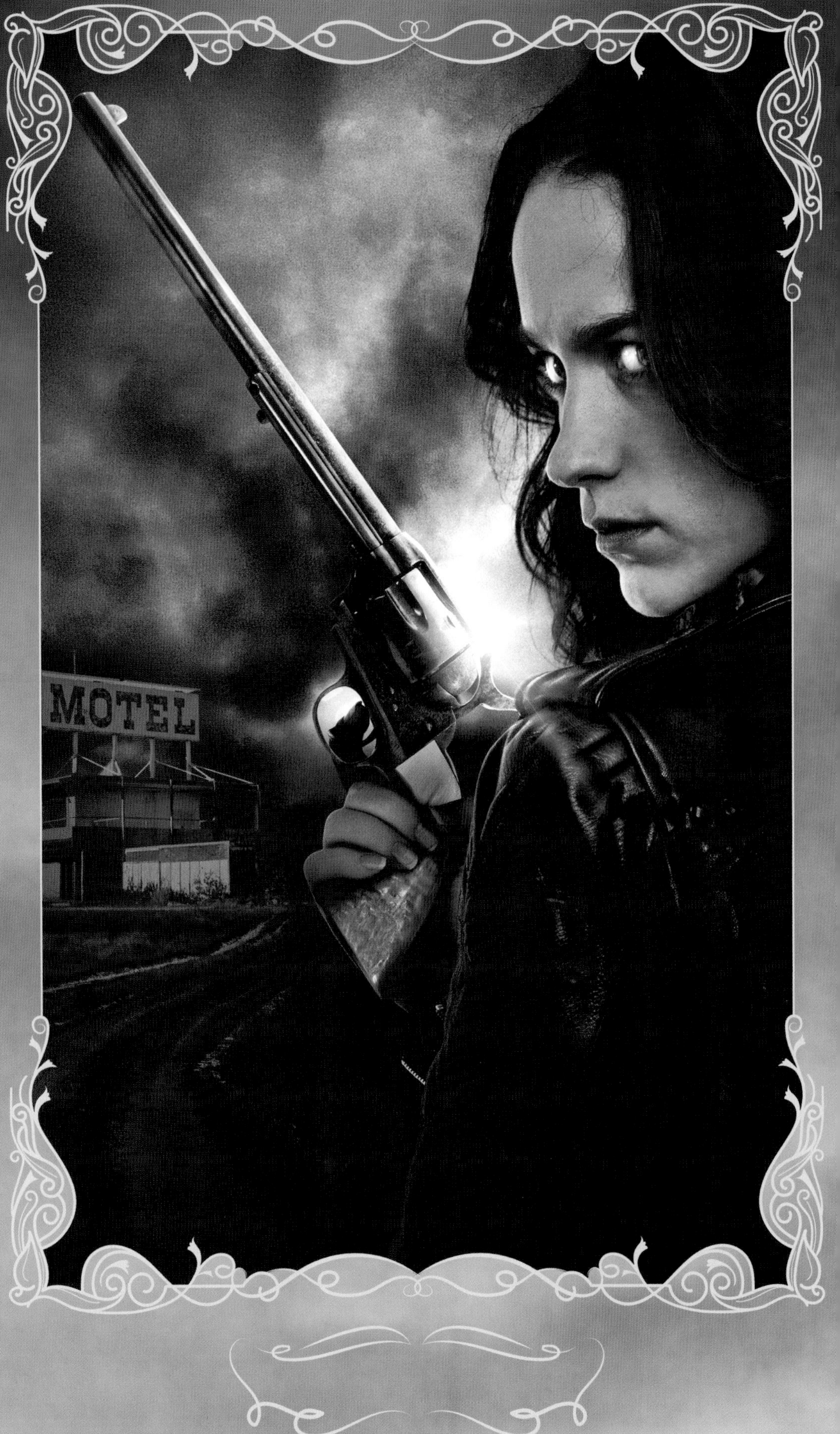
MOTEL

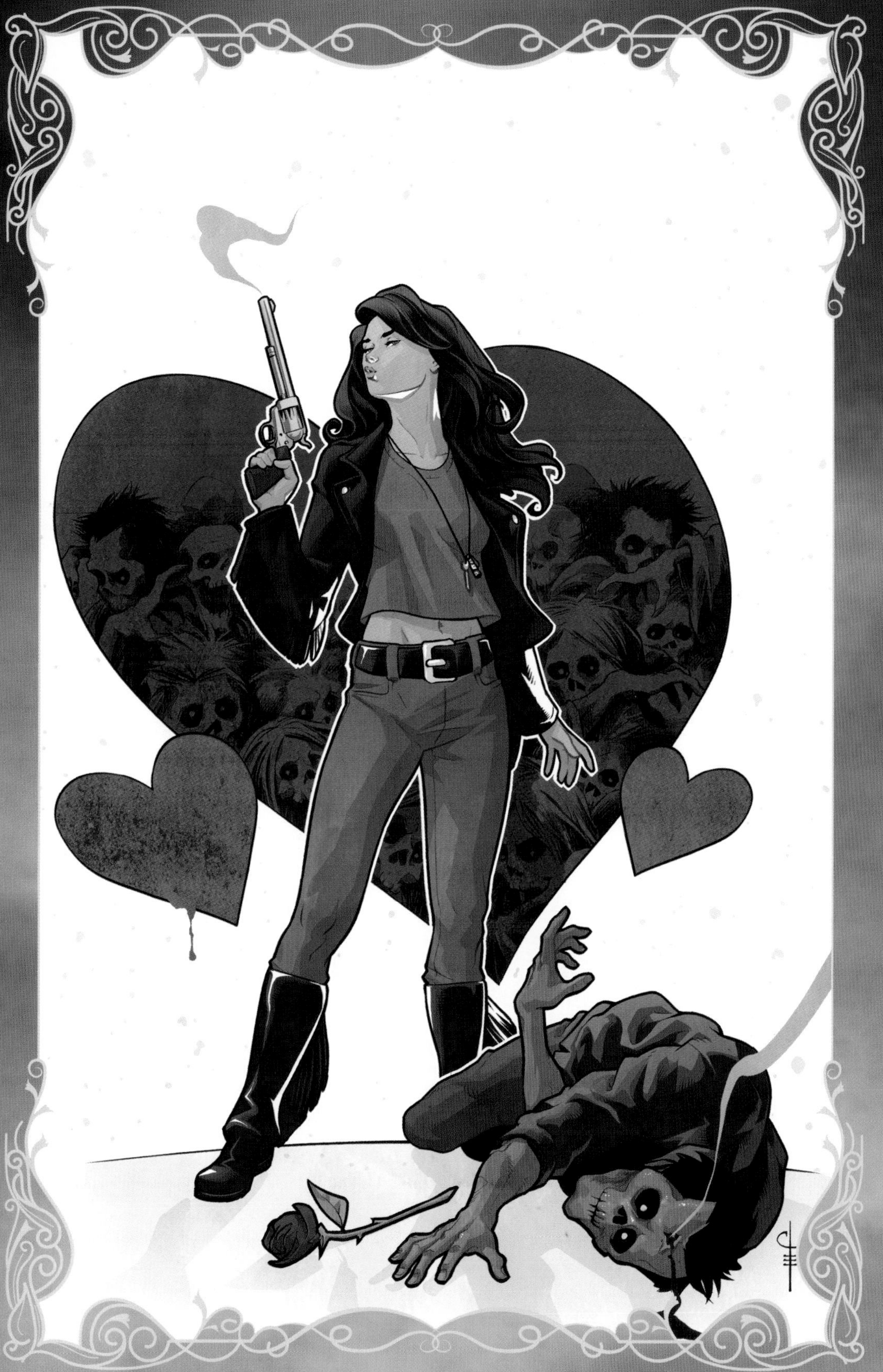

Art by **Chris Evenhuis**

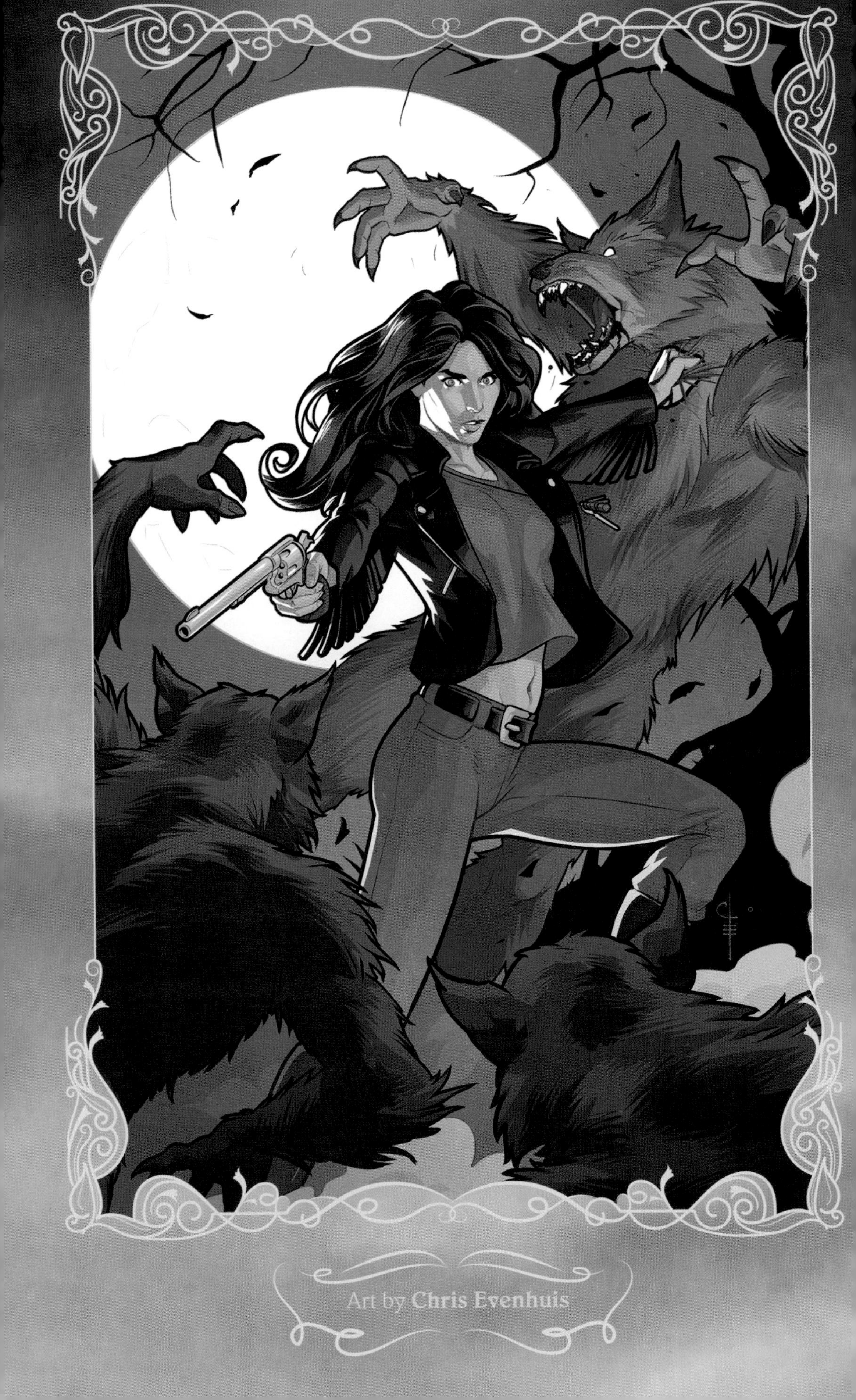

Art by **Chris Evenhuis**

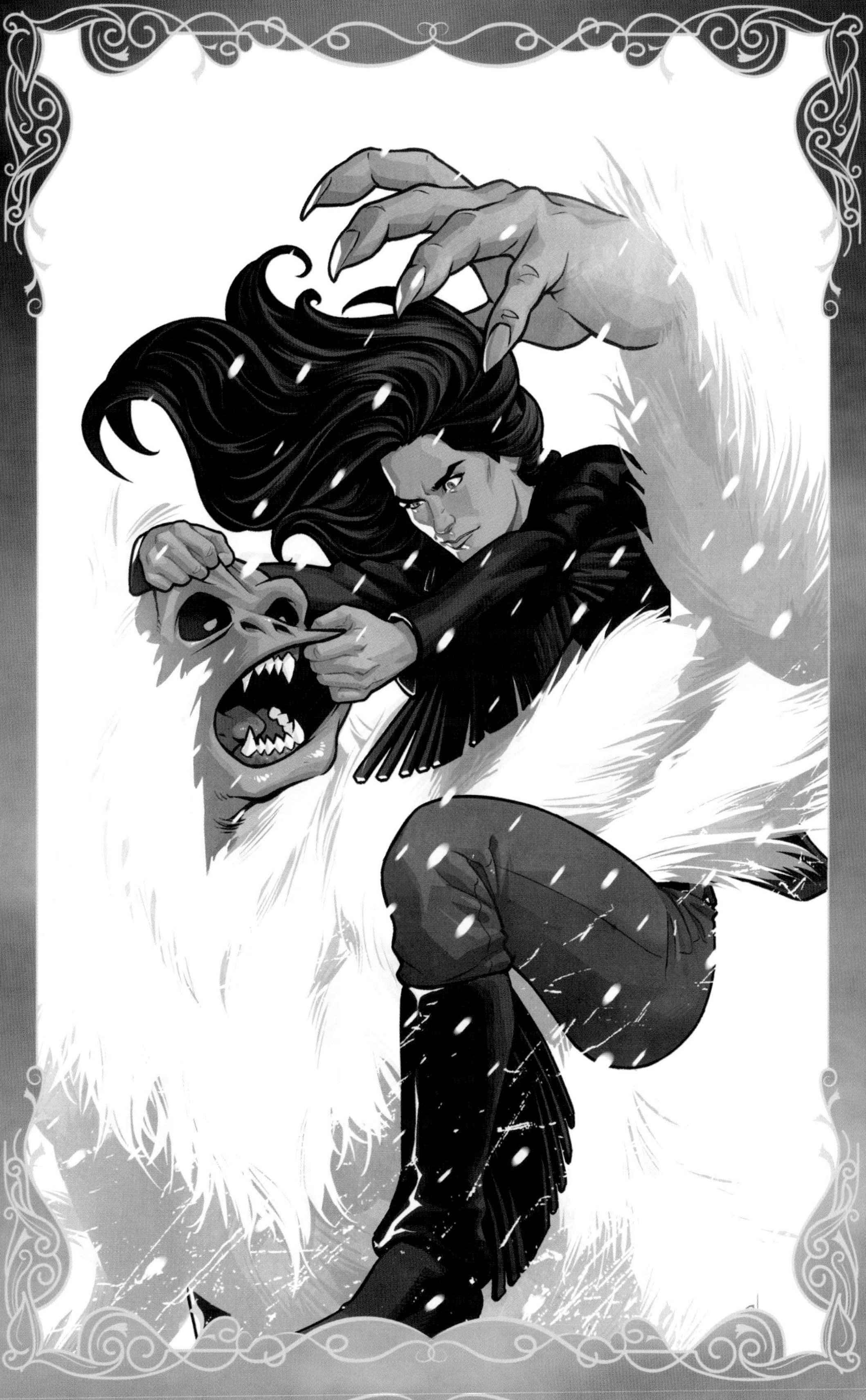

Art by **Chris Evenhuis**

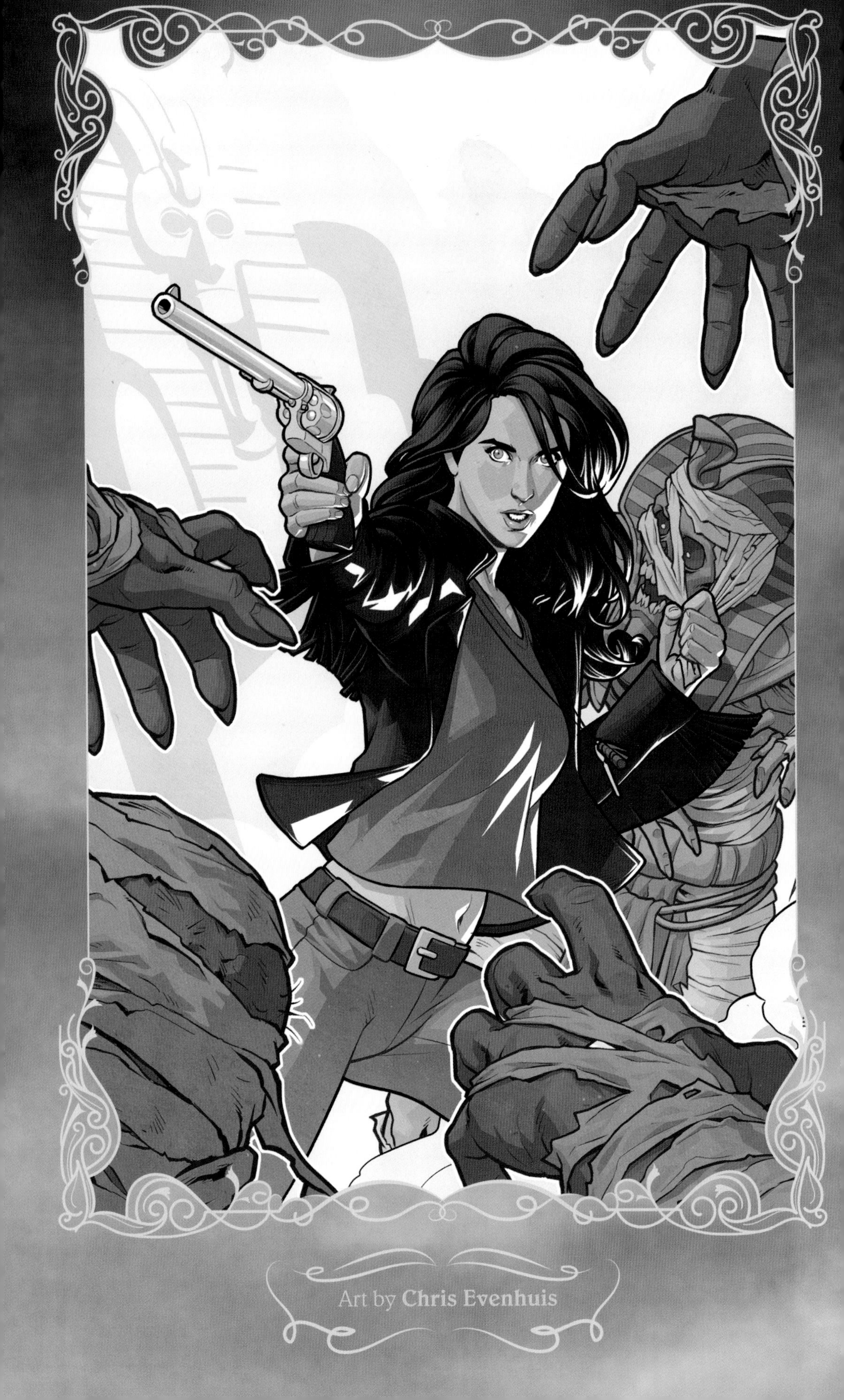

Art by **Chris Evenhuis**

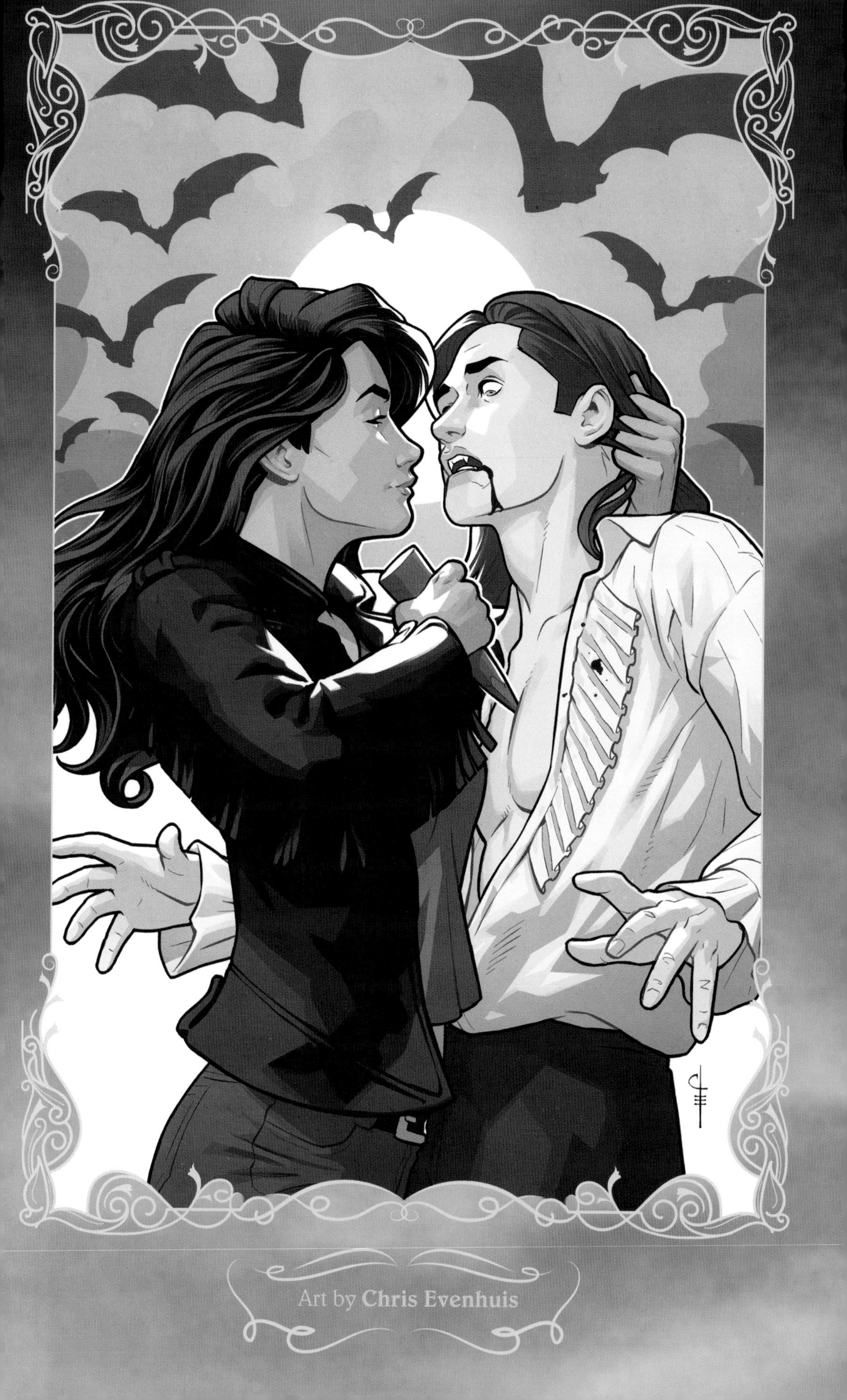

Art by **Chris Evenhuis**

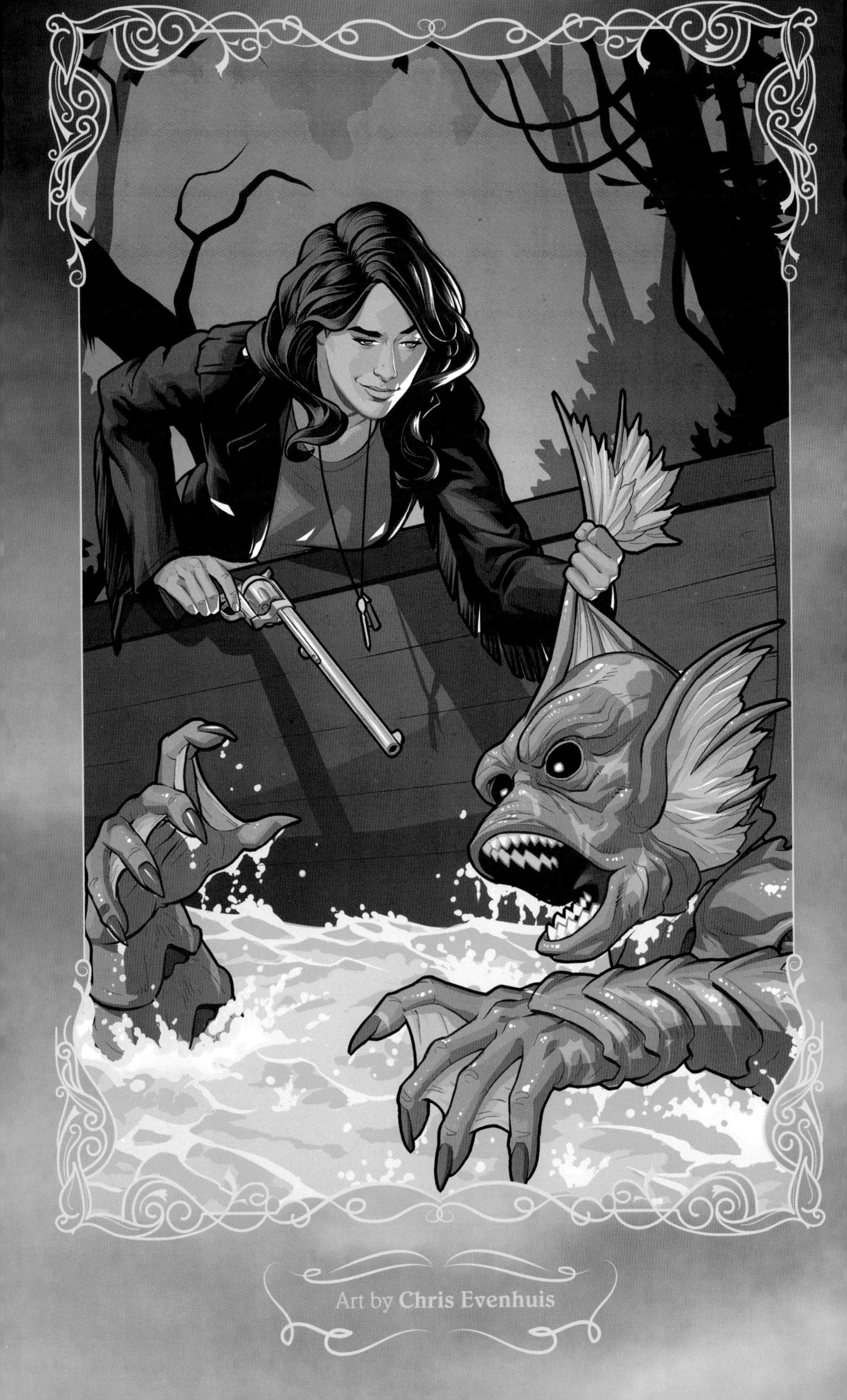

Art by **Chris Evenhuis**

CHARACTER
DESIGNS
By Lora Innes

Wynonna Earp

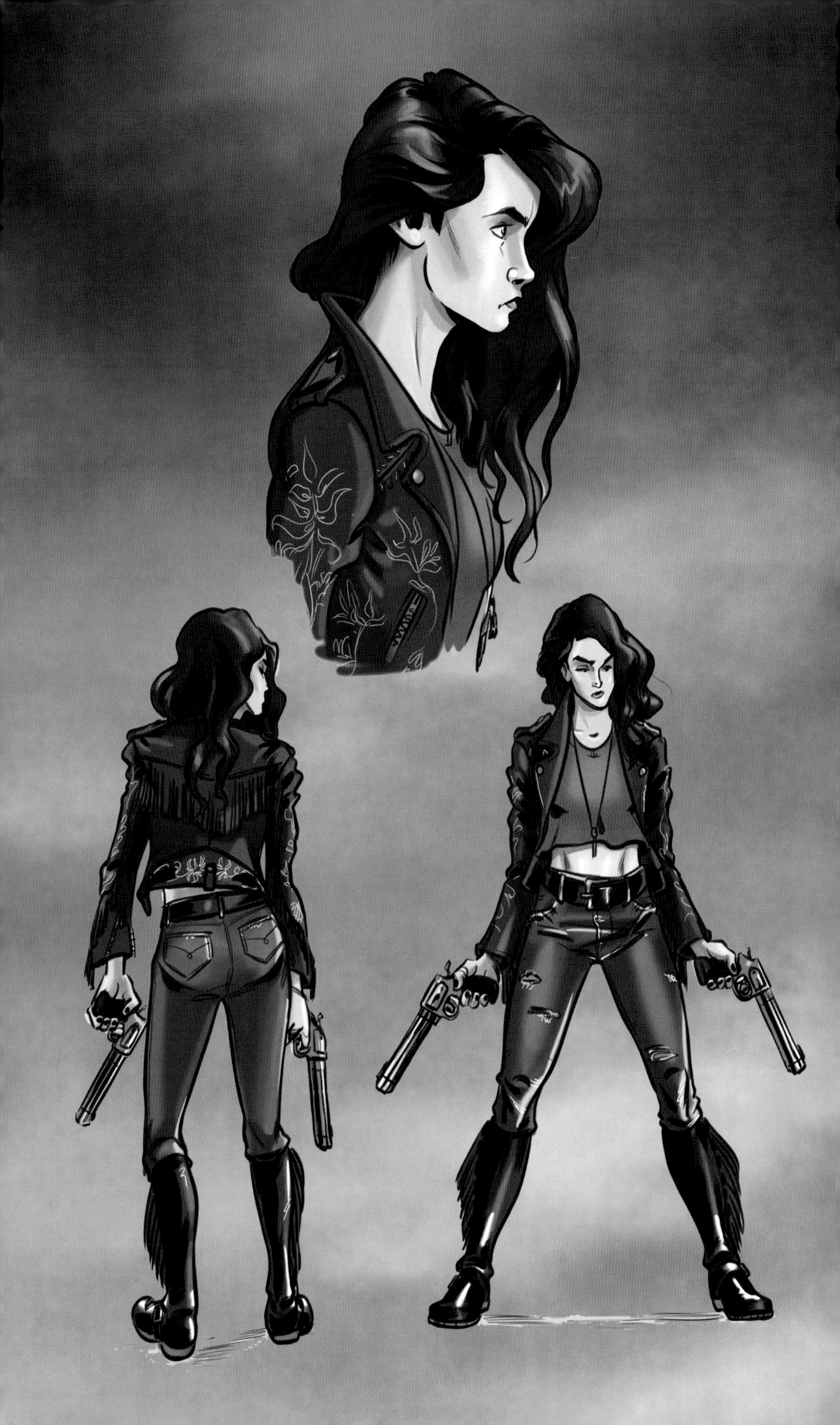

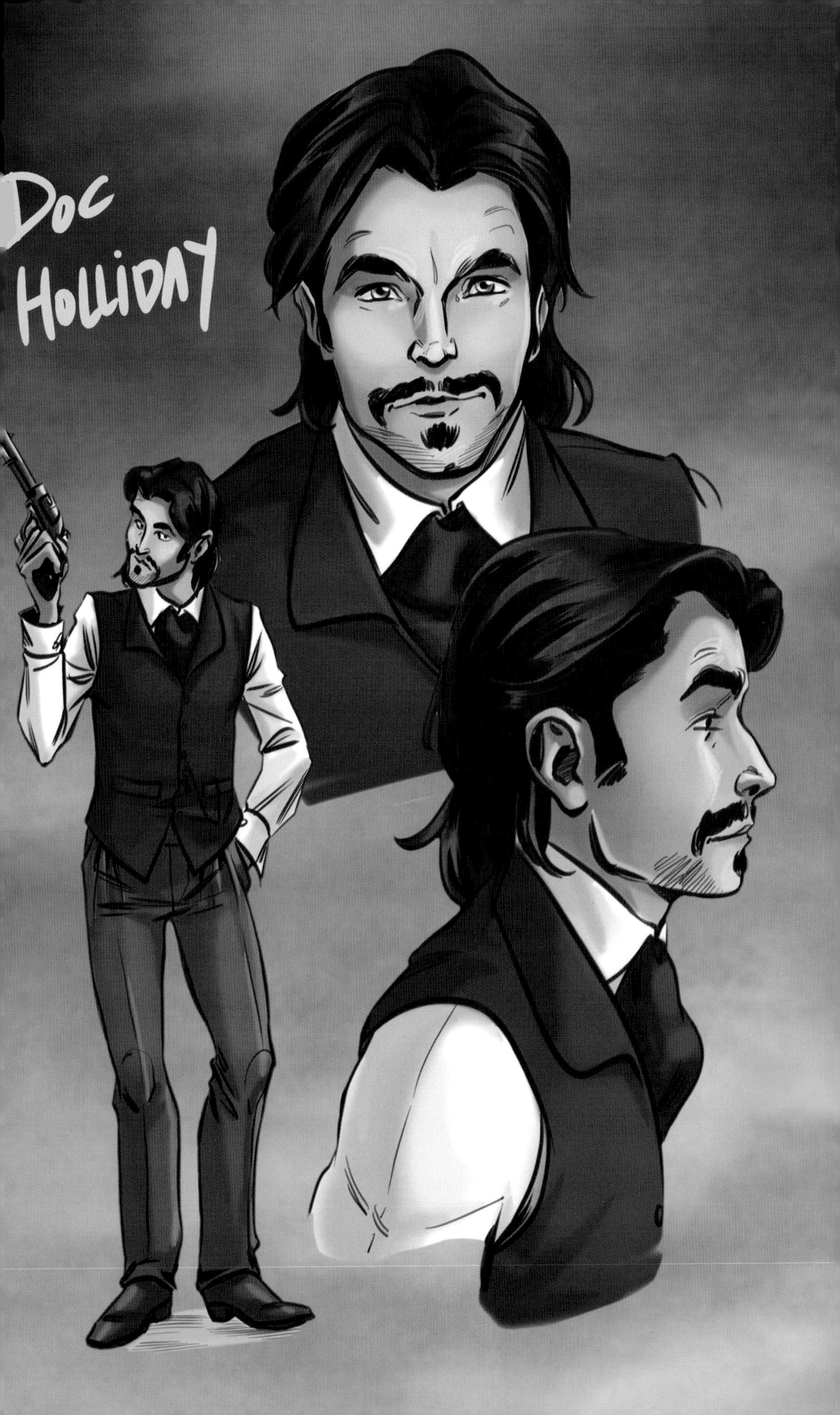
Doc
Holliday

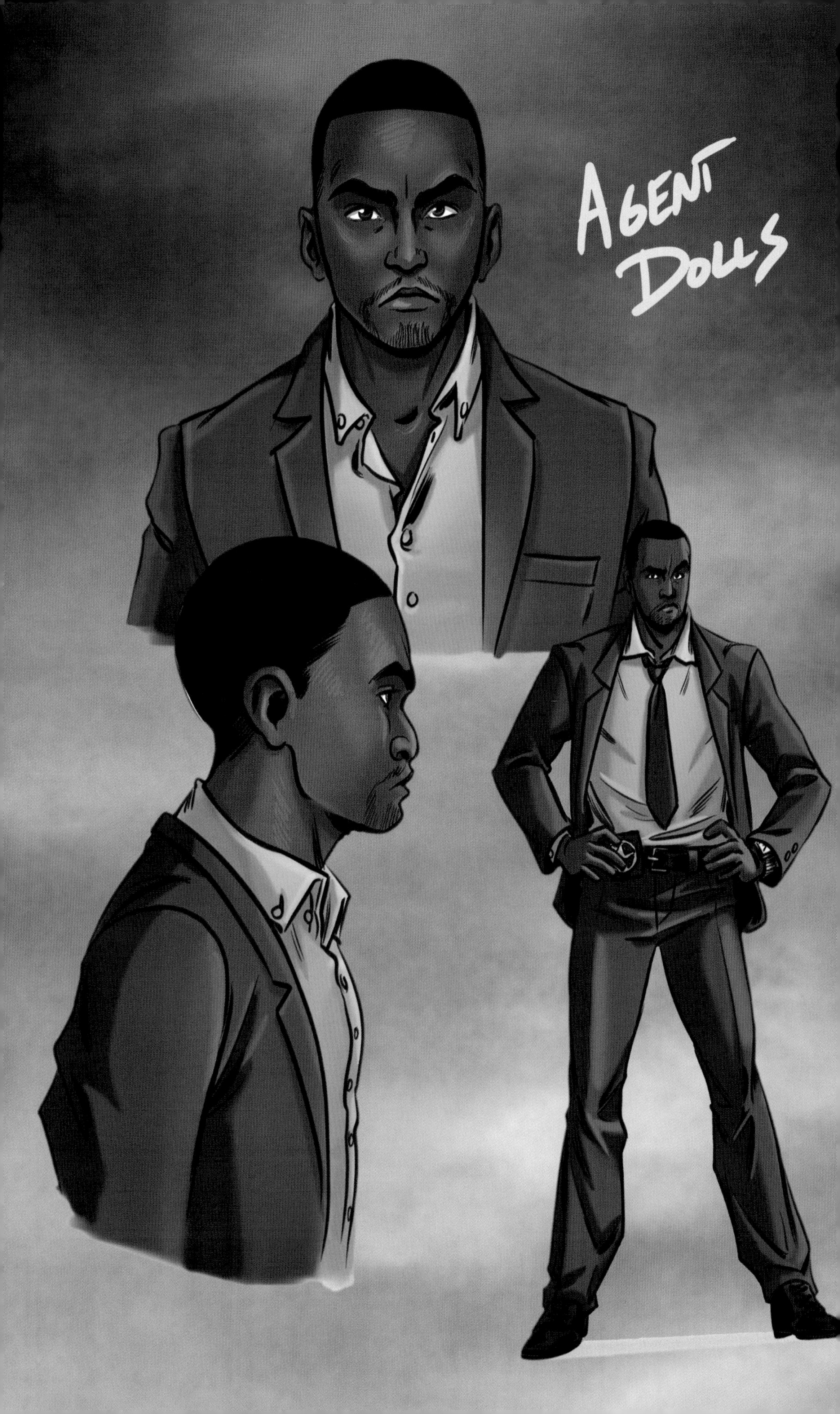
AGENT DOLLS

Wynonna Earp: "Make My Day."

By Beau Smith

I don't like to travel.

I don't have what you call "The Fear Of Flying," being on a jet is fine with me, driving doesn't bother me. My problem with travel is the preparation.

I've been a writer and marketing guy in comic books since 1987. I was VP of marketing for Eclipse Comics, Image Comics, McFarlane Toys, IDW Publishing and Jun Planning. There was a time when I would be traveling at least two weeks out of every month, sometimes more. After a couple of decades of that, travel wasn't so amusing. So for the last decade, I've tried to cut back on it as much as possible.

Only a few things can pull me away from The Flying Fist Ranch. This past year, Ted Adams, CEO of IDW Publishing, was one of those things.

Ted and I have been brother-like friends since 1990, when he was the Distribution Manager at Eclipse Comics and I was the VP of Marketing. Our mutual love of comic books and books has always been our common bond. His brains and my BS have gotten us through a lot in the comic book business through the years.

In 2015, Ted pulled me out of my bunker twice, the first time to be a groomsman in his wedding to the lovely Paula Beerman in April in La Jolla—and then in December when my wife, Beth, and I traveled to Calgary, Alberta, Canada to be on the set of the SyFy TV series *Wynonna Earp*.

Let me testify here and now about two things. If you were to have told my 10-year-old self that one day I would be writing

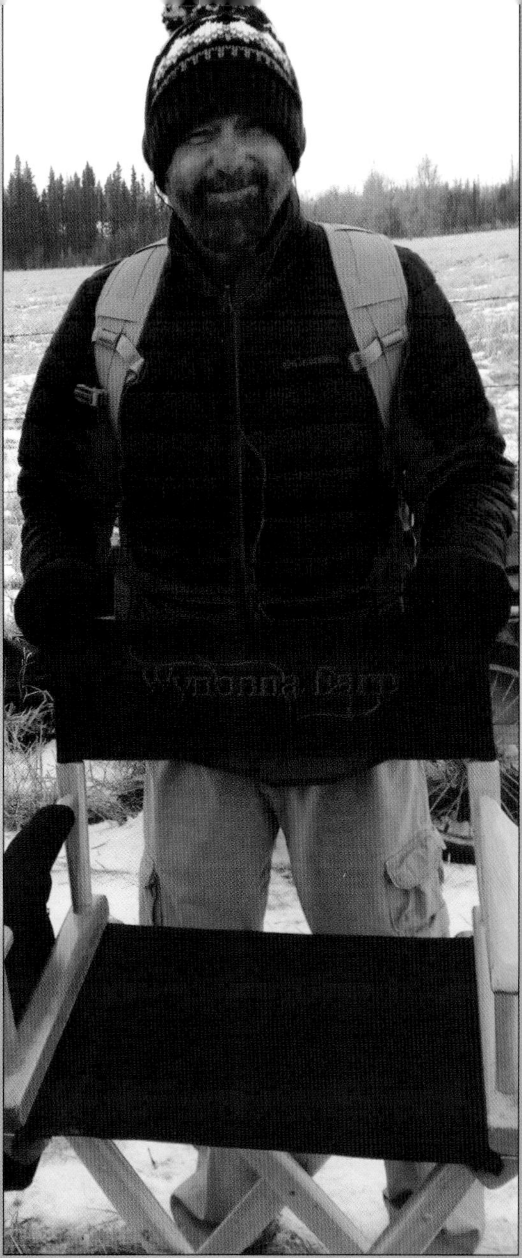
Wynonna Earp

Beau Smith and his director's chair.

comic books—Including some of my all-time favorite characters—my head would've exploded. Top that off by telling me that one day one of my own characters would not only be a comic book series, but a TV series as well, I would've exploded AND taken the neighborhood with me.

Excluding travel days, I was on the set/offices of *Wynonna Earp* for 48 hours. Other than my faith and family, it was the best 48 hours of my life. As much as I enjoy being the center of attention, this was overwhelming. From the moment we walked into the offices, everyone I met was nice, super nice. It was also overwhelming to see

Beth Smith, Melanie Scrofano, Beau, Emily Andras, Tim Rosan, and Shamier Anderson.

the name WYNONNA EARP everywhere, on walls, notes, scripts, papers, props, and also coming out of the mouths of everyone. What I created, alone, in my office, at my 100-plus-year-old desk, was everywhere.

The moment we walked in we were greeted by Producer Jordy Randall as well as a film crew that was recording most everything that went on from that moment forward. Jordy acted as our tour guide, introducing me to some of the most creative people in television I have ever met. The best part was the fact that these young, creative folks were working on a character that I created, that was hard to wrap my feeble mind around.

I met everyone from accounting to transportation. Everyone was so keyed in on *Wynonna Earp* and what was going on, and the best part was that they were fans of the character. It was like we all spoke in a shorthand language that didn't need a translator. It instantly brought us all together. Production Designer Ingrid Jurek was just amazing taking us through all the props, set designs and much more. My pointy little head was swimming as I saw and held some of the coolest props and gadgets that they had created for the show. The art designs that I saw should be framed. Even my beady little eyes were wide in awe.

Highlight moment was when I met *Wynonna Earp* Showrunner/Producer/Writer Emily Andras. We had communicated back and forth online for a few months, but getting to meet Emily in person was the best. She was just as smart and quick-witted as her writing. So generous and so creative. She took me to the writer's room and introduced me to the other writers on the show. I could've spent days there. The white boards on the wall

were filled with tons of info on Wynonna Earp and the series. I felt like Indiana Jones discovering historical artifacts, minus a giant ball rolling to crush me. We all spent time seeing who could ask who the most questions. The best part was that the topic was always creating and, of course, Wynonna Earp.

The rest of the afternoon was spent on the interior set for Wynonna Earp. A 64,000-plus-square-foot warehouse was home to most of the interior sets and scenes for *Wynonna Earp*. There was Shorty's Bar, Wynonna's home, The Black Badge Division HQ, the Torture Barn and more. I found myself walking in and out of the sets, just to make sure I wasn't really in the bar, the barn, and Black Badge HQ. The detail to everything was amazing. I even tried the beer taps a few times hoping real beer would flow.

One of the most surreal moments came

Ted Adams, Paula Adams, Beau, Emily, and Beth.

Allison Baker and Ted.

when I had to go to "Hair and Makeup" for the interviews—both video and print—that I needed to do. I was kinda excited at first, I thought they were gonna "make up some hair" for the top of my head, but alas, I was mistaken. Allison Baker of IDW headed up all the interviews and the schedule for the day. Allison is one of the most amazing people I have met. If I had just a thimble full of her organizational skills, then my secret plans of world domination would be a reality. I still think that Allison invented silk, because everything that happened there was THAT smooth.

Along with Ted and myself, the main cast for *Wynonna Earp* started to roll in for interviews as well: Melanie Scrofano (Wynonna Earp), Shamier Anderson (Agent Dolls), and Tim Rozon (Doc Holliday). Again, like Emily, I had communicated with all of them before we came to Calgary, but meeting them all was a real blast. Melanie is one entertaining person, she is a true hoot! Free spirit doesn't even come close, pretty and full of energy. We hugged and she called me "Daddy." She turned to everyone and said, "It's Daddy Beau! He created us all!" I was flattered and blushing at the same time. (Good thing I still had my makeup on, eh?)

Shamier Anderson as Agent Dolls in the series is a very serious, authoritative figure. In real life, he is one of the sweetest, coolest guys you'll ever meet. It was like we had been friends for years. We talked about almost every kinda topic you could think of, we laughed and shared some good stories, some so good they had to ask us to keep it down as other interviews were going on. We had THAT much of a good time.

Meeting Tim Rozon was great. Let me tell you, the guy is as movie-star handsome as it gets. He can charm the bark off of wood with his Doc Holliday southern accent that he can kick into without pause. Tim is also a HUGE comic book fan. He truly knows his stuff when it comes to comics. He also knows how to impress the ladies with his smile. When my wife Beth was introduced to him, she was like a teenage girl meeting Justin Bieber. "I really enjoy watching the dailies, Tim, but I think I like looking at you a little more than I should," Beth said. It was a priceless moment that I will tease her with for many years to come.

That night, as it snowed, we had a wonderful dinner with Jordy and Emily. The conversation of creativity was one for the ages. It just couldn't have gone any better.

The next day was cold, snowy and really showed off Calgary. Ted and I enjoyed the beautiful scenery as we were driven about 45 minutes out of town to the outside shoot location for the day, one of the most amazing middle of nowhere places we've ever seen. We saw bison on the way, cattle and the Canadian Rockies in the background. Mike, our driver, was a great host and filled us in on everything.

The previous day, I had a small taste of

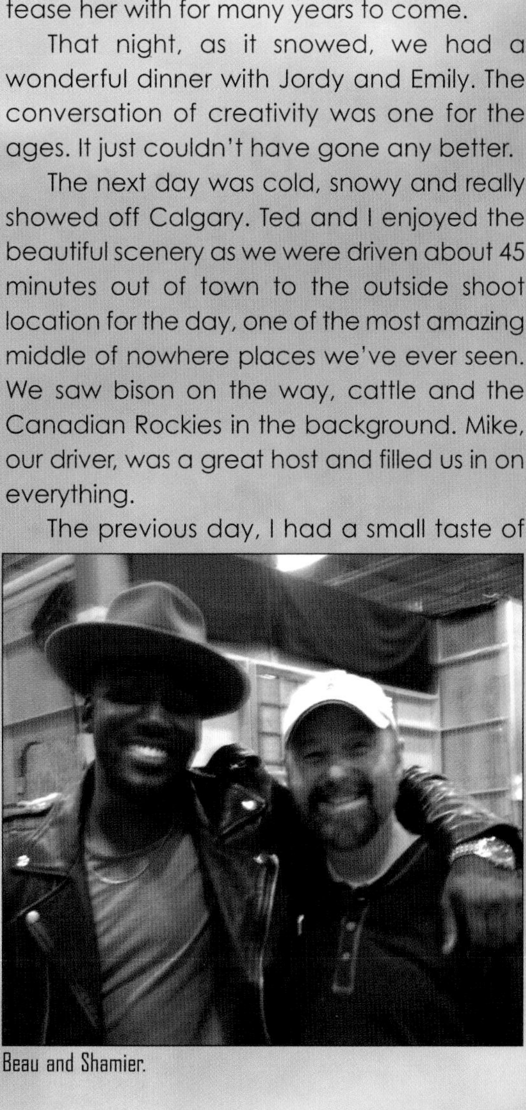

Beau and Shamier.

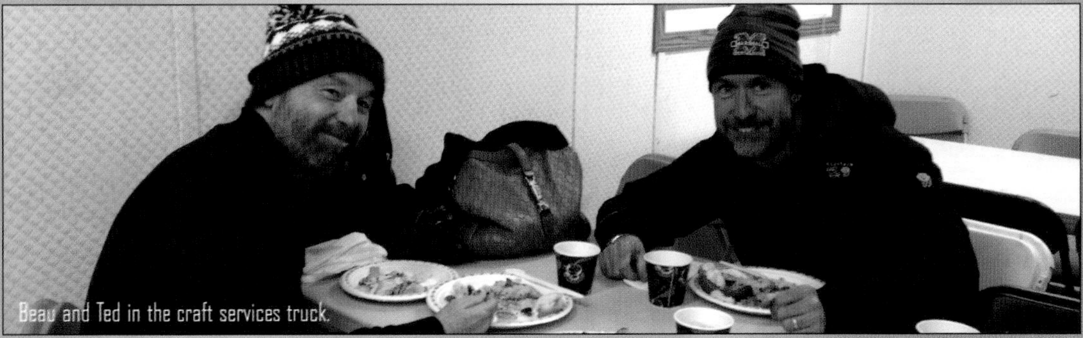

Beau and Ted in the craft services truck.

just how many people it takes to produce a TV show. In the offices, there must have been 50 people. As we arrived at the location shoot, I REALLY started to find out. A circle of trailers, buses, trucks and other vehicles all lined up and in their places. Husky men hauling equipment, lumber, props and such. Then we head down a snow-covered road to where they were shooting a scene with Dominique Provost-Chalkley (Waverly Earp) and Katherine Barrell (Deputy Nicole Haught). As soon as we got out of the truck, the assistant director downloaded us with everything that was going on, provided us with remote headphones so we could hear the actors and director, Ron Murphy, and then gave us director chairs. I thought to myself that any minute they were gonna figure out it was just me and throw me out of the coolest party ever. What a great time I was having!

After the scene, I hung out with Dominique and Katherine a bit. Dominique is British, so it was really neat to hear her go in and out of her British, then American, accent without effort. Such a sweet person, you are gonna love her as Waverly Earp, Wynonna's sister in the TV series. Katherine looked every bit the deputy as she was in her law enforcement outfit. We got to talk about her recent overseas travels and her love for basketball. Both Katherine and Dominique are much tougher than I, they didn't act as if it was cold at all.

The next scene they were shooting involved two of the main villains in a confrontation. That also included a flame thrower and an Uzi. They had me hooked! It all took place on a torchlit bridge with thugs, guns and a mutant/zombie that was at least 6-foot-8. It was evening by now and even colder. They had made us a production tent complete with heater, monitors and chairs. I felt like King For The Day!

The scene is a real Mexican standoff between main bad guy Bobo Del Rey, whom I created in *Wynonna Earp* #1, played by the intense and amazing Michael Eklund, and

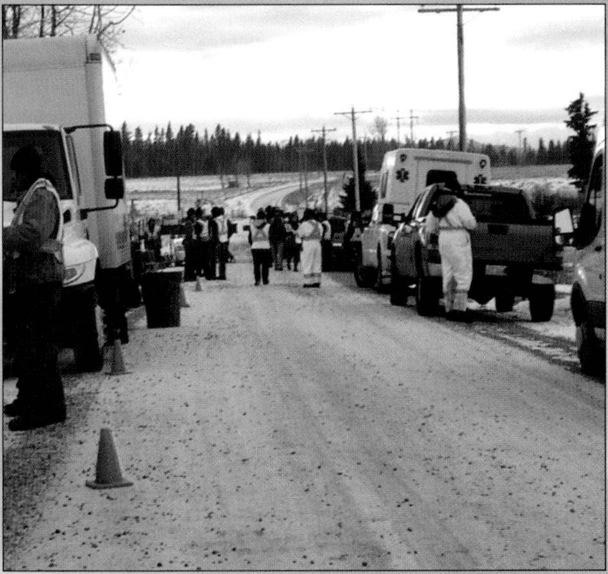

On location set for *Wynonna Earp*.

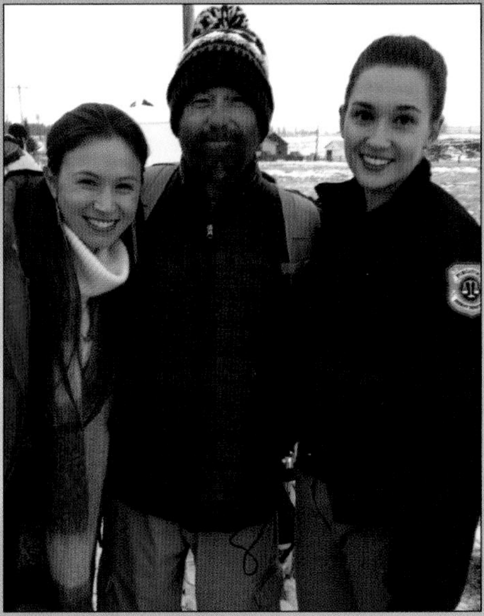

Dominique Provost-Chalkley, Beau, and Katherine Barrell.

Michael Eklund on location shoot.

Constance Clootie, the Stone Witch (the really lovely Rayisa Kondracki). Again, these people were out here in the freezing cold (The same area where the movie *The Revenant* with Leonardo DiCaprio was mostly shot), yet none of them acted like it was even chilly. They are all such pros. Seeing the flame thrower and the Uzi go off was really fun. I felt like I was 12 years old. At one point, while in the tent, they called out that the director wanted to see me. At this point, I figured they finally caught on to me and were gonna boot me out, but that wasn't it. Ron Murphy, the director, asked me if I wanted to help him direct this scene. I laughed, figured he had to be joking, but he was not.

I got to place actors, frame the shot, get everything rolling and call "Action." I was so stoked. A few days later, when I got home, I checked the dailies and sure enough, there I was, behind the camera, and you could hear me call "Action." Never in a million years did I ever think that would happen. Ron was also kind enough to take 30 minutes to

really talk writing and directing with me. It was so neat to hear about how everything was put together. He asked me about how I write comics and the creativity that goes behind that. It really made my day.

It was getting late, and we were all getting hungry. Ted suggested that we eat there on set at the catering trailer. I was all for that. Their menu was great, and the atmosphere was even better. We sat there in a trailer like I used to eat in when I worked construction. The cast, crew, director, everybody was with us! We talked, laughed and just had a great time.

By the time we got back to the hotel it was late, and all of us had early flights out in the morning, so we said our goodbyes and crashed. I enjoyed all of it so much and so much more happened, but there just isn't enough room here to capture it all. I'm sure my editor Carlos is already yanking out his hair by seeing just how long I've gone on here. Sorry, Carlos. [Ed. Note: It's like the *War and Peace* of set-visit essays!]

It was neat to see and be a part of the entire location trip. I'll never forget it, much like anyone never forgets "the first time." Most of all, I enjoyed spending time with my buddy, Ted on the road again. He has believed in Wynonna Earp from day one, and that faith has never waned.

As Beth and I were in the airport, waiting for them to call us for boarding, I picked up a local Calgary paper. I skimmed through it as we waited. On the front page of the entertainment/arts section there was the headline "Creator of Wynonna Earp Okays Local Production."

My trip was made.

On location shoot for *Wynonna Earp*.

"*Wynonna Earp* breaks the box so many female comic characters are commonly put into..."

— *Project Nerd*

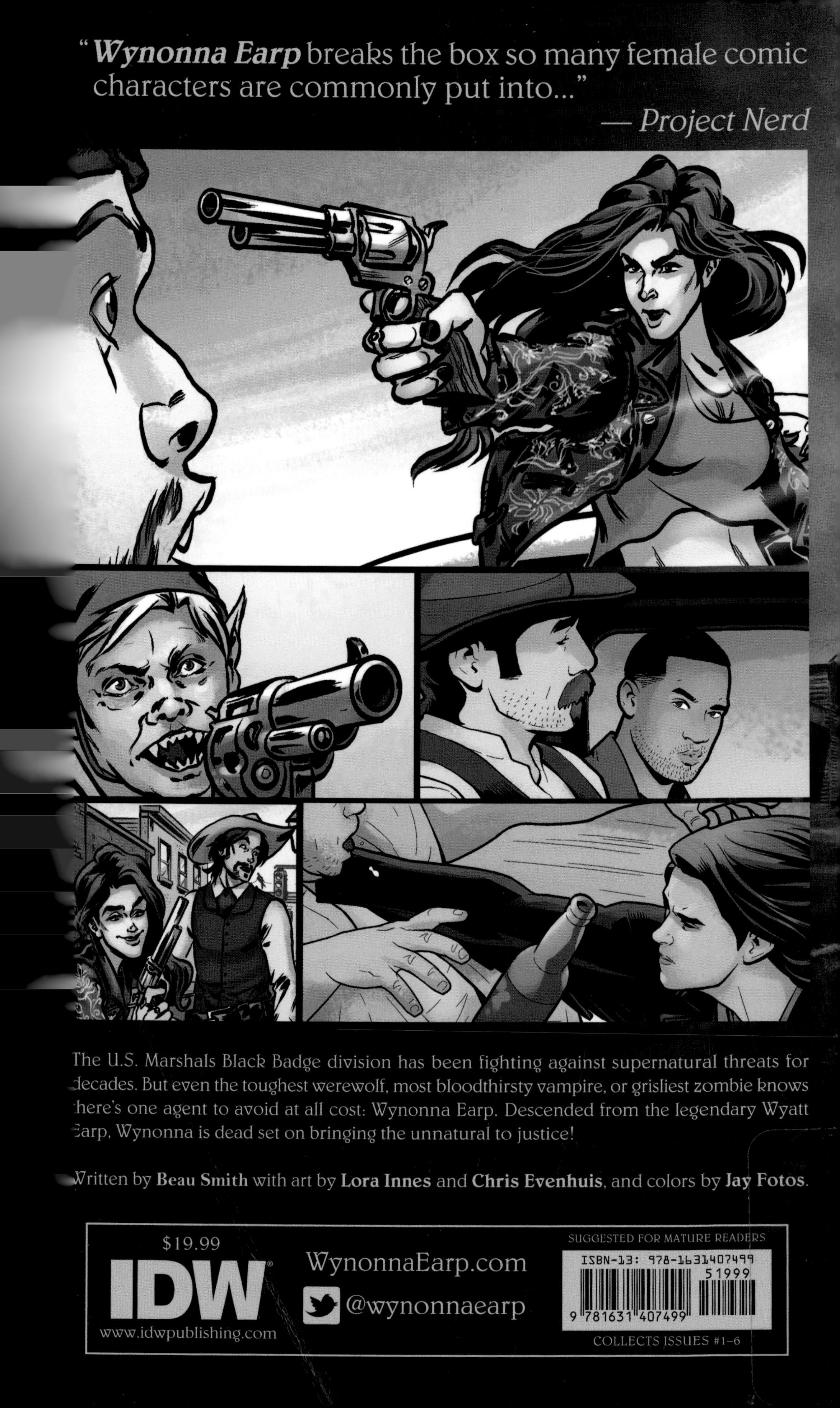

The U.S. Marshals Black Badge division has been fighting against supernatural threats for decades. But even the toughest werewolf, most bloodthirsty vampire, or grisliest zombie knows there's one agent to avoid at all cost: Wynonna Earp. Descended from the legendary Wyatt Earp, Wynonna is dead set on bringing the unnatural to justice!

Written by **Beau Smith** with art by **Lora Innes** and **Chris Evenhuis**, and colors by **Jay Fotos**.

$19.99

IDW

www.idwpublishing.com

WynonnaEarp.com

@wynonnaearp

SUGGESTED FOR MATURE READERS

ISBN-13: 978-1631407499

51999

9 781631 407499

COLLECTS ISSUES #1–6